THE FAITH
of the
EARLY FATHERS

Volume Two

A source-book of theological and historical passages from the Christian writings of
the Post-Nicene and Constantinopolitan
eras through St. Jerome

selected and translated

by

W. A. JURGENS

The Liturgical Press   Collegeville, Minnesota

Nihil obstat: Rev. Joseph C. Kremer, S.T.L., *Censor deputatus*. *Imprimatur*: ✝ George H. Speltz, D.D., Bishop of St. Cloud. January 25, 1979.

ISBN 0-8146-1007-2

Dedicated to the Memory

of

His Grace

**ARCHBISHOP
EDWARD F. HOBAN**

TABLE OF CONTENTS

FOREWORD

The first volume of *The Faith of the Early Fathers* appeared eight years ago. The excellent reception that it received is attested by the fact that it is about to be released again in its third edition. When volume one of the work, covering the patristic period up to about the end of the fourth century, was put to press in March 1970, I promised on its good reception to provide a second volume, which I supposed would suffice to cover the second half of the patristic age.

The pressure of other writing and translating has delayed the completion of the work, which at the same time has grown so that now not only a second but a third volume, the two to appear simultaneously, are necessary for the adequate treatment of the period.

Volume two, which you have in hand, is devoted to the post-Nicene and Constantinopolitan eras, and stops short of Augustine. Besides a number of secondary lights its principal luminaries are SS. Basil, the two Gregory's, Chrysostom, Ambrose, and Jerome. Volume three covers from St. Augustine inclusive to the end of the patristic period, marked by the deaths of St. Isidore of Seville († 636 A. D.) in the West and of St. John Damascene († 749 A. D.) in the East.

The format of volume 2 is precisely that of volume 1, which is explained at some length in the introduction to volume 1. Each selection is numbered; and the numerical order of passages is the same as that established by M. J. Rouët de Journel in his *Enchiridion patristicum*. Passages not to be found in Rouët de Journel are given a number with an alphabetic postscript. The marginal numbers pertaining to each passage refer to the numbered theological propositions in the Doctrinal Index (pp. 227-254). With the numbered theological propositions in the Doctrinal Index are the reference numbers of all the passages which in some way pertain to the theological propositions. In this second volume the Scriptural, Doctrinal, and General Indices cover all three volumes.

Properly used and with its mechanism understood this work will be of immense help to students, especially in their research and classroom papers and exercises in any area of theology and Christian antiquity. The seminarian and theological student who takes but a few minutes to understand the mechanics of the Doctrinal Index will benefit immeasurably thereby. Testimonials to the utility of the work have been received from all over the United States, from Africa, India, and Australia. Several priests have told me that they use it to supplement the readings in their recitation of the Liturgy of the Hours. It is likewise a work much used by the laity in study clubs and for their private reading.

As with volume one the source of the texts I translate is regularly that which is currently reckoned as the standard or best available edition. At the same time, however, and as a convenience, I refer also to the proper place in Migne's *Patrologiae cursus completus*.

In using *The Faith of the Early Fathers* it is important to remember that this is a work which presents a view of the faith in its formation and development. It is proper, therefore, that it includes the writings of heretics; and not every isolated statement in the texts presented is to be taken as a sound declaration of the faith. Passages which contradict or seem to contradict the theological propositions of the Doctrinal Index are numbered there in parentheses.

Not the least of the lessons to be learned from a work of the present kind is how marvellously the faith is a seamless robe. Cut it here, tear it there, excise a piece from it anywhere, and the whole of it unravels. It is not possible to deny any one dogma of the faith without ultimately having to deny them all. If there is no original sin, neither is there any redemption. If the Word did not become flesh, Scripture is not inspired and there was no death on the cross. If Christ be not Man, Mary is not the Mother of God. If Christ be not God, we have been deceived and the Church is not infallible. *If Christ be not risen our faith is in vain and we are still in our sins*.

W. A. JURGENS

Cleveland, Ohio
June, 1978

INDEX OF SELECTIONS

TABLE OF ABBREVIATIONS

AND OF LATIN TERMS

A.D. = year or years [of the Lord].

ante = before.

apud = in, among, with.

aut = or [else].

ca. = circa = about.

Ch. = chapter.

Chs. = chapters.

CSEL = *Corpus scriptorum ecclesiasticorum latinorum.* Series of Latin texts of the
Fathers, edited by the Wiener Akademie der Wissenschaften, 1866ff. Commonly called the *Vienna Corpus.*

CSCO = *Corpus scriptorum christianorum orientalium.* Series of the writings of the
Fathers in the various oriental languages, each accompanied by a translation in a
more commonly understood language. Publication began at Paris in 1903, and
continues, now at Louvain. The corpus has seven sub-series: Syriac, Coptic,
Arabic, Armenian, Georgian, and Ethiopic texts and translations; and *Subsidia*,
embracing various monographs and linguistic treatises.

et postea = and afterwards.

fl. = *floruit* = flourished.

forte = perhaps.

GCS = *Die griechischen christlichen Schriftsteller der ersten [drei] Jahrhunderte.* Series
of Greek texts of the Fathers, edited by the Preussische Akademie der Wissenschaften, 1897ff. Commonly called the *Berlin Corpus.*

iter = among, between

.isi forte = or maybe.

paulo post = soon after.

PG = Abbé J. P. Migne, *Patrologiae cursus completus: Series graeca.* 161 volumes,
Paris, 1857–1866. Greek texts with Latin translation.

PL = Abbé J. P. Migne, *Patrologiae cursus completus: Series latina.* 221 volumes
including 4 of indices, Paris, 1844–1855.

post = after.

postea = afterwards.

regn. = *regnavit* = reigned.

seu = or [also].

sive = or [also].

Vs. = verse.

VV. = verses.

The Faith of the Early Fathers

EVAGRIUS OF PONTUS [A. D. 345–A. D. 399]

Evagrius Ponticus, born at Ibora in the Pontus, was ordained a lector by St. Basil the Great and a deacon by St. Gregory of Nazianz. In Jerusalem he was acquainted with the Roman lady Melania; and in his self-imposed exile in the deserts of Egypt he knew well Macarius the Alexandrian and Macarius the Egyptian, the latter called also the Great.

It is extremely unfortunate that Evagrius' very numerous writings have not survived in a better state of preservation. The loss of his works is probably attributable in large part to his condemnation as an Origenist in 553 A. D. at the Fifth Ecumenical Council, the Second of Constantinople. We catch glimpses of him in John Climacus, Maximus the Confessor, Philoxene of Mabbug, Isaac of Nineveh, John bar Caldun, John Cassian, and the Bar Hebraeus.

Very little of his works has survived in the original Greek; somewhat more in Latin, Syriac, Armenian, Arabic and Ethiopic translations—just enough to whet the appetite for his many insights, and to make us regret that we have not his works complete.

LETTERS [ante A. D. 399]

About sixty-seven letters of Evagrius are extant in Syriac, and have been published by W. Frankenberg in his *Evagrius Pontikus*, Berlin, 1912, an edition embracing the Syriac text along with Frankenberg's own retranslation back into Greek. We are concerned here with only one of the letters: the only one extant also in what is presumably the original Greek. As early as 1909 J. Schäfer chose to regard letter no. 8 in the corpus of the letters of St. Basil as unauthentic. In 1922 J. Bessières showed that the letter did not pertain to the general tradition of Basil's letters; and in 1923 W. Bousset (*Apophthegmata*, Tübingen, 1923, pp. 335–336) and R. Melcher (in his article *"Der achte Brief des Basilius, ein Werk des Evagrius Pontikus,"* in the *Münsterische Beiträge zur Theologie*, No. 1, 1923) showed independently of each other that the reputed letter 8 of Basil, bearing the heading "An Apology to the People of Caesarea for His Withdrawal, and a Defense of the Faith," is in fact a letter of Evagrius Ponticus to some monks near Caesarea. The Maurist editors had already perceived the unlikelihood of the heading and had judged that it was addressed to a monastery. It is all a little embarrassing in regard to Basil, since this letter no. 8 has so often formed the core, as Quasten notes (*Patrology*, Vol. 3, p. 224), of studies on the theology of Basil.

The letter is not merely anti-Arian but anti-Pneumatomachian, and is an excellent Trinitarian source, to be dated near the end of the fourth century, perhaps in 381 *A.D.*, or soon thereafter, if, as seems probable to some, Evagrius shows in it an awareness of the fifth theological oration of St. Gregory of Nazianz. The text of the letter is found in the corpus of Basil's letters, where it is no. 8: In Migne, PG 32, 245-263. The present standard, however, is Y. Courtonne's critical edition of Basil's letters, Vol. 1, Paris 1957, pp. 22-37. The Syriac version is in Frankenberg's *Evagrius Pontikus*, Berlin 1912, pp. 620-635.

A new edition of all the remains of Evagrius is presently being prepared by A. and C. Guillaumont.

DOGMATIC LETTER ON THE MOST BLESSED TRINITY

911

[*Apud Bas. Ep.* 8, 2]

[The heretics] ought to be confessing that the Father is God, that the Son is God, and that   237
the Holy Spirit is God, just as is taught by the divine words and by those who have   238

a better understanding of the Scriptures. To those who accuse us of a doctrine of   151
three Gods, let it be stated that we confess one God, not in number but in nature (1).
For all that is said to be one numerically is not one absolutely, nor is it simple
in nature. It is universally confessed, however, that God is simple and not composite.

912

[Apud Bas. Ep. 8, 3]

In accord with the true teaching we do not speak of the Son as being either like (2) or   257
unlike (3) the Father. Each of these terms is equally impossible; for likeness and unlikeness
are predicated in respect to quality, and divinity is not restricted by quality. We, however,
confess the identity (4) of nature, accept the consubstantiality (5), and shun any
compositeness in the Father, God according to substance (6), who begot the Son, God
according to substance. It is from the fact of their both being God according to substance
that their consubstantiality is shown.

914

[Apud Bas. Ep. 8, 10]

You call the Holy Spirit a creature. And every creature is the servant of its creator.   277
"All things," it is said, "serve You" (7). But if He is a servant, His holiness is acquired;
and anything which acquires its holiness is capable also of evil. It is because the Holy
Spirit is holy in substance, however, that He is called the "font of sanctification" (8).
The Holy Spirit, therefore, is not a creature. And if not a creature, He is consubstantial
(9) with God.

1. τῇ φύσει.
2. ὅμοιον.
3. ἀνόμοιον.
4. ταυτότητα.
5. τὸ ὁμοούσιον.
6. κατ' οὐσίαν.
7. Ps. 118 [119]:91.
8. See Rom. 1:4.
9. ὁμοούσιον.

ST. BASIL THE GREAT [*ca A. D.* 330–Jan. 1, 379]

The three great lights who are so often referred to as the Three Cappadocians are Basil the Great of Caesarea, his friend Gregory of Nazianz, and his own brother, Gregory of Nyssa. Basil was born about the year 330 A. D. at Caesarea in Cappadocia to a most illustrious family. His father Basil was the son of St. Macrina the Elder, a zealous pupil of St. Gregory the Thaumaturge of Neocaesarea. His mother Emmelia was the daughter of a martyr. Of the ten children in the family three became bishops: Basil himself, made bishop of Caesarea in 370, Gregory, bishop of Nyssa, and Peter, bishop of Sebaste. The oldest daughter, St. Macrina the Younger, was a model of the ascetical life.

As a student in Athens Basil first met Gregory of Nazianz, joining with him in a friendship so close that in his eulogy to Basil in 381 A. D., Gregory could say that they were "one soul with two bodies."

Soon after his baptism, which was postponed until his adult years, Basil sought for a more perfect way of life, journeying throughout Egypt and the Middle East inspecting the various ascetical and eremitical establishments. Finally upon coming home he met Eustathius of Sebaste, who seemed to Basil to have discovered already that for which he had himself been searching for so long. The history of his friendship with Eustathius is rather like that of Jerome with Rufinus. And if Basil's love lacked the glutinous quality of Jerome's, when at last the friendship was dissolved its aftermath of accusations and counteraccusations was scarcely less venomous and scarcely less a scandal to the Christian world.

The history of Basil's conflicts with Arianism in its various forms and with Pneumatomachianism is virtually synonymous with the history of the Trinitarian dogma in the second half of the fourth century. He saw Arianism reach its ultimate and disastrously logical conclusion in Eunomian anomoianism, while a portion of the homoiousian party passed through a brief period of orthodoxy only to fall victim to a second Arianism, the Macedonian denials of the divinity of the Holy Spirit.

In the time of the Emperor Valens Basil was virtually the only Orthodox bishop in all the East who succeeded in retaining charge of his see. He did it by sheer force of character, combined with the courage to withstand the Emperor when needful and to ignore him when practicable. This was a period when, throughout the world, the orthodox bishops who remained in charge of Churches could be counted on one's fingers, and probably on the fingers of one hand.

Ask a Catholic today what is the greatest tragedy ever to befall Christ's Church and he will probably reply that it was the Reformation in the sixteenth century, which so rent the seamless robe that its schism is with us still. But the historian knows that in its own time Arianism was far more general than Protestantism has ever been. If it has no other importance for modern man, a knowledge of the history of Arianism should demonstrate at least that the Catholic Church takes no account of popularity and numbers in shaping and maintaining doctrine: else, we should long since have had to abandon Basil and Hilary and Athanasius and Liberius and Ossius and call ourselves after Arius.

Basil is accounted the founder of Eastern monasticism; and with St. John Chrysostom, he is one of the two pillars of the Oriental Church. Other pillars there may be in other contexts; but in the presence of Basil and Chrysostom they become mere pilasters.

LETTERS [*inter ca. A. D.* 357-378]

The corpus of St. Basil's letters, running to some 368 items, is perhaps our most valuable source for biographical details about himself. The letters reveal the saint as a

polished and cultured gentleman of excellent education; and, unwittingly no doubt, they reveal also certain minor weaknesses of character—Jerome's barbed remark about Basil's pride does not really miss the mark—when their author treads the thin line between not telling the whole truth and engaging in outright untruth; and that other thin line between obsequiousness and hypocrisy. In writing to Demosthenes, a certain civil official, no praise is too great (Letter 225); but in writing about Demosthenes to others, he calls him "the first and greatest of our evils" (letter 237) and "a fat sea monster" (Letter 231). Through his letters, in short, we find that Basil is a real man of flesh and blood, not just a plaster saint.

As might be expected, the corpus contains letters to Basil as well as those written by him. And naturally there are questions about authenticity in regard to some of the letters. In my article "A Letter of Meletius of Antioch", in the *Harvard Theological Review*, Vol. 53, no. 4 (Oct., 1960), I showed that letter 92 in the corpus should in all probability be attributed to Meletius, although Basil too, with several others, signed it. In regard to questions of authenticity and chronology, however, we can only refer the reader to more specialized studies such as those of F. Loofs, J. Bessières, S. Y. Rudberg, and Prestige (ed. Chadwick), while affirming that we will cite only such letters as are generally accepted as authentic.

The text of Basil's letters can be found in Migne, PG 32, 219-1112. There is also a four volume bilingual edition, Greek and English, in the Loeb Classical Library, the work of Roy Deferrari. The present standard is Y. Courtonne's *Saint Basile. Lettres,* in three volumes, Paris 1957, 1961 and 1966 respectively.

LETTER OF BASIL TO HIS BROTHER GREGORY (1) *A. D.* 369 *aut* 370.

915

[38, 4]

Since, therefore, the Holy Spirit, from whom the whole abundance of good things is   285
poured out upon creation, is linked with the Son, with whom He is inseparably joined,   269
and has His existence from the Father as from a source, whence also He proceeds, He has this as the characteristic mark of the individuality of His Person (2): that He was made known after the Son and with Him, and that He subsists from the Father.
But the Son, who of Himself and through Himself makes known the Spirit who proceeds   281
from the Father, and who alone shines forth as the Only-begotten from the Unbegotten Light, has in common with the Father or with the Holy Spirit none of the characteristic marks by which He is Himself known; rather, it is He alone who is recognized by the stated signs. The Supreme God alone has as the special mark of His Person by which   250
He may be known, that He is the Father and subsists from no other source; and   259
again it is through this mark that He is recognized individually. . . . But anyone
who perceives the Father both perceives Him by Himself and likewise includes the Son   238
in that perception. And anyone who perceives the Son does not separate Him from the Spirit but, sequentially in order and conjointly in nature, expresses the faith so commingled in himself in the Three together. And anyone who makes mention of the Spirit alone, does also embrace in this confession Him of whom He is the Spirit. And since the Spirit is of Christ and of God, as Paul says (3), just as a man who grasps one end of a chain at the same time draws the other end to himself, so too, anyone who draws the Spirit, as the Prophet says (4) thereby draws also the Son and the Father. And if anyone truly receives the Son, he will hold Him on both sides, while the Son   270
draws toward him on one side His own Father and on the other His own Spirit. . . .   237
It is quite impossible to conceive of any sort of separation or division by which the Son could be thought of apart from the Father, or the Spirit be disjoined from the Son;

rather, the communion and the distinction apprehended in Them, are, in a certain
sense, inexpressible and unimaginable, since the continuity of their nature is never   239
broken by the distinction of Persons (5), nor are their notes of proper distinction ever
confessed in Their community of essence (6).

LETTER OF BASIL TO A PATRICIAN LADY CAESARIA. ca. A. D. 372.

916

[93]
   To communicate each day and to partake of the holy Body and Blood of Christ is   873
good and beneficial; for He says quite plainly: "He that eats My Flesh and drinks My   850
Blood has eternal life (7)." Who can doubt that to share continually in life is the same   877
thing as having life abundantly (8)? We ourselves communicate four times each week, on
Sunday, Wednesday, Friday, and Saturday (9); and on other days if there is a
commemoration of any saint. It were needless to point out that for anyone in times of   868
persecution to be obliged, in the absence of a priest or deacon (10), to receive
communion by his own hand is certainly not a serious offence, because long custom
sanctions this practice in such cases. Indeed, all the solitaries in the desert, where
there is no priest, reserving Communion at home, receive it from their own hands.   865
In Alexandria and in Egypt everyone, even of the laity, reserves Communion in his
own home and receives by his own hand whenever he is pleased to do so.

THE TRANSCRIPT OF FAITH DICTATED BY THE MOST HOLY BASIL AND SIGNED BY EUSTATHIUS, BISHOP OF SEBASTE. A. D. 373.

917

[125, 3]
   We neither say that the Holy Spirit is unbegotten,—for we know one Unbegotten   250
and one Beginning of beings, the Father of our Lord Jesus Christ,—nor do we say that   276
He is begotten; for in the tradition of the faith we have been taught that there is one
Only begotten. We have been taught that the Spirit of Truth proceeds from the Father,   100
and we confess that He is uncreatedly from God. . . . We must add this also, that   269
they must be shunned as evidently hostile to piety who overturn the order given us   234
by the Lord and place the Son before the Father, and the Holy Spirit before the Son.
Indeed, we must preserve unaltered and inviolate the order which we have received
from the very words of the Lord when He said: "Going forth, make disciples of all
nations, baptizing them in the name of the Father and of the Son and of the Holy Spirit
(11)." ✠ I, Bishop Eustathius, having read this aloud to you, Basil, have understood
and have agreed with what is written above. I have signed it in the presence of my
brothers, our Fronto, and the Chorbishop Severus, and some others of the clergy (12).

A LETTER OF BASIL TO DIODORE, A PRIEST OF ANTIOCH AND AFTERWARDS BISHOP OF TARSUS. A. D. 373 aut 374.

918

[160, 1]
   A letter has reached us which bears the name of Diodore, but which seems in its   980
content to belong to anyone except Diodore. It really appears to us that some clever

fellow, masquerading in your person, wanted, by using your name, to make himself
seem reliable to his audience. Asked by someone if it was permissible for him to marry
the sister of his dead wife, he did not tremble in horror at the question but listened
calmly, and very nobly and gloriously supported the wanton desire! . . . [2] First of
all, then, a point of greatest importance in such matters, we have a custom which we can
interpose; and it has the force of law, because its regulations were handed down to us
by holy men. It is simply this: If anyone, overcome by impurity, falls into unlawful
intercourse (13) with two sisters, neither is it to be regarded as a marriage, nor are they
to be admitted at all to the assembly of the Church until they have separated from
each other.

OF BASIL TO AMPHILOCHIUS, BISHOP OF ICONIUM: THE FIRST CANONICAL LETTER (14). A. D. 374.

919

[188, 1]
   It seemed best to the men of former times,—Cyprian and our Firmilian, I mean, and   950
their colleagues,—to subject all of these, whether Cathari, Encratites, or Hydroparastates
(15), to a like judgment, because their separation had been initiated through schism,
and because those who had separated themselves from the Church no longer had in
themselves the grace of the Holy Spirit, when His being imparted ceased through   803
the breach of its continuity. For those who first withdrew had their ordination from the   962
Fathers, and through the imposition of their hands they had the spiritual charism.   792
But, having broken away, they became laymen, and had the power neither to baptize   951
nor to ordain (16) nor could they any longer confer on others that grace of the Holy
Spirit from which they themselves had fallen away.

919a

[188, 2]
   A woman who has deliberately destroyed a fetus must pay the penalty for murder.   969

919b

[188, 3]
   A deacon who has committed fornication after being admitted to the diaconate is to   951
be dismissed from the ministry; but, reduced to the rank of the laity, he is not barred
from the reception of communion.

919c

[188, 4]
   In regard to trigamists and polygamists the same canon is laid down as in the case   979
of digamists, but in proper proportion: for digamists, one year, or, as some say, two
years, while trigamists are excommunicated for three years and often for four years.
Moreover, such a state is no longer called marriage but polygamy or, indeed, a
moderate fornication. . . . We have accepted as our usual practice, not from the
canons but in conformity with our predecessors, a separation of five years in the case
of trigamists. Yet, there is no need to separate them entirely from the Church.
Rather, in two or three years, consider them worthy of being hearers, and after this
allow them to stand with the rest at prayer, while excluding them from Holy

Communion. Restore them to their place of Communion only after they have shown
some fruitful repentance.

919d

[188, 6]
   The fornications of canonical persons must not be considered marriage; rather,   980
their union must certainly be broken (17).   964

919e

[188, 8]
   A man who, in a fit of temper, used an axe on his wife is a murderer.   902

919f

[188, 8]
   Those also who give drugs causing abortions are murderers themselves, as well as   969
those who receive the poison which kills the fetus (18).

919g

[188, 9]
   The Lord's declaration about the prohibition of departing from a marriage except   974
for the reason of fornication, consistent with its meaning, applies equally to men and
to women. Yet, such is not the practice; on the contrary, we find a greater strictness
in regard to women. Custom orders adulterous men and fornicators to be retained by
their wives (19). . . . She that left her husband is an adulteress if she went to another
man. But the husband she abandoned is to be pardoned, and the woman who cohabits
with such a man is not condemned. But if a man who separates from his wife goes to
another woman, he is himself an adulterer, because he has made her commit adultery;
and the woman cohabiting with him is an adulteress because she has taken another's
husband to herself.

919h

[188, 12]
   The canon absolutely excludes digamists from the ministry.   964

919i

[188, 13]
   Our Fathers did not reckon killings in war as murders, but granted pardon, as it   902
seems to me, to those who were fighting in defence of virtue and piety. Perhaps,
however, they should be advised that, since their hands are not clean, they should
abstain from Communion for a period of three years (20).

*OF BASIL TO AMPHILOCHIUS, BISHOP OF ICONIUM: THE SECOND CANONICAL
   LETTER. A. D. 375.*

921a

[199, 21]
   When a man living with a wife becomes dissatisfied with his marriage and falls into   975
fornication, we call such a man a fornicator and we keep him longer under penalty. We do

not, however, have any canon by which to bring against him a charge of adultery if his sin
is with an unmarried woman (21). . . . He that has committed fornication is not excluded
from cohabitation with his wife. A wife, therefore, will receive her husband when he
returns from fornication; but the husband will send away from his home a defiled wife. The
reasoning for this is not easy, but custom has so ruled.

921b

[199, 37]

A man who marries after another man's wife has been taken away from him will   974
be charged with adultery in the case of the first woman; but in the case of the second he
will be guiltless.

921c

[199, 46]

A woman who marries a man, not knowing at the time that he was deserted by a wife,   974
and who is afterwards dismissed because his former wife has returned to him, has   975
committed fornication, though it be in ignorance. She will not on this account be
barred from marriage; but it will be better if she remain unmarried (22).

922

[199, 48]

A woman who has been abandoned by her husband ought, in my opinion, remain   974
[alone]. For when the Lord says, "If anyone dismisses his wife, except on account of   975
immorality, he causes her to commit adultery (23)," by her being named an adulteress
she is barred from union with another. For how were it possible for the man to be
responsible, as the cause of adultery, and the woman be blameless, whom the Lord
calls an adulteress because of her intercourse with another man?

OF BASIL TO AMPHILOCHIUS, BISHOP OF ICONIUM: THE THIRD CANONICAL LETTER. A. D. 375.

922a

[217, 75]

Let him who has been defiled with his own sister, the daughter of his father or   904
mother, not be permitted to be present in the house of prayer until he cease from his
iniquitous and unlawful conduct. After coming to an awareness of that dread sin,
let him be a weeper for three years (24), standing at the door of the houses of prayer
and begging the people entering there for the purpose of praying to offer in sympathy
for him, each one, earnest petitions to the Lord. After this let him be admitted for
another three years among the hearers only (25); and when he has heard the Scriptures
and the teachings let him be put out and not be deemed worthy of prayer. Then, if he
has sought it with tears and has cast himself down before the Lord with a contrite
heart and with great humility, let him be given submission for another three years
(26). And thus, when he has exhibited worthy fruits of repentance, let him be admitted
in the tenth year to the prayer of the faithful without Communion. And when he has
assembled for two years in prayer with the faithful, then let him finally be deemed
worthy of the Communion of the good (27).

LETTER OF BASIL TO AMPHILOCHIUS, BISHOP OF ICONIUM. A. D. 376.

923

[234, 1]

    The operations of God are various, but His essence (28) is simple. We say, however,   151
that we know our God from His operations; His essence itself, we do not undertake   179
to approach. His operations come down to us, but His essence remains inaccessible.   174
[2] . . . Know that it is the voice of scoffers that says: "If you are ignorant of the
essence of God, you adore what you do not know." I know that He is; but what His   173
essence is, that I regard as beyond understanding. How, then, am I saved? Through
faith. Faith suffices in itself to know that God is, not what He is. And He is the Rewarder   550
of those who seek Him (29). Knowledge of the divine essence consists in our perceiving   564
His incomprehensibility; and the object of our worship is not that of which we
comprehend the essence, but that of which we comprehend that the essence exists.

LETTER OF BASIL TO AMPHILOCHIUS, BISHOP OF ICONIUM, A. D. 376.

924

[235, 1]

    Which is first, knowledge or faith? We say that in general, in the case of the   564
mathematical sciences (30), faith precedes knowledge. But if, in our teaching, anyone
say that knowledge comes before faith, I raise no objection, rather taking knowledge
as referring to the knowledge that is within the limits of human comprehension.

LETTER OF BASIL TO AMPHILOCHIUS, BISHOP OF ICONIUM. A. D. 376.

926

[236, 6]

    Essence and person (31) differ as the general and the specific, as living being and   238
particular man. In the Godhead, therefore, we confess one essence, so as not to give a   281
varying definition of being; but we acknowledge a particularization of person, so that
our notion of Father and Son and Holy Spirit may be unconfused and clear. For if we
do not consider the separate qualities of each,—I mean paternity, filiation, and
sanctification,—but confess God only, from the general concept of existence, we   277
cannot possibly offer a sound explanation of our faith. It is necessary, therefore, to
confess our faith by adding the particular to the general. Godhead is general, while
paternity is particular. Joining the two, we must say: "I believe in God the Father."
Again in our confession of the Son we must do the same, joining the particular to the
general, to say: "I believe in God the Son." Likewise in the case of the Holy Spirit we   266
must make our utterance conform to His appellation and say: "I believe also in the
Divine Holy Spirit." This we do so that the [divine] unity may be safeguarded
throughout by the confession of one Godhead, while the particularization of Persons
(32) is confessed in the distinction of the characteristics recognized in each.

LETTER OF BASIL TO OPTIMUS, BISHOP OF ANTIOCH IN PISIDIA. A. D. 377.

927

[260, 9]

    Since, therefore, every soul was, at the time of the Passion, subjected, as it were, to   785 a kind of doubt, in accord with the Lord's word when He said: "You will all be scandalized in Me (33)," Simeon prophesies also of Mary herself that, standing beneath the cross and seeing what was happening and hearing His words, even after the testimony of Gabriel (34), even after her secret knowledge of the divine conception (35), and after the great showing of miracles,—she too, he says, will experience a certain unsteadiness in her soul (36). For the Lord must taste of death for the sake of all; and to become a propitiation for the world, He must justify all men in His blood. "Some doubt, therefore, will touch even you yourself, who have been taught from above about the Lord." That is the sword (37).

386

LETTER OF BASIL TO THE PEOPLE OF SOZOPOLIS IN PISIDIA. A. D. 377.

928

[261, 2]

If the coming of the Lord in the flesh did not take place, the Redeemer did not pay Death the price for us (38), and did not by Himself destroy the reign of Death. For if that which is subject to Death were one thing and that which was assumed by the Lord were another, then neither would Death have stopped doing his own works nor would the suffering of the God-bearing flesh have become gain for us. He would not have destroyed sin in the flesh; we who had been dying in Adam would not have been made alive in Christ; that which had fallen apart would not have been repaired; that which was shattered would not have been restored; that which had been alienated from God by the deceit of the serpent would not have been made God's own again.

310
384
314
374
376

929

[261, 3]

It is evident, then, that the Lord took on natural feelings (39) in order to confirm that the Incarnation was a true one and not phantasmal, but rejected as unworthy of the Godhead the feelings which arise from vice and which soil the purity of our lives. That is why it is said that He was made "in the likeness of sinful flesh (40)"; not in the likeness of the flesh, as some suppose, but "in the likeness of sinful flesh." Thus did He take our flesh with its natural feelings; yet, "He did not sin (41)."

349
343

345

1. This letter is found also in the manuscript tradition of the letters of Basil's brother, Gregory of Nyssa, addressed to another brother, Peter of Sebaste. Its ascription to Gregory is the more likely, but modern scholarship has not yet arrived at a firm solution to the problem of its authorship. The content of the letter describes the difference between the terms οὐσία and ὑπόστασις (See also § 926 below). Prior to Basil's time most of the Eastern authors used the terms οὐσία and ὑπόστασις as synonymous terms for essence, also called substance. For Basil, and largely since his time, οὐσία is essence or substance, while ὑπόστασις is person, the subsisting πρόσωπον.
2. τὴν ὑπόστασιν.
3. Rom. 8:9.
4. Ps. 118 [119]:131. In the Psalm, however, the phrase does not mean to draw the Holy Spirit, but simply to draw breath.
5. τῶν ὑποστάσεων.
6. τῆς κατὰ τὴν οὐσίαν κοινότητος.
7. John 6:55.
8. ζῆν πολλάκως. Lit., life manifoldly or in many ways. An old Latin translation renders the passage as having a multiplex basis for living—multiplici ratione vivere.
9. ἐν τῇ κυριακῇ, ἐν τῇ τετράδι, καὶ ἐν τῇ παρασκευῇ, καὶ τῷ σαββάτῳ.
10. μὴ παρόντος ἱερέως ἢ λειτουργοῦ.
11. Matt. 28:19.
12. See W. A. Jurgens, Eustathius of Sebaste, Rome 1959, pp. 65-66.
13. ἄθεσμον κοινωνίαν.
14. Nos. 188, 199 and 217 in the corpus of Basil's letters are responses to questions posited by Amphilochius, Bishop of Iconium. They are termed respectively the First, Second, and Third Canonical Letters of Basil, because they have been arranged, though by a later hand, in the form of canons or legal prescriptions. It seems probable to me that the questions and answers were directed not to abstract principles but to actual concrete cases with which Amphilochius was confronted.

15. The Cathari are the Novatianists. The Council of Nicaea acknowledged the validity of their sacraments. The Encratites, under a gnostic influence, condemned marriage, the use of wine and animal foods. The Hydroparastates were such a sect who interpreted the Encratite teaching so strictly that they used no wine even at Mass, but only water.
16. χειροτονεῖν.
17. The Canonists Balsamon and Zonaras think that "canonical persons" means all who are enumerated on the rolls: clerics, monks, nuns, and girls living at home in professed virginity. Aristenus and, with him, the Maurist editors, find that Basil uses the term specifically for professed virgins.
18. This is similar in content to the 21st Canon of the Council of Ancyra of 314 A. D.
19. An influence, no doubt, of the civil law which allowed a man to obtain a divorce, but not a woman.
20. According to Balsamon and Zonaras the advice of this Canon was never put into practice. The bishops did, however, appeal to this Canon against the Emperor Phocas (602-610 A. D.) when he wanted all his soldiers who were killed in battle to be honored as martyrs.
21. Roman Law was much concerned with property rights and inheritance. It is apparently under this influence that Basil would seem to define as adultery the intercourse of a married or unmarried man with a married woman not his wife, and fornication the intercourse of a married or unmarried man with an unmarried woman; whereas the intercourse of an unmarried woman with an unmarried man is fornication, of an unmarried woman with a married man—not quite logically—adultery; and the intercourse of a married woman with any man not her husband, married or unmarried, adultery. Basically, it makes the distinction of fornication or adultery depend entirely upon the marital status of the woman in the illicit union. The rationale behind these distinctions must have been the danger of a woman's presenting her husband with a putative offspring not really his own, with the consequent danger of dispersing his properties in inheritance to one who is not his own blood.
22. This canon, combined with nos. 31 and 36 from this same source, is found later as Can. 93 of the celebrated Synod in Trullo. N.B. The Trullo or Trullanum is not a city, but a domed meeting room in the imperial palace at Constantinople.
23. Matt. 5:32.
24. τριετίαν προσκλαιέτω.
25. ἄλλην τριετίαν εἰς ἀκρόασιν μόνην παραδεχθήτω
26. διδόσθω αὐτῷ ἡ ὑπόπτωσις ἐν ἄλλοις τρισὶν ἔτεσιν.
27. The four classes of penitents enumerated by Basil are the same as those listed in the 11th Canon of the *Canonical Letter* of St. Gregory the Miracle-Worker (§ 611a above in Volume I).
28. ἡ οὐσία.
29. See Heb. 11:6.
30. ἐπὶ τῶν μαθημάτων.
31. οὐσία δὲ καὶ ὑπόστασις.
32. τῶν προσώπων.
33. Matt. 26:31.
34. See Luke 1:32-33.
35. See Luke 1:35.
36. This is Basil's highly questionable interpretation, in which he but follows Origen, of the sword that would pierce Mary's soul. Simeon's prophecy was: "Thy own soul a sword shall pierce."
37. See Luke 2:35.
38. Another of Origen's wretched opinions accepted by Basil: that the blood price was paid by the Savior not to His own Father but to Satan or Death.
39. τὰ μὲν φυσικὰ πάθη παραδεξάμενος.
40. Rom. 8:3.
41. 1 Peter 2:22. See also Is. 53:9.

AGAINST EUNOMIUS [*inter A. D.* 363-365]

St. Basil's *Against Eunomius* or, as it is called in Greek, *Refutation of the Apology of the Impious Eunomius,* in three books, is the earliest of his dogmatic writings. Eunomius, Bishop of Cyzicus since *ca.* 360 A.D. and the friend and pupil of Aëtius of Antioch, is accounted the father of the radical Arians. It was he who brought to prominence the faction which supported Anomoianism, Arianism brought to its ultimate logical consequence, holding that Father and Son are unlike (ἀνόμοιος) in all things. The party in fact are often called Eunomians, the term being used as synonymous with Anomoians.

Eunomius' *Apology* had been published about the year 361 A.D. Basil's refutation deals in book 1 with the argument that God's essence consists in His not being born, innascibility or ἀγεννησία, this being the major of the syllogism leading to the conclusion that the Word cannot be true Son of God, since He is generated. Book 2 defends the Nicene proposition of the Son's consubstantiality (ὁμοουσία) with the Father. Book 3 does the same for the Holy Spirit, against the Macedonian or Pneumatomachian position. Published editions of the work usually have five books, but books 4 and 5 are actually appended works of Didymus the Blind.

The older Nicenes had used the terms *ousia* and *hypostasis* as synonymous, meaning being or essence; and this did lead to a certain confusion. Without subscribing at all to von Harnack's position that the Cappadocians were never truly Nicene but actually succeeded in canonizing the homoian view, I am inclined to believe that in his very early career Basil did tend toward the acceptance of homoiousian terminology. If this latter be the fact, it is very likely his wrestling with this problem of sameness and likeness that put him on the path to genuine advance in Trinitarian theology. At any rate, for Basil *hypostasis* is not a synonym for *ousia*; it does not mean *being*. Rather, it means *person* and is a better term for this than the older *prosopon* which was subject to severe misunderstanding through its use by Sabellius in a modalist context. As late as 362 A. D. a synod of Alexandria presided over by Athanasius admitted that one could speak legitimately either of one *hypostasis* or of three *hypostaseis*. Basil's formula, and he is the first to insist on it, is μία οὐσία, τρεῖς ὑποστάσεις–one being, three hypostases, *i.e.*, one essence, three persons.

The Migne edition of Basil's works, largely a re-editing of the older Maurist edition of J. Garnier and Pr. Maran, always enjoyed a reputation of special excellence. The Migne text of the *Against Eunomius*, PG 29, col. 297-669, remains the standard.

930

[1, 10]

There is no one name sufficiently broad to take in the whole nature of God. There are names, however, many and varied, obscure and of little importance in view of the whole, but each of its own special significance, which, when assembled together, convey to us a sufficient understanding of God's nature. Among these names which are ascribed to Him, some signify what qualities are inherent in God, whereas others indicate what qualities are not found in Him. From these two categories, from the denial of what is absent and from the confession of what is present, we find expressed for us a certain character, as it were, of God.

175

181

931

[1, 14]

I reckon that the comprehension of God's essence is beyond not just men alone but beyond every rational nature. When I say rational, however, I mean created. For the Father is known by the Son alone, and by the Holy Spirit. "No one," the Scriptures say, "knows the Father except the Son," and "the Spirit probes all things, even the depths of God (1)." . . . It follows, then, that the essence of God is not perceivable by any except the Only-begotten and the Holy Spirit. From such operations of God, however, as fall under our gaze, and from created things, we recognize a Creator, and in this way too we perceive His goodness and His wisdom. What is known about God, He has manifested to all men (2).

173

188

179

932

[1, 15]

    When our mind considers whether or not the God who is over all things (3) can   141
have some cause to which He is Himself subject, and can think of none, it terms His   250
life, since it is without beginning, unbegotten (4). . . . When, therefore, Luke says that
Adam is from God (5), do we not ask ourselves, "From whom, then, is God?" And
is there not in the mind of each of us a ready answer, "from no one"? But that which
is from no one is without beginning; and what is without beginning is unbegotten.

    Just as the from-another-ness of men is not their essence, neither with the God of
the whole universe can we say that His essence is His unbegottenness (6), though in fact
He is from none.

933

[2, 9]

    Is there anyone who does not know that with names there are some which signify   181
their underlying realities absolutely and by their very utterance, whereas there are others
with whose utterance there is made apparent only a relationship to something else? For
example, with man, horse, cow, each indicates the very thing named. But son, servant,
friend signify only the affinity they have with that to which, by name, they are related.
Thus when one hears of the begotten, his mind is drawn not to some essence, but he is
made to know its relationship to another. For that is called begotten which is the product
begotten of something.

934

[2, 12]

    The God of the whole universe is the Father even from infinity, and never at any   256
time did he commence to be the Father. He was not restrained by any lack of power in
the carrying out of His will, nor did He have to await the passage of certain times, as do
men and the rest of the animals, to achieve the faculty of generating only with the completion
of a certain age, so that He might then carry out what He intended (really, it is the part of
madmen to think and speak thus), but had ever His paternity, if I may so speak, coextensively
with His eternity. The Son too, therefore, existing before time and existing always,
never began to be; but if there is father, there is son, and as soon as there is thought of father
thought of son enters in. For father plainly bespeaks father of son. Of the Father, then,
there is no origin, and the origin of the Son is the Father; nor is there any interval   250
between them.

935

[2, 14]

    [Eunomius:] God begot the Son, when the Son was either existing or not existing. If I   292
choose not existing, no one will accuse me of rashness. If existing,—well, such
a statement would go quite beyond not just absurdity and blasphemy, but outright
silliness; for what already exists has no need of being begotten.

    [Basil:] . . . At the very outset we warned our audience about the difficulty in   256
these expressions for a considerable number of people who, out of ignorance, think
of the generation of the Son after a human fashion.

936

[2, 17]

    What Eunomius is asking is really nothing else but whether we cannot inquire as to   256

whether or not the Father existed before His own subsisting. The question, you see, 250
is senseless. To inquire after something superior to Him who has no beginning and is
unbegotten, and to posit questions of temporal priority when inquiring after Him
who is with the Father from eternity and in whose regard there is no interval between
Himself and the One begetting Him,—well, plainly the one course is just as
mindless as the other. It makes little difference whether he ask what will happen
after the death of one who is immortal, or if he ask what existed before the generation
of one who is eternal. These people think that because the lack of a beginning in the
Father is called eternity, the lack of a beginning is the same thing as eternity; and
they suppose that since the Son is not unbegotten they are to declare that He is
not eternal. Yet these terms differ greatly in significance. For unbegotten says that
something has neither beginning of its own nor a cause of its existing (7); but
eternal says that, in respect to its being, it is older than all time and age. The Son,
accordingly, though He is not unbegotten, is eternal.

937

[2, 18]
    It is evident to everyone that whenever the same person is termed both an angel 236
and God, it is the Only-begotten who is manifested, making Himself
visible to men generation after generation and proclaiming the will of the Father to His
saints. So too it can be understood that the One who in Moses' presence called Himself
the Really Existing (8), is none other than God the Word, who in the beginning was with
God (9).

940

[3, 1]
    The Son is second in order from the Father, because He is from Him; and in dignity, 259
because the Father is His origin and cause, whereby the Father is His Father, and
because it is through the Son that access and approach is had to God the Father. The 268
Son is not, however, second to the Father in nature, because the Godhead is one in
each of them, and plainly, too, in the Holy Spirit, even if in order and in dignity He
is second to the Son (yes, this we do concede!), though not in such a way, it is clear, 492
that He were of another nature. All the angels, having but one appellation, have 493
likewise among themselves the same nature, even though some of them are set over
nations, while others of them are guardians (10) to each one of the faithful.

941

[3, 2]
    Principalities and Powers (11) and all the rest of the creatures of the same sort, who 489
are shown by attention and study to have holiness, cannot be said to be holy of 740
their very nature. Yearning to possess the good, they receive a measure of holiness in
proportion to their love of God (12). . . . This is how they differ from the Holy
Spirit: His nature is holiness, whereas the holiness that is in the angels is there by 277
reason of their participating in it.

1. Matt. 11:27 and 1 Cor. 2:10.
2. See Rom. 1:19.
3. See Rom. 9:5.
4. ἀγέννητον.

5. Luke 3:38; so far back does Luke trace the genealogy of Christ.
6. οὐδὲ ἐπὶ τοῦ θεοῦ τῶν ὅλων οὐσίαν ἐστὶν εἰπεῖν τὸ ἀγέννητον.
7. Apparently Basil felt no necessity of pointing out again to an audience perhaps more accustomed to philosophical discussion than we are in our times that neither of these notions, beginning (ἡ ἀρχὴ) and cause (ἡ αἰτία), does of itself imply anything temporal. The difficulty, of course, is that we are human beings, not gods; and we have no experience of any beginning or cause of being that is apart from time.
8. ὥστε καὶ ἐπὶ τοῦ Μωϋσέως ὄντα ἑαυτὸν ὀνομάσας.
9. John 1:2.
10. παρεπόμενοι: literally, *followers-at-the-side*.
11. ἀρχαὶ . . . καὶ ἐξουσίαι.
12. κατὰ τὴν ἀναλογίαν τῆς πρὸς τὸν θεὸν ἀγάπης.

THE HOLY SPIRIT [*A. D.* 375]

Arianism ultimately taught that the Three Persons of the Trinity were wholly unlike each other both in essence and in glory. They were, in fact, unlike in all things; and when one of the Arian preachers declared that "the Son is pious, but the Father is impious," a grumbling among the people was kept from advancing toward riot by his quick and facile explanation that the Son is pious because he reveres the Father; but the Father is impious because he has none to revere. To see the point of this more clearly, the reader may need to remind himself that the virtue of piety is not the ill-defined religious feeling that the term usually describes today but is, in its more precise sense, the virtue of a son's reverencing his father.

If in its earlier development Arianism had little or nothing to say of the Holy Spirit, this phase did not long perdure. It was Macedonius, a homoiousian, who initiated the direct attack on the Holy Spirit; and the Arianism that directly denies the divinity of the Spirit is variously termed Macedonianism, Marathonianism (from Marathonius of Nicomedia) and Pneumatomachianism (the -ism of those who fight against the Holy Spirit). Macedonius was expelled from the See of Constantinople in 360 A. D., and with his expulsion the fight grew more intense and came more into the open.

Basil has been suspected and was held suspect by some in his own time of harboring Semi-Arian (homoiousian) views. It is quite possible that he at one time thought the term homoiousios more apt than homoousios; but certainly he was never Arian or Semi-Arian in his thinking. And in a letter (9, 3) from the year 361 A. D., he declares his preference for homoousios, while stating that he will accept the terminology "ἀπαραλλάκτως ὅμοιον κατ᾽ οὐσίαν — invariably like in substance."

Basil's treatise on *The Holy Spirit*, written in 375 A. D., scandalized many because nowhere in it does he say explicitly that the Holy Spirit is God; yet, he says it implicitly throughout the treatise. And even so orthodox a fighter as St. Athanasius defended Basil and said that he was simply "becoming weak with the weak to gain the weak."

It is one of the paradoxes of history that an important work specifically on the Holy Spirit by a theologian who made such great advances in the theology of the Trinity in general and of the Spirit in particular should have been so bitterly resented by so many of the rigidly orthodox whose positions it supported and explained. But of course, those who make progress must necessarily be to some extent and in a certain sense innovators.

The treatise in fact opens with Basil's defense of his having used in the public celebration of the Liturgy the formula "Glory be to the Father with (μετὰ) the Son together with (σὺν) the Holy Spirit," instead of ". . . through (διὰ) the Son in (ἐν) the Holy Spirit." The work, a single book of 30 chapters, is dedicated to Amphilochius, Bishop of Iconium, the cousin of Basil's friend Gregory of Nazianz.

The Migne text is in PG 32, col. 67-217. The standard edition is that of B. Pruche in the series *Sources Chrétiennes*, Paris 1947, and now in its second edition in the same series, Vol. 17-bis, Paris 1968.

943

[8, 21]

The fact that the Father does His work of creation through the Son does not mean   286
that the Father's creating is imperfect nor does it demonstrate any enfeeblement of the   284
energy of the Son; rather, it but indicates their unity of will. The term "through whom"
contains a confession of the antecedent Cause, and is not adopted because of any objection
to the efficient Cause.

944

[9, 22]

To each who receives the Spirit it is as if he alone received Him; yet, the grace the   753
Spirit pours out is quite sufficient for the whole of mankind. All who share in Him   754
share not according to the measure of His power but according to the capacity of their own
nature. [23] . . . Shining upon those who are cleansed of every blemish, He renders them
spiritual in a communion (1) with Himself. Just as a sunbeam, falling on light and transparent
bodies, makes them exceedingly bright and causes them to pour forth a brilliance from
themselves, so too souls which bear the Spirit and which are illuminated by the Spirit
become spiritual themselves and send forth grace to others. Hence comes to us foreknowledge
of the future, understanding of mysteries, discernment of what is hidden, sharing of good
gifts, heavenly citizenship, a place in the choir of angels, joy without cease, abiding in
God, likeness unto God, and that which is best of all, being made God (2).

945

[12, 28]

Let no one be misled by the fact that the Apostle frequently omits the name of the   826
Father and of the Holy Spirit when mentioning baptism; nor let anyone suppose that   827
the invocation of the Names is a matter of indifference. "Those of you," he says, "who
have been baptized in Christ have put on Christ (3)"; and again, "Those of you who have
been baptized in Christ have been baptized in His death (4)." The naming of Christ,
you see, is the confession of the whole; it bespeaks the God who anoints, the Son who is
anointed, and the Spirit who is the anointing (5). . . . If, then, in baptism the separation
of the Spirit from the Father and the Son is perilous to the one baptizing and useless
to the one receiving, how can it be safe for us to separate the Spirit from the Father   279
and the Son? . . . We believe in a Father, a Son, and a Holy Spirit; so too, then, are
we baptized in the name of the Father and of the Son and of the Holy Spirit.

946

[15, 35]

The design (6) of our God and Savior in regard to mankind is a calling back from the   376
fall and a return to familiar friendship with God (7) from the alienation brought about
by disobedience. This is the reason for Christ's sojourning in the flesh, for the models
of His Gospel actions, the suffering, the cross, the tomb, the resurrection: that man,
who is being saved through his imitation of Christ, might receive that old adoption   755
as son.

947

[15, 35]

This then is what it means to be born again of water and Spirit (8): just as our dying   800
is effected in the water, our living is wrought through the Spirit. In three immersions   825
and in an equal number of invocations the great mystery of baptism is completed
(9) in such a way that the type of death may be shown figuratively, and that by the

handing on of divine knowledge the souls of the baptized may be illuminated (10).
If, therefore, there is any grace in the water, it is not from the nature of water but from the
Spirit's presence there (11).

948

[15, 36]

Our restoration (12) to paradise, our ascent to the kingdom of heaven, our return to   755
the adoption of sons, our vocal freedom to call God our Father, our being made   285
sharers in the grace of Christ, our being termed children of light, our being participants
in eternal glory, and in a word, our being brought into the fullness of blessing (13) in
this world and in the future, is through the Holy Spirit. We await the full enjoyment of all
those good gifts in store for us; and, since they are promised us, it is as if they were already
present, and we contemplate grace represented as if in a mirror.

949

[16, 38]

The manner of the creation of the heavenly powers is passed over in silence, for   283
the historian of the creation of the world has disclosed to us only the creation of things   284
that can be perceived by the senses. You, however, are able to draw an analogy from   285
things that are visible to those that are invisible; glorify, then, the Creator by whom all   286
things were made, visible and invisible, Principalities and Powers, Virtues, Thrones   488
and Dominations (14), and all other rational natures whom we cannot name. In the
creation of the angels, I would have you recall that their original cause is the Father,
their creating cause is the Son, and their perfecting cause the Spirit; thus the ministering
spirits (15) subsist by the will of the Father, are brought into being by the operation
of the Son, and are perfected by the Spirit. The perfection of angels, moreover, is
sanctification and perseverance therein. Let no one suppose that I am affirming three
original hypostases (16), or that I am calling the Son's operation imperfect. The
cause of existing things is One, creating through the Son and perfecting through the
Spirit. The operation of the Father, who effects all in all, is not imperfect, nor is
the Son's creating incomplete if not perfected by the Spirit. The Father, creating
simply by willing, could stand in no need of the Son; nevertheless He wills through
the Son; nor could the Son, working in accord with His likeness to the Father,
have any need of cooperation; but the Son too wills to bring to perfection through
the Spirit.

950

[16, 38]

The Virtues (17) of the heavens are not holy by their very nature; for if this were   285
the case they would not differ from the Holy Spirit. It is in proportion to the relative   489
excellence they have among themselves that they have a measure of sanctification from   740
the Spirit. Although a branding iron is thought of along with fire, it is one notion,   277
nevertheless, and the fire another. This is the case too with the heavenly Virtues,   483
whose substance is perhaps wind in the upper air (18) or immaterial fire, according to
what is written: "Who makes winds His angels, and a flame of fire His ministers (19)."
They exist, therefore, in place and become visible, appearing in their proper bodily forms
to those who are worthy. But sanctification, which is outside their essence, is a perfection
superadded to them through the communion of the Spirit. They maintain their worthiness
by their perseverance in the good; and while they retain their freedom of choice they   486
never fall away from their close attendance upon the Really Good.

951

[17, 43]

The Spirit is spoken of together with the Lord in the same way that the Son is   270
spoken of with the Father. The name of the Father and of the Son and of the Holy   274
Ghost is delivered in like manner. According to the order of the words delivered in
baptism, the relation of Spirit to the Son is the same that the Son has to the Father. And
if the Spirit is ranked with the Son, and the Son with the Father, it is obvious that
the Spirit too is ranked with the Father. What room is there, then, for speaking
either of connumeration or of subnumeration, when the names are ranked in one and
the same coordinate series?

951a

[18, 44]

When the Lord gave us the formula of the Father, the Son, and the Holy Spirit (20),   268
He did not connect the gift with number. . . . Let the Unapproachable be altogether   257
above and beyond number, in the same way that the ancient reverence of the Hebrews
wrote the unutterable name of God in characters reserved, attempting thereby to proclaim
its infinite excellence. Count if you must; but you must not by your counting do
damage to the faith.

952

[18, 45]

In worshiping God of God we profess the distinction of Persons (21) and abide still   257
by the monarchy, not scattering the divine attributes (22) in a divided multiplicity;
for we contemplate one form, so to speak, in God the Father and in God the   258
Only-begotten, displayed in the invariableness of the Godhead. The Son is in the Father
and the Father in the Son. Such as the latter is, so too the former, and such the former,
so the latter; and herein lies the unity. According to distinction of Persons there is
One and One; but according to common nature, both are One. How then, if one and
one, are there not two Gods? It does not follow that there are two kings because we   264
speak of a king and a king's image. The authority is not split nor is the glory divided.
The sovereignty and power to the authority of which we are subject is one, just as   124
the glory we ascribe thereto is not plural but one; for the honor paid the image passes
to the prototype. What, in this example, the image has by imitation, the Son has,
in the point under discussion, by nature.

953

[18, 47]

The path to the knowledge of God lies *from* one Spirit *through* one Son *to* one   238
Father; and conversely the goodness of nature, the holiness of nature and the royal   272
dignity reach *from* the Father *through* the Only-begotten *to* the Holy Spirit. Since
we confess the Persons in this manner. There is no infringing upon the holy dogma
(23) of the monarchy.

954

[27, 66]

Of the dogmas and kerygmas (24) preserved in the Church, some we possess from   100
written teaching and others we receive from the tradition of the Apostles, handed on

to us in mystery (25). In respect to piety both are of the same force. No one will
contradict any of these, no one, at any rate, who is even moderately versed in matters
ecclesiastical. Indeed, were we to try to reject unwritten customs as having no great
authority, we would unwittingly injure the Gospel in its vitals; or rather, we would
reduce kerygma to a mere term. For instance, to take the first and most general example,   125
who taught us in writing to sign with the sign of the cross those who have trusted in
the name of our Lord Jesus Christ? What writing has taught us to turn to the East in   898
prayer? Which of the saints left us in writing the words of the epiclesis at the consecration   863
(26) of the Bread of Eucharist and of the Cup of Benediction? For we are not content
with those words the Apostle or the gospel has recorded, but we say other things
also, both before and after; and we regard these other words, which we have received
from unwritten teaching, as being of great importance to the mystery.

Where is it written that we are to bless the baptismal water, the oil of anointing,   822
and even the one who is being baptized? Is it not from silent and mystical tradition?   841
Indeed, in what written word is even the anointing with oil taught? Where does it say   842
that in baptizing there is to be a triple immersion (27)? And the rest of the things done   825
at Baptism,—where is it written that we are to renounce Satan and his angels? Does this
not come from that secret and arcane teaching (28) which our Fathers guarded in a   810
silence not too curiously meddled with and not idly investigated, when they had
learned well that reverence for the mysteries is best preserved by silence. . . .
In the same way the Apostles and Fathers who, in the beginning, prescribed the Church's
rites, guarded in secrecy and silence the dignity of the mysteries; for that which is
blabbed at random and in the public ear is no mystery at all. This is the reason for our
handing on of unwritten precepts and practices: that the knowledge of our dogmas
may not be neglected and held in contempt by the multitude through too great
a familiarity. Dogma and kerygma are two distinct things. Dogma is observed in
silence; kerygma is proclaimed to all the world.

954a

[27, 66]
We all look toward the East when we pray; but few know that it is because we are   898
looking for our own former country, Paradise, which God planted in Eden in the East
(29). On the first day of the week, we stand when we pray; but not
all of us know why. The reason is that on the day of resurrection, by standing at prayer,
we remind ourselves of the grace we have received (30).

1. τῇ πρὸς ἑαυτὸ κοινωνίᾳ πνευματικοὺς ἀποδείκνυσι.
2. θεὸν γενέσθαι. St. Athanasius in his *Treatise on the Incarnation of the Word* 54, 3 (§ 752 above in volume 1) says of
    the Word: "He became man that we might become God."
3. Gal. 3:27.
4. Rom. 6:3.
5. ἡ γὰρ τοῦ Χριστοῦ προσηγορία . . . δηλοῖ . . . τόν τε χρίσαντα θεόν, καὶ τὸν χρισθέντα υἱόν, καὶ τὸ χρίσμα
    τὸ πνεῦμα.
6. οἰκονομία.
7. εἰς οἰκείωσιν θεοῦ.
8. See John 3:5.
9. τὸ μέγα μυστήριον τοῦ βαπτίσματος τελειοῦται. See § 406 above, with its note 2, in regard to τέλειον.
10. τὰς ψυχὰς φωτισθῶσιν οἱ βαπτιζόμενοι. See again § 406 and its note 2, in regard to φώτισμα.
11. ἐκ τῆς τοῦ πνεύματος παρουσίας.
12. ἀποκατάστασις.
13. Rom. 15:29.
14. εἴτε ἀρχαί, εἴτε ἐξουσίαι, εἴτε δυνάμεις, εἴτε θρόνοι, εἴτε κυριότητες.
15. τὰ λειτουργικὰ πνεύματι.
16. τρεῖς . . . ἀρχικὰς ὑποστάσεις. Basil can hardly be denying that he affirms τρεῖς ὑποστάσεις, since he does not use
    the word ὑπόστασις as a synonymn for ὀυσία, but as meaning Person. He will not be denying that there are three
    Persons, then; and the negative must be taken in view only of ἀρχικάς. They are not all three original, because the Son

is begotten and the Spirit is spirated. This were as good a place as any for the student to review quickly his theology of the Trinity: in God there is one being, two processions, three persons, four relations, and five notions. The one being or essence is Divinity, belonging equally and undividedly to each of Three Persons. The two processions are generation, by which the Son proceeds from the Father, and spiration, by which the Holy Spirit proceeds from the Father [and the Son]. The Three Persons are Father, Son, and Holy Spirit. The four relations are paternity, the Father's relationship to the Son; filiation, the Son's relationship to the Father; active spiration, the relationship of the Father and the Son to the Holy Spirit; and passive spiration, the relationship of the Holy Spirit to the Father and the Son. The five notions are a) unbegottenness and b) paternity, belonging to the Father alone; c) filiation, belonging to the Son alone; d) active spiration, belonging to the Father and the Son; and e) passive spiration, belonging to the Holy Spirit alone. I only sandwich this in, but if one make it food for meditation it becomes a genuine spiritual banquet.

17. αἱ . . . δυνάμεις.
18. ἀέριον πνεῦμα.
19. Ps. 103[104]:4.
20. Matt. 28:19.
21. τὸ ἰδιάζον τῶν ὑποστάσεων ὁμολογοῦμεν.
22. τὴν θεολογίαν: for which I freely admit that *divine attributes* is a weak translation, capturing only a part of the idea. "The theology" here embraces all that pertains to the Godhead.
23. τὸ εὐσεβὲς δόγμα.
24. τῶν . . . δογμάτων καὶ κηρυγμάτων. See Basil's own definition, at the end of the present passage, of what he means in the present instance by dogma and kerygma.
25. What St. Basil means in this place by ἐν μυστηρίῳ is not clear. The notion of mystery is, with the Greek Fathers, very broad; and it is probably significant that Basil employs in this passage numerous examples of liturgical and reverential practices, all of which, in Greek thought, are "mysteries."
26. τὰ τῆς ἐπικλήσεως ῥήματα ἐπὶ τῇ ἀναδείξει. The words ἀνάδειξις and ἀναδείκνυσθαι constitute a technical terminology in regard to the consecration of the Eucharist. Since their usual meaning is in reference to showing or displaying, some have supposed that the passage refers to an elevation of the consecrated elements; but this is certainly not the case; and ἀναδείκνυσθαι already had the meaning of *consecrare*, in the sense of *dedicare*, in such authors as Strabo and Plutarch.
27. Literally, "Whence that a man is to be thrice baptized?"
28. ἐκ τῆς ἀδημοσιεύτου ταύτης καὶ ἀπορρήτου διδασκαλίας. Note that ἀπορρήτου (arcane) = *not to be spoken*. Reference, of course, is to the *disciplina arcana* or *disciplina arcani*.
29. Gen. 2:8. See also Heb. 11:14.
30. The interplay of words here is lost in translation. Resurrection is ἀνάστασις = *standing again*. That it was in fact by regulation and decree that one was not to kneel for prayer but to stand on Sunday, see § 367 and § 651 above.

HOMILIES ON THE PSALMS [*ante A.D.* 370]

St. Basil's exegetical writings are confined entirely to homilies; and they are not purely literary homilies, but his actual preaching. The homilies on the Psalms belong to the period of his priesthood prior to his elevation to the episcopate, that is, between 364 and 370 A.D.

The Maurist corpus of Basil's homilies on the Psalms contains eighteen such sermons, of which, however, only thirteen are generally regarded as authentic: homilies on Psalms 1, 7, 14, 28, 29, 32, 33, 44, 45, 48, 59, 61, 114 (as numbered in the Septuagint). The five unauthentic homilies, relegated to an appendix in Migne (PG 30, col. 71-118), are on Psalms 14, 28, 37, 115, and 132.

The standard edition for the thirteen authentic homilies is still that of Migne, PG 29, col. 209-494. To it might be added some fragments of others of Basil's homilies on Psalms, especially Ps. 17, that Cardinal Pitra was able to extract from the catena on the Psalms, of Nicetas of Heraclea: in Pitra's *Analecta sacra et classica*, Paris 1888, part 1, pp. 76-103. A new critical edition is presently being prepared by E. Amand de Mendieta and S. Y. Rudberg.

955

[On Ps. 1, no. 1]

I would say that the exercise of piety is rather like a ladder, that ladder which once was 543 seen by the Blessed Jacob, of which one end was near the earth and reached to the ground, while the other end extended above and reached to heaven itself. What is necessary is that those who are being introduced to the virtuous life should put their feet on the first steps and from there mount ever to the next, until at last they have ascended by degrees to such heights as are attainable by human nature.

956

[On Ps. 7, no. 2]

A man who is under sentence of death, knowing that there is One who saves, One who   1000
delivers, says: "In You I have hoped, save me" from my inability "and deliver
me" from captivity (1). I think that the noble athletes of God, who have wrestled all
their lives with the invisible enemies, after they have escaped all of their persecutions
and have come to the end of life, are examined by the prince of this world (2); and   995
if they are found to have any wounds from their wrestling, any stains or effects
of sin, they are detained. If, however, they are found unwounded and without stain,
they are, as unconquered, brought by Christ into their rest.

957

[On Ps. 7, no. 5]

I think that not all who have received this earthly body will be judged in the same way   634
by the just Judge; for there are external circumstances far different with each of us which
must cause judgment to vary for each of us. The combination of circumstances to which
we are subject and which are not in our power but are involuntary, makes our sins more
grievous or even renders them lighter. Suppose it is fornication that is brought to judgment.
But the one who committed this sin was trained from the beginning in wicked practices;
for he was brought into life by licentious parents and was reared with bad habits, in
drunkenness, reveling, and with obscene stories. If someone else, however, had many
invitations to better things,—education, teachers, hearing more divine discussions,
salutary readings, advice of parents, stories which shape character to seriousness and self-
control, an orderly way of life,—if he falls into the same sin as the other, how were
it possible, when he is called to account for his life, that he would not be regarded as
deserving of a more severe penalty than the other?

958

[On Ps. 28, no. 6]

"The voice of the Lord divides the flame of fire (3)." . . . I believe that the fire   1032
prepared in punishment for the devil and his angels is divided by the voice of the Lord.
Thus, since there are two capacities in fire, one of burning and the other of
illuminating, the fierce and punitive property of the fire may await those who deserve
to burn, while its illuminating and radiant part may be reserved for the enjoyment
of those who are rejoicing.

959

[On Ps. 32, no. 3]

"All His works [are] in faith (4)." What does this mean? "If you see the heavens   131
and their orderliness," it means, "they are a guide to faith"; for by themselves they
show their Artisan. If you see the ornamentation of the earth, these things too increase
your faith in God. Yet it is not by our being led to God by our carnal eyes that we believe in
Him; rather by the power of the mind we have perceived through things that are visible
Him who is invisible. "All His works," therefore, "are in faith."

960
[On Ps. 32, no. 4]

Nothing is made holy except by the presence of the Spirit (5). The Word, the Artisan   285
and Creator of the universe, gave to the angels their entry into existence; the Holy   489
Spirit added their holiness to them. The angels were not created infants, to be gradually   740
perfected by exercise until they became worthy of the reception of the Spirit; rather,
in their initial formation and, as it were, mixed into the very substance of their
being, they had holiness.

961
[On Ps. 48, no. 4]

Do not look to a brother for your redemption, but to someone who exceeds your   363
own nature; not a mere man, but to the Man God Jesus Christ, He that alone is able
to give ransom to God for all of us. . . . What is a man able to find so valuable
that he can give it for the ransom of his soul? Yet one thing was found that was worth
as much as all men together. It was given as the ransom price for our souls, the
holy and most precious blood of our Lord Jesus Christ, which He poured out for all
of us; we were, therefore, "bought dearly (6)." If then a brother cannot redeem,
can any man redeem? But if a man is not able to redeem us, the one who did
redeem us is not a man. Do not suppose that because He sojourned among us "in
the likeness of sinful flesh (7)," that our Lord is mere man; do not fail to observe
the power of His divinity. He had no need to give God a ransom for Himself, nor
to redeem His own soul; for "He did no sin, nor was deceit found in His mouth (8)."

962
[On Ps. 114, no. 5]

"Turn to your rest; for the Lord has been kind to you (9)." Eternal rest awaits   774
those who have struggled through the present life observant of the laws, not as
payment owed for their works, but bestowed as a gift (10) of the munificent God on
those who have hoped in Him.

1. Ps. 7:2.
2. ἐρευνῶνται ὑπὸ τοῦ ἄρχοντος τοῦ αἰῶνος. That Satan should be our judge is not, of course, a tenable view. The idea
   is much akin to that in regard to the *telónai*, the demon tax-collectors who beset a soul on its passage to heaven. This long
   discredited and mythological intrusion was never a firm tradition, though it is encountered not infrequently in the history
   of the Liturgy. See under *telónai, telónia,* and *telonía* in the index (p. 993) to Cyprian Vagaggini's *Theological
   Dimensions of the Liturgy,* Liturgical Press, 1976.
3. Ps. 28[29]:7.
4. Ps. 32[33]:4.
5. εἰ μὴ τῇ παρουσίᾳ τοῦ πνεύματος.
6. 1 Cor. 6:20.
7. Rom. 8:3.
8. 1 Peter 2:22.
9. Ps. 114[115]:7.
10. κατὰ χάριν.

EULOGIES ON THE MARTYRS AND SERMONS ON MORAL
AND PRACTICAL SUBJECTS [*ante A. D.* 379]

Under the above title we group all the surviving sermons of Basil that are not directly
exegetical, drawing the descriptive title itself from St. Gregory of Nazianz, who

mentions them in this way in his *Orations* 43, 67. The title refers specifically to a traditional grouping of twenty-four sermons in the Maurist edition, in Migne, PG 31, col. 163–618, generally regarded as authentic, though the authenticity of several has at times been questioned. More recent critical editions are available for a few of the individual sermons; but as a collected edition, Migne's Maurist reprint is still the standard.

In this collection of twenty-four sermons, no. 22, *To the Youngsters, on the Advantage of Reading the Pagan Classics*, while certainly authentic, is not actually a sermon at all, but a treatise written for his young nephews, counseling them on how to proceed with their education in the pagan schools of the grammarians and rhetoricians.

Besides the twenty-four sermons (or twenty-three sermons and a treatise, if the reader insist) of the present collection, there is a considerable body of other sermons associated with Basil in one way or another, many of which may be found in Migne, but including also a fair body of material not found in Migne. This whole body of Basilian sermons and homilies needs to be reorganized and re-edited. Probably some authentic items might be extracted from it. A good starting place would be Otto Bardenhewer's brief conspectus in his *Geschichte der altkirchlichen Literatur*, Vol. 3, pp. 151-153, even though it was written more than 50 years ago. It will at least give an idea of what to look for and what to expect, not only in Greek but also in translation in Latin, Armenian, Coptic and Slavonic. Stig Rudberg's studies of the manuscript tradition are, of course, indispensable to any further work.

966

[*On the Wealthy* 7, 8]

Tell me, the reward which you expect, does it depend on the time when you lived,   770
or on the time which follows after your death? . . . No, when life is over there is no   991
longer any opportunity for the improving of piety.

967

[*At a Time of Famine and Drought* 8, 7]

Little given, much gotten; by the donation of food the original sin is discharged (1).   614
Just as Adam transmitted the sin by his wicked eating, we destroy that treacherous food when we cure the need and hunger of our brother.

968

[*On Baptism* 13, 5]

For prisoners, Baptism is ransom, forgiveness of debts, death of sin, regeneration   836
of the soul, a resplendent garment, an unbreakable seal, a chariot to heaven, a   798
protector royal, a gift of adoption.

969

[*On the "In the Beginning was the Word"* 16, 3]

What was in the beginning? "The Word," he says (2). . . . Why the Word? So   260
that we might know that He proceeded from the mind. Why the Word? Because   265
He was begotten without passion (3). Why the Word? Because He is Image of   264
the Father who begets Him, showing forth the Father fully, in no way separated from Him, and subsisting perfectly in Himself, just as our word entirely befits our thought.

970

[Against the Sabellians and Arius and the Anomoians 24, 3]

One God and Father, One God and the Son, and not two gods, since the Son has   258
identity with the Father. I do not perceive one Godhead in the Father and another in   257
the Son; not one nature in one and another in the other. You may make the individuality
of the Persons clear by numbering the Father and the Son separately, but confess
one essence (4) in both, so as not to divide them into a multiplicity of gods.

971

[Ibid. 24, 4]

When I speak of one essence, do not think of two separated from one, but of a Son   258
subsisting from the Father from the beginning (5), not of Father and Son emerging
from one essence. Indeed, do not speak of brothers; we confess Father and Son. There   251
is identity of essence because the Son is from the Father; not made by His decree, but   255
born of His nature; not separated from the Father, but the Entire shining forth
while abiding still in the Entire (6).

1. λῦσον τὴν πρωτότυπον ἁμαρτίαν.
2. John 1:1.
3. ὅτι ἀπαθῶς ἐγεννήθη. Ultimately the notion is probably that the Son's being begotten implies no change nor liability to change in the Father; no one was acted upon. But English being what it is, we cannot translate the clause "He was begotten impassively" or "apathetically." These English terms correspond only etymologically to the Greek term. At the same time, it may be that "without passion" is just what Basil means; for a word is begotten in the mind truly without passion—unless, of course, one be about to deliver himself of impassioned speech.
4. μίαν ὁμολόγει ἐπ' ἀμφοῖν τὴν οὐσίαν.
5. ἀλλ' ἐκ τῆς ἀρχῆς τοῦ πατρὸς τὸν υἱὸν ὑποστάντα.
6. ἀλλὰ μένοντος τελείου τέλειος ἀπολάμψας.

FAITH *[inter A. D.* 370 / 378]

St. Basil's *Moralia or* Τὰ ἐθικὰ, an extensive introduction to the Christian life, is apparently the product of intermittent endeavor over a period of years, and probably was not published as a full and independent work until after Basil had become a bishop, that is, after 370 A. D.

The treatise *De fide* is in fact one of several prefaces, prologues, or introductions to the *Moralia*. It was probably added to the latter by Basil himself, but only after the *Moralia* had already been published.

Faith is found along with another foreword to the *Moralia*, the *Judgment of God*, in Migne, PG 31, cols 653-699, immediately before the *Moralia* (cols. 700-869). The original of our selection 972 is at col. 677.

972

[1]

Faith, therefore, is unhesitating assent, in the fullest conviction of their truth, to the   554
things heard in what is, by God's grace, proclaimed. . . . Plainly it is a falling away   566
from faith and an offense chargeable to pride, either to reject any of those things that   104
are written or to introduce things that are not written (1).

1. The terms ἀθετεῖν τι τῶν γεγραμμένων and ἐπεισάγειν τῶν μὴ γεγραμμένων may be taken as equivalent to "to reject anything that is in Scripture" and "to introduce anything that is not in Scripture."

RULES BRIEFLY TREATED [post A.D. 370]

Of the several ascetical writings of St. Basil, the chief are the *Moralia*, the *Rules Treated at Length,* and the *Rules Briefly Treated*. Both of the *Rules* are in question and answer form. The *Rules Treated at Length* or *Regulae fusius tractatae* has fifty-five headings of lengthier content, but is really substantially shorter than the *Rules Briefly Treated* or *Regulae brevius tractatae*, with three hundred and thirteen headings of briefer content.

The two *Rules* are not so organized a monastic rule as is that of St. Benedict. They are in fact collections of questions and answers in regard to the conduct of the ascetical and monastic life. It is probable that the two *Rules* are actually composed of the questions put to Basil by his monks when he was visiting his monasteries, along with his immediate and unconsidered replies, the whole taken down by shorthand stenographers.

The ascetical writings of Basil have been very closely studied by J. Gribomont and no serious work can any longer be done on them without taking into account Gribomont's findings as published in his several writings on the subject, notably his *Histoire du texte des Ascétiques de saint Basile*, Louvain 1953; *"L'exhortation au renoncement attribuée a saint Basile,"* in *Orientalia Christiana Periodica*, Vol. 21 (1955, pp. 375-398 (that the *De renuntiatione saeculi* is not authentic); *"Obéissance et Evangile selon saint Basile le Grand,"* in *La Vie Spirituelle*, suppl. 21 (1952), pp. 192-215; and *"Les Règles Morales de saint Basile et le Nouveau Testament,"* in *Studia Patristica*, Vol. 2, or in *Texte und Untersuchungen*, Vol. 64, Berlin 1957, pp. 416-426.

The Migne edition of the *Regulae brevius tractatae* is still the standard text, and is in PG 31, col. 1080-1305.

974

[172]

Question: What is the fear with which the Body and Blood of Christ are to be received by us? A kind of certainty, or a kind of feeling?   875

Answer: The Apostle teaches us this fear when he says, "Anyone who eats and drinks unworthily eats and drinks judgment on himself (1)." Certainty is effected   852
by faith in the words of the Lord, when He says, "This is My Body, which is given for you; do this in remembrance of me (2)."

975

[229]

Answer: The same rationale is observed in the declaring of one's sins as in the   920
detection of physical diseases. Just as the diseases of the body are not divulged to all, nor haphazardly, but to those who are skilled in curing them, so too our declaration of our sins should be made to those empowered to cure them, even as it is written,   925
"You that are strong, bear the infirmities of the weak (3)"; that is, carry them by means of your diligent care.

976

[267]

In one place the Lord declares that "these shall go to eternal punishment (4),"   1034
and in another place He sends some "to the eternal fire prepared for the devil and his angels (5)"; and speaks elsewhere of the fire of gehenna, specifying that it is a place "where their worm dies not, and the fire is not extinguished (6)"; and even of old and through the Prophet it was foretold of some that "their worm will not die,

nor will their fire be extinguished (7)." Although these and the like declarations are
to be found in numerous places of divinely inspired Scripture (8), it is one of the   20
artifices of the devil, that many men, as if forgetting these and other such statements
and utterances of the Lord, ascribe an end to punishment, so that they can sin the more
boldly. If, however, there were going to be an end of eternal punishment, there would
likewise be an end to eternal life. If we cannot conceive of an end to that life, how   1043
are we to suppose there will be an end to eternal punishment? The qualification of
"eternal" is ascribed equally to both of them. "For these are going," He says,
"into eternal punishment; the just, however, into eternal life." If we profess these
things we must recognize that the "he shall be flogged with many stripes" and   1035
the "he shall be flogged with few stripes (9)" refer not to an end but to a distinction
of punishment.

977

[288]
It is necessary to confess our sins to those to whom the dispensation of God's   920
mysteries (10) is entrusted. Those doing penance of old are found to have done it   925
before the saints. It is written in the Gospel that they confessed their sins to John
the Baptist (11); but in Acts they confessed to the Apostles, by whom also all were
baptized (12).

978

[293]
Question: How are they to be dealt with who avoid the greater sins but do not   633
hesitate to commit the lesser ones?
Answer: First of all it must be understood that this distinction has no basis in the New
Testament. A single declaration is made against all sins, when the Lord says, "He that
sins is the slave of sin (13)." . . . If, however, we can safely speak of small and great
sin, it is incontrovertibly evident to everyone that a great sin is one that holds anyone in
its power, whereas a small sin is one which does not get the upper hand; just as with
athletes, it is the stronger who is victor, while the weaker is conquered by the superior,
whichever he be.

1. 1 Cor. 11:29.
2. Luke 22:19. *Remembrance* is ἀνάμνησις.
3. Rom. 15:1. § 977 below is a surer statement of personal restriction of sacramental ministry.
4. Matt. 25:46.
5. Matt. 25:41.
6. Mark 9:45.
7. Is. 66:24.
8. πολλαχοῦ τῆς θεοπνεύστου γραφῆς.
9. Luke 12:47-48.
10. τὴν οἰκονομίαν τῶν μυστηρίων τοῦ θεοῦ. These mysteries, of course, are the sacraments; in fact, the Greek term
   μυστήριον is not infrequently translated by the Latin *sacramentum*.
11. Matt. 3:6.
12. Acts 19:18.
13. John 8:34.

ST. GREGORY OF NAZIANZ [*ca. A. D.* 330 – *ca. A. D.* 389]

Gregory, the second of the three great Cappadocian Fathers, was the close friend of the other two, Basil of Caesarea especially, and Basil's brother, Gregory of Nyssa.

Gregory's only claim to the name "of Nazianz" is custom. He was born at Arianz, not far from Nazianz, about the year 330 A. D. His father, Gregory also, had been a member of the Hypsistarian sect, but soon after his conversion he was made Bishop of Nazianz; so it is really the elder Gregory who ought rightly be called Gregory of Nazianz.

Seldom have two friends been closer than Gregory and Basil. Yet they were not at all matched in temperament. Basil tended to be somewhat arrogant, of a fiery character and volatile. Gregory however was a mild and gentle soul. Otto Bardenhewer remarks that "Basil was the elm and Gregory the vine that wraps itself about the elm."

The friends did quarrel occasionally. Basil could write a caustic letter. In his replies Gregory never backs down and never compromises. He can be just as severe as Basil, but caustic and outraged never. His letters are filled with warm words and cold logic. Gregory's severity is couched in a smoother and even tender language; and in the face of his logic and sentiment, which says in effect, "We don't have to agree, but if you will only be reasonable about it there is no need for it to alter our love for each other," the quarreling is, if not forgotten, at least ignored.

Too much, I think, has been made of their quarrels. They were both men of such magnanimity that they could see each other's faults quite clearly and love each other anyway. If there was a difference even in their magnanimity I would have the impression that Gregory had two trump more than Basil: Gregory saw also his own faults, and Basil was not likely to; and Gregory would never insist on trying to change his friend's views, whereas Basil was certain to take a difference of viewpoint, even a legitimate one, as a personal affront.

Basil and Gregory were students together in Caesarea, Alexandria, and Athens; and their close association continued through Gregory's lengthy visits to Basil's monastery on the Iris.

It was about the year 362 A. D. when Gregory, at the demands of his father's congregation in Nazianz and somewhat against his own will, was ordained to the priesthood. As a priest, after a short flight to the Iris and back, he assisted his father in Nazianz.

When about the year 371 A. D. a division of the civil boundaries of Cappadocia into two provinces, Caesarea and Tyana, precipitated a dispute between Basil and Anthimus of Tyana, who now claimed to be a metropolitan there in his own right, Basil sought to consolidate his own authority by hastily establishing new bishoprics in Tyana. It was very nearly by force that Basil consecrated Gregory Bishop of Sasima, a miserable desert crossroads. Gregory said that Sasima was "without water, without grass, a frightfully horrible and narrow little village" (*Carm. de vita sua* 439).

He never took charge of the place. As a bishop he continued on at Nazianz, assisting his father until the latter's death in 374 A. D. When he saw that if he remained at Nazianz no new bishop would be appointed there he withdrew to Seleucia in 375 A. D.

In 379 the Nicene community in Constantinople, a see long in the hands of Arians and oppressed by numerous other heresies, invited Gregory to come there as bishop, and he accepted. When the second ecumenical council, First Constantinople, opened there in May of 381, it recognized Gregory as legitimate bishop. But before the council was over the objections to his nomination on the grounds that it was uncanonical for a bishop to be transferred from one see to another, as indeed it was, were so great that Gregory simply resigned. He went back to Nazianz and took charge there for about two years until Eulalius was appointed bishop. Then he retired to the family estate at Arianz, where he remained in solitude until his death in 389 or 390 A. D.

Gregory was a gentle and peaceful man. Most of his life was quietly spent, out of the public eye. The loftiness of his writing and the acuity of his theological insights, as exemplified in his *Orations*, are virtually unparalleled. Not prolific but extraordinarily profound, he alone among the Fathers is given St. John's title, the Divine, *i.e.*, the Theologian.

Gregory's writings are assembled under three headings, *Orations, Letters*, and *Poems*. A new edition, badly needed, was promised by the Cracow Academy of Sciences already about 65 years ago; but it has not yet appeared.

ORATIONS

The greater part of Gregory's *Orations*, the collection of which numbers forty-five items, belongs to the years 379 to 381 A.D., that is, to his Constantinopolitan period. The collection is extant in the original Greek; and there are versions extant in whole or in part in Latin, Syriac, Armenian, Coptic, Georgian, Arabic, Old Slavonic (Old Bulgarian) and Old Russian. No. 35 in the collection is usually regarded as spurious.

It is, of course, mostly upon the *Orations*, for the most part sermons and talks that he actually delivered, that Gregory's reputation as a theologian of greatest excellence justly depends. Something of the varied content of the *Orations* may be inferred from the nature of our selections below.

Nine of the forty-five *Orations* are extant also in Latin, Rufinus' translation of nos. 2, 6, 16-17, 26-27, 38, and 40. The translation is rather careless.

Lacking a newer critical edition, the Migne reprint (PG 35-36) of C. Clémencet's edition of 1778 is the standard. For the five theological orations, however, which are nos. 27-31 in the collected orations, the better edition is A. J. Mason, *The Five Theological Orations of Gregory of Nazianz*, Cambridge 1899, in the series *Cambridge Patristic Texts*. Clémencet's edition, incidentally, Vol. I of Gregory's works, contains only the *Orations*. The second and final volume of the *Opera* did not appear until 62 years later, edited by A. B. Caillau and containing the *Letters* and *Poems* (1840).

IN DEFENCE OF HIS FLIGHT TO PONTUS AFTER HIS ORDINATION. A. D. 362.

979

[2, 105]

We who extend the accuracy of the Spirit to every letter and serif [of Scripture] 23 will never admit, for it were impious to do so, that even the smallest matters were recorded in a careless and hasty manner by those who wrote them down. We hold that even these matters have been kept in mind to the present time.

ON THE DESTRUCTION OF THE CROPS BY HAIL AFTER A PROLONGED DROUGHT AND A DEADLY CATTLE PLAGUE. A. D. 373.

980

[16, 7]

I know the trembling and the staggering and the heaving and the wrenching of the   1030
heart and the palsied knees and the like that are the punishments of the impious. But I do not mean to speak of the judgments to come, to which indulgence in this life will deliver us; for it is better to be punished and cleansed now than to be sent to the torment to   991
come, when it will be time for punishing only, and not for cleansing.

981

[16, 15]
We must know, of course, that to commit no sins is really superhuman   658
and pertains to God alone.

FUNERAL ORATION ON HIS FATHER, DELIVERED IN THE PRESENCE OF BASIL THE GREAT OF CAESAREA. A. D. 374.

982

[18, 6]
He was ours even before he was of our fold. His manner of life made him one of us.   413
Just as there are many of our own who are not with us, whose lives alienate them from
the common body, so too there are many of those outside who belong really to us, men
whose devout conduct anticipates their faith. They lack only the name of that which in
fact they possess. My father was one of these, an alien shoot but inclined to us in
his manner of life (1).

IN PRAISE OF HERO THE PHILOSOPHER. A. D. 379.

983

[25, 16]
We do not call the Son Unbegotten; for one only is the Father; nor the Spirit the Son,   250
for one only is the Only-begotten. They too have this divinity, which is singular, the   275
Son by filiation and the Spirit by a procession that is not filiation.   276
The Father is truly father, and more truly than many of us who have the name. He   281
is singularly and properly father, but not in a corporeal way: He is singularly Father,
because His fatherhood is not by a union; and Father of a singular, for His Son is
the Only-begotten; and Father singular, for there is no Son before. He is Father wholly and
completely, not needing any acknowledgment from us; Father from the beginning,
not from a later time.
The Son is truly Son, because He is singular Son, and Son of a singular, and singularly,
and Son singular; for He is not Father also, who is wholly and completely Son, Son
from the beginning, so that never does He commence to be the Son. For their Godhead is
not from a change of plan, nor a progressive deification, as if the one were at any time
not the Father, and the other at any time not the Son.
The Holy Spirit is truly holy. No other is such, not in the same way; for He is holy not   277
by an acquiring of holiness but because He Himself is Holiness; not more holy at one
time and less holy another time; for there is no beginning in time of His being holy, nor
will there ever be an end of it.
Common to Father and Son and Holy Spirit is their having no coming into being, and   269
their divinity. Common to Son and Holy Spirit is their coming from the Father. Proper
to the Father alone is His unbegottenness; to the Son alone, His begottenness; to the
Spirit alone, His being sent forth (2).

SECOND THEOLOGICAL ORATION, A. D. 380.

984

[28, 5]

"I will see the heavens, the works of your fingers, the moon and the stars (3)," and   131
the rational order that is in them; but this is said not as if he were seeing them now, but
because he is going to see them hereafter. Ahead of them, however, is That Nature which
is above them and from which they are, That Nature which is illimitable and unbounded;
and I say this not of the fact that He exists, but of what He is who exists. . . . It is one   173
thing to be persuaded of the existence of something, and another thing entirely to know
what it is. [6] That God does exist and that He is the efficient and sustaining Cause of all   130
things is taught us by our eyes and by the order in nature (4): our eyes, because they light
upon visible objects and behold in them their beautiful stability and progress, immovably
moving and revolving if I may so express it; and the order in nature, because upon
beholding these visible and orderly things we reason back to their Author.

985

[28, 9]

When we say that God is incorporeal this does not set forth nor contain within itself   175
His essence, anymore than do unbegotten and unoriginate and unchangeable and
incorruptible and any of the other terms that we might predicate about God or use in
reference to Him. How, indeed, should it pertain to His Being, in reference to His nature
and substance (5), that He has no beginning, does not change, and is not subject to
any limitation?

986

[28, 12]

We who are prisoners of the earth, as the divine Jeremias puts it (6), and covered with   170
this dense flesh, know this much at least: . . . that it is no more possible for those
who are in the body to be conversant with objects of thought apart from bodily objects
than it is for a man to step over his own shadow, be he ever so quick.

987

[28, 16]

Let us suppose that the existence of the universe is spontaneous. To what will you   131
ascribe its order? If you like, we will grant even that. But to what then will you ascribe its   132
preservation and its being maintained in the terms of its first existence? Something else,   530
or is that also spontaneous? Surely to something other than chance! But what else can
this be, except God? Thus reason, which is from God and is implanted in all of us,   135
which is our first law and is participated in by all, leads us to God through the things
we can see.

988

[28, 17]

What God is in nature and essence no man has ever yet discovered nor can discover.   174
Whether it will ever be discovered is a point which they who are so inclined may
investigate and philosophize about. In my opinion it will be discovered when our   172
godlike and divine portion, I mean our mind and reason, shall have been mingled with
that to which it is akin, when the image shall have ascended to its Archetype, to do which

it even now desires. It seems to me that this is the solution to that whole philosophical problem of our being about to know even as we have been known (7). But in our present mode of existence all that is apparent to us is but an effluence, like a little radiance from a great light.

989

[28, 31]

[An angel], then, is called spirit and fire (8): spirit, as being of an intellectual nature;   482
and fire, as being of a purifying nature. I know that these same names are given to the   483
First Essence; but in relation to ourselves, at least, we must call the angelic nature
incorporeal, or as nearly such as possible. You see how this reasoning dizzies us, and we
can make no progress in it, except only to this point: we know that there are certain   488
Angels and Archangels, Thrones, Dominations, Principalities, Powers, Splendors,
Ascents, Intelligent Virtues or Intelligences (9), natures pure and unalloyed; immovable to
evil, or so moved only with difficulty; circling ever in chorus around the First Cause   490
(10). . . . They sing the praises of the divine majesty and contemplate eternally the   172
eternal glory, not that God may thereby have an increase of glory, for nothing can be
added to what is already full, to Him that supplies all good things to others, but that there
may never be an end of blessings to those first natures after God.

THIRD THEOLOGICAL ORATION, A. D. 380.

990

[29, 16]

They say that Father is the name either of an essence or of an action. . . . Well, you   281
clever fellows, I would indeed be frightened by your distinction (11), were it really
necessary to accept one or the other of the alternatives, rather than to discard both and state
a third and truer one: Father is the name neither of an essence nor of an action, but of
the relation which describes how the Father stands to the Son, and the Son to the Father.
With us these names make known a genuine and real relation; and here too they signify an
identity of nature of the Begotten to the Begetter.

FOURTH THEOLOGICAL ORATION. A. D. 380.

991

[30, 2]

Of all beings that exist, who is without cause? The Godhead. None can tell the cause   141
of God; else he were older than God. What is the cause of the manhood that, for our   370
sakes, God assumed? Surely it was for our being saved. What else could it be?

992

[30, 15]

Their tenth objection is ignorance, the statement that the final day and hour is known   351
to none, not even the Son, except the Father (12). But how is it possible that Wisdom   261
should be ignorant of any of those things that are? . . . How indeed could He know
so accurately those things which are to precede that hour and which are to take place at the
end, but be ignorant of the hour itself? This thing would be like a riddle, as if one
were to say that he knows accurately everything that is in front of a wall, but does not
know the wall itself; or that he knows well the end of the day but knows not the beginning

of the night, whereas knowledge of the one necessarily brings with it knowledge of the other. If, then, we may proceed from the example of what is seen to what is known, is it not perfectly plain to everyone that He does know as God, but says that, as Man, He knows not?

993

[30, 18]

So far as we can proceed, *He Who Is* and *God* are the special names of His essence;   140
and of these two, especially *He Who Is*, not only because when He was speaking to Moses   141
on the mountain, and Moses asked Him by what name He was to be called, this is what
He called Himself when He commanded Moses to say to the people, "*He Who Is* sent me
(13)''; but also because we find that name more appropriate (14). . . . We are
inquiring into the nature whose being is absolute and not conjoined to another. In its
proper sense *being* is peculiar to God and belongs entirely to Him; nor is God's *being*
limited or cut short by any such terms as *before* or *after*; for with Him there is neither
was nor *will* be.

994

[30, 20]

It seems to me that He is called Son because He is identical to the Father in essence;   257
and not only this, but also because He is of Him. He is called Only-begotten not
because He is singular Son, Son of a singular, and Son singular, but because He is Son in   260
a singular fashion and not in a corporeal way. He is called Word because He is to the   265
Father what a word is to the mind; not only because of His passionless generation, but
also because of His union and because of His conveying information.

995

[30, 21]

[Some of Christ's names] are peculiarly our own, and belong to the nature He assumed.   373
Thus He is called Man . . . so that He may of Himself sanctify all mankind, becoming
as it were a leaven to the whole lump (15), and, by uniting to Himself the whole that
was condemned, may release it from condemnation, becoming for all men all that we   345
are, except sin: body, soul, mind, all through which death comes; and thus He became   311
Man, the combination of all these; God in visible form, because He kept that which is   312
perceived by mind alone. He is Son of Man, both because of Adam and because of the   313
Virgin. From them He was born, from the one as His forefather, from the other as His   781
Mother; in accord with the law and not in accord with the law of generation. He is Christ   341
because of His Godhead; for the anointing of His Manhood is not a sanctifying by an
action as it is with all others anointed, but a sanctifying by the sanctifying presence
of the fullness of the Anointing One (16). The effect of this is that That Which Anoints is
called Man, and it makes that which is anointed God (17).

FIFTH THEOLOGICAL ORATION. A. D. 380.

996

[31, 8]

[Scripture speaks of] "the Holy Spirit, who proceeds from the Father (18)": who,   266
since He proceeds from there, is not a creature; who, since He is not begotten, is not a   275

Son; who, since He is between the Unbegotten and the Begotten, is God. . . . What,   276
then, is procession? Tell me first what is the unbegottenness of the Father, and then
I will physiologize for you on the generation of the Son and the procession of the Spirit;   239
and we will both be frenzy-stricken for prying into God's mysteries. . . . [9] "What is   281
there," they say, "that is lacking to the Spirit, for Him to be a Son? For if there were
not some lack, would He not be a Son?" "No," we reply, "there is nothing lacking; for
God has no deficiency." But, if I can put it like this for the sake of clarification, the
difference of their relation to each other (19) gives rise to the difference of their name.
Certainly nothing is lacking to the Son for His being the Father (indeed, sonship
is not a deficiency), but still, He is not the Father. By that line of reasoning the
Father would have to lack something for His being the Son; for the Father is
not the Son. But this is certainly not because of any deficiency nor of any subordination in
respect to essence. Rather, the very fact of not being begotten, of being begotten, and
of proceeding has effected that one is called Father, another Son, and another, the
one of whom we are speaking, Holy Spirit; and thus the distinction of the three Persons
(20) may be preserved in the one nature and dignity of the Godhead.

The Son is not the Father, for the Father is One; but He is what the Father is. Nor is the
Spirit, because He is of God, the Son; for the Only-begotten is One; yet He is what
the Son is. The Three are One in their Godhead; and in peculiar properties the One is
Three. Thus the One is not a Sabellian unity, nor are the Three a Trinity by the wicked   293
division now in vogue (21). [10] What then? Is the Spirit God? Absolutely! What then,   268
consubstantial too (22)? If He is God, He has to be!

997

[31, 14]
For us there is One God, because the Godhead is One; and though we believe in Three,   238
we refer to One whatever has its source (23) in Him. It is not as if one were more God
and another less God; nor is there an earlier and a later. Neither are they separated in will,
nor divided in power, nor are any of the qualities of divisible things to be found here.
Rather, to put it concisely, the Godhead remains undivided in its divisions (24); and there
is one mingling of light, as if in three suns joined to each other. When we look at the
Godhead, or the First Cause, or the Monarchy, that which we perceive is One; but when
we look at the Persons in whom the Godhead resides, . . . there are Three whom we
worship.

AGAINST THE ARIANS AND ABOUT MYSELF. A. D. 380.

997a
[33, 1]
Where are they who revile us for our poverty and pride themselves in their riches?   420
they who define the Church by numbers and scorn the little flock (25)?

998
[33, 9]
I am so old fashioned a philosopher that I still believe the heavens are one and common   386
to all, that there is a common coursing of the sun and moon. . . . And what is more
than this, we have in common reason, law, prophets; and the very suffering of Christ, by
which we are recreated, not this one or that one, but all who are participants in the
same Adam and were led astray by the serpent and slain by sin, and are saved again by   376

the heavenly Adam and are led back by means of the tree of shame to the tree of life
from which we had fallen away.

999

[33, 15]
   I am not afraid for my little flock, for it is seen at a glance. I know my sheep and mine   238
know me (26). . . . My sheep hear my word, which I have heard from the oracles
of God, which I have learned from the holy fathers. . . . [16] I call them by name . . .
and they follow me. . . . They worship the Father and the Son and the Holy Spirit,
One Godhead; God the Father, God the Son, God—I hope it doesn't choke you—the   266
Holy Spirit (27), One Nature in Three Personalities (28), intelligent, perfect, subsisting
of themselves, numerically divided, but not divided in their Godhead.

1000

[33, 17]
   Remember your profession of faith. In whose name were you baptized? In the Father's   826
name? Jewish, but good. In the Son's name? Good; no longer Jewish, but not yet
perfect. In the Holy Spirit's name? Excellent! This is perfect!

ON THE WORDS OF THE GOSPEL IN MATTHEW 19:1. A. D. 380.

1001

[37, 2]
   What [Christ] was He laid aside. What He was not, He assumed. Not that He became   323
two; rather, He deigned to be made one out of two. Both are God, that which assumed
and that which was assumed; two natures concurring in one, not two Sons. Let not
the commingling be falsified.

1002

[37, 6]
   Their laws are unequal and irregular. Why did they restrain the woman but indulge   974
the man? A woman who practices evil against her husband's bed is guilty of adultery,
and for this the penalties of the law are very severe; but a husband committing
fornication against his wife, has he no account to give? I do not accept this legislation
nor do I approve this custom. They who made the law were men, and their legislation
is hard on women. . . . This is not how God acts. He says, "Honor thy father and
thy mother," the first time there is a commandment to which a promise is joined:
"that it may be well with thee (29)." . . . See the equality of the legislation. There
is one Maker of man and woman; one and the same debt is owed by children
to both their parents (30).

1003

[37, 13]
   "It is a question not of him who wills nor of him who runs, but of God's showing   650
mercy (31)." . . . There are some people who are so proud of their successes that
they attribute everything to themselves and nothing to Him who made them and gave
them wisdom and supplied them. with good things. Let them learn of this saying

that even to wish someone well requires God's help; or rather, that even to
choose what is right is something divine and a gift of God's benevolence to man.
That we be saved requires something from us and from God. That is why it says,
"Not of him who wills"; that is, not *only* of him who wills; and not *only* of him
who runs, but *also* of God's showing mercy. Since to will is also from God, it is
reasonable that Paul attributed the whole to God. However well you may run, however
well you may wrestle, you still need Him who gives the crown.

1004

[37, 15]

    I fear lest some absurd reasoning arise to propose that the soul has lived elsewhere,   1004
and is afterwards bound to this present body; and that it is from that other life that
some receive the gift of prophecy, and that some are condemned, having lived
wickedly. . . . But this is all too absurd, and belongs in no way to the teachings of
the Church.

ON THE THEOPHANY OR BIRTHDAY OF CHRIST. A. D. 380.

1005

[38, 9]

    Since a movement to contemplation of Self could not alone satisfy the Goodness   465
that is God, and since it was the part of the Highest Goodness that good must be
poured out and go forth as multiplying the objects of its beneficence, He first conceived
the heavenly and angelic powers (32). This conception was a work carried out by
His Word and perfected by His Spirit. Thus did the secondary splendors come into   482
being, as ministers of the First Splendor, whether they are to be regarded as intelligent   483
spirits, or fire of an immaterial and incorporeal kind, or as being of some other nature
which closely approaches this.

1006

[38, 13]

    [When, because of their greater crimes, men] were in greater need of help, greater   363
help was given them; and this was the Word Himself of God, . . . the unchangeable   264
Image, the Rule and Word (33) of the Father. To his own image He came (34), and
took on flesh for the sake of flesh, and mingled Himself with an intelligent soul for
the sake of my soul, purifying like by Like. In all except sin He was made Man (35).   345
Conceived by the Virgin who first was purified in soul and body by the Spirit, for it   313
was needful that birth be honored and that virginity be honored even more, He then
came forth as God with that which He had assumed, one from two opposites, flesh and   322
spirit, of which the one was deifying, the other deified.

1007

[38, 16]

    You shall see . . . Jesus . . . crucified and crucifying my sin, as a Lamb offered   374
and as a Priest offering, as a Man buried and as God rising again, and afterwards   382
ascending, whence He will come again in His own glory. How many festivals there
are in each of the mysteries of Christ! And all of them have one main point: my
perfection and reformation, and return to the [original condition of the] first Adam.   376

ORATION ON THE HOLY LIGHTS. A. D. 381.

1008

[39, 11]

When I say "God," you must be illuminated in a flash by One Light and by Three: 238
Three in Personalities or Hypostases or, if anyone prefer to call them so, Persons (36),
for we will not quarrel about names if the syllables convey the same meaning; One by
reason of essence or Godhead. They are distinguished among themselves indivisibly,
if I may put it thus; and connected among themselves undividedly. The Godhead is
One in Three, and the Three are One, in whom the Godhead is, or, to put it more
precisely, who are the Godhead.

1009

[39, 12]

The Father is Father, and without beginning; for He is from no one. The Son is Son,   281
and not without beginning; for He is from the Father. Yet, if you take the word beginning   250
in a temporal sense, He too is without beginning; for He is the Creator of times and is   256
not subject to time. The Holy Spirit is truly Spirit, coming forth from the Father, not   269
in the manner of a Son, however, for the Spirit's coming forth is not by generation   275
processionally, if, for the sake of clarity, it be necessary to coin a word (37).   276

1010

[39, 17]

[Besides the Baptisms of Moses, John, and Jesus], I know also a fourth Baptism,   833
that by martyrdom and blood, by which also Christ Himself was baptized. This one is
far more august than the others, since it cannot be defiled by later stains.

ORATION ON HOLY BAPTISM. A. D. 381.

1011

[40, 7]

Just as [God] gave existence to what did not exist, so too He gave new creation to   752
what did exist, creation more divine and lofty than that which existed before, a seal   798
for those only just entering life, and for those of more mature age a gift (38) and a
restoration of the image obliterated through wickedness.

1011a

[40, 17]

Do you have an infant child? Allow sin no opportunity; rather, let the infant be   835
sanctified (39) from childhood. From his most tender age let him be consecrated by   836
the Spirit. Do you fear the seal because of the weakness of nature? O what a pusillanimous
mother, and of how little faith! . . . Give your child the Trinity, that great and noble
Protector.

1012

[40, 23]

Of those who fail [to be baptized] some are utterly animal or bestial, according to   618
whether they are foolish or wicked. This, I think, they must add to their other sins,

that they have no reverence for this gift, but regard it as any other gift, to be accepted
if given them, or neglected if not given them. Others know and honor the gift; but
they delay, some out of carelessness, some because of insatiable desire. Still others
are not able to receive it, perhaps because of infancy (40), or some perfectly involuntary
circumstance which prevents their receiving the gift, even if they desire it. . . .

I think that the first will have to suffer punishment, not only for their other sins, but
also for their contempt of Baptism (41). The second group will also be punished, but
less because it was not through wickedness as much as through foolishness that they
brought about their own failure. The third group will be neither glorified nor punished
by the just Judge; for though unsealed they are not wicked. They are not so much
wrong-doers as persons who have suffered a loss. . . . If you are able to judge a man   832
who intends to commit murder solely by his intention and without there having been
any act of murder, then you can likewise reckon as baptized one who desired Baptism
without having received Baptism. But if you cannot do the former, how the latter?
I cannot see it. If you prefer, we will put it like this: if in your opinion desire has
equal power with actual Baptism, then make the same judgment in regard to glory.
You will then be satisfied to long for glory, as if that longing itself were glory. Do
you suffer any damage by not attaining the actual glory, as long as you have a desire
for it?

1012a
[40, 28]

"Well enough," some will say, "for those who ask for Baptism; but what do you   835
have to say about those who are still children, and aware neither of loss nor of   836
grace? Shall we baptize them too?"

Certainly, if there is any pressing danger. Better that they be sanctified unaware,
than they depart unsealed and uninitiated.

1013
[40, 36]

I know a cleansing fire which Christ came to hurl upon the earth (42); and He   1032
Himself is called Fire in words anagogically (43) applied. . . . I know also a fire   1034
that is not cleansing but avenging, that fire either of Sodom, which, mixed with a
storm of brimstone, He pours down on all sinners (44), or that which is prepared   1033
for the devil and his angels (45), or that which proceeds from the face of the Lord
and burns up His enemies all around (46). And still there is a fire more fearsome
than these, that with which the sleepless worm is associated (47), and which is never
extinguished but belongs eternally to the wicked. All these are of destructive power,   1015
unless even here someone may prefer to understand this in a more merciful way,   1014
worthy of Him who chastises (48).   1000

1014
[40, 45]

Believe that the whole universe, that which is visible and that which is invisible,   460
was made out of nothing by God, and is governed by the providence of its Creator,   461
and will receive a change to a better state. . . . Believe in the Son of God, the   195
Word before the ages, who was begotten of the Father apart from time and incorporeally,   256
who in these last days was, for your sake, made Son of Man, born of the Virgin   782
Mary in an indescribable and stainless way,—for there is no stain where God is and   320
whence salvation comes,—whole man and at the same time God also, on behalf of

the whole of suffering man (49), so that He might bestow salvation on the whole of   314
you (50), taking away the whole of sin's condemnation; in His Godhead not subject   374
to suffering (51), but suffering in what He assumed; made Man as much for your   347
sake as you are made God for His; who was led to death on behalf of the lawless,
crucified and buried so as to taste of death; who rose again on the third day, and
ascended into heaven so that He might take you with Him who were prostrate; who   391
will come again in His glorious parousia, to judge the living and the dead; who then   392
will be no longer in the flesh nor yet incorporeal, but will have a more divine body
of a kind that He alone knows.

SECOND ORATION ON EASTER, A. D. 383.

1015

[45, 3]
God always was, and is, and will be; or better, He always is. *Was* and *will be* are   156
portions of time as we reckon it, and are of a changing nature. He, however, is ever
existing; and that is how He names Himself in treating with Moses on the mountain   140
(52). He gathers in Himself the whole of being, because He has neither beginning nor
will He have an end. He is like some great sea of Being, limitless and unbounded,   173
transcending every conception of time and nature. Only His shadow falls across the   175
mind, and even that but dimly and obscurely, as shadow produced not by what He
truly is, but only by the things around Him, partial images gathered from here and
there and assembled into one, some sort of presentation of the truth, but which flees
before it is grasped and escapes before it is conceived.

1016

[45, 22]
To whom was that Blood paid out that was shed for us, and why was it shed,   384
that great and precious Blood of our God, High Priest, and Victim? We were in bondage   382
to the Evil One, sold under sin, and receiving pleasure in exchange for wickedness.
If a ransom belongs not to someone else but to him who holds in bondage, I ask you,
to whom was this paid, and for what reason? If to the Evil One, O, what an outrage! . . .
If to the Father, first I ask, how can that be? For we were not being detained by Him;
and second, why would He be delighted by the Blood of His Only-begotten Son? . . .
Surely it is evident, however, that the Father did receive [the sacrifice of His Son],
though neither asking nor demanding it, but because of His plan of redemption (53)   375
and so that man might be sanctified by the Humanity of God; so that He Himself
might free us, that He might overcome the tyrant by force, and that He might lead   387
us back to Himself through the mediation of His Son.

1. Gregory's father was, of course, Gregory the elder, Bishop of Nazianz. He had been converted to Catholicism only
   shortly before his ordination, having formerly been a member of a rather obscure sect known as the Hypsistarians. Even
   in its own time the sect was little known outside the neighborhood of Arianz. It was apparently a syncretistic mishmash
   of Judaism, Christianity, and paganism.
2. ἡ ἔκπεμψις: that is to say, His passive spiration.
3. Ps. 8:4.
4. ὁ φυσικὸς νόμος might be rendered very literally *natural law*; but I think that such a translation, in a sense more
   accurate, would only distort and confuse the meaning, which, in the context seems clearly to mean *the order that is
   visible in the arrangement of the physical universe*, or *the order in nature*.
5. τὴν ὑπόστασιν has here its older meaning of *essence* or *substance* and not the meaning *person* to which Basil of
   Caesarea reserves it. Gregory seems in general to be still content to have *hypostasis* mean either *person* or *substance*, the
   distinction to be gathered from the context.

6. Lament. 3:34.
7. 1 Cor. 13:12.
8. Ps. 103[104]:4; Heb. 1:7.
9. ἀγγέλους τίνας καὶ ἀρχαγγέλους, θρόνους, κυριότητας, ἀρχάς, ἐξουσίας, λαμπρότητας, ἀναβάσεις, νοερὰς δυνάμεις ἢ νόας.
10. τὸ πρῶτον αἴτιον.
11. If he were to admit either alternative offered, he would have to deny the Son's divinity; for if Father name the divine essence, and since Son is not Father, Son were not of the divine essence. And if Father name an action, and since action requires an effect, Son were an effect, and therefore created.
12. Mark 13:32.
13. Ex. 3:14.
14. More appropriately that is, than *God*, which, Gregory points out in the few lines we are omitting, is thought by some to derive from such etymologies as even Gregory finds dubious; for example, θέειν = *to run* and αἴθειν = *to blaze*.
15. See 1 Cor. 5:6.
16. This will be a little clearer if we recall St. Paul's words, "God was in Christ," 2 Cor. 5:19.
17. This seems to me to be another way of saying that He became Man so that man might become God.
18. John 15:26.
19. τὸ δὲ τῆς ἐκφάνσεως, ἵν' οὕτως εἴπω, ἢ τῆς πρὸς ἄλληλα σκέσεως διάφορον . . . .
20. Here the τῶν τριῶν ὑποστάσεων certainly means *of the three Persons*. See note 5 above, for an instance of Gregory's use of *hypostasis* in the sense of *substance* or *essence*.
21. ἵνα μήτε τὸ ἓν Σαβέλλιον ᾖ, μήτε τὰ τρία τῆς πονηρᾶς νῦν διαιρέσεως. Sabellianism is a variety of modalism. Sabellius did nominally teach a Trinity; but he so emphasized the Oneness of God that the Sabellian Trinity is not a Trinity of Divine Persons but a Trinity of the Monad's manifestations.
22. τί οὖν, ὁμοούσιων;
23. If *source* seems less than adequate, it is the best I can do with τὴν ἀναφοράν. It might also be translated *origin*, or *point of referral*.
24. ἀλλὰ ἀμέριστος ἐν μεμερισμένοις . . . ἡ θεότης.
25. The Church does not take a popularity poll in determining her teaching. No matter that today we are so often informed by the newspapers of the majority percentages of "Catholics" who think contraception a matter of indifference and of no moral consequence. At one point in the Church's history, only a few years before Gregory's present preaching, perhaps the number of Catholic bishops in possession of sees, as opposed to Arian bishops in possession of sees, was no greater than something between 1% and 3% of the total. Had doctrine been determined by popularity, today we should all be deniers of Christ and opponents of the Spirit. Who were those great men who knew the truth and preserved it? Basil of Caesarea, Hilary of Poitiers, Athanasius of Alexandria, Liberius of Rome, Ossius of Cordova. By careful thought we might name a few others who were never Arian; and this of perhaps half a thousand bishops! So few, so brave;—but do not question the orthodoxy of the centenarian Ossius, who signed away his faith only when they wrenched his bones and when he was already twice as old and thrice as old as most who confronted him. History will be kinder to his memory than Hilary was. Liberius was perhaps not so brave as he ought to have been; but neither was he so cowardly as he might have been, and Rome knew no Arian Pope.
26. John 10:14.
27. θεόν (εἰ μὴ τραχύνῃ) τὸ πνεῦμα τὸ ἅγιον.
28. Or *in Three Peculiarities*, if you prefer: μίαν φύσιν ἐν τρισὶν ἰδιότησι.
29. Deut. 5:16. See also Ex. 20:12.
30. See § 1352, note 15, below.
31. Rom. 9:16.
32. δυνάμεις. When this term is the name of a specific choir of angels, it is translated *Virtues*, and the ἐξουσίαι are the *Powers*; but here it seems to be generic of the various choirs, and in this usage it is usually translated *powers*.
33. ὁ ὅρος καὶ λόγος.
34. Here the image is man, made in God's image and likeness.
35. See Heb. 4:15.
36. ἰδιότητας, εἴτουν ὑποστάσεις, . . . εἴτε πρόσωπα.
37. His coining of a word is only of the adverbial form, ἐκπορευτῶς. The substantive is used in earlier writings, and even in Gregory's own *Fifth Theological Oration*. He has already used other terms for the same idea, such as ἔκπεμψις and πρόοδος, and the verbs προέρχεσθαι and προϊέναι.
38. χάρισμα.
39. *I. e.,* baptized.
40. Gregory does not reject infant Baptism. His statement here must be taken as meaning simply that the infant has not the ability to ask for Baptism or to seek it. See §§ 1011 and 1011a, immediately above, and § 1012a, immediately below, where it is clear that he does encourage infant Baptism. And in point of fact, even the present statement declares the same; for how should he reject infant Baptism and yet hold, as will shortly appear, that the infant who dies unbaptized is, though not punished, yet excluded from glory?
41. Throughout the present passage Gregory has been referring to Baptism as χάρισμα; now he calls it λουτρόν. See St. Clement of Alexandria, § 407 with its note 2.
42. Luke 12:49.

43. Anagoge is a mystical or spiritual meaning or application of words. The old Latin translation by Rufinus has it simply that Christ "is Himself mystically called Fire."
44. Gen. 19:24. Ps. 10[11]:6.
45. Matt. 25:41.
46. Ps. 96[97]:3.
47. Is. 66:24. Mark 9:44.
48. Gregory seems to leave open to possibility the view that the fire even of hell is more cathartic than punitive. This would seem to deny the eternity of hell's punishment, at least in the case of some lesser sinners. It is, of course, the notion of purgatory; yet he has not developed the idea further, has presented no clear distinction of fires between a purgatory and a hell, and we can scarcely claim him as admitting the former. The fact is that by making a purgatory out of hell, he is an Origenist; and that he is an Origenist in this respect is generally admitted.
49. ὑπὲρ ὅλου τοῦ πεπονθότος.
50. He becomes whole Man that he may redeem the whole of man. Apparently this is an application of the principle that what were not assumed were not healed.
51. ἀπαθῆ θεότητι.
52. Ex. 3:14.
53. ἀλλὰ διὰ τὴν οἰκονομίαν.

LETTERS

Gregory himself published a collection of his letters, apparently the first Greek author to do so, at the request of Nicobulus, the grandson of his sister Gorgonia.

The letters are models of clarity and brevity. Valued in general for their autobiographical details, a few of them have also a considerable theological importance. Nos. 101 and 102 to the priest Cledonius are of set purpose anti-Apollinarian. The Ecumenical Council of Ephesus of 431 A. D. published a lengthy extract from letter no. 101, and the Ecumenical Council of Chalcedon twenty years later published the whole of the same letter.

The edition of A. B. Caillau of 1840 contains 243 letters. In reprinting Caillau's text Migne added letter 244, first discovered by G. Mercati. Letters 41-43 are actually letters of Gregory's father, also Gregory of Nazianz; but the younger Gregory's collection can rightly claim them, especially since they probably came from his own hand in his father's name. Of these, no. 42 is found also in the corpus of Basil's letters, where it is no. 47, addressed to Gregory. Its ascription as a letter of the elder Gregory through the younger Gregory and to Eusebius of Samosata seems the more likely. Letter no. 243 is probably a letter of St. Gregory the Miracle-worker (the Thaumaturge).

The Migne edition is in PG 37, cols. 20-396. It is superseded by Paul Gallay's critical edition in the Berlin Corpus, GCS Vol. 53, Berlin 1969. The Berlin Corpus edition does not contain letters 101-102, 202, and 243, the last being omitted as unauthentic, and the other three as being discourses not properly belonging in a collection of letters. Gallay has also published an edition of Nos. 101-102 and 202, however, as Vol. 208 in the series *Sources Chrétiennes*, Paris, 1974. No. 101 has so long been known as a letter that I shall continue to call it such.

LETTER OF GREGORY TO CLEDONIUS THE PRIEST, AGAINST APOLLINARIS.
A. D. 382.

1017

[101]
If anyone does not agree that Holy Mary is the Mother of God (1), he is at odds with   780
the Godhead. If anyone asserts that Christ passed through the Virgin as through a   781
channel, and was not shaped in her both divinely and humanly, divinely because without man and humanly because in accord with the law of gestation, he is likewise godless.

If anyone assert that His manhood was formed, to be clothed over afterwards with   329
divinity, he too is condemned; for this were not a generation of God, but a flight from
generation. . . . If I am to speak concisely, the elements of which the Savior consists   324
differ from one another; for invisible is not the same as visible, nor is the timeless the
same as that which is subject to time. But He is not two Persons (2)! Far be it! Both
are one by their conjunction, the divine made man and the human deified, or however
you wish to express it. I say diverse elements (3), contrary to what is had with the   238
Trinity. There we acknowledge different Persons (4) so as not to confound the
hypostases, and not different elements (5), for the Three are one and the same in their
Godhead.

1018

[101]
   If anyone has hoped in Christ as a Man lacking a mind, he is truly mindless and is   314
quite unworthy of being saved. That which was not assumed has not been healed; but
that which is united to God, the same is saved. If only half of Adam fell, then what is
assumed and saved may also be only half; but if the whole of Adam fell, it must be
united as a whole to Him that is born, in order to be wholly saved.

LETTER OF GREGORY TO AMPHILOCHIUS, BISHOP OF ICONIUM. ca. A. D. 383.

1019

[171]
   Cease not to pray and plead for me (6) when you draw down the Word by your word,   890
when in an unbloody cutting you cut the Body and Blood of the Lord, using your
voice for a sword.

1. θεοτόκον τὴν ἁγίαν Μαρίαν.
2. οὐκ ἄλλος δὲ καὶ ἄλλος.
3. λέγω δὲ ἄλλο καὶ ἄλλο.
4. ἄλλος καὶ ἄλλος.
5. οὐκ ἄλλο δὲ καὶ ἄλλο.
6. ἡμῶν here is merely the editorial plural

POEMS [inter ca. A. D. 383-389]

   Gregory's *Poems* belong mostly to the late years of his life when he was in retirement
at Arianz. Critics differ severely on their literary worth and even on the historical
precedents of their poetical forms. The collection numbers 507 items arranged in
sections in the Maurist edition: I.) *Theological poems*, subdivided into 1) *dogmatic* and
2) *moral*; and II.) *Historical poems*, subdivided as 1) *about himself* and 2) *about others*.
In an appendix are numerous *epitaphs* and *epigrams*, and a drama entitled *Christ
Suffering*.
   As might be expected, many spurious items have found their way into the collection;
and the drama or tragedy *Christus patiens* belongs only to the High Middle Ages.
   A critical edition of the *Poems* was prepared by L. Sternbach; but the manuscript was
destroyed during the second world war before the work could be published. A. B.
Caillau's edition of 1840 is reprinted in Migne, PG 37-38; and this remains at present
the standard. I am quoting only Carm. 1, 1, 12, however; and a separate edition of this
can be found in P. Joannou's *Fonti. Vol. II. Les canons des Pères grecs*, Rome 1963,
pp. 229-231.

1020

[1, 1, 12]

. . .

    These are all twelve of the historical books   41
10 Of the most ancient Hebrew wisdom:
    First there is Genesis, then Exodus, Leviticus too.
    Then Numbers, and the Second Law.
    Then Josue and Judges. Ruth is eight.
    Ninth and Tenth the Acts of Kings,
15 And Paralipomenon. Last you have Esdras.
    The poetic books are five: Job being first,
    Then David; and three of Solomon,
    Ecclesiastes, Canticle and Proverbs.
    And five prophetic, likewise inspired.
20 There are the twelve written in one book:
    Osee and Amos, and Micheas the third;
    Then Joel, and Jonas, Abdias
    And Nahum, and Habacuc, and Sophonias,
    Aggeus, and Zacharias, Malachias.
25 All these are one. The second is Isaias.
    Then the book called Jeremias, of the New-born Babe.
    Then Ezechiel, and Daniel's gift.
    I reckon, therefore, twenty-two old books,
    Corresponding to the number of the Hebrew letters.
30 Now count also those of the new mystery.   42
    Matthew wrote the miracles of Christ for the Hebrews,
    Mark for Italy, Luke for Greece;
    John for all, the great herald reaching to the heavens.
    Then the Acts of the wise Apostles.
35 Of Paul too the fourteen Epistles.
    And the seven Catholic, which are one of James,
    Two of Peter, three of John again;
    And Jude is the seventh. You have them all.
    And if there are others besides these, they are not germane (1).

1. Gregory's Old Testament Canon, as we would expect, lacks Maccabees and the deuterocanonical five: Wisdom, Sirach, Tobias, Judith and Esther. His canon, then, of the Old Testament, is identical to that of Athanasius. Unlike Athanasius, Gregory still omits the Apocalypse from the New Testament. See § 791 with its notes.

ST. GREGORY OF NYSSA [ca A. D. 335 – A. D. 394]

    Gregory of Nyssa is the younger brother of Basil of Caesarea, born about the year 33 A. D., and the third of the Three Cappadocians. Unlike Basil, he was not a very good administrator or leader; and unlike Gregory of Nazianz, he was not a particularly attractive preacher. But he was an extraordinarily gifted man as mystic, theologian, and writer. In fact, in the versatility of his writings, he far surpasses the other two.

    Gregory was educated for the most part by his older brother Basil. After having advanced in the Church as far as lector, he decided on a worldly career as a teacher of rhetoric, and he married. The other Gregory convinced him to retire to Basil's monastery on the Iris.

    In the autumn of 371, Basil, trying to consolidate his ecclesiastical authority as metropolitan, consecrated Gregory bishop of Nyssa, just as he was sending the other Gregory to Sasima.

Gregory of Nyssa, like Nazianz, was consecrated rather much against his preferences, if not literally against his will. Nyssa, however, at least agreed to take possession of his see; but other than that, he disappointed his brother just as much as did Nazianz, and Basil criticized and blamed him rather constantly for lack of firmness, politico-ecclesiastical unfitness, and poor fiscal administration.

Gregory had furthermore to contend with the considerable opposition of the Arians, who falsely accused him of misappropriation of funds and in a synod at Nyssa in 376 deposed him *in absentia*. But when the Emperor Valens died two years later, Gregory was able to return to Nyssa. In 379 the Synod of Antioch made him visitator in the Pontus and while on this mission he was, in 380, elected Bishop of Sebaste. In 381 at Constantinople he was outspoken in his defense of Gregory of Nazianz. We find him again at Constantinople to preach the funeral panegyric over the Princess Pulcheria in 385, and shortly afterwards he did the same for her mother, the Empress Flaccilla.

He was present in a synod convened at Constantinople in 394, and is then heard of no more among the living.

The first collected edition of Gregory's works was the folio edition in two volumes edited by Fronto Ducaeus, Paris 1615. J. Gretser supplied an extensive appendix to it in a third volume, Paris 1618. G. Morelli republished the whole in three folio volumes but in a less elegant style and with numerous errors, Paris 1638. Previously unpublished works of Gregory were edited by L. A. Zacagni, Rome 1698; by J. B. Caraccioli, Florence 1731. An edition of the works lacking in the 1615 and 1638 editions was published by A. Gallandi in his *Biblioteca veterum Patrum*, Vol. 6, pp. 515-716, Venice 1770. Previously unpublished works were edited also by Angelo Cardinal Mai in 1833 and 1847; and, during the period 1835-1840, by J. G. Krabinger.

The Migne edition, Paris 1858, in PG 44-46 sought to bring together all Gregory's authentic writings and to separate therefrom the spurious. The Abbé was not in all respects successful.

An edition promised by Ulrich von Wilamowitz-Moellendorf in 1909 began to bear fruit in the 1920's and is now nearly completed. The general editor from the beginning was Werner Jaeger, succeeded at his death by Hermann Langerbeck, and at his death succeeded in turn by Hadwiga Hörner. The series is now very nearly completed, and is published, with reprints of the earlier volumes, by the E. J. Brill company of Leiden, under the auspices of the Harvard Institute for Classical Studies.

VIRGINITY [*A. D.* 370 *aut* 371]

The treatise on *Virginity*, which might well have been an author's crowning achievement of ascetical writing, is in fact the earliest of St. Gregory's writings, belonging to the period after Basil's consecration as Bishop of Caesarea in 370 A. D., before his own consecration as Bishop of Nyssa in 371.

It is probable that after publishing the work Gregory continued to revise it, which will account for the fact of the two slightly different versions known through the manuscripts. It was a rather widely read work in the Middle Ages, as is shown by the existence of an unusually large number of manuscripts. The *editio princeps* is that of Johannes Livineius, Antwerp 1574. The text in Migne, PG 46, cols. 317-416, is now replaced as standard by that of J. P. Cavarnos in Werner Jaeger's Wilamowitz-Moellendorf, Vol. 8/1, first published in 1952 and republished at Leiden, 1963, pp. 215-343.

1020a

[14(13): *Jaeger*, pp. 306-307]*

Death begins at birth; but those who have, through virginity, remained aloof from this   984
process, have drawn within themselves the boundary line of Death, and have by
their own deeds checked his advance. They have, as it were, made of themselves a kind
of frontier between Death and Life, and a barrier too, which thwarts him. If,
therefore, Death is unable to pass beyond virginity, but in virginity is checked and
thwarted, it is plainly demonstrated that virginity is stronger than Death. . . . It was
not possible that Death should cease his works so long as mankind by marriage was
working too; he walked the path of life in all generations past; he started with every
new-born child and accompanied it to the end; but he found at last in virginity a barrier
beyond which he could not pass. Just as in the time of Mary, the Mother of God (1), the   780
Death who had reigned from Adam until then found, when he came to her and dashed   783
his forces against the fruit of her virginity as against a rock, that he was himself
shattered against her, so too in every soul that passes through this life in flesh that is
protected by virginity, the strength of Death is shattered and annulled, when Death finds
no place in which to fix his sting.

*Because the works of Gregory have in general never had a standard division into verses or any sort of convenient reference
 units, I will cite the Harvard edition as *Jaeger*, with pertinent page numbers.
1. ἐπὶ τῆς θεοτόκου Μαρίας. The term theotókos is found also in Gregory's *Letter* 17: *To Eustathia, Ambrosia, and the
 Basilissa*.

THE MAKING OF MAN [*A. D.* 379]

Gregory's short treatise on *The Making of Man* is somewhat in the style of a homily,
and belongs to a period shortly after Basil's death, probably to the Eastertime of 379
A. D. It is intended to supplement and complete Basil's *Homilies on the Hexameron*.
The work is an anthropological-dogmatic investigation of Gen. 1:26, addressed to the
brother of Gregory and Basil, Peter of Sebaste.

The Migne text in PG 44, 125-256, is supplanted by that of G. H. Forbes in his
edition of Gregory's works, Burntisland 1855–1861, Vol. 1, pp. 96-319. A new edition
is being prepared by Hadwiga Hörner, to appear in Vol. 4 of Jaeger's
Wilamowitz-Moellendorf, the collected edition of which she is presently the general
editor.

1021

[14, 2]

Since reasoning has discovered three different varieties within our vital faculty,—   503
one which is nourished but has not perception; one which is nourished and is capable   504
of perceiving, but lacks all rational activity; and a third which is rational, perfect, and
co-extensive with the whole faculty, so that among these varieties superiority belongs to the
intellectual,—let no one suppose from all this that there are three souls welded together in
the human compound, each contemplated within its own boundaries, so that one might
regard the human nature as a concoction of several souls. Rather, the true and perfect soul
is by nature one, the intellectual and immaterial, which mingles with our material nature
through the agency of the senses.

THE LIFE OF MOSES [*ca. A. D.* 390]

In *The Life of Moses* Gregory engages in rather extreme allegorical interpretation in order to provide, from Moses' life, a pattern of conduct for the life of his own young friend, Caesarius. It is still, if not a work of valuable scientific instruction, a work of profound edification.

The Migne edition, PG 44, cols. 297-430, is rendered obsolete by Jean Card. Daniélou's edition in the series *Sources Chrétiennes*, 2nd edition, Paris 1955 (the first edition had not the text but only a French translation), and 3rd edition, Vol. 1-ter, Paris 1968. There is also a recent critical edition by Herbert Musurillo in Vol. 7/1 of Langerbeck's Jaeger's Wilamowitz-Moellendorf, Leiden 1964.

1022

[2: *Jaeger*, pp. 45-46]

There is a certain opinion, having credence from its having been handed down from the Fathers, which says that when our nature fell into sin God did not leave us without protection in our misery. Rather, a certain angel from among those to whom is allotted an incorporeal nature, was appointed by Him to assist in the life of each man; but contrariwise, too, the corrupter of our nature, destructive of human life, fights against the same by the agency of a certain evil and malicious demon. Between these two, in the middle is man. The goal of each of these companion spirits is directly opposed to that of the other, their goal being to prevail more effectively over the other. The good offers to man's consideration the good prospects of virtue, which are viewed aright through hope; the other, material delights, in which there is not the hope of good things but things already present and possessed, visible things enslaving the senses of the very foolish.

493
492

494

613

1023

[2: *Jaeger*, pp. 86-87]

The mind goes on ahead and, through ever greater and more perfect attention, it achieves an understanding of the truly intelligible, thereby drawing closer to the vision by which it may better discern the indiscernibility of the divine nature. . . . In this matter true vision belongs to Him who is sought; and in this matter, not seeing is itself the seeing (1).

173

1. καὶ ἐν τούτῳ τὸ ἰδεῖν ἐν τῷ μὴ ἰδεῖν.

HOMILIES ON ECCLESIASTES

Gregory's eight *Homilies on Ecclesiastes*, covering the texts of that Book from its beginning up to 3:13, provide no clue as to the time of their writing. The Migne texts, PG 44, 615-754, are now superseded by Paul Alexander's edition in Jaeger's Wilamowitz-Moellendorf, Vol. 5, Leiden 1962, pp. 195-442.

1024

[8: *Jaeger*, pp. 433-434]

Paul, joining righteousness to faith and weaving them together, constructs of them the breastplates for the infantryman (1), armoring the soldier properly and safely on

758
760

both sides. A soldier cannot be considered safely armored when either shield is disjoined
from the other. For faith without works of justice is not sufficient for salvation (2);
neither, however, is righteous living secure in itself of salvation, if it is disjoined from
faith.

1. τῷ ὁπλίτῃ τὸν θώρακα, literally, *the cuirass for the hoplite*. The well-armored soldier had a cuirass with plates both
front and back, a fact upon which Gregory's figure depends.
2. See James 2:14.

COMMENTARY ON THE CANTICLE OF CANTICLES

The fifteen homilies on the Canticle of Canticles really constitute a commentary on
that Book from its beginning to 6:8, with, for the unifying theme of the work, the thesis
that the biblical book displays, under the figure of a marriage feast, the union of the
human soul with the Godhead. The introduction complains of "certain Churchmen"
who fail to see the anagogical character of the book. Though they are unnamed by
Gregory, they must include Theodore of Mopsuestia, who sees in the book no more than
a wedding poem.
The homilies can be dated only to the extent that the last of them is later than
Gregory's *In psalmorum inscriptiones*.
Migne's edition, in PG 44, 755-1120, is supplanted by H. Langerbeck's edition in
Jaeger's Wilamowitz-Moellendorf, Vol. 6, Leiden 1960.

1025

[1: *Jaeger*, pp. 15-16]
He that desires all men to be saved and to come to a knowledge of the truth (1) shows   591
thereby the most perfect and blessed way of salvation, the way, I say, of love. For
some, salvation may come through fear, when, in the face of threats of punishment in   914
gehenna, we keep aloof from wickedness. There are some too who practice the virtue of   585
hope in view of the reward promised those who live piously, not possessing the
good of love, but the expectation of recompense.

1. 1 Tim. 2:4.

THE LORD'S PRAYER

The work entitled *The Lord's Prayer*, of uncertain date, consists of five homilies, the
first on prayer in general and the last four on the Lord's Prayer in particular.
The Migne edition, PG 44, 1119-1194, is still standard. John F. Callahan has a new
edition under preparation, to appear in Vol. 7/2 of Jaeger's Wilamowitz-Moellendorf.

1026

[4]
All rational creation is divided into incorporeal and corporeal nature. The incorporeal   483
is the angelic, and the other kind is we men. The intellectual, however, which is remote
from the cumbersome body,—I say this in respect to its being opposed to the earth with its
gravity,—has its allotted portion above, sojourning in the light and ethereal places, because
it is so nimble and agile. The other nature, however, because of the kinship that our body,
a kind of muddy sediment, has with the earthy, is necessarily allotted this earthly life.

THE BEATITUDES

The Beatitudes is an exegetical work consisting of eight homilies on Matt. 5:1-10. The text in Migne, PG 44, 1193-1302, is still standard. A new edition is presently in preparation by John F. Callahan, scheduled to appear in Vol. 7/2 of Jaeger's Wilamowitz-Moellendorf.

1027

[7]

Man, who among the things that exist is reckoned as nothing, as ashes, as grass, as   740
vanity, is made the familiar of such and so great a Majesty as can neither be seen, nor
heard, nor reckoned. Man is received and accounted as son by the God of the universe.
Who can discover a way of giving thanks worthily for such a gift? With what
voice, with what thought, what movement of the heart, can a man sing the praises of
this superlative gift? Man transcends his own nature: from mortal he is made immortal,
from brazen, unalloyed (1), from ephemeral, eternal, and in short, from man, a
god. For if he is made worthy of becoming a son of God he will have entirely in himself
the dignity of the Father, and will be heir to all the paternal goods. O, the liberality of
that wealthy Master!

1. ἐξ ἐπικήρου ἀκήρατος. The pun in the Greek concerns beeswax, from cut to pure: and it limps just as badly as mine on
   metal.

THE GREAT CATECHISM [*post A. D.* 383]

Gregory's dogmatic writings are of two kinds, the polemical and the positive. *The Great Catechism*, written soon after the year 383 A. D., is of the latter sort. In this, the best of Gregory's positive dogmatic works, the chief dogmas of Christianity are treated: the Trinity of the Godhead, the Redemption of mankind through the Incarnation of the Logos, and the personal acceptance of redeeming grace through Baptism and Eucharist. The method of offering biblical-theological proofs is left entirely in the background by speculative-theological argumentation.

The text in Migne, PG 45, 9-106, has long since been antiquated by the edition of J. R. Srawley in the series *Cambridge Patristic Texts*, Cambridge 1903, 2nd edition 1956. An edition by L. Méridier, *Grégoire de Nysse. Discours catéchétique*, was published at Paris in 1908. A new edition by Hilda Polack is intended for publication in Vol. 3/2 of Jaeger's Wilamowitz-Moellendorf.

1028

[1]

A certain strength and life and wisdom is observed in what is human; yet no one would   177
suppose, because of the similarity of terms, that with God, life or strength or wisdom
are to be understood as being the same. Rather, the meaning of all such terms is
lowered in accord with the standard of our nature. Our nature is weak and subject to
corruption because our life is short, our strength is not lasting, and our word is unstable.   180
In the Supreme Nature, however, everything that is said about it is at the same time
elevated to the greatness of that which is contemplated.

1029

[3]

Anyone who studies closely the depth of the mystery receives into his soul in modest   238
degree some understanding of the doctrine about the divine nature (1), but not so   239
much as to enable him to explain clearly in words the unfathomable depth of this
mystery: how the same thing is numbered even while it eludes enumeration, how it is
observed with distinctions even while it is apprehended as a monad, how it is
distinguished in reference to hypostasis and not separated in its essence (2).

1030

[8]

Since both soul and body have a common bond of fellowship in their sharing in the   990
misfortunes which derive from sin, so too is there a certain analogy of corporeal death to
that death which is of the soul. Just as in reference to the flesh we pronounce that death
which is cessation of sentient life, so too in regard to the soul we term that death which   639
is separation from true life.

1031

[11]

If you inquire how divinity is conjoined to humanity, you will have first to inquire   320
as to what the coalescence is of the soul with the flesh. If you do not know the manner
by which your soul is united to your body, do not imagine that that other question
needs to be understood by you either. In the case of the soul and body, while we believe
that the soul is something other than the body because the flesh, when the soul is   990
isolated from the body, becomes dead and inert, we still do not know the manner of their
union. So too in that other inquiry, while we confess that the divine nature differs in
majesty from a nature that is mortal and perishable, we are not capable of perceiving
the manner of the conjunction of the divine and the human. Yet the miracles recorded   82
do not permit us to doubt that God was born in the nature of a man.

1032

[12]

When we consider the universe and survey the orderly operation of the world (3)   132
and the benefits that are providentially (4) operative in our lives, we perceive the
existence of some power effective of what comes to be and conservative of what is. So
too in regard to God's being manifested to us in the flesh, we make the miracles of His
operation satisfactory proof of the divine epiphany, recognizing everything through   82
His recorded works on which the divine nature has left its hallmark.

1033

[26]

The Adversary himself will not doubt that what took place [in the Incarnation] was   1014
both just and salutary, if it be that he is to attain to the enjoyment of its benefit. Those who
are cut and cauterized for the sake of a cure are angry with those who are curing
them, and they wince in pain at the incision. But if a cure is effected by these means,
and the pain of the cauterizing pass away, they are grateful to those who have worked
this cure in them. In this same manner, when, after periods of time, the evil in our
nature, which now is mixed with it and has coalesced with it, is expelled from it,
and when those now lying prostrate in wickedness have been restored to their promordial

condition (5), all creation will give thanks in one voice, those who have been punished
in purgation (6) as well as those who from the beginning had no need of purgation (7).

1034

[31]
    Some are saying that God, if He wanted to, could by force bring even the disinclined   700
to accept the kerygmatic message. But then where would their free choice be? Where
their virtue? Where their praise for their having succeeded? To be brought around
to the purpose of another's will belongs only to creatures without a soul or irrational (8).

1035

[37]
    Since it has been shown that it is not possible for our body to become immortal   879
except it be made participant in incorruption through communion with the Immortal, it
is necessary to consider how it is possible for that One Body, though distributed
always to so many myriads of the faithful throughout the world, to be whole in its   859
apportionment to each individual, while yet it remains whole in itself. . . . This
Body, by the indwelling of God the Word, has been made over to divine dignity (9).
Rightly then, do we believe that the bread consecrated by the word of God (10) has been   856
made over into the Body of God the Word (11). For that Body was, as to its potency
(12), bread; but it has been consecrated (13) by the lodging there of the Word, who
pitched His tent in the flesh. From the same cause, therefore, by which the bread that was
made over (14) into that Body is made to change into divine strength (15), a similar
result now takes place. As in the former case, in which the grace of the Word made holy   864
that body (16) the substance (17) of which is from bread, and in a certain manner
is itself bread, so in this case too, the bread, as the Apostle says (18), "is consecrated by
God's word and by prayer"; not through its being eaten does it advance to become
the Body (19) of the Word, but it is made over (20) immediately into the Body by means
of the word, just as was stated by the Word, "This is My Body (21)!" . . . In the plan   878
(22) of His grace He spreads Himself to every believer by means of that Flesh, the   871
substance (23) of which is from wine and bread, blending Himself with the bodies of
believers, so that by this union with the Immortal, man, too, may become a participant
in incorruption. These things He bestows through the power of the blessing which
transforms (24) the nature of the visible things to that [of the Immortal] (25).

1036

[40]
    The life of torment allotted to sinners is in no way equivalent to anything that torments   1032
the sense here. If one or the other of those torments is named in terms of something
well known here, there is still no small difference. When you hear the word fire, you
have been taught to understand something else than the fire that we know of, because of
that fire's having a quality which our fire has not; for that fire is never quenched,
whereas experience has discovered many ways of quenching our fire. There is a great
difference between fire that can be quenched and fire that is unquenchable (26).

---

1. κατὰ τὴν θεογνωσίαν.
2. τῷ ὑποκειμένῳ. William Moore, in his translation in the *Nicene and Post-Nicene Fathers, Second Series*, renders this
phrase "as to subject matter." In his note to the same passage, however, he states that with Gregory ὑποκείμενον is
"always equivalent to οὐσία, and οὐσία generally to φύσις."
3. τὰς κατὰ τὸν κόσμον οἰκονομίας ἐπισκοποῦντες.
4. θεόθεν.

5. ἐπειδὰν ἡ εἰς τὸ ἀρχαῖον ἀποκατάστασις τῶν νῦν ἐν κακίᾳ κειμένων γένηται.
6. ἐν τῇ καθάρσει.
7. καθάρσεως. No doubt there is in this passage something of the notion of purgatory; but that is only or largely because the Origenist position which Gregory shares is in some respects a step in that direction. See note 2 at § 1060 below.
8. τῶν ἀψύχων ἢ τῶν ἀλόγων.
9. πρὸς τὴν θεϊκὴν ἀξίαν μετεποιήθη.
10. τὸν τῷ λόγῳ τοῦ θεοῦ ἁγιαζόμενον ἄρτον.
11. εἰς σῶμα τοῦ θεοῦ λόγου μεταποιεῖσθαι.
12. τῇ δυνάμει.
13. ἡγιάσθη.
14. μεταποιηθείς.
15. εἰς θείαν μετέστη δύναμιν.
16. Christ's incarnational body, which grew and got its material substance from bread, and could therefore in a sense be called bread.
17. σύστασις.
18. 1 Tim. 4:5.
19. Now Gregory speaks not of the incarnational body but of the Eucharistic Body.
20. μεταποιούμενος.
21. Matt. 26:26; Mark 14:22; Luke 22:19.
22. τῇ οἰκονομίᾳ.
23. σύστασις. Gregory is not using *substance* as we now use the term in speaking of *substance and accidents*. That were *ousia*; this is *sýstasis*. Here our word *substance* means the visible and tangible, the material; in fact, this is an instance where *substance* very nearly means *accidents*. That is to say, substance here is not essence, but matter. The same applies to the word *sýstasis* where we call attention to the term in note 17 on the present passage.
24. μεταστοιχειώσας implies the change of a thing's elementary nature. Some English translations render it *transelementates*.
25. The final and theologically very important statement reads: ταῦτα δὲ δίδωσι τῇ τῆς εὐλογίας δυνάμει πρὸς ἐκεῖνο μεταστοιχειώσας τῶν φαινομένων τὴν φύσιν.
26. In connexion with this passage, read also § 1033, § 1060, and § 1061, with note 2 at § 1060.

TO ABLABIUS: THAT THERE ARE NOT THREE GODS

The present short work is in response to a difficulty posed by a certain Ablabius, in sum: I Peter, James, and John, of one human nature, are called three men, why are not Father, Son, and Holy Spirit, of one divine nature, to be called three Gods?

Among Gregory's literary remains are two letters to a Bishop Ablabius. The Ablabius to whom the present work is addressed is not a bishop. In some manuscripts of *To Ablabius*, the man is referred to as a monk. The address calls him a "noble soldier of Christ," which were a suitable address to a monk, but not to a bishop, who would, in Greek custom, be given a grander title. .

In the introduction to the present work Gregory's reference to himself and the bishops of his generation as "we old men" can provide but little clue to the dating of the work, since Gregory was wont from rather early in life to class himself among the elderly.

The Migne text in PG 45, 115-136 is replaced as standard by F. Mueller's edition in Jaeger's Wilamowitz-Moellendorf, Vol. 3/1, Leiden 1958, pp. 35-57.

1037

[*Jaeger*, pp. 47-48]

Every divine operation touching on creation and named according to our various 283
conceptions of it has its origin from the Father, proceeds through the Son, and is
perfected in the Holy Spirit. For this reason the name of the operation is not divided by
the number of those operating: the action of each in regard to anything is not separate and
peculiar; rather, whatever takes place, whether in regard to the acts of His providence
on our behalf or in reference to the establishment and governing of the universe,
takes place by the action of the Three.

1038

[*Jaeger*, pp. 55-56]

While we confess the invariableness of the [divine] nature we do not deny the   274
distinction of cause and of caused, by which alone we perceive that one Person is
distinguished from another, in our belief that it is one thing to be the cause and another to
be from the cause; and in that which is from the cause, we recognize yet another
distinction. It is one thing to be directly from the First Cause, and another to be through
Him who is directly from the First, so that the distinction of being Only-begotten abides
undoubtedly in the Son, nor is it doubted that the Spirit is from the Father; for the middle   269
position of the Son is protective of His distinction as Only-begotten, but does not
exclude the Spirit from His natural (1) relation to the Father.

1. In speaking of a natural relation he means of course a relation in respect to nature. He is referring to the procession of the
   Spirit from the Father; and the Spirit's relation to the Father is one of passive spiration.

TO THE GREEKS: FROM UNIVERSAL IDEAS

This short work deals with the expressions and terminology used in describing the
Trinity. Gregory shows herein a willingness to accept, "following the tracks of Plato," as
Otto Bardenhewer put it, the real existence of the universal idea.

The Migne text, PG 45, 175-186, is replaced as standard by F. Mueller's edition in
Jaeger's Wilamowitz-Moellendorf, Vol. 3/1, Leiden 1958, pp. 17-33. Mueller's edition
restores the introduction and conclusion lacking in all prior editions.

1039

[*Jaeger*, p. 25]

It is one and the same Person of the Father (1) by whom the Son is begotten and from   252
whom the Holy Spirit proceeds. Therefore and fittingly, there being One Cause of   269
Those whom He has caused, we boldly say there is One God, since also He co-exists
(2) with Them. For the Persons of the Godhead are separated one from another neither   283
in time, nor place, nor will, nor practice, nor operation, nor passivity, nor any of
the like things such as are perceived with men, but only in that the Father is Father and   281
not Son, and the Son is Son and not Father, and likewise the Holy Spirit is neither Father
nor Son.

1. πρόσωπον τοῦ πατέρος.
2. συνυπάρχει.

AGAINST EUNOMIUS [*inter A. D.* 380/384]

The most important of Gregory's polemical dogmatic writings, the *Against Eunomius*
consists in most reckonings of twelve books or thirteen, the thirteenth called also 12 B.

In its original form the work was in three books, corresponding directly to the three
books of Eunomius' Ὑπὲρ τῆς ἀπολογίας ἀπολογία, (itself a reply to Basil's
Ἀπολογία), against which it was written. In the course of time Book 2 of Gregory's
Against Eunomius was replaced by a second work which he wrote against Eunomius, the
Refutation of the Creed of Eunomius, and was placed at the end of the work, where it
became Book 12 B or 13, since the original Book 3 had now been divided into Books 3
to 12.

The text in Migne, PG 45, 237-1122, has the displaced order of books as noted above. W. Jaeger's edition, first published at Berlin in 1921, the firstfruits, Vols. 1 and 2, of the Wilamowitz-Moellendorf project, entirely supplants Migne and does us the great service of restoring the original order of the books. This 1921 edition of Jaeger has been reprinted as Vols. 1 and 2 in Jaeger's Wilamowitz-Moellendorf, published under the auspices of the Harvard Institute for Classical Studies by the Brill company of Leiden, 1960. Volume 1 contains the original Books 1 and 2 (later reckoned as 1 and 12 B, now restored). Volume 2 contains Book 3 (later reckoned as Books 3-12, and now restored). Also in Volume 2 is the *Refutatio confessionis Eunomii* which in Migne and for centuries before his time had been reckoned as Book 2, and is now once more regarded properly as the separate work that it is.

1040

[Bk 1: *Jaeger*, Vol. 1, p. 138]

Father conveys the notion of unoriginate, unbegotten, and Father always; the only-begotten Son is understood along with the Father, coming from Him but inseparably joined to Him. Through the Son and with the Father, immediately and before any vague and unfounded concept interposes between them, the Holy Spirit is also perceived conjointly. The Spirit is not later than the Son in His existence, as if the Only-begotten could be thought of as ever having been without the Spirit. Rather, since the Spirit is from the God of all things, He has for the cause of His being that from which the Only-begotten is Light, through which True Light He shines forth. Neither on grounds of duration nor by reason of an alien nature can He be separated from the Father or from the Only-begotten.

250
256
272

268

1041

[Bk 1: *Jaeger*, Vol. 1, p. 222]

But there neither is nor ever shall be such a dogma in the Church of God, that would prove the simple and incomposite to be not only manifold and variegated, but even constructed from opposites. The simplicity of the dogmas of the truth proposes God as He is: not to be comprehended by a name nor by a concept nor by any mental apprehension. He remains superior not only to human but also to angelic and to every supramundane apprehension. He is unutterable and indescribable, above any meaning that can be invested in a word.

151

173

1042

[Bk 3: *Jaeger*, Vol. 2, p. 38]

If anyone should ask for some kind of interpretation and description and explanation of the divine essence, we will not deny that in such wisdom as this we are untutored. This only do we profess, that what is by nature infinite cannot be comprehended in any conception expressed in words.

173

153

1043

[Bk 3(4): *Jaeger*, Vol. 2, pp. 84-85]

Let [Eunomius] first show, then, that the Church has believed in vain that the Only-begotten Son truly exists, not made such through adoption by a Father falsely so-called, but existing as such according to nature, by generation from Him Who Is, not estranged from the nature of Him who begot Him. . . . And let no one interrupt me and say that what we confess should be confirmed by constructive reasoning

252

257

(1). It suffices for the proof of our statement that we have a tradition coming down
to us from the Fathers, an inheritance as it were, by succession from the Apostles   102
through the saints who came after them.

1044

[Bk 3(5): *Jaeger*, Vol. 2 pp. 130-131]
   We know that the divine nature is always one and the same and continues ever as it is.   332
The flesh by itself is that which reason and sense apprehend concerning it; but
commingled with the divine (2) it no longer remains in its own bounds and properties,
but is taken up to that which is overwhelming and transcendent. Our contemplation of the
properties of the flesh and the properties of the Godhead remains free of confusion,
so long as each of these is contemplated by itself, as in the saying, "The Word existed
before the ages, but the flesh was made in the last days." . . . What form is
struck in the Passion, and what form is glorified from eternity? This much is clear even
if one does not pursue the argument further: that the blows belong to the servant
in whom the Master was, and the honors to the Master whom the servant surrounded.
Thus, by reason of their connexion and their growing together, what belongs to each   334
becomes common to both (3): the Master takes upon Himself the stripes belonging to
the servant, the servant is glorified by the glory of the Master. That is why the cross
can be called the cross of the Lord of Glory, and why every tongue can confess, to the
glory of God the Father, that Jesus Christ is Lord (4).

1045

[Bk 3(7): *Jaeger*, Vol. 2, p. 163]
   Divinely inspired Scripture, as the Divine Apostle calls it, is the Holy Spirit's writing.   20
Its purpose is usefulness to men. "All Scripture," he says, "is inspired of God   22
and useful (5)."

1046

[Bk 3(8): *Jaeger*, Vol. 2, p. 186]
   The word of Holy Scripture indicates one mark of the true Godhead, which Moses   140
learned from the Voice from above, when he heard it saying: "I am He that exists (6)."
We judge it proper, therefore, to believe that that alone is truly divine whose existence
is found to be eternal and infinite, and in whom all that is contemplated is ever the   155
same, neither increasing nor diminishing.

1047

[Bk 2(12B): Jaeger, Vol. 1, p. 263]
   We have from reasoning but a dull and inexact perception of the divine nature. By   175
means of the names, nevertheless, which may piously be spoken of that nature,   176
we gather knowledge that is sufficient for our limited capacity. We do not say, however,
that all of these names are of uniform significance; on the contrary, some of them are   181
expressive of qualities inherent in God, while others place an emphasis on what He is   178
not. We say, for example, that God is just and that He is incorruptible. By *just* we
indicate that justice is in Him; by *incorruptible*, that corruption is not in Him.

1048

[Bk 2(12B): *Jaeger*, Vol. 1, pp. 265-266]
   Human thought, busying itself with solicitous inquiry through such reasoning as is   175

available to it, reaches out and just touches His inaccessible and sublime nature;   174
for its discernment is neither so sharp nor so clear that it can see the invisible, nor is it
yet so remote of approach that it is unable to catch a glimpse of what it is seeking. . . .
Not that the human mind is able to see precisely what that nature is, about which
it is reasoning, but from the knowledge of the properties which that nature has and the   180
properties which it has not, it sees as much only as can be seen. . . . From the negation   178
of properties not inherent in that nature, and from the confession of what may
piously be inferred about that nature, the human mind grasps something of what it is.

1049
[Bk 2(12B): *Jaeger*, Vol. 1, p. 267]
From the things we predicate of Him, we do not learn what God is in essence (7).   174
While we avoid in every way the admitting of any absurd concepts into the notions   175
we form about God, we apply to Him many and varied surnames, adapting these   181
appellations according to the direction taken by our thoughts.

1050
[Bk 2 (12B): *Jaeger*, Vol. 1, p. 290]
Since, as the Apostle says, "His eternal power and divinity are clearly seen,   131
understood through the creation of the world (8)," all creation, therefore, and above all,   179
as the Scripture says, the orderly arrangement in the heavens demonstrates the
wisdom of the Creator through the skill displayed in His works (9).

1051
[Bk 2 (12B): *Jaeger*, Vol. 1, p. 298]
The thing that exists is, in its subsisting, a work of the Creator's power; but the names   524
by which things are known, and by which reason designates each with a clear and
accurate description, are the work and invention of our rational power. This same
rational power, however, and its nature, is a work of God.

1. κατασκευή, constructive reasoning, is a technical term in logic.
2. ἀνακραθεῖσα δὲ πρὸς τὸ θεῖον. Gregory's terminology does sometimes give a handle to Monophysitism. Gregory
   seems never to be able to rid himself entirely of the notion of a transformation of Christ's human nature into the divine.
   The Latin translator who rendered ἀνακραθεῖσα as *coniuncta* was much too kind to Gregory. ἀνακεράννυμι is *to mix
   so as to blend*.
3. I am not entirely comfortable with the terms συνάφεια and συμφυΐα—connection and growing together; but possibly
   Gregory was not happy with them either. It is extremely difficult to find terms that are satisfactory. Other than these
   troublesome terms, the statement is creditable enough of the *communicatio idiomatum*, in spite of what might be called
   Gregory's anticipated Monophysitism.
4. Phil. 2:11.
5. 2 Tim. 3:16.
6. Ex. 3:14.
7. κατ᾽ οὐσίαν.
8. Rom. 1:20.
9. See Ps. 18[19]:2-4. It is this passage to which Gregory has been referring in the context of the present selection.

REFUTATION OF THE VIEWS OF APOLLINARIS [*post A. D.* 385]

Gregory's work against Apollinaris belongs to his late years, after 385 A. D. It begins
with a rather vehement invective against Apollinaris' *Demonstration of the Incarnation*

of God in the Likeness of Man, no longer extant as such, but the content of which can be reconstructed through Gregory's refutation. He combats especially the Apollinarist notions that the body of Christ came down from heaven, and that in Christ the place of a human spirit (νοῦς) is supplied by the Divine Logos. (I think that I was, as a child, an unwitting Apollinarist; for the Jesus of my simple faith was a human body activated by the Divine Spirit in place of a soul. I wonder if that disastrous notion is not still common among less sophisticated Catholics?)

The Migne text, PG 45, 1123-1270, which reprints Zacagni's edition of 1698, is entirely supplanted as standard by F. Mueller's edition in Jaeger's Wilamowitz-Moellendorf, Vol. 3/1, Leiden 1958, pp. 129-233.

1052

[17: Jaeger, p. 154]

The only-begotten God Himself raised up the man mingled (1) with Himself, 314
separating the soul from the body and uniting both again; and thus He brought about the 312
common salvation of our nature. Hence He is called the Author (2) of life. For in His 374
dying and rising again for us, the only-begotten God reconciled the world to Himself,
redeeming such captives as we were, all who have flesh and blood in common with Him, 313
buying us back with the blood of our own common heritage.

1053

[29: Jaeger, p. 176]

"The Father raises up the dead and gives them life, and the Son gives life to whom He 258
will (3)." We do not understand by this that some are rejected by the will of the
Lifemaker. Because, however, as we have heard and do believe, all things that are the
Father's are the Son's also, it is obvious that we perceive in the Son the will also of the
Father, which is one of these things. If, therefore, the paternal will is in the Son,
but the Father, as the Apostle says, "wills that all men be saved and come to knowledge 200
of truth (4)," certainly He that possesses all things that are the Father's and has the
Father wholly in Himself, has entirely within Himself along with the other good things of
the Father the whole salvific will. If, therefore, He does not lack the perfect will,
it is fully evident that those whom the Father wills to make live He too makes alive. He
does not skimp in any way in the loving-kindness of His will toward men, as
Apollinaris would have it; He does not will that only some and not all should be made
alive. It is not the will of the Lord that is the reason why some are saved and some
are lost; were that the case, the cause of their perdition would have to be referred to His 215
will. That some are saved and some perish depends rather upon the deliberate choice
of those who hear the word.

1054

[42: Jaeger, p. 201]

Just as happens in the open sea, if someone throw a drop of vinegar into the sea, and 321
the drop, made over into a marine quality, becomes the sea, so too with the true Son and
only-begotten God, . . . who, through flesh, is manifested to men. Flesh which by its
own nature is flesh, is made over in accord with the sea of incorruptibility,—just
as in the saying of the Apostle, that "mortality is swallowed up by life (5),"—and all
those things that are manifested according to the flesh are changed to accord with the
divine and undiluted nature.

1055

[55: *Jaeger*, pp. 225-226]

Godhead, though not subject to death, is raised from the dead (6). Godhead is not 322
mortal because what is not composed is not dissolved; and It is raised because, existing 329
in that which was dissolved, It is prepared to raise up with Itself that which had
fallen in accord with the law of human nature, so that while each part continues to 334
exhibit its natural qualities, It heals the nature of bodies by the body, and the nature of 314
souls by the soul. Uniting again through Itself what had been separated, It is raised
up in Him who is the Exalted.

1. ἀνακραθέντα. The Latin translator simply cannot convince himself that Gregory would really use this word. Now he
translates it *unitum*. See note 2 to § 1044 above, and the text of § 1054 below.
2. ἀρχηγός. See Acts 3:15.
3. John 5:21.
4. 1 Tim. 2:4.
5. 2 Cor. 5:4.
6. ἡ θεότης καὶ οὐ τέθνηκε καὶ ἐγήγερται. Note the peculiar force of καὶ . . . καὶ . . . ; literally, *Godhead (is) not
only not-mortal but also is-raised*. Actually, this is no more than an example of the corresponsive καὶ . . . καὶ . . . ,
the οὐ simply presenting a confusing appearance, since it belongs not with the καὶ but with the τέθνηκε; and as
corresponsive, the καὶ . . . καὶ . . . has already the force of *not only . . . but also . . . .*

DIALOGUE ON THE SOUL AND RESURRECTION [*A. D.* 379 *aut* 380]

Returning from the Synod of Antioch at the end of 379 A. D., Gregory went to visit
his elder sister, St. Macrina the Younger, who was superioress of the women's
monastery on the Iris. He found her ill, and by evening of the first day after his arrival
she was dead.

The dialogue is the conversation that Gregory had with Macrina as she lay dying. In
the course of their conversation Macrina declares her views on the soul, death,
immortality, resurrection, and the restoration of all things. It would be grossly impolite
to ask whether this is really the dying dialogue of Macrina, or whether Gregory
afterwards wrote down what he thought a dying person of exemplary life ought to be
saying. That is why no one ever asks.

The Migne text, PG 46, 11-160, reprints that of J. G. Krabinger, Leipzig 1837, and is
still the standard. An edition by Hilda Polack is expected in Vol. 3/2 of Jaeger's
Wilamowitz-Moellendorf.

1056

[Migne, PG 46, col. 29]

Macrina: The soul is an essence created, a living essence (1), intellectual; to an 503
organic and sentient body it is the power of living (2) and the faculty of perceiving
sensible objects, so long as a nature capable of all this endures.

1057

[Migne, PG 46, col. 96]

Macrina: Hope is operative only so long as the enjoyment of the things hoped for is not 580
in possession; and faith, likewise, is a support against the uncertainty of the things 582
hoped for. This is what Paul says when he defines it: "Faith is the substance (3) of 567
things hoped for (4)." When the thing hoped for actually comes, all the other faculties 546
are idled and love alone remains active, finding nothing to succeed itself.

1058

[Migne, PG 46, col. 125]

Macrina: The question was, "If souls exist prior to their bodies, when and how   507
do they come into existence?" . . . If it be granted that the soul lives in some
condition peculiar to itself prior to the body, it is altogether necessary for us to think that
there is some value to those absurd dogmatizations which explain the souls' inhabiting
of bodies as a consequence of wickedness. . . . We can only suppose, however,
that soul and body have a single beginning.

1. οὐσία γεννητή, οὐσία ζῶσα.
2. δύναμιν ζωτικήν.
3. ὑπόστασις.
4. Heb. 11:1.

ON THE UNTIMELY DEATHS OF INFANTS

This rather short work belongs to Gregory's later years, and is addressed to Hierius, the
Prefect of Cappadocia. The treatise tries to find an explanation for the deaths of infants
in God's foreknowledge, coupled with His mercy.

The text in Migne is in PG 46, 161-192. Probably this will be included among the
"certain minor works" that are to be included in Vol. 3/2 of Jaeger's Willamowitz-
Moellendorf.

1059

[Migne, PG 46, col. 184]

It is a reasonable supposition that God, who knows the future just as well as the past,   189
checks the advance of an infant to perfect maturity of life so that the evil which, by   194
virtue of His foreknowledge, He has detected in the future, may not actually develop.
. . . This, we suspect, is the reason for the deaths of infants: He who does all things
rationally withdraws the material of evil in His great love for men, granting no
time for the actual doing of evil works to one whom, by virtue of his foreknowledge, He
knows would indulge a propensity to evil.

AGAINST THOSE WHO RESENT CORRECTION

This work, known also as the *De castigatione* or *On Chastisement* belongs to
Gregory's lesser ascetical writings. It was occasioned by the fact that some of his flock so
resented his correction that they left the Church.

The Migne text, PG 46, 307-316, is still the standard. Presumably an edition
will be included in Vol. 3/2 of Jaeger's Wilamowitz-Moellendorf, which is announced
as going to contain, in addition to the *Dialogue on the Soul and Resurrection* and the
Great Catechism, also "certain minor writings."

1060

[Migne, PG 46, col. 312]

The doorkeepers of the [heavenly] kingdom are careful and they do not play games.   1034
They see the soul bearing the marks of her banishment (1). . . . Then the miserable
soul, accusing herself severely of her own thoughtlessness, and howling and wailing and

lamenting, remains in that sullen place, cast away as if in a corner, while the incessant and inconsolable wailing takes vengeance forever (2).

1. τοῦ ἀφορισμοῦ.
2. εἰς αἰῶνας. Nevertheless, Gregory's eternity of punishment must, in view of his numerous fuller statements elsewhere, be taken only in a relative sense. Gregory's ἀποκατάστασις is the Origenist ἀποκατάστασις πάντων, except that Gregory's is really final, whereas Origen's repeats itself in endless cycles. Gregory seems to be convinced, at any rate, that ultimately all men and the fallen angels with them shall return to God. See above, § 1033, § 1036, and below, § 1061.

ORATIONS AND SERMONS

Besides the homilies which make up the commentaries on Ecclesiastes and on Canticle of Canticles, the treatises on the Beatitudes and on the Lord's Prayer, all treated above, and a grouping of two homilies on 1 Corinthians, of which I will not treat, there is also a small collection of other *Orations and Sermons*, embracing liturgical sermons, panegyrics on martyrs and saints, funeral orations, encomia, moral sermons, and dogmatic sermons.

The Migne edition, PG 46, 431-1000, contains thirty-one such sermons, and remains the standard text except for the fifteen that have now been edited in *Sermones, Pars Prior*, in Jaeger's Wilamowitz-Moellendorf, Vol. 9. Presumably the rest will follow in another volume.

The *Oratio in diem luminum sive in baptismum Christi* was probably delivered on the Feast of Epiphany in the year 383 A. D. (§ 1062 below). The collection includes five sermons *In sanctum Pascha sive in Christi resurrectionem*, of which no. 1, belonging to Easter of A. D. 382 (§ 1063 below), no. 3 (§ 1064 and 1065 below), and no. 5 are regarded as authentic. No. 2 is invariably regarded as unauthentic, and no. 4 is still questionable. All our citations below are from sermons presently regarded as authentic.

The chronology of the *Orations and Sermons* has been closely studied by Jean Card. Daniélou.

SERMON ON THE DEAD

1061

[*Jaeger*: Vol. 9, pp. 55-56]

If a man distinguish in himself what is peculiarly human from that which is irrational,   1000
and if he be on the watch for a life of greater urbanity for himself, in this present
life he will purify himself of any evil contracted, overcoming the irrational by reason.
And if he have inclined to the irrational pressure of the passions, using for the
passions the cooperating hide of things irrational, he may afterwards in a quite different
manner be very much interested in what is better, when, after his departure out of the
body, he gains knowledge of the difference between virtue and vice, and finds that
he is not able to partake of divinity until he has been purged of the filthy contagion in his
soul by the purifying fire (1).

SERMON ON THE DAY OF LIGHTS or ON THE BAPTISM OF CHRIST

1062

[*Jaeger*: Vol. 9, pp. 225-226]

The bread again is at first common bread; but when the mystery (2) sanctifies it, it is   860

called and actually becomes the Body of Christ. So too the mystical oil, so too the   856
wine; if they are things of little worth before the blessing, after their sanctification by the   841
Spirit each of them has its own superior operation. This same power of the word   791
also makes the priest (3) venerable and honorable, separated from the generality of men   950
by the new blessing bestowed upon him. Yesterday he was but one of the multitude,   951
one of the people; suddenly he is made a guide, a president, a teacher of piety, an   965
instructor in hidden mysteries.

SERMON ON THE INTERVAL OF THREE DAYS BETWEEN THE DEATH AND RESURRECTION OF OUR LORD JESUS CHRIST, or SERMON ONE ON THE RESURRECTION OF CHRIST

1063

[*Jaeger:* Vol. 9, p. 287]

He offered Himself for us, Victim and Sacrifice, and Priest as well, and "Lamb of   382
God, who takes away the sin of the world (4)." When did He do this? When He   890
made His own Body food and His own Blood drink for His disciples; for this much is   849
clear enough to anyone, that a sheep cannot be eaten by a man unless its being eaten be   851
preceded by its being slaughtered. This giving of His own Body to His disciples
for eating clearly indicates that the sacrifice of the Lamb has now been completed.

ON THE HOLY PASCH or SERMON THREE ON THE RESURRECTION OF CHRIST

1064

[*Jaeger:* Vol. 9, pp. 258-259]

Just as seed, existing formlessly in the beginning, is shaped into a design and increases   1011
in bulk, prepared as it is by the indescribable skill of God, so too it is not at all absurd
but entirely consistent that the material enclosed in tombs and which once was
possessed of shape should be restored anew to its ancient structure, and dust become
man again in the same way that man originally took his birth from dust.

1065

[*Jaeger:* Vol. 9, p. 268]

If in illustrious deeds the body toils along with the soul, and in sinful deeds it is not   1011
absent, how do you manage to pilot the incorporeal alone to the dicastery? But that
were not at all a just view, nor do wise men hold such. If the soul sinned naked and alone,
let it alone be punished; but if it has an evident accomplice, the just Judge will not
dismiss that accomplice. I hear Scripture too saying that for the condemned just   1032
punishments are ordered: fire and darkness and a worm. All of these are punishments
suited to composite and material bodies. . . . By such consistent reasonings from all
sides we are compelled to assent to the resurrection of the dead, which God will
bring about at its appointed time, when in His works He will make good His own
promises.

1. τοῦ καθαρσίου πυρός. That is, the *purgatorial fire*, or so it might be translated. But it is highly doubtful that the reference is to a purgatory as Catholic teaching knows it. Gregory seems indisputably to follow Origen in assigning a medicinal quality to the fire of hell, virtually turning hell into purgatory.
2. ἱερουργήσῃ.
3. τὸν ἱερέα.
4. John 1:29.

DIDYMUS THE BLIND [ca. A. D. 313 – ca. A. D. 398]

Didymus, born at Alexandria about the year 313 A. D., was blind from about the age of four. Yet he became one of the most learned men and one of the most prolific authors of his age. Under St. Athanasius, Didymus was made head of the catechetical school at Alexandria and was in fact its last head. At his death the school removed to Sid and shortly closed. Among Didymus' more famous students were Jerome and Rufinus.

Didymus was not an especially original thinker; but his prodigious memory enabled him to gain a masterful knowledge of philosophy and theology, along with geometry, astronomy and arithmetic.

The contemporaries of Didymus knew him as a man of considerable insight and extreme kindness. There is nothing of invective in his writings—apparently Jerome learned that without a teacher—and he is able to show a rather angelic disposition even when dealing with heresies, condemning the doctrine but never the person. Consequently he was well-liked and on good terms even with the Arians. He remained always a layman; and he lived as an ascetic outside Alexandria even when he was head of the catechetical school.

Didymus' Trinitarian writings are a model of soundness, and his doctrine is correct in general, except that he followed Origen in regard to the preexistence of souls and the ultimate salvation of all, or *apokatástasis pánton*. In the sixth and seventh centuries the writings of Didymus suffered the same fate as those of Evagrius of Pontus: anathematization because of their Origenist tendencies. This no doubt accounts for the fact that the holy man himself was never accorded the title of saint, as well as for the loss of the major part of his writings.

The only collected edition of Didymus' writings is that of Migne, PG 39, 131-1818. Migne's edition did inadvertently omit a few things known already in his time, but it is in general a rather careful and circumspect edition. With the findings of more recent studies, however, a new collected edition would be most welcome. It would, of course, have to include a substantial body of fragmentary remains of Didymus that were found at Toura in 1941 in the course of excavating for a munitions dump.

THE HOLY SPIRIT [ante A. D. 381]

St. Ambrose made use of the Greek text of Didymus' work in writing his own *De Spiritu sancto* in the year 381 A. D., for which St. Jerome, in his usual dudgeon, accused him, in the introduction to his translation of Didymus' treatise, of plagiarism. Jerome's translation was prepared at the suggestion of Pope Damasus, between the years 384 and 392 A. D.

The treatise is regarded as one of the best monographs on the Holy Spirit written in the fourth century. The Greek text has perished, but Jerome's translation survives. It is found twice in Migne, *apud* Jerome at PL 23, 101-154, and at PG 39, 1031-1086. It is my impression that an edition by G. Bardy, to be a critical edition with translation and notes under the title *Didyme, Traité du Saint-Esprit*, planned for the series *Sources Chrétiennes*, was foiled by Bardy's untimely death in 1955 and has never appeared.

1066

[35]

God is simple and of an incomposite and spiritual nature, having neither ears nor   151
organs of speech. A solitary essence and illimitable, He is composed of no numbers   152

and parts. This, indeed, is likewise to be accepted in respect to the Son and the Holy
Spirit.

1067

[37]

"Of mine He shall receive (1)." Just as we have understood discussions, therefore,   273
about the incorporeal natures, so too it is now to be recognized that the Holy Spirit
receives from the Son that which He was of His own nature, and not as one substance
giving and another receiving, but as signifying one substance. So too the Son is said to   281
receive from the Father the very things by which He subsists. For neither has the Son
anything else except those things given Him by the Father, nor has the Holy Spirit
any other substance than that given Him by the Son. And on that account we do
affirm those propositions according to which we believe that in the Trinity the nature
of the Holy Spirit is the same as that of the Father and the Son.

1. John 16:15.

THE TRINITY [*inter A. D.* 381-392]

Didymus' three books on *The Trinity* is his principal writing, and it has survived intact,
probably because it contains nothing of the author's Origenism. The work satisfied
even Jerome, who remarks, "On the Trinity, certainly he is Catholic." The work fully
defends the consubstantiality of the Three Persons, has no taint of subordinationism,
and answers the objections of the Arians and Macedonians.

The authenticity of the work has been disputed in recent years but is now rather
generally acknowledged.

The Migne text is in PG 39, 269-992, a reprint of J. A. Mingarelli's edition
of 1769; and it is still the standard.

1068

[1, 15]

Just as it is impossible for the Father not to be without beginning and yet be truly   237
Father,—for He has this name not from time nor as an addition to something else,—so
too it is impossible for the Son, the Word, and His Holy Spirit, not to be without
beginning, and still be, by nature, of His substance (1); for at the same time that the
Father was,—if I may be allowed to phrase it thus,—the Son was uninterruptedly
begotten and the Spirit was made to proceed. And there has been no cessation of His   276
being Father of the Only-begotten, nor of His having His Spirit proceed from Him;   273
and by being Father He differs neither in time nor in essence from the Son and His Spirit.

1069

[2, 4]

How is the Holy Spirit spirit from spirit? The fact that it is written is proof enough   239
(2). The how of it is beyond our mind and reason, beyond even the intelligence of
the angels. For even though the Father is spirit, God the Word was begotten of Him;
and thus too the Holy Spirit shines forth from Him and with Him. . . . It is not
possible for the Spirit not to be consubstantial (3) and equal to Him from whom He   268
exists; He too, therefore, is by His nature holy (4).   277

1070

[2, 6, 2]

Nothing created can fill the whole world, nor contain all things and be in all things.   484
On the contrary, even for intellectual Powers there is a boundary and a defined quantity.   154
To fill all and contain all and be in all are properties only of the Godhead. But the Holy   267
Spirit's majesty, perpetuity, limitlessness, His being everywhere, through all and in
all, is forever. He does indeed fill the world and subsist divinely (5), and is
unrestricted (6) as to power, measuring indeed, but not being measured.

1071

[2, 6, 7]

The creature does not participate substantially in the rational soul, as if by indwelling   267
in it; for so to participate (7) is proper to God alone. But the Holy Spirit, in His   753
subsisting, participates substantially (8), as do the Father and the Son. . . . From
the very beginning of the Father's indwelling in those who are worthy, is it not of   283
necessity, in view of the unity of the divine nature and its fullness in its indwelling
in us, that the Son and the Holy Spirit join and concur in that incursion? Surely
no one would ever want to say that it is as if a multiplicity of gods were indwelling   238
in us, but one God, the three Persons subsisting quite as One (9) in the unity of the
Godhead.

1072

[3, 2, 8]

If the Only-begotten is, as Paul writes to the Hebrews, "the Splendor of the   257
glory and the exact stamp of the substance (10)" and the Image of the   263
shapeless and invisible and beginningless God, and if He speaks truly when   264
He says, "Whoever sees Me sees the Father (11)," and "I and the Father
are one (12)," He is consubstantial with God the Father, and with Him
co-beginningless and equal and invariable. For light, begotten of light, is not
of another nature nor later; and an exact stamp of an essence shows
sameness and invariability of nature and glory and omnipotence.

1073

[3, 4]

It helps us to understand the terms first-born and only-begotten when the   783
Evangelist tells that Mary remained a virgin "until she brought forth her
first-born son (13)"; for neither did Mary, who is to be honored and
praised above all others, marry anyone, nor did she ever become the Mother of
anyone else, but even after childbirth she remained always and forever
(14) an immaculate virgin (15).

1074

[3, 12]

The saying, "I came down from heaven, not to do My will but that of the   330
Father who sent Me (16)," is to be taken in this sense: "In the Incarnation
I am not doing the will of My humanity, but that of My divinity." For the will
of the Beloved Son is not separate from the will of God the Father. In the
Trinity there is one and the same will.

1075

[3, 16]

God, subsisting above the invisible and most hidden, and above every 170
mind, not only does not fall under sight or any kind of sense at all, but neither 173
is He, since He is illimitable and unapproachable, to be observed by the
mind of the angels.

1076

[3, 21]

How would you know that [Christ] truly became flesh with a living soul, 310
and was not a mere phantasm, whereas the Manicheans think that He had a 312
body only in appearance and the Arians that He was without a soul, if
He had not said, "My soul is exceedingly sorrowful (17)," and showed a
certain fear, and if He had not partaken of food and drink and sleep? For these
things pertain neither to divinity nor to flesh without a soul. In reference to 349
the body those things only which pertain to the corruptibility of the body are
regarded as passions, not, however, what arises in us through failure to
use the rational faculties; in reference to the soul, the cares resulting from the
passions are included.

1. ἐκ τῆς ὑποστάσεως αὐτοῦ.
2. ὅτι δὲ τοῦτο γέγραπται, δέδεικται.
3. ὁμοούσιον.
4. ἅγιον φυσικῶς.
5. συνέχουσα κατὰ τὴν θεότητα. Literally, *subsisting according to* (or in accord with) *the Godhead*. The effect of this usage of κατά is to make of the prepositional phrase an adverb: and *in accord with the Godhead = divinely*. This is not in fact an exceptional usage and grammarians sometimes term it the κατά *of fitness*, in which the preposition is followed by a term in the accusative.
6. ἀχώρητος.
7. τὸ οὕτως μετέχεσθαι. If the manner of expression be somewhat offensive to anyone's pious ear, it is probably possible to translate the Greek, doing it no real violence, in this fashion: "The creature is not made to enjoy, of his substance, a participation in the rational soul, as if by indwelling in it; for that manner of enjoyment is proper to God alone." But I am not certain whether the problem, if there is one, is thereby cured or only obscured.
8. Note that the term οὐσιωδῶς = *substantially* is of very precise meaning: *by reason of essence*.
9. κατά γε τὸ ἕν.
10. Heb. 1:3. Here ὑποστάσεως, with Paul, means substance or essence, whereas the same term at the end of § 1071 immediately above meant person.
11. John 14:9.
12. John 10:30.
13. Matt. 1:25.
14. ἀεὶ καὶ διὰ παντὸς might also mean *always and in every respect*.
15. ἄμωμος παρθένος.
16. John 6:38.
17. Matt. 26:38.

AGAINST THE MANICHEANS

The treatise *Against the Manicheans*, not datable with any useful precision, is extant in the original Greek. It is a work of eighteen rather short chapters. It is possible that what we actually have is only an excerpt from a more extensive work. Didymus does engage in similar polemics against the Manicheans in his other writings, and there is no reason to be suspicious in respect to his authorship of the present work.

The standard text is still that of Migne, PG 39, 1085-1110.

1077

[8]
  If Christ had received His body from a marital union and not in another   781
way it would be supposed that He too is liable to an accounting for that sin,   614
which, indeed, all who are descended from Adam contract in succession. But   615
if the Manicheans are saying, "If it is the flesh of sin that is the issue of
the intercourse of man and woman, then marriage is wicked," let them hear
that before the coming of the Savior who takes away the sin of the world, all
men did indeed, just like other things they did with malice, enter upon
marriage sinfully. Hence the understanding about bodies begotten in
marriage; and thus, since the coming together of Adam and Eve came about
after sin (1), the flesh is for that reason called the flesh of sin. . . . But when
the Savior was sojourning here, just as there was a taking away of sin from   374
other things, so too from marriage. . . . [9] And in a different way it   983
may be said even more naturally that virginity is something divine, and is   984
accounted among the virtues. If, therefore, someone compares virginity to
marriage, the latter may be called sin; but it is not sin in the absolute sense.

1. I have the impression that many of the Fathers supposed that the sin of Adam and Eve was an act of sexual intercourse. At
first blush that would seem not to have been Didymus' view of the matter, when he says that the coming together of
Adam and Eve took place after sin. Closer examination, however, will make it clear that in this passage he says nothing
whatever of what the nature of their sin may have been. That is not what he is discussing. And he really only says that
their *marital relationship*, chronologically, was established after they had committed the original sin. He might (or might
not) consider that their sin was a sin of fornication, after which sin their marriage was established. At any rate, his view is
that had sin not come first, presumably there would never have been an institution of marriage. The establishment of
marriage, then, is, as it were, a result of sin; and that is why the flesh which is begotten in marriage is called the flesh of
sin. That, it seems to me, is Didymus' reasoning.

ST. AMPHILOCHIUS OF ICONIUM [*ca. A. D.* 340/345 – *post A. D.* 394]

  Amphilochius was born a Cappadocian, probably a cousin of Gregory of Nazianz, and
certainly the close friend of the great Cappadocians, Basil and the two Gregory's. At
Antioch he studied under the great rhetorician Libanius, and went about the year 364 A. D.
to Constantinople to practice law. About the year 370 he began to incline more and
more to an eremitical way of life; but his yearnings in that direction were never fulfilled,
because at the end of 373 A. D. Basil consecrated him a bishop, making him the
somewhat reluctant metropolitan of Lycaonia with Iconium for his see. Amphilochius is
last mentioned among the living when he attended a synod at Constantinople in 394.
Presumably he died shortly thereafter.
  Apparently Amphilochius was a very capable administrator, and he was a prominent
figure in the theological controversies of his time. Much respected by his
contemporaries, among whom he enjoyed a certain eminence, he was recognized as a
patristic authority within a generation after his death, being quoted by ecumenical
councils from Ephesus onwards.
  The writings of Amphilochius were undoubtedly rather extensive; but most of them,
unfortunately, have been lost. Somehow in later years he slipped into a kind of oblivion
from which he has been partially rescued only in modern times, largely through the
efforts of K. Holl and G. Ficker.
  A synodal letter, written by him at Iconium in 376 A. D., has survived intact, along
with a few sermons and a lengthy poem *To Seleucus*. The rest of his remains consists
only of a large body of fragments.
  The texts in Migne, PG 39, 9-130, must be supplemented by the further texts
published by Karl Holl, *Amphilochius von Ikonium in seinem Verhältnis zu den grossen*

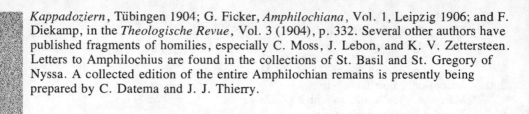

Kappadoziern, Tübingen 1904; G. Ficker, *Amphilochiana*, Vol. 1, Leipzig 1906; and F. Diekamp, in the *Theologische Revue*, Vol. 3 (1904), p. 332. Several other authors have published fragments of homilies, especially C. Moss, J. Lebon, and K. V. Zettersteen. Letters to Amphilochius are found in the collections of St. Basil and St. Gregory of Nyssa. A collected edition of the entire Amphilochian remains is presently being prepared by C. Datema and J. J. Thierry.

TO SELEUCUS

Cosmas Indicopleustes knows that Amphilochius wrote an *Iambic Letter to Seleucus*. This *To Seleucus* or *Iambics to Seleucus* has been preserved for us, a poem of 340 verses (the poem itself declares at the end that it consists of 333 iambic lines; but it does not count the last seven, consisting of four lines of greetings, two for its self-counting, and one line, a blessing), among the *Poems* of St. Gregory of Nazianz, book 2, section 2, number 8. The text in Migne is in PG 37, 1577-1600. A better edition is that of E. Oberg, *Amphilochii Iconiensis Iambi ad Seleucum*, Berlin 1969.

The *Iambics to Seleucus* is undoubtedly a genuine work not of Gregory but of Amphilochius, and perhaps the only poem he ever wrote. An instruction to Seleucus on what should be his life of study and virtue, it includes an important listing of the Canon of Scripture. Seleucus is identified as the grandson of Trajan the General, and the nephew of St. Olympias.

1078

[*Apud Greg. Naz. Carm*. 2, 2, 8]

. . .

I will review for you each gift of these
Divinely inspired books; and that you may clearly know,   20
I will first review those of the Old Testament.   41
The Pentateuch has Creation, then Exodus,
265   And Leviticus, the middle book,
After which is Numbers, then Deuteronomy.
Add to these Josue, and Judges.
Then Ruth, and of Kingdoms four
Books, and Chronicles yoked together;
270   After these, Esdras, one and then the second.
Then will I review for you five in verse:
Job, crowned in the contests of many sufferings,
And the Book of Psalms, soothing remedy for the soul,
Three of Solomon the Wise, Proverbs,
275   Ecclesiastes, Canticle of Canticles.
Add to these the Prophets Twelve,
Osee first, then Amos the second,
Micheas, Joel, Abdias, and the type
Of Him who three days suffered, Jonas,
280   Nahum after those, and Habacuc; and ninth,
Sophonias, Aggeus and Zacharias,
And angel twice-named Malachias (1).
After these prophets learn yet another four:
The great intrepid Isaias,
285   Jeremias, ready to sympathize, and mysterious

Ezechiel, and Daniel last,
Most wise in his deeds and words.
To these some add Esther.

Now I am to read the books of the New Testament.   42
290 Accept only four Evangelists,
Matthew, then Mark, to which add Luke
The third, count John in time as
Fourth, but first in sublimity of teachings.
Son of Thunder (2) rightly he is called,
295 Who loudly announced the Word of God.
Accept from Luke a second book also,
That of the Catholic Acts of the Apostles.
Add to these besides that Vessel of Election (3),
The Herald of the Gentiles, the Apostle
300 Paul, writing wisely to the Churches
Twice seven Epistles, one to the Romans,
To which must be added two to the Corinthians,
And the one to the Galatians, and that to the Ephesians, after which
There is the one to the Philippians, then those written
305 To the Colossians, to the Thessalonians two,
Two to Timothy, to Titus and to Philemon
One to each, and to the Hebrews one.
Some call that to the Hebrews spurious,
But not rightly do they say it; for the gift is genuine.
310 What then is left? Of the Catholic Epistles
Some say seven need be
Accepted, others only three:
One of James, one of Peter, one of John,—
Or three of John and with them
315 Two of Peter,—the seventh that of Jude.
The Apocalypse of John again
Some accept, but most will
Call it spurious. Here then most certainly
You have the Canon of the divinely inspired Scriptures (4).

1. The name Malachias means angel. The opening words of the book are "The burden of the word of the Lord that came to Israel by the hand of Malachias." The Septuagint, having placed the name Malachias at the head of the book, then translates the opening line, "The burden of the word of the Lord that came to Israel by the hand of His angel." Thus Malachias is, in the Septuagint, angel twice-named.
2. Mark 3:17.
3. Acts 9:15.
4. κανών. . . τῶν θεοπνεύστων γραφῶν.

FRAGMENTS

1079

[No. 9, in PG 39, 105]*
During the time of suffering, in His willing acceptance of the three days in   321
the tomb, the temple of the body is set free. He raises it up again, and it   329
is joined to Himself, to the Word inexpressible and unutterable. He does not

*According to Karl Holl, this fragment should be attributed to Cyril of Alexandria rather than to Amphilochius.

blend it in Himself, nor does He reject the flesh; rather, He preserves unmingled in Himself the separate identity (1) of the two natures of the different essences (2).

1080

[No. 12, in PG 39, 109]

Henceforth distinguish for me the two natures, that of God and that of   322
Man. For neither is Man produced of God by being detached from Him, nor God from Man by advancement. I am saying God *and* Man. But whenever you attribute the sufferings to the flesh and the miracles to God, you must   332
necessarily, whether you want to or not, attribute the humble words to the Man born of Mary, but the more sublime and divinely suitable, to the Word who existed in the beginning.

1. τὴν ἰδιότητα.
2. τῶν δύο φύσεων τῶν ἑτερουσίων.

ST. EPIPHANIUS OF SALAMIS [*ca. A. D.* 315 – May 12, 403]

St. Epiphanius was born about the year 315 in Palestine, near Eleutheropolis and not far from Gaza. His episcopacy was on the Island of Cyprus, however, at Constantia, now called Salamis.

Epiphanius is a strange figure. He was fully as testy as Jerome, and yet Jerome was friendly to him and held him in great reverence. It is Jerome who calls him a Pentaglot, for his knowledge of Greek, Syriac, Hebrew, Coptic and Latin. Jerome says also in his treatment of him in the *De viris illustribus* 114 that Epiphanius' works were eagerly read not only by the learned, because of their subject matter, but also by the plain people, on account of their language.

There is a basis beyond Jerome's adulation for this last remark. The fact is, Epiphanius despised the classical learning of Hellenism and viewed with suspicion the elegant writings of those who had studied rhetoric. When the Emperor Julian's disenfranchisements of Christians prevented them from any longer teaching rhetoric and the classics, Epiphanius alone among the bishops thought it a sign of progress and rather rejoiced over it. Karl Holl's judgment of Epiphanius' language is that it is an "elevated Koine." Ulrich von Wilamowitz-Moellendorf, however, thought it simply exhibited a great many vulgarisms, that is, colloquialisms. Photius said that Epiphanius' writings were careless and verbose; and it is commonly considered that they display the author's characteristic shallowness. Quasten in his *Patrology*, Vol. 3, p. 385, says that they are "hasty, superficial and disorderly compilations of the fruits of his extensive reading."

Two things at least may be said in favor of Epiphanius' writings: they preserve much valuable history otherwise lost, and they permit reconstruction of lost writings of other authors, particularly Irenaeus and Hippolytus.

St. Epiphanius combined a fiery zeal for Nicene orthodoxy with an incredibly rude lack of judgment, moderation, and tact. He was a vehement iconoclast (literally) before anyone else was; and he hated Origen passionately.

Epiphanius joined with Theophilus of Alexandria in expelling the Origenist monks from Nitria, and when the Tall Brothers took refuge with Chrysostom, Epiphanius went personally to Constantinople to confront Chrysostom with being a protector of heretics.

An unreliable legend records one of those wonderful incidents which are really too good not to be true: At their last confrontation Epiphanius blessed Chrysostom with a remarkably well-honed oriental curse: "I hope you will not die—a bishop!" And Chrysostom responded in kind: "To return home safely—do not expect!" Within a few days, Epiphanius died at sea when his boat sank on the way back to Cyprus. Scarcely more than a year later, Chrysostom was sent into an exile from which he never returned.

How strange that Epiphanius, that rude and violent man whose thought was too shallow ever to risk his falling into heresy, was anti-Origenist and is accounted a saint, whereas Didymus, that sweet, humble, and holy blind man, was pro-Origenist and hence is not! None will deprive Epiphanius of his prize; but it is impossible to believe that Didymus did not arrive home safely too.

THE MAN WELL-ANCHORED [*A. D.* 374]

St. Epiphanius' earliest extant writing, dating from 374 A. D., is his *Agkyrotós*, or *The Man Well-Anchored*. What else should a curmudgeon who dwelt by the sea call his book? In defense of the consubstantiality of the Holy Spirit and against the Macedonians or Pneumatomachians, the work has so many digressions that it is virtually a compendium of dogma.

Chapters 119 and 120 of the work are two creeds which Epiphanius recommends for use in baptism. The first (ch. 119) is the baptismal creed in use at Salamis and had been introduced there only shortly before Epiphanius' election to the see. It is this first creed that is the so-called Nicene-Constantinopolitan. See § 910a in the present work, with the remarks preceding it on page 398, where I explained with a singular lack of clarity that this creed, the so-called Nicene-Constantinopolitan, known to Epiphanius already in 374 A. D., is apparently a reworking of the Baptismal Creed of Jerusalem, which in turn was a reworking of the Nicene.

The second creed, in chapter 120, is longer, and was composed by Epiphanius himself. This is offered below in § 1089a.

The text of Migne, PG 43, 17-236, and that of F. Oehler, in his *Corpus haereseologicum*, Vol. 2, Berlin 1859, are both happily superseded by that of Karl Holl in the Berlin Corpus (GCS), Vol. 25 (1915), pp. 1-149.

1081

[7]

The Father is unbegotten, increate, and illimitable. The Son is begotten, but   250
is also increate and illimitable. The Holy Spirit is eternal, not begotten,   251
not created, not a brother, not a paternal uncle, not a forefather, not a   276
descendant, but Holy Spirit, of the same substance of the Father and Son. "For   268
God is spirit (1)."

1082

[8]

Each of the names is singular in significance, and has no secondary   281
significance. The Father is father, and has none against whom He might be compared, nor is He linked to any other father, so that there are not two gods. The Son is Only-begotten, true God of true God; He has not the name Father, nor is He foreign to the Father; rather, He subsists from the One Father. He is called Only-begotten as a singular appellation indicating that He is the Son; and God from God, because there is one God, Father and Son. The only-begotten Holy Spirit (2) has neither the name of Son nor the appellation

of Father, but is called Holy Spirit, and is not foreign to the Father. For
the Only-begotten Himself calls Him "the Spirit of the Father (3)," and says   269
of Him that "He proceeds from the Father (4)," and "will receive of mine
(5)," so that He is reckoned as not being foreign to the Father nor to the Son,   268
but is of their same substance, of the same Godhead; He is Spirit divine, . . .
of God, and He is God. For He is Spirit of God, Spirit of the Father, and   270
Spirit of the Son, not by some kind of synthesis, like soul and body in us, but
in the midst of Father and Son, of the Father and of the Son, a third by
appellation.

1083

[33]
   How could it be discovered that the Incarnation (6) is carried out in truth, if [Christ]   310
had not the necessary habitation of humanity? . . . Those passages [of Scripture]   311
which speak of Christ's eating and drinking show that He had true flesh. . . .   312
When the Word came, He had the whole economy of humanity, both flesh and soul and
whatever else is in a man.

1084

[57]
   We see that the Savior took [something] in His hands, as it is in the Gospel, when He   852
was reclining at the supper; and He took this, and giving thanks, He said: "This is really   810
Me (7)." And He gave to His disciples and said: "This is really Me." And we see that It   857
is not equal nor similar, not to the incarnate image, not to the invisible divinity, not to
the outline of His limbs. For It is round of shape, and devoid of feeling. As to Its power,
He means to say even of Its grace, "This is really Me"; and none disbelieves His
word. For anyone who does not believe the truth in what He says is deprived of grace
and of Savior.

1085

[65]
   Inasmuch as I was weak by reason of the flesh, the Savior has been sent to me in the   374
likeness of the flesh of sin (8) to conduct a very special business deal, so that He
might redeem me from slavery, from corruption, and from death. And for me "He
became righteousness and sanctification and redemption (9)"; righteousness because
by His fidelity He atoned for sin; sanctification because He acquitted through water
and Spirit, and in His word; redemption, because He gave Himself, His blood,   380
the blood of the true Lamb, as a price for me.

1086

[75]
   The Father always existed and the Son always existed, and the Spirit breathes from   251
the Father and the Son; and neither is the Son created nor is the Spirit created. . . .   273
Indeed, through the Word Himself all created things exist, through the heavenly King,   284
the subsisting Word, our Savior and Benefactor. For this is the Holy Savior who   781
came down from heaven, who deigned to fashion our salvation in a virginal workshop,   322
. . . who did not change His nature when He took on humanity along with His   311
divinity, . . . who took on the human flesh and soul; being perfect at the side of the   312

Father and incarnate among us, not in appearance but in truth, He reshaped man to   310
perfection in Himself, from Mary the Mother of God (10) through the Holy Spirit. . . .   780
The Word Himself became flesh (11), not ceasing to be God, not changing divinity into   321
humanity, but with the proper fulness of His divinity and with the proper Person
(12) of God the Word, He joined together in His existence the being that is man's and
whatever man is. I mean perfect man, whatever is present in man, and whatever sets man
apart.

1087

[80]
What do those people think they can say if we assert that Christ, born of Mary, is   345
perfect Man, or endowed with a mind? Do we suspect that He was burdened with
sin? Far be it!

1088

[87]
As for those who profess to be Christians but are followers of Origen, and who   1013
confess the resurrection of the dead, of our body and of the body of the Lord, of that holy
body received from Mary, but who at the same time say that the same flesh does
not rise, but other flesh is given in its place by God: are we not to say that this opinion
exceeds all others in its impiety?

1089

[93]
From men like ourselves there is no hope of salvation. For no one of all the men who   370
come from Adam is able to effect our salvation. . . . In His coming, therefore,   310
the Lord took flesh from our flesh, and God the Word became a Man like us, so that in
His divinity He might give us salvation, and that in His humanity he might suffer for
the sake of us men, doing away with suffering by His suffering and by His own   334
death putting death to death. . . . In Him the suffering of the flesh is attributed to the
divinity, which really cannot suffer at all, so that the world will not place its hope in
man, but in the Lordly Man, since divinity itself undertakes to attribute the suffering to
Itself.

1089a

[120]
We believe in one God, the Father almighty, maker of all things, both visible and   157
invisible; and in one Lord Jesus Christ, the Son of God, begotten of God the Father,   158
Only-begotten, that is, of the substance of the Father; God of God, Light of Light,   460
true God of true God; begotten, not made; consubstantial (13) with the Father; through   252
whom all things were made, both those in heaven and those on earth, both visible   257
and invisible; who for us men and for our salvation came down and took flesh, that is,   284
was born perfectly of the holy ever-virgin Mary by the Holy Spirit, was made   370
man, that is, He received perfect man, soul and body and mind and all that man is, except   302
sin, not from the seed of man nor as is usual with men (14), but He reshaped flesh   783
into Himself, into one holy unity; not in the way that He inspired the prophets, and both   346
spoke and acted in them, but He was made Man perfectly; for "the Word was made   344
flesh (15)," not undergoing change, nor converting His own divinity into humanity;—   345
joined together into the one holy perfection and divinity of Himself;—for the Lord   347

Jesus Christ is one and not two, the same God, the same Lord, the same King; and He   391
suffered in the flesh, and rose again and ascended into heaven in the same body,   392
and sits in glory on the right of the Father, about to come in the same body in glory to   1043
judge the living and the dead; whose kingdom will have no end; and we believe in the   20
Holy Spirit, who spoke in the Law and proclaimed in the Prophets and descended at the   267
Jordan, speaking in the Apostles and dwelling in the saints; thus do we believe in   268
Him: that the Spirit is Holy, Spirit of God, Spirit perfect, Spirit Paraclete, increate, and 269
is believed to proceed from the Father and to receive from the Son.   266
    We believe in one Catholic and Apostolic Church, and in one Baptism of repentance,   418
and in the resurrection of the dead and the just judgment of souls and bodies, and   836
in the kingdom of heaven, and in eternal life.   1011
    But those who say that there was a time when the Son or the Holy Spirit was not, or   251
was made out of nothing or of another substance or essence (16), who say the Son   256
of God or the Holy Spirit is liable to change or to becoming different, these people the   257
Catholic and Apostolic Church, your Mother and ours, anathematizes; and again   268
we anathematize those who do not confess the resurrection of the dead, and all heresies
which are not consistent with this, the true faith (17).

1. John 4:24.
2. τὸ πνεῦμα τὸ ἅγιαν μονογενές. Terminology has not yet frozen. We had rather said *only-spirate;* but that is not what
   Epiphanius said. In our accepted terminology there are two processions: generation and spiration. The Son is begotten
   and is the Only-begotten. The Spirit is spirated, which means breathed.
3. Matt. 10:20.
4. John 15:26.
5. John 16:15.
6. The term οἰκονομία has by this time come to mean purely and simply the *Incarnation*. Nor is this just one of
   Epiphanius' linguistic peculiarities. The same usage is found in numerous authors of this period. See note 3 to § 2138
   below. The word *economy* further on in the present passage might also be read as *incarnation*; thus, "He had the whole
   incarnation of humanity, ..."
7. τοῦτό μού 'εστι τάδε. Probably it is because of the arcane discipline that Epiphanius scrupulously avoids mentioning
   bread and body.
8. Rom. 8:3.
9. 1 Cor. 1:30.
10. ἀπὸ Μαρίας τῆς θεοτόκου.
11. John 1:14.
12. τῇ ἰδίᾳ ὑποστάτει.
13. ὁμοούσιον.
14. ὐὐκ ἀπὸ σπέρματος ἀνδρὸς οὐδὲ ἐν ἀνθρώπῳ.
15. John 1:14.
16. ἢ ἐξ ἑτέρας ὑποστάσεως ἢ οὐσίας.
17. This final statement will seem less a tautology if we remember that the etymological significance of *heresy* is *choice*.
    Thus, *we anathematize . . . all choices [of belief] that are not consistent with . . . the true faith*.

PANACEA AGAINST ALL HERESIES [*inter A. D.* 374/377]

    This work has the strange title *Panárion* which is not really a Greek word at all, but
just a Hellenization of the Latin term *panarium*, which means a breadbox. So the *pan-*
of the term does not refer to *all* of anything, but to *bread*. I would suspect that
Epiphanius knew the word used colloquially for a medicine chest; at any rate, that seems
to be how he understands it. And his medicine chest contains remedies and antidotes
against all heresies. I shall call it in English the *Panacea* or *Panacea against All
Heresies*, which is etymologically unsound but, I think, nonetheless a happy thought. At
any rate, the problem is not so large as a breadbox.
    In 375 A. D. Epiphanius was already writing the work. By 376 or 377 he was on
chapter 66. Probably he finished the work in 377 A. D.

The *Panacea* deals with eighty heresies, not all of which really deserve the title. Twenty of these heresies, like Barbarism and Hellenism, are pre-Christian. The notion that there are eighty heresies is probably dependent upon the four score concubines of the Canticle of Canticles 6:7. But Epiphanius had to search deeply to find them all. Among his eighty is a certain Aërius, who is known chiefly and, if I do not err, solely from chapter 75 of the *Panacea*. Msgr. Duchesne, in his *Histoire ancienne*, Vol. 2, pp. 497-498, remarked that when Epiphanius stumbled upon Aërius he dutifully lamented the latter's errors; but secretly, in his heart of hearts, he was delighted to find one more heretic to add to his collection.

A spurious epitome of the work is found in Migne, PG 42, cols. 833-886, and has been published also in an Old Armenian version (J. Dashian, Vienna 1895).

The edition of Migne in PG 41-42 and that of F. Oehler in his *Corpus haereseologicum*, Vols. 2-3, Berlin 1859 and 1861 are superseded by that of K. Holl in the Berlin Corpus: GCS Vol. 25 (1915), pp. 153-464, heresies 1-33; Vol. 31 (1922), heresies 34-64; and Vol. 37 (1933), heresies 65-80.

1090

[8, 5]

The Law of God given to [the Jews] . . . prescribed . . . that they know God   232
only and worship Him. The Name was heralded in monarchy; in the monarchy the
Trinity was announced and was believed in by the best of those men, that is, the prophets
and the saints.

1092

[27, 6]

At Rome the first Apostles and bishops were Peter and Paul; then Linus, then Cletus;   431
then Clement, the contemporary of Peter and Paul, whom Paul remembers in his   432
Epistle to the Romans (1). It should surprise no one that others received the episcopate
from the Apostles before him, who was the contemporary of Peter and Paul; for He was,
at any rate, the contemporary of the Apostles. . . . The succession of the bishops
in Rome is as follows: Peter and Paul, Linus and Cletus, Clement, Evaristus,
Alexander, Sixtus, Telesphorus, Hyginus, Pius, Anicetus, whom I have already
mentioned above in my enumerating of the bishops.

1093

[33, 9]

What Moses wrote he did not write apart from the will of God; rather, the   50
Law was given him by the Holy Spirit. . . . And that the legislation is   51
God's, that is clear. All that God had anywhere ordained by law, whether in
times, in figures, in apocalypses of future good things, was clarified when
our Lord Jesus Christ came and showed its fulfillment in the gospel.

1094

[51, 30]

Two reasons can be advanced to explain why the marriage was celebrated   968
with external festivities in Cana of Galilee, and why the water was truly   972
changed into wine: so that the tide of Bacchanalian frenetics in the world
might be turned to chastity and dignity in marriage, and so that the rest might
be directed aright to the enjoyment both of wine free of toil and of the

favor that presented it; so that in every way it might stop the mouths of those
aroused against the Lord, and so that it might show that He is God with the   82
Father and His Holy Spirit.

1095

[59, 2]
   Just as one who has lost virginity has not the ability of regaining it   928
physically, that being a physical impossibility (2), so too it is with those who
fall into some great transgressions (3) after Baptism (4); and just as one who
falls from virginity can have the secondary honor of continence, so also one
who commits transgressions of the graver kind after his Baptism has a
secondary remedy.

1096

[59, 4]
   In point of fact a call to the holy priesthood of God, since the coming of   964
Christ and because of the exceeding greatness of the honor of the priesthood,
is not approved for those who, after a first marriage, and their wife having
died, enter upon a second marriage. And this the holy Church of God
has kept watch over unfailingly and strictly. But even one who is husband of
one wife, if she is still living and still bearing children, is not approved; but
after one marriage, if a husband keep continent or, if his wife has died,
he remain a widower, he may be approved as both deacon and presbyter and
bishop and subdeacon, especially where the ecclesiastical canons are
precise (5).

1097

[59, 4]
   Because of the weakness of the people and their inability to be content   979
with a first wife, it is possible to tolerate their marrying a second after the
death of the first. But the man who has one wife only is held in greater
approval and honor by all the deliberations of the Church. . . . Nor do we   977
mean that anyone might have two wives, taking a second while the first is
still around, but after being severed (6) from the first he may legitimately, if he
please, marry a second.

1098

[61, 6]
   It is not necessary that all the divine words have an allegorical meaning.   100
Consideration and perception is needed in order to know the meaning of   101
the argument of each. It is needful also to make use of Tradition; for not
everything can be gotten from Sacred Scripture. The holy Apostles handed
down some things in the Scriptures, other things in Tradition.

1099

[62, 4]
   The Spirit is always with the Father and the Son, not a brother to the   273
Father, not begotten, not created, not a brother of the Son, not a descendant of

the Father; but proceeding from the Father and receiving of the Son, not
foreign to the Father and the Son, but of the same substance, of the same
Godhead, of the Father and the Son, He is with the Father and the Son, Holy
Spirit ever subsisting, Spirit divine, Spirit of glory, Spirit of Christ, Spirit of
the Father. "It is the Spirit of the Father who speaks in you (7)"; "My   270
Spirit has stood by in your midst (8)." He is third in appellation, equal in
divinity, not different as compared to Father and Son, connecting Bond of the   279
Trinity, Ratifying Seal of the creed (9).

1100

[64, 35]
   Resurrection is not posited of that which has not fallen, but of that which   1011
has fallen and has risen up again. . . . For it is not that which has not died
but that which has died that is said to be laid to rest. But it is flesh that   502
dies; the soul is immortal.

1101

[65, 5]
   The word of God clearly signifies that the angels were created not after   480
the stars nor before the earth and sky. The statement is plainly   481
incontrovertible that before the earth and sky nothing of created things
existed; that "in the beginning God created the heavens and the earth (10)," as
the beginning of creation, and before this nothing at all had been created.

1102

[69, 26]
   But you will certainly tell me, "He begot either willingly or else   253
unwillingly!" But I am not like you, you contentious fellow, that I should have 254
to probe the why and the wherefore of God! For if not willing He begot,
He begot involuntarily; and if willing He begot, did this will, then, exist   256
before the Son (11)? It may be, if ahead of the Son there was a moment of
time for a decree of the will. With God, however, there is not a time involved
in intention, nor a will in consideration. He begets neither willing nor not   255
willing, but in His nature, which is superior to intention.

1103

[69, 52]
   God the Word, the uncaused Creator who, with the Father and with His   362
Holy Spirit, created man, though He was immortal and undefiled, when   320
it seemed good to Him, became Man by a certain hidden mystery of wisdom;
and because of His exceedingly great love of mankind He took upon Himself perfectly 372
the whole of what He had molded, not out of necessity, but by voluntary   374
purpose, so that in the flesh He might condemn sin, and on the cross   381
discharge the curse, and in the tomb (12) take away corruption from our   390
midst, and that in His divinity, going down into hell with His soul, He might
break the sting of death and dissolve the covenant in regard to hell (13).

1104

[69, 62]

The Divinity decided to fulfill all that pertained to the mystery of the   390
Passion, and to go down with His soul into the depths, to effect there the
salvation of those who had fallen asleep beforehand; I mean to say, the holy
patriarchs.

1105

[70, 5]

Reject also the opinion of those who say the body is in the image of God.   152
For how were it possible for the visible to be close to the invisible? How the   154
corporeal to the incorporeal? How the tangible to the illimitable?

1106

[70, 7]

And it is impossible, especially for a human nature, to see God. It is not   170
allowed the visible to see the invisible. But the invisible God, in His love of   172
mankind and strengthening the powerless with power, will bring about by
His own power a way that it may see the invisible, and that it may see
both the invisible and the infinite, not as the infinite is, but accordingly as our
nature has been enabled to do so, and to the extent of the power in which
the powerless shall have been empowered. And nothing of discrepancy will   25
be found in Sacred Scripture, nor will there be found any statement in
opposition to any other statement.

1107

[73, 34]

[The Antiochians] confess that Father, Son, and Holy Spirit are   102
consubstantial (14), three Persons, one substance, one God (15), because that   231
faith is true which is handed down by those who came first, that faith which
is both prophetic and evangelic and apostolic, that faith which our fathers and
bishops confessed, when they met in the Synod of Nicaea in the presence
of Constantine, the great and blessed king.

1108

[75, 4]

To those who have any intelligence it is clear that to say that bishop and   953
priest (16) are equal is the utter fullness of stupidity. And how should this   960
be possible? This order [of episcopate] is a begetting of fathers; for it
begets fathers to the Church; but the other, not able to beget fathers, begets   828
children for the Church, through the rebirth of Baptism (17), but not fathers
or teachers. And how were it possible for someone to ordain (18) a priest, if he
did not himself have hands laid on him for the laying on of hands (19),   958
or to say that he is equal to the bishop?

1109

[75, 8]

Furthermore, as to mentioning the names of the dead, how is there   1001
anything very useful in that? What is more timely or more excellent than that   996

those who are still here should believe that the departed do live, and
that they have not retreated into nothingness, but that they exist and are alive
with the Master? And so that this most august proclamation might be told
in full, how do they have hope, who are praying for the brethren as if
they were but sojourning in a foreign land? Useful too is the prayer fashioned
on their behalf, even if it does not force back the whole of guilty charges
laid to them. And it is useful also, because in this world we often stumble
either voluntarily or involuntarily, and thus it is a reminder to do better (20).
For we make commemoration of the just and of sinners: of sinners, begging
God's mercy for them; of the just and the Fathers and Patriarchs and
Prophets and Apostles and Evangelists and martyrs and confessors, and of
bishops and solitaries, and of the whole list of them, so that we may set the   121
Lord Jesus Christ apart from the ranks of men because of the honor due Him,
and give reverence to Him, while keeping in mind that the Lord is not to be
equated with any man, even if that man live in a justice that is boundless
and limitless (21).

1110

[77, 29]
   We have not two Christs, not two royal Sons of God, but the same who is   324
God, the same is Man; not as indwelling in man, but He is made whole
Man. . . . "The Word became flesh (22)." For he did not say, "The flesh   310
became Word," so that he can show that the Word first came down from
heaven, made the flesh from the womb of the holy Virgin subsist in Himself,   311
and reshaped the whole humanity perfectly into Himself.

1111

[78, 6]
   Was there ever anyone of any breeding who dared to speak the name of   783
Holy Mary, and being questioned, did not immediately add, "the Virgin?" For
by such added names the positive proofs of merit are apparent (23). . . .
And to Holy Mary, Virgin is invariably added, for that Holy Woman remains
undefiled.

1112

[79, 3]
   It is true that in the Church there is an order of deaconesses (24), but not for   957
being a priestess, nor for any kind of work of administration (25), but for
the sake of the dignity of the female sex, either at the time of Baptism, or of
examining the sick or suffering, so that the naked body of a female may
not be seen by men administering sacred rites, but by the deaconess (26).

1. "Romans" is an error here. Clement is mentioned in Paul's Epistle to the Philippians 4:3; in fact, however, there is no
   good reason for identifying the Clement of Paul's Epistle with St. Clement of Rome, and it is generally assumed that
   their identification is most unlikely.
2. μὴ ἐνδεχομένης τῆς φύσεως. Some may prefer to translate *that being impossible in the very nature of things*.
3. ἐν μεγάλοις τισὶ παραπτώμασι.
4. ἀπὸ τοῦ λουτροῦ. See § 407 above.
5. No doubt this is to be understood as saying "this is the situation where the canons are precisely observed." The whole
   final sentence of the passage is so concise in the Greek as to preclude much arguing about fine points—or perhaps, to
   foster it. It would read in a fairly literal translation: "But also the husband of one wife, she being still living and
   child-bearing, is not approved, but after one, keeping continent or remaining a widower, both deacon and presbyter and

bishop and subdeacon, especially where the ecclesiastical canons precise.'' The rest in my translation is supplied of my own ingenuity.

6. ἀποσχισθείς. It is obvious in the context that this means "severed by her death."
7. Matt. 10:20.
8. Aggeus 2:5.
9. σύνδεσμος τῆς τριάδος ἐπισφραγὶς τῆς ὁμολογίας.
10. Gen. 1:1.
11. Reading ἄρα instead of ἆρα.
12. What Epiphanius actually says is *in the monument* or *in the memorial: ἐν τῶ μνήματι.* This is an interesting example of a word's becoming of such common usage that one no longer thinks of its primary sense. The tomb in which Christ was laid was certainly not intended as a monument to his memory.
13. καὶ διαλύσῃ τὴν πρὸς τὸν ᾅδην διαθήκην.
14. ὁμοούσιον.
15. τρεῖς ὑποστάσεις, μίαν οὐσίαν, μίαν θεότητα.
16. ἐπίσκοπον καὶ πρεσβύτερον. In this passage I am departing from my usual practice of translating πρεσβύτερος as *presbyter*, and rendering it *priest*, since to use the term *presbyter* in the present text might only obscure the meaning.
17. τοῦ λουτροῦ.
18. πρεσβύτερον καθιστᾶν.
19. μὴ ἔχοντα χειροθεσίαν τοῦ χειροτονεῖν. This may also be translated *not ordained for ordaining*.
20. ἵνα τὸ ἐντελέστερον σημανθῇ.
21. κἂν τε μυρία καὶ ἐπέκεινα ἐν δικαιοσύνῃ ὑπάρχῃ ἕκαστος ἀνθρώπων.
22. John 1:14.
23. My translation is quite literal. I suspect that Epiphanius is only making one of those ridiculously obvious abstract pronouncements, this one to the effect that "it is by surnames that identification is made certain, since surnames point out one's special and peculiar merits."
24. διακονισσῶν τάγμα.
25. ἀλλ' οὐχὶ εἰς τὸ ἱερατεύειν οὐδέ τι ἐπιχειρεῖν ἐπιτρέπειν.
26. ἵνα μὴ ὑπὸ ἀνδρῶν ἱερουργούντων θεαθείη ἀλλ' ὑπὸ τῆς διακονούσης.

THEODORE OF MOPSUESTIA [† *A. D.* 428]

Theodore was a fellow student of John Chrysostom under Libanius, the pagan and sophist rhetorician, and afterwards under Diodore of Tarsus, the great Christian teacher at Antioch.

The friendship of Theodore with Chrysostom began already in their school days under Libanius, and lasted throughout their lives. It was Chrysostom who persuaded Theodore, not yet twenty years of age, to enter a monastery at Antioch. And when shortly Theodore left, intending to pursue a career as a lawyer, it was Chrysostom again who, with his two eloquent letters *To the Fallen Theodore*, persuaded him to return.

In 383 A. D. Flavian of Antioch ordained Theodore to the priesthood and in 392 Theodore became Bishop of Mopsuestia in Cilicia. Theodore survived his friend Chrysostom by more than twenty years, dying in 428 A. D.

About ten years after Theodore's death Cyril of Alexandria, who was then much involved in the Nestorian controversy, accused Diodore († 392) and Theodore of having been the more remote but nonetheless guilty progenitors of Nestorianism. With numerous suspicions voiced and condemnations levelled over the years, Theodore was finally condemned in the fifth ecumenical Council of Constantinople of 553 A. D., which Council issued the condemnation of the Three Chapters. The celebrated Three Chapters were in fact the Christological letter of Ibas of Edessa to Maris of Chalcedon, certain writings of Theodoret of Cyr, and the person and writings of Theodore of Mopsuestia.

The writings of Theodore were quite numerous. Sixty are listed by title in a catalogue by the Nestorian Ebedjesu from the early fourteenth century. Another such catalogue, from the first half of the thirteenth century, is found in the *Chronicle of Seert*.

For the most part Theodore's writings are extant only in a multitude of fragments. Their general loss is undoubtedly the unfortunate result of his condemnation in the Three Chapters.

Theodore stands condemned of Nestorianism; and the Nestorians themselves have always appealed to his authority, regarding him even yet as their greatest exegete. It is obvious, of course, that he was never formally a Nestorian. The date of his death precludes that. In the light of modern scholarship it has become highly questionable whether he ought in any sense be regarded as a proponent, even an unwitting one, of Nestorianism. The great triple play which made him a Father of Nestorianism, Diodore to Theodore to Nestor, is failing.

Critical analysis of Theodore's fragmentary remains show him orthodox enough for his period. It is not to be expected that he would use a Chalcedonian terminology. Berthold Altaner (*Patrology*, 1961, p. 371) has noted that critical studies by M. Richard, E. Amann, R. Devreese, and A. Grillmeier have shown that Theodore had done well in the struggle against Apollinarianism; ". . . moreover, Richard and Devreese have proved that the texts which were the cause of his condemnation as the father of Nestorianism in 553 are mostly spurious." Grillmeier in fact has concluded that none contributed more than Theodore to the growth of a sound Christology in the period between the second ecumenical Council of Constantinople in 381 A. D. and the third ecumenical Council of Ephesus in 431 A. D. His teaching is not without certain dangerous tendencies; but it does actually point the way to the fourth ecumenical Council of Chalcedon in 451 A. D. At the fifth ecumenical Council of Constantinople in 553 A. D., he was perhaps more deserving of tribute than condemnation.

The Migne edition of Theodore's writings, MG 66, 9-1020 is still the closest thing to a collected edition, but for the most part it is hopelessly outmoded. H. B. Swete's two volume edition of Theodore, Cambridge 1880 and 1882 (republished in 1969), contains complete commentaries on Paul's Epistles to the Galatians, Ephesians, Philippians, Colossians, First and Second Thessalonians, First and Second Timothy, Titus and Philemon, in a Latin translation dating from the fifth century and formerly attributed to Ambrose, published from the two ninth and tenth century manuscripts discovered by Swete himself. Included also are the pertinent Greek fragments of the same, found in *Cod. Coisl*. 204. Swete's second volume contains in an appendix all the then known fragments of Theodore's directly dogmatic writings. For what it contains, the two volume Swete edition is generally regarded as standard. More recent authors have published very considerable numbers of other fragments, perhaps the largest body of these being in Syriac. Bibliographical sources for much of this material can be gleaned from Quasten, *Patrology*, Vol. 3, pp. 401-423.

THE INCARNATION

The work on *The Incarnation* was perhaps the best known of Theodore's writings; at any rate, it is the most frequently quoted. According to Gennadius in his *De viris illustribus* 12, it was a work of fifteen books and about fifteen thousand lines. It survives, however, only in a substantial number of fragments in Latin, Greek, and Syriac. The fragments must be used with care, since many of them come from sources interested in proving Theodore the father of Nestorianism. The complete text of a Syriac translation was discovered at Seert in 1905 by Addai Scher, and it ought to have been a major tool in deciding to what extent the texts of *The Incarnation* that have come to us from interested sources have been tampered with. What a terrible tragedy, then, that this precious document was completely destroyed during the first world war, before it could be published and before any copy was made of it.

The fragments in Migne, MG 66, still need to be sorted out in a more critical fashion.

The fragments in Swete, Vol. 2, pp. 290-312, are more useful, but still must be read with a very critical eye. It is on these that my translated passages are based. Twenty short fragments from the British Museum's Codex Additional 12156 can be found in P. A. de Lagarde's *Analecta Syriaca*, Leipzig 1858, pp. 100-108. Fragments from Codex Additional 14669 are published in E. Sachau's *Theodori Mopsuesteni fragmenta Syriaca*, Leipzig 1869, pp. 28-57. Sachau's work has Syriac text and Latin translation, and includes on pages 63-68 a Latin translation of the texts published by Lagarde.

1113

[7]

When [God] is said to indwell either in the Apostles or wholly in the just, it is as if He   324
were well-pleased to make His dwelling in the just, as if He were in some way
gratified by those excelling in virtue. We have never been so insane, however, to say
that [in the Incarnation] there was this kind of an indwelling in Christ; there, rather,   326
it is as in the Son. That is how He was pleased to indwell. But why is this indwelling
"as in the Son?" Because when He indwelt He united to Himself all that He had
assumed, and He prepared it to share with Him in all the honor which He, by nature the
indwelling Son, so held in common that it was accounted as in one Person (1); and, in
accord with the union with what He had assumed, He communicated to it all
sovereignty. So too in the assumed [He wanted] to do all things, so that even the
judgment and examination of all would take place through [the assumed] and through its
presence (2), [even while] the difference [of natures] was plainly perceptible in
the characteristics proper to nature.

1113a

[8]

When we distinguish the natures [in Christ] we say that the nature of God the Word   326
is perfect, and the Person (3) is perfect; for one cannot speak of subsistence without
person (4). Perfect too is His human nature, and the Person likewise. When, however,
we look to their being conjoined, we say that there is one Person (5).

1113b

[15]

When, therefore, they ask, "Is Mary Mother of Man or Mother of God (6)?" we   326
answer, "Both (7)!" The one by the very nature of what was done, and the other by   780
relation (8). Mother of Man, because it was a Man who was in the womb of Mary
and who came forth from there; and Mother of God, because God was in the Man who
was born (9), not in Him in a circumscribable way according to nature (10), but existing
in Him by the intention of will (11).

1. Jesus Christ, the incarnate Son.
2. διὰ . . . τῆς αὐτοῦ παρουσίας. Here I doubt the *parousia* refers to the second coming, though in fact what is spoken of will take place at the *parousia*. Still I think it makes more sense here to understand the term in its more common meaning of *presence*.
3. τὸ πρόσωπον.
4. οὐδὲ γὰρ ἀπρόσωπόν ἐστιν ὑπόστασιν εἰπεῖν. For Theodore *person* is *prosopon;* *hypostasis* here is *subsistence* or that by which a nature or substance really exists. Or again, *hypostasis* might in some vague way be thought of as *personality*, or something logically but not really apart from *person*. The statement itself gives a great handle to Nestorianism.
5. ἓν πρόσωπον.
6. ἀνθρωποτόκος ἢ θεοτόκος ἡ Μαρία;
7. Nestorius asks the same question; but his answer, purely and simply, is, "of man!" See § 2057a, below.

8. τὸ δὲ τῇ ἀναφορᾷ.
9. See 2 Cor. 5:19.
10. κατὰ τὴν φύσιν.
11. κατὰ τὴν σχέσιν τῆς γνώμης.

THE BOOK OF PEARLS

The title of this work is found in two catalogues of Theodore's writings, that of Ebedjesu and that of the *Chronicle of Seert*, which catalogues make it clear that *The Book of Pearls* was simply a collection of Theodore's letters. Very few fragments of his letters are extant, perhaps only three. The fragment below is translated from a text in Swete, Vol. 2, p. 339. The same fragment is found in Migne, PG 66, 1013.

FRAGMENT OF A LETTER TO DOMNUS

1113c

Since the manner of the union [of the two natures in Christ] is according to the [divine] good pleasure, and the natures guard against any commingling, one Person is exhibited, indivisibly of both; and one will, and one operation, with one authority and dominion due to them (1).

326
322
330

1. In attempting to guard against a monophysite commingling of natures, Theodore has apparently opened a door to monothelitism.

AGAINST APOLLINARIS

Ebedjesu refers in his catalogue to a work of Theodore entitled *De assumente et assumpto*, which is probably to be identified with the *De Apollinario et eius haeresi* referred to by Facundus of Hermiane. Theodore's refutation of Apollinaris consisted of at least four books, of which seventeen fragments survive from books three and four, mostly in sources attempting to prove his alleged Nestorianism.

The fragments are to be found in H. B. Swete's Vol. 2, pp. 312-322, with Syriac fragments in E. Sachau, *Theodori Mopsuesteni fragmenta Syriaca*, Leipzig 1869, p. 60 and in the *Patrologia orientalis*, Vol. 13, p. 188.

The passage I quote below (§ 1113d) is translated from a Swete text, Vol. 2, p. 314, found also in Migne at PG 66, 997. It was such passages as this which secured Theodore's condemnation as a Nestorian. I cite the passage because it is one often quoted; but I have the gravest doubts of its authenticity. The Nestorianism of the passage is rather patent; and the passage does not accord well with § 1113b, which might be Nestorian in its tenor, but which with a little good will can be accepted as Catholic. More telling, however, is § 1113d's total lack of accord with the *Catechetical Homilies* of Theodore, discovered by A. Mingana, which see below at §§ 1113f-1113p.

1113d

[3]
It is unreasonable to say that God was born of the Virgin. For this is nothing else than saying He was born of the seed of David, brought forth of the substance (1) of the Virgin and shaped in her. We say, therefore, that what was of the seed of

326
779

David and of the substance (2) of the Virgin, what was framed in the maternal womb and formed by the power of the Holy Spirit, was born of the Virgin.

1. ἐκ τῆς οὐοίας.
2. ἐκ τῆς οὐσίας.

COMMENTARY ON MATTHEW

According to Ebedjesu, Theodore wrote a *Commentary on Matthew*, of which, in fact, there are numerous fragments extant. The texts of the Matthew fragments can be found in Migne, PG 66, 703-714, and in J. Reuss, *Matthäus-Kommentare aus der griechischen Kirche*, Vol. 61 in the series *Texte und Untersuchungen*, Berlin 1957, pp. 96-150. Syriac fragments are available in P. de Lagarde, *Analecta Syriaca,* Leipzig 1858, pp. 107-108, and in E. Sachau's *Theodori Mopsuesteni fragmenta Syriaca*, Leipzig 1869, pp. 69-70.

The fragment below is translated from a text in Migne, PG 66, 713. Its authenticity is established through the almost identical statement, of undoubted authenticity, in Theodore's fifth catechetical homily, § 1113f.

1113e

[On Matt. 26:26]
He did not say, "This is the symbol of My Body, and this, of My Blood," but, "This is My Body and My Blood (1)," teaching us not to look upon the nature of   852
what is set before us, but that it is transformed (2) by means of the Eucharistic action   856
(3) into Flesh and Blood.

1. Matt. 26:26, 28.
2. μεταβάλλεσθαι.
3. διὰ τῆς γενομένης εὐχαριστίας.

CATECHETICAL HOMILIES

Until the discovery and publication in 1932 and 1933 by A. Mingana of a complete text in Syriac of Theodore's *Catechetical Homilies*, these sermons were known only from a few isolated fragments. With Mingana's discovery of a seventeenth century manuscript of the Syriac translation made shortly after Theodore's death, it could be seen that there were in fact sixteen catecheses, the first ten (part 1) explaining the articles of faith as presented in the Creed, and the last six (part 2) explaining the Lord's Prayer (no. 11), and dealing with the baptismal liturgy (nos. 12-14) and the Eucharist (nos. 15-16). Thus the division into preliminary catecheses for the catechumens and mystagogic catecheses for the neophytes closely parallels the form of the *Catechetical Lectures* of Cyril of Jerusalem. The manuscript in which Mingana discovered the *Catechetical Homilies* is *Codex Mingana Syriaca* 561 in the library at Selly Oak College in Birmingham.

The baptismal creed commented on in the homilies does not vary significantly from the so-called Nicene-Constantinopolitan Creed, our familiar Mass Creed. In the explanation of the Lord's Prayer, our *daily bread* is ordinary food for daily sustenance and not the *supersubstantial* Eucharistic Bread of Origen and Cyril of Jerusalem (see § 853e with its note 133).

With Mingana's publication of the Syriac text, accompanied by an English

translation, the revival of interest in Theodore and the continuing efforts toward understanding him as an orthodox teacher received their initial impulse. The Mingana editions, text and translation, are in the series *Woodbrooke Studies*, Vols. 5 and 6: *Commentary of Theodore of Mopsuestia on the Nicene Creed*, Cambridge 1932, and *Commentary of Theodore of Mopsuestia on the Lord's Prayer and on the Sacraments of Baptism and the Eucharist*, Cambridge 1933. Translations have appeared also in Latin, German, and French, the French edition by R. Tonneau and R. Devreese, Vol. 145 in the series *Studi e Testi*, Vatican City, 1949, having the special merit of being accompanied by a photomechanical reproduction of the Syriac manuscript.

The translations of the passages below are based on the Mingana edition. Along with the material on the Eucharist, Theodore has some very valuable remarks on the Sacrament of Penance.

1113f

[5]

It is proper, therefore, that when [Christ] gave the Bread He did not say, "This   851
is the symbol of My Body," but, "This is My Body." In the same way when He   852
gave the Cup He did not say, "This is the symbol of My Blood," but, "This is   860
My Blood"; for He wanted us to look upon the [Eucharistic elements] after their
reception of grace and the coming of the Holy Spirit not according to their nature,
but [that we should] receive them as they are, the Body and Blood of our Lord.
We ought . . . not regard the [Eucharistic elements] merely as bread and cup, but as the
Body and Blood of Christ, into which they were transformed by the descent of
the Holy Spirit (1).   863

1113g

[5]

The followers of Arius and Eunomius, however, state that [Christ] assumed a body   312
but not a soul, saying that the nature of the Godhead stood in place of the soul.
Those men lowered the divine nature of the Only-begotten inasmuch as, by the
greatness of that nature, it was the divine nature itself that moved and performed the
actions of the soul, it having imprisoned itself in the body to do everything needful
for the body's sustenance. But see, if the Godhead had stood in place of the soul,
[Christ] would not have been hungry or thirsty, nor would He have become tired or
been in need of food. . . . Our blessed Fathers warned us and said, "He was incarnate
and became a man," so that we might believe that the one who was assumed and in
whom God the Word dwelt was a perfect man, complete in all that pertains to the
nature of man, and composed of a mortal body and a rational soul, because it was for
man and his salvation that [God the Word] came down from heaven.

1113h

[6]

[In receiving the Eucharist] each of us takes a small portion, but we believe that in   859
that small portion we receive all of Him.

1113j

[6]

In the profession of faith which our blessed Fathers wrote [at Nicaea] . . . they   324
followed the divine Scriptures, which speak of the natures as different, while they   326

referred them to one Person (2) because of the close union that was effected between them, so that it might not be supposed that they were separating that perfect union between the one who was assumed and the one who was assuming. If this union were destroyed, the one who was assumed would not be seen as more than a mere man like ourselves.

1113k

[8]

He is neither God alone nor man alone; rather, He is truly both by nature, that is to say, God and Man: God the Word, the one assuming, and Man, the one assumed. . . . The one assuming is the divine nature, which does everything for us; and the other [the one assumed], is the human nature, which was assumed on behalf of all of us, and is united to [the divine nature] in an indescribable union which will never be severed. . . . From the fact that we say two natures we are not constrained to say two Lords nor two Sons; that would be utter foolishness. With all things that in a certain respect are two and in another respect one, the union by which they are one does not obviate the distinction between their natures, nor does the distinction between their natures prevent their being one.

322
326

329
324

321
323

1113m

[16]

[If we have sinned], the Body and Blood of our Lord . . . will strengthen us, . . . if we committed [those sins] involuntarily, and they came to us against our will from the weakness of our nature, and we fell into them against our desire, and on their account have been filled with remorse and have prayed to God in great repentance for our lapses. . . . If with diligence we do good works and turn from evil deeds and truly repent of the sins that befall us, undoubtedly we shall obtain the grace of the remission of our sins in our receiving of the holy Sacrament (3).

929
930

1113n

[16]

At first [the offering] is laid upon the altar as mere bread, and wine mixed with water; but by the coming of the Holy Spirit it is transformed into the Body and the Blood, and thus it is changed into the power of a spiritual and immortal nourishment.

860
861
856
877

1113p

[16]

If we commit a great sin against the commandments . . . we must first induce our conscience with all our power to make haste and repent our sins as is proper, and not permit ourselves any other medicine. . . . This is the medicine for sins, established by God and delivered to the priests of the Church, who make diligent use of it in healing the afflictions of men. You are aware of these things, as also of the fact that God, because He greatly cares for us, gave us penitence and showed us the medicine of repentance; and He established some men, those who are priests, as physicians of sins. If in this world we receive through them healing and forgiveness of sins, we shall be delivered from the judgment that is to come. It behooves us, therefore, to draw near to the priests in great confidence and to reveal to them our sins; and those priests, with all diligence, solicitude, and love, and in accord with the regulations

900

920

mentioned above, will grant healing to sinners. [The priests] will not disclose the   921
things that ought not be disclosed; rather, they will be silent about the things that
have happened, as befits true and loving fathers who are bound to guard the shame of
their children while striving to heal their bodies.

1. This last clause reflects the view that the epiclesis is consecratory. Several passages in other places of the *Catechetical Homilies*, notably in *Homily* 16, reflect or make explicit this same view.
2. ܦܪܨܘܡܐ in the Syriac is simply a transliteration of the Greek term *prósōpon*.
3. From this same homily, passage § 1113p treats of the Sacrament of Penance, and confession of "great" sins. It seems apparent, therefore, that what Theodore terms "involuntary sin" is what we call *venial sin*.

ST. JOHN CHRYSOSTOM [*inter A. D.* 344/354–*A. D.* 407]

Some will say that John Chrysostom is unparalleled anywhere, while others will say that he is matched only by Augustine. To compare levels of greatness is a foolish task which can end only in slighting some; so of John let us believe only that he was utterly unique, and there is none other like him.

Though Chrysostom had more early biographers and panegyrists than any other of the Fathers, we still do not know when he was born, except within the ten year period of 344-354 A. D.

His native place was Antioch. His earliest education came from his mother Anthusa, who was widowed at the age of twenty. John studied philosophy under Andragathius and rhetoric under the celebrated Libanius, in whose school he met and formed a lifelong friendship with Theodore of Mopsuestia. Sozomen (*H. E.* 8, 2) knows the legend, generally regarded as historical, that Libanius, on his deathbed, was asked who his successor should be; to which he replied, "John, if only the Christians had not stolen him!"

When John was about eighteen years of age he met Meletius, the Bishop of Antioch, who apparently saw in the boy something of a promise of his grand future. He baptized John, who became Meletius' rather constant companion; and three years after his Baptism, during which time also he had been studying theology under Diodore of Tarsus, John was ordained lector.

In spite of his mother's begging him to remain at home with her, for except for him she was alone in the world, John sought solitude and the ascetical life outside Antioch. There he spent four years living with a hermit, after which he found his own cave, where he remained another two years. During this latter period he never lay down to sleep, night or day. As a consequence his gastro-intestinal system refused anymore to function properly, and the cold and dampness caused malfunctioning of his kidneys. Unable to care for his physical ailments in solitude, he returned again to society.

In 381 A. D. he was ordained a deacon by Meletius, and in 386 A. D. a priest by Flavian, the successor of Meletius. Under Flavian John was assigned for twelve years, 386 to 397, as preacher in the main church of Antioch. It is to his preaching, of course, that his principal fame attaches, and by reason of his eloquence that he is called Chrysostom, which means "gold mouth."

In 397 A. D. Nectarius died, he that had succeeded Gregory of Nazianz as Bishop of Constantinople; and the Emperor Arcadius had John brought to the capital where, on Feb. 26, 398 A. D., John was the somewhat unwilling recipient of episcopal consecration at the hands of the at least equally unwilling Theophilus of Alexandria.

As Metropolitan of Constantinople John immediately set about a much needed reform of clergy and laity. The happy period of his life was over. Reformers, whatever the power of their eloquence or authority of their hand, are never much loved. And if John's preaching now often showed but little tact and consideration, it was because for a man of such nobility and integrity as were Chrysostom's, tact and tempering of words could only have been a betrayal of duty in the face of the incredible worldliness that surrounded the court and the capital.

In 401 A. D. at a synod in Ephesus he deposed six bishops as guilty of simony, with the result that all forces opposed to him, at home and abroad, consolidated in a united effort to destroy him. The power of the court was vested more in the Empress Eudoxia than in the somewhat feeble-minded Arcadius; and John had already earned her enmity by his preaching against the luxury and depravity of the court.

Theophilus of Alexandria had resented John ever since Arcadius had forced John's consecration as Bishop of Constantinople. Theophilus' dislike of John turned to an active hatred when he had to come personally to Constantinople in 402 A. D. to answer charges brought against him by the desert monks of Nitria, before a synod presided over by John. Theophilus had expelled from Egypt considerable numbers of the desert monks on grounds of their being Origenists in their theology; and some fifty of them, including the four so-called "Tall Brothers," had taken refuge with Chrysostom. I have always wondered whether these Tall Brothers might perhaps have been blacks, like the famous Abba Moses; and if tall and black, whether they had perhaps come up to Nitria from the south, members of the Watussi tribe. But however that may be, it was on the complaints of the Tall Brothers and the other banished monks who had come to Constantinople, that Chrysostom called Theophilus to trial.

Theophilus in turn called together thirty-six bishops, all enemies of Chrysostom and mostly Egyptians, to a synod in the outskirts of Chalcedon, the celebrated Synod of The Oak. At The Oak John was condemned on twenty-nine charges; and when he refused three times to appear in his defense, he was declared deposed.

Arcadius then exiled John to Bithynia, but he grew so frightened of the threatened rioting of the people and of an earthquake that very night which was taken as an omen, that he recalled John the next day. John came back into Constantinople in triumph, a fleet going out to meet his ship. He delivered a jubilant address in the Church of the Apostles. The next day he spoke again, now in eloquent praise of the Empress.

The uneasy peace lasted only two months. When a silver statue of the Empress was erected near his Cathedral, John complained of the noise and of the indecent amusements and dancing. The Empress was encouraged by John's enemies to take his complaints rather personally, and her hostility to John was renewed.

On the Feast of St. John the Baptist, John preached his famous sermon which, according to Socrates (*H. E.* 6, 18) and Sozomen (*H. E.* 8, 20), began with the words, "Again Herodias raves, again she rages, again she dances, again she demands the head of John on a platter." No matter that a sermon beginning with those words is judged spurious by the best authorities (Savile, Montfaucon, and Tillemont). No matter that John knew his Scripture better than that. It is probable enough that he said something very like it. His enemies declared that he meant Eudoxia; and I suppose he did. He was charged with resuming his pastoral duties after canonical deposition. The Emperor ordered him to retire and he refused. The Emperor then forbade him the use of any church. On the Easter Vigil of 404 A. D. John and his followers assembled in the baths of Constans to confer solemn Baptism. Armed intervention drove the faithful from the place, but not before the baptismal waters were mixed with blood.

On June 9, 404 A. D., Chrysostom was ordered into exile to Cucusus in Lesser Armenia, where he remained three years. When his enemies saw his success in that place, and that his followers still visited him, they secured from Arcadius an order for his further banishment to a more distant place, Pityus, on the eastern shore of the Black Sea. Forced to travel on foot in severe weather, Chrysostom never reached his destination. He died en route at Comana in the Pontus, on September 14, 407 A. D.

No one else among the Greek Fathers has so large a body of extant writings as has

Chrysostom. His works, moreover, survived almost in their entirety. He wrote a few practical and moral treatises, and a considerable number of letters; but by far the largest body of his writings is in sermon form.

There are three great collected editions of Chrysostom's works. The oldest is that of the Jesuit Fronton du Duc or Fronto Ducaeus, in twelve folio volumes of Greek and Latin, Paris 1609–1633. Sir Henry Savile, a provost of Eton, published his Greek edition in eight folio volumes at Eton in 1612. It is said that Sir Henry expended £ 8,000 of his own funds in preparing his edition, and that Lady Savile was so jealous of her husband's devotion to Chrysostom that she threatened to burn Sir Henry's manuscripts. Let that be a warning to scholars everywhere.

The third of the great editions is that of the Maurist, Dom Bernard de Montfaucon, in thirteen folio volumes, Greek and Latin, Paris 1718–1738. Montfaucon labored on this edition for twenty years. He died three years after its completion († Dec. 21, 1741), at the age of eighty-six. The Montfaucon edition is perhaps not quite so judicious a text as Savile's, but the content is more complete. It has been reprinted in thirteen folio volumes at Venice, 1734–1741; in 1755; and again in 1780, this last in fourteen volumes; at Paris, the Gaume edition with some additions by F. de Sinner, in thirteen octavo volumes, 1834–1839. It is this last, with the addition of a *Supplementum* of dubious authenticity, and with the substitution of Frederick Field's texts (1839) for the homilies on Matthew, that is reprinted by Migne in his PG 47–64.

Some will still prefer Savile as the best edition. Others regard the Montfaucon as superior, especially in Migne's edition with its substitution of Field's texts of the homilies on Matthew. Without entering into the unproductive arguments about whether or not Migne's Montfaucon-Field is superior or inferior to Savile, I will employ Migne as the basis of my translations, except where noted to the contrary; for whatever the relative merits of the two texts, it must be acknowledged that it is Migne that is almost always used and the much more readily available to those who may wish to compare my English with the Greek. I do, however, have a Savile available, and will keep one eye on that text also while translating from Migne.

All will agree that a new collected critical edition of Chrysostom is much to be desired. Neither Montfaucon nor Savile, and much less Fronto, showed any specially enlightened judgment in their comparison of manuscripts and choice of readings. A new critical edition, if one can speak of it in a purely ideal way and with no thought of the monstrous financial problems which it must entail, ought to take into account mountains of nearly untouched manuscripts, manuscripts unconsulted by the earlier editors, along with early translations in Syriac, Armenian, Coptic, Arabic, Ethiopic, Georgian, Old Russian, and Old Slavonic. Furthermore, there are still upwards of five hundred unauthentic sermons that have never been edited at all. And who can say whether or not a few gems may yet lie hidden even in the supposed dross?

TO THE FALLEN THEODORE [*inter A. D.* 371/378]

The *To the Fallen Theodore* consists of two admonitory writings. Though usually termed letters, the first has the form of a treatise, and only the second that of a letter. But whatever the original literary genre, the two works are invariably treated as two books of a single writing, and that too is how I shall treat them.

John's fellow-student Theodore, later Bishop of Mopsuestia, had entered upon a monastic life, only to abandon it after a short time, intending instead to become a lawyer and to marry. No doubt it was John who had persuaded Theodore to become a monk in the first place; and the present work or works constitutes John's successful plea "to the

fallen Theodore'' to return to his monastic refuge. In becoming a monk, Theodore
became a bride of Christ. Should he abandon his purpose now and marry he is guilty of
adultery. Marriage is a legitimate estate, but it is no longer an option available to one
who is already married; and the condition of one who has once promised virginity is
much the same as that of one who has married: he can marry no more. Theodore must
abide by his choice of Christ and flee away from his comely Hermione.

Dom de Montfaucon dated these writings in 369 A. D. G. Rauschen has gained more
acceptance in attributing them to Chrysostom's own monastic or eremitic period,
between 371 and 378 A. D.

The text in Migne, PG 47, 277-316, is now superseded by that of Jean Dumortier in
Volume 117 of the series *Sources Chrétiennes*, Paris 1966.

1114

[1, 11]

Hear what the Blessed Peter says: "It is good for us to be here (1)!" but if he, when   172
he beheld some indistinct image of future things, immediately put everything else out
of his soul because of the pleasure produced in his soul by that vision, what will
anyone be able to say when the very truth of those things is presented, when the
royal halls are thrown open and it is possible to gaze upon the King Himself, no longer
in a shadowy way nor in a mirror, but face to face (2); no longer by faith, but by
actual sight?

1115

[2, 3]

I do agree with you that marriage is legitimate. For it is written, "Marriage is   983
honorable, and the marriage-bed is undefiled; but fornicators and adulterers God
will judge (3)." But it is no longer possible for you to preserve the legitimate conditions
of marriage. For if a person who has been joined to the heavenly Bridegroom afterwards   982
deserts Him and joins himself to a woman, the act is adultery even if you call it marriage
a myriad times over; or rather, it is as much worse than adultery as God is better
than man. Do not be deceived by anyone's saying, "God has not forbidden marriage."
I know that as well as you. He has not forbidden marriage; but He has forbidden
adultery, which is what you are contemplating.

1. Matt. 17:14.
2. 1 Cor. 13:12.
3. Heb. 13:4.

VIRGINITY [*ante ca. A. D.* 392]

Chrysostom's treatise on *Virginity* was written at Antioch and is earlier than his
homilies on First Corinthians, preached at Antioch, in which the treatise is mentioned; but
it is not otherwise datable. It is a work of some length, and in its greater part (chapters
24-84) it is a rather ample explanation of 1 Cor. 7. Chrysostom defends, in his generally
rather passionate manner, St. Paul's proposition that while marriage is good, virginity
is better.

The text in Migne, PG 48, 533-596, is superseded by that of H. Musurillo and
B. Grillet in Volume 125 of the series *Sources Chrétiennes*, Paris 1966.

1116

[10]

That virginity is good I do agree. But that it is even better than marriage, this I do   983
confess. And if you wish, I will add that it is as much better than marriage as heaven   984
is better than earth, as much better as the angels are better than men. And if there were
any other way in which I could say it even more emphatically, I would do so.

HOMILIES ON THE DEVIL

The three *Homilies on the Devil* belong to Chrysostom's Antiochian period but are not
otherwise datable. It is clear from the opening words of number three that it was preached
two days after number two; but where number one belongs in the series we do not
know.

John insists that we cannot simply blame our failings on the devil. We have free
will and choice and must resist temptation. If the establishing of this point seems,
in some of its expressions, to bring him dangerously near to Pelagianism, that is only
a hazard of the subject matter; for he is certainly in no way minded to Pelagianism, and
he is quite forcible in his insistence that man has of himself no sufficiency to avoid sin,
and for this he stands ever in need of divine grace. Chrysostom is equally certain,
however, that our nature is not of itself evil; rather, sin is the result of defective moral
purpose.

The text of the three homilies in this series is in Migne, PG 49, 241-276.

1117

[2, 3]

Creation is not evil. It is both good and a pattern of God's wisdom and power and   131
love of mankind. . . . Hear what Paul says: "Ever since the creation of the world
the invisible properties of God are seen, perceived in the things He has made (1)."
For each of these (2), by which He speaks, declares that it leads us to the knowledge
of God, that it makes us know the Master better.

1. Rom. 1:20.
2. *I. e.*, His creatures, or elements of His creation.

THE PRIESTHOOD [*paulo post A. D.* 386]

Chrysostom's treatise on *The Priesthood*, undoubtedly the most celebrated of his
works, has been assigned to various dates; but I think by no reasoning so cogent as that
of J. Arbuthnot Nairn, who shows that it belongs to the period 386-390 A. D., and most
probably to the year 387.

The treatise is a dialogue between Chrysostom and his friend Basil. John had
conspired in a deceit, tricking Basil into consenting to be consecrated a bishop. When
Basil, who had been led to believe that John had already allowed himself to be
consecrated, discovered that in fact John had fled into hiding but had helped to deceive
him, he came to John in tears to reproach him. The dialogue, in six books, is John's
defense of his conduct, and a treatise on the exalted dignity of the priestly and episcopal
office.

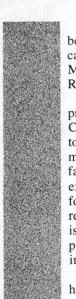

Over the years and from quite early times a considerable amount of paper and ink has been expended on the problem of the identity of Chrysostom's friend Basil. The usual candidates for this identity are Basil of Seleucia, Basil the Great, Basil of Raphanea, and Maximus of Mopsuestia, with the only apparent likelihood belonging to Basil of Raphanea.

When I published my translation of the treatise in 1955, I recall that I stated a preference for Basil of Raphanea, which had been the preference too of Fronto Ducaeus, Cardinal Baronius, Tillemont, Montfaucon, Bardenhewer, and Nairn. I suppose I was too awed by such names to dare differ with them. Whatever the case, I have changed my mind. I am inclined now to believe that the whole incident is a pleasant fiction, fabricated to provide a literary occasion for the dialogue. Basil, then, does not really exist at all. Yet, in another sense, he does. There is far too much passion in the telling for it to be an empty fabrication. It is a tender dialogue, and the model of Basil must be real. Basil is the memory of someone whom John has loved very much. I suspect that he is Theodore of Mopsuestia; and if John's deception or "clever management" as he prefers to call it has not conspired in Theodore's consecration, it is at least John's importuning that has returned the fallen Theodore to his monastery.

The Migne edition, PG 47, 623-692 is no longer used for the text of *The Priesthood*, having been succeeded by J. Arbuthnot Nairn's edition in the series *Cambridge Patristic Texts*, Cambridge 1906. I have before me Nairn's own copy, with two of his holograph letters laid in. Nor has the critical edition of S. Colombo in the series *Corona patrum Salesiana*, Turin 1934, dislodged Nairn from its position as standard text.

The passages quoted below are translated from Nairn's text, and are in the English of my *The Priesthood: A Translation of the Peri Hierosynes of St. John Chrysostom*, The Macmillan Co., New York 1955.

1118

[3, 4, 177]

When you see the Lord immolated and lying upon the altar, and the priest (1) bent   890
over that sacrifice praying, and all the people empurpled by that precious blood, can   895
you think that you are still among men and on earth? Or are you not lifted up to heaven?

1119

[3, 5, 182]

They who inhabit the earth, they who make their abode among men, are entrusted   900
with the dispensation of the things of heaven! Priests have received a power which God   925
has given neither to angels nor to archangels. It was said to them: "Whatsoever   965
you shall bind upon earth shall be bound in heaven; and whatsoever you shall loose, shall
be loosed (2)." [183] Temporal rulers have indeed the power of binding; but they
can bind only the body. Priests, however, can bind with a bond which pertains to the soul
itself, and transcends the very heavens. Whatever priests do here on earth, God
will confirm in heaven, just as the master ratifies the decisions of his servants. [184]
Did He not give them all the powers of heaven? "Whose sins you shall forgive,"
He says, "they are forgiven them: whose sins you shall retain, they are retained (3)."
What greater power is there than this? The Father has given all the judgment to the
Son (4). And now I see the Son placing all this power in the hands of men. They are
raised to this dignity as if they were already gathered up to heaven, elevated
above human nature, and freed of its limitations.

1120

[3, 6, 190]

The priests of Judaism had power to cleanse the body from leprosy—or rather, not to   925

cleanse it at all, but to declare a person as having been cleansed (5). And you know 965
how much contention there was even in those times to obtain the priestly office. Our
priests have received the power not of treating with the leprosy of the body, but with
spiritual uncleanness; not of declaring cleansed, but of actually cleansing (6). . . .
[193] What mean-souled wretch is there who would despise so great a good? None,
I dare say, unless he be urged on by a devilish impulse. [194] . . . God has
given to priests powers greater than those given to our parents; and the differences
between the powers of these two is as great as the difference between the future life and
the present. [195] Our parents begot us to temporal existence; priests beget us to
the eternal. The former are not able to ward off from their children the sting of death, nor
prevent the attack of disease; yet the latter often save the sick and perishing soul—
sometimes by imposing a lighter penance, sometimes by preventing the fall. Priests
accomplish this not only by teaching and admonishing, but also by the help of
prayer. [196] Not only at the time of our regeneration [in baptism], but even afterward, 828
they have the authority to forgive sins. "Is there anyone among you sick? Let him call in 940
the priests of the church, and let them pray over him, anointing him with oil in the
name of the Lord. And the prayer of faith shall save the sick man, and the Lord shall raise
him up, and if he have committed sins, he shall be forgiven (7).

1. τὸν ἀρχιερέα.
2. Matt. 18:18.
3. John 20:23.
4. John 5:22.
5. Lev. 14:2-3.
6. This is a clear statement from Chrysostom of the priestly power of forgiving sins, and is directly opposed to the erroneous opinion known to theologians as the *vis clavium declaratoria* attributed to certain followers of Abelard. Abelard himself held a view known as *vis clavium proprie nulla*, signifying that no power of the keys had been passed on by the Apostles. His view was condemned by the Council of Sens in 1140 or 1141. Abelard's followers modified his doctrine somewhat, holding that the power of the keys consisted merely in giving a declaratory sentence; *i.e.*, the priest-confessor did not himself forgive sins, but merely declared to the penitent that God himself had already forgiven the penitent's sins, in view of the penitent's contrition. Among those who held this latter view was St. Raymond of Peñafort. See Ludwig Lercher, *Institutiones theologiae dogmaticae*, Vol. 4/2/2, Innsbruck 1950, p. 53. This latter view likewise was preached as recently as 1500 or 1501 in Strassburg, by Geiler von Kaysersberg in his celebrated *Ship of Salvation* sermons, inspired by Sebastian Brant's *Ship of Fools*, first published in 1494. See Philip de Lorenzi's *Geilers von Kaisersberg ausgewählte Schriften* (4 volumes, Trier, 1881–1883), Vol. 4, p. iii. In a footnote in de Lorenzi, Vol. 4, p. 127, Geiler is quoted: *Unde sacerdos absolvendo confitentem pronunciat eum absolutum, non remittit peccatum*. In Vol. 1, p. vi, de Lorenzi notes that Geiler's opinion smacks of heresy; and he cites that opinion as being *dass der Priester nie einen Sünder lospreche, der nicht zuvor von Gott losgesprochen sei, und dass somit der Priester bei der Absolution die Sünde nicht eigentlich nachlasse, sondern nur die Nachlassung derselben durch Gott ausspreche*. Geiler von Kaysersberg held with the followers of Abelard that the priest did not forgive sins; rather, he declares to penitents that, by virtue of their perfect contrition, God has already forgiven their sins. Thus he gives a declaratory sentence, having no more real power over sins than the Jewish priests had over leprosy. On the contrary, Chrysostom held, and the Church has always declared, that the priest himself, by the power invested in him, forgives sins. The Church also holds, of course, that by perfect contrition sins are immediately forgiven; and in this instance she requires the confession of grave sin as a legal form and as a deterrent. In the instance, then, in which a penitent has actually achieved *contritio* or perfect contrition, his sins are already forgiven, and no doubt it is effectively a declaratory judgment that the priest is giving, when he pronounces absolution. I suppose the Abelardians did not admit a possibility of forgiveness without *contritio*, which is sorrow for sin because it is an offense against the Divine Majesty of God. The Church, however, is more merciful than they. She allows that, coupled with sacramental confession and absolution, *contritio* is not necessary, but *attritio* (which is called imperfect contrition) is sufficient, *attritio* being sorrow for sin for baser reasons than its being an offense against God's majesty, the classical reason in *attritio* being fear of punishment.
7. James 5:14-15.

HOMILIES AGAINST THE ANOMOIANS AND ON THE INCOMPREHENSIBLE NATURE OF GOD [*A. D.* 386-387]

Montfaucon and Migne have a series of twelve homilies under the title *Homiliae duodecim contra anomoeos de incomprehensibili*. Migne's text of the twelve is in PG

48, 701-812. Actually at least two separate series of homilies seem to be represented in this collection: five in the first series and seven beyond.

Under the present heading I shall draw selections only from the series of five homilies. For selections from the latter seven see below, §§ 1133-1134, under the heading *Homilies against the Anomoians and on the Consubstantiality of the Father and the Son*.

The Migne text for the present grouping of five homilies is in PG 48, 701-748. The more acceptable text for scholarly purposes, however, is that of A. M. Malingrey, *Jean Chrysostome. Sur l'incompréhensibilité de Dieu*, now in its second edition in the series *Sources Chrétiennes*, Vol. 28-bis, Paris 1970.

1121

[1, 3]

After having said, "When I was a child (1)," [Paul] continues, "We see now by means   174
of a mirror in an obscure manner (2)." Here we have a second example of our present   551
weakness, and of our imperfect knowledge. A third example is found again with the
words "in an obscure manner." For the child sees much, and he hears and he speaks;
but he neither sees nor hears nor speaks anything very distinctly; and though he thinks,
his thoughts are not much organized. So too I know many things, but the manner of
these things I do not know. I know that God is everywhere and I know that He is
everywhere in His totality (3); but how He achieves this, I do not know. That God is
without beginning and unbegotten and eternal, I know; but how, I do not know. For
reasoning is unable to grasp how some essence (4) can exist without having existence
either from itself or from another. I know that the Son has been begotten, but the how
of it I do not know. I know that the Spirit is from Him, but the how of His being from
Him I do not know.

1122

[1, 5]

[Paul] knows [God] in part (5). But he says "in part," not because he knows   174
something of God's essence (6) while something else of His essence he does not know;   175
for God is simple. Rather, he says "in part" because he knows that God exists; but   151
what God is in His essence (7) he does not know.

1123

[1, 6]

But if you prefer, let us put Paul and the Prophets aside and go up to heaven, to see   170
if perhaps there are any there who know what the essence (8) of God is. Most certainly
if some are found there who know, they have nothing in common with us; for great is
the difference between angels and men. Nevertheless, so that you may have an
abundant understanding of the fact that not even in heaven is there any creature who is   174
able to know God's essence, let us hear about the angels. What about them? Do they
discuss this essence (9) there, and inquire about it among themselves? Certainly not!

1124

[2, 3]

A man has dared to say, "I know God even as God knows Himself!" Does this require   173
any refutation? Does it deserve any argumentation? Or does not the very utterance
alone of those words display their whole impiety? Indeed, the insanity of this is clear,

this madness is inexcusable, this newest kind of impiety! No one—not never no how—
has at any time dared either to harbor such an idea in mind or to let it have access to
his tongue (10).

1125

[3, 1]

We therefore call God Himself the indescribable, the unfathomable, the invisible,   173
the incomprehensible, the one who surpasses the power of the human tongue, who   170
exceeds the comprehension of the mortal mind, who is inscrutable even to the angels,   488
who is unseen by the Seraphim, who is unfathomable to the Cherubim, who is invisible
to Principalities, Powers, and Virtues, and to every creature without exception, known
by the Son alone and the Holy Spirit.

1126

[3, 3]

"And the Seraphim stood around [the throne of God], six wings to this one and six   170
wings to that one, with two [wings] covering their faces and two their feet (11)."
For what reason, pray tell, did they extend their wings and cover their faces? For what
reason could it be, except that they could not bear the lightning and the flashes of
radiance leaping from the throne? Anyone who is not himself light unalloyed does not
see the pure essence itself (12); but the things he sees are condescensions (13). And
what is a condescension? Whenever God appears not as He is, but shows Himself in
such a way as to enable Himself to be seen, measuring Himself to the weak vision
of those seeing Him, that display of Himself is a condescension.

1127

[4, 2]

And I, therefore, as if I had opened the book of your memory and had pointed my   173
finger to the proofs of those things already examined by reason, will amble on to what 170
remains. And what is there that is left? To show that neither Principalities, nor Powers, 488
nor Dominions, nor any other creature is able to comprehend God perfectly.

1128

[4, 3]

Why does John say, "No one has ever seen God (14)?" So that you might learn   173
that He is speaking about the perfect comprehension of God and about the precise   170
knowledge of Him. For that all those incidents were condescensions and that none of
those persons saw the pure essence (15) of God is clear enough from the differences of
what each did see. For God is simple and non-composite and without shape; but they   151
all saw different shapes. . . . When, therefore, you hear that "no one has ever seen   152
God," consider it the same as hearing that no one can know God in an utterly perfect
manner, as to His essence (16). . . . When, therefore, the Prophet says that although
God was condescending, [the Seraphim and Cherubim] could not bear to look at
Him, it means nothing else but that they were not able to have a clear knowledge and
an accurate comprehension of Him, nor did they dare to gaze intently upon His pure
and perfect essence (17), nor even upon this condescension. For to gaze intently
is to know.

1129

[5, 3]

When [Paul] specifies the One God as the Father (18) he does not exclude the Son   232
from the Godhead; and when he specifies the One Lord as the Son he does not exclude
the Father from Lordship. Rather, Paul does this to correct the weakness of the
[Corinthians], and because he wanted to provide them with no occasion [for doubting].
This too is why the Son of God is not made known to the Jews through the Prophets
in a clear and manifest way, but only rarely and in an obscure manner. For when they
were being released from the error of polytheism, if they had heard of God [the
Father] and God [the Son] they would have relapsed into that same illness. That is
why the Prophets say repeatedly, "There is one God, and besides Him there is no other
(19)." It is not that they deny the Son,—perish the thought!—but they wanted to cure
the infirmity of those men and persuade them to rid themselves of a multiplicity of
gods who did not really exist.

1130

[5, 5]

That we are required only to know that God exists, and not to meddle needlessly   130
into His essence (20), hear what Paul has to say: "He that is coming to God must believe   174
that God exists (21)." And again the Prophet, accusing someone of impiety, does not
accuse him of not knowing *what* God is but of not knowing *that* God is. "For," he
states, "the fool says in his heart, 'There is no God (22)!'"

1131

[5, 7]

I implore and I beseech and I exhort you to confess to God frequently (23). I do not   917
lead you into a theater of your fellow-servants, nor do I compel you to reveal your sins
before men. Open your conscience in the presence of God, and show Him your wounds,
and seek medications from Him. Show them not to one who will reproach you but to one
who will heal you; for even if you remain silent, He knows all (24).

1. 1 Cor. 13:11.
2. 1 Cor. 13:12. The phrase *in an obscure manner* is ἐν αἰνίγματι.
3. ὅτι ὅλως ἔστι πανταχοῦ.
4. οὐσίαν.
5. 1 Cor. 13:9.
6. τῆς οὐσίας.
7. τὴν οὐσίαν.
8. τὴν οὐσίαν.
9. τῆς οὐσίας ταύτης.
10. My translation is perhaps a little loose: but the Greek is highly idiomatic; and Chrysostom, anxious to deny thoroughly
     any such possibility, allows himself five negatives in his sentence: οὐδεὶς τοιοῦτον οὐδὲν οὐδέποτε οὔτε εἰς νοῦν
     βαλέσθαι, οὔτε διὰ τῆς γλώττης προενεγκεῖν ἐτόλμησεν.
11. Is. 6:2. With their other two wings they flew.
12. αὐτὴν ἀκραιφνῆ τὴν οὐσίαν.
13. The term I render *condescension* is ἡ συγκατάβασις. It can also be translated *accommodation*. In ecclesiastical usage
     from the time of Eusebius it refers to God's dealings with men; and the term is found in Gregory of Nazianz in the
     particular context of reference to the Incarnation. I do not know an ecclesiastical usage earlier than Eusebius, *H. E.* 7,
     24.
14. John 1:18.
15. ἀκραιφνῆ τὴν οὐσίαν.
16. οὐσιωδῶς.
17. πρὸς τὴν ἀκραιφνῆ καὶ ἀκέραιον οὐσίαν.
18. 1 Cor. 8:6.
19. Deut. 4:35.
20. τὴν οὐσίαν.

21. Heb. 11:6.
22. Ps. 13[14]:1.
23. ἐξομολογεῖσθαι τῷ θεῷ συνεχῶς.
24. Most modern authors are much more certain than I am that Chrysostom knew nothing of confession before a priest. That he is never very explicit or unambiguously explicit is surely true enough. The celebrated passage in *The Priesthood* on the power of the keys (§ 1120) is said to relate only to Baptism and the anointing of the ill. Yet, there are others who do not so interpret it. P. Martain and P. Galtier in the early years of the present century appealed to Chrysostom as a witness to private confession to a priest. I find it difficult to believe that such passages as § 1119 and § 1120 do not have sacramental confession as their presupposition, even if such is not explicitly mentioned therein. Furthermore the present passage § 1131 is supposedly one in which he very clearly specifies a confession to God alone and not to the priest. But again, is that entirely clear? Is it not equally possible that when he says "I do not lead you into a theater of your fellow-servants, nor do I compel you to reveal your sins before men," he may mean that he does not require a *public* confession? Is it not possible that the line should be interpreted, "[When I hear your confessions] I do not lead you into a theater of your fellow-servants nor do I compel you to reveal your sins before [the generality of] men?" It will be said, of course, that such an interpretation is gratuitous. Perhaps it is; but so too is it gratuitous to insist that it cannot mean such; and I offer it only as a possible interpretation and not as the interpretation that is solely possible. I simply contend that they say too much who say that such a passage as § 1131 excludes the possibility of confession before a priest. Furthermore I note that the translation of this same passage in Johannes Quasten's *Patrology*, Vol. 3, p. 479 (generally an excellent work and one to which I am certainly very much indebted) has a line: "Unfold your conscience to God alone." The Greek of the line reads: τὸ συνειδὸς ἀνάπτυξον ἔμπροσθεν τοῦ θεοῦ. The word *alone* has no prototype in the Greek. Quasten is playing with educated dice. He has added to the text the very word he wants to prove. On the other hand it is only proper to point out that in similar passages elsewhere in Chrysostom the word *alone* does occur. See below, passages 1132, 1136, 1157, 1169, and 1230, with their pertinent notes.

HOMILIES ON LAZARUS [*A. D.* 388]

The Suidas speaks of a commentary by Chrysostom on Luke's Gospel. He does in fact state that Chrysostom wrote commentaries or courses of homilies on all four of the Gospels. Of any homilies that John may have written on Mark's Gospel, we have nothing. All that is left of any lengthier commentary that may have existed on Luke is the seven *Homilies on Lazarus*, the poor man of the parable in Luke 16:19-31. Nor is it evident that the seven *Homilies on Lazarus* are not a complete unit in themselves. It is generally presumed that the Suidas erred in attributing to Chrysostom full courses of sermons on Mark and Luke.

The *Homilies on Lazarus* are to be dated at Antioch in 388. Their text is found in Migne, PG 48, 963-1054.

1132

[4, 4]

If we have been neglectful to the present moment, let us proceed immediately to the work of destroying sin through confession and tears, and by accusing ourselves of our sins. For there is nothing more destructive of sin than [self-]accusation and [self-]condemnation, joined to repentance and tears. Have you condemned your sin? You have put aside your burden! Who says so? God Himself, who renders judgment. "First tell your sins, so that you may be justified (1)." Why, pray tell, are you ashamed, why do you blush to tell your sins? Do you tell them to a man, such as might reproach you? Do you confess them to a fellow-servant,.such as might make them public? No, you expose your wound to the Master, to the Guardian, to the Benefactor of mankind, to the Physician. . . . Unless you tell the magnitude of your debt, you do not experience the abundance of grace. "I do not oblige you," He says, "to come into the middle of a theater and to be surrounded by many witnesses. Tell your sin to Me alone in private, so that I may heal your wound and release you from your pain (2)."

917
911
920
921

1. Is. 43:26 in the Septuagint. Chrysostom reads ἁμαρτίας for Rahlfs' Septuagint's ἀνομίας. The thought is different in the Hebrew, and seems to have been better captured by the Vulgate. The more correct notion of the passage would seem to be something to the effect of: "If you have anything by which to justify yourself, tell it now!"
2. See § 1131 above, with its note 24. There is perhaps the barest possibility that the last sentence is not to be placed in the mouth of God, and the *Me* refers to Chrysostom; but I think it may be taken as virtually certain that such is not the case. It is still God speaking, and the *to Me alone* is God. Nevertheless, I still think that this is rhetoric. Chrysostom is teaching his people that the priest-confessor is no more than God's ear; and as such, he is an organ of hearing but not of speaking. Otherwise, why so much encouragement not to be ashamed? And why the admonition to frankness? Was anyone ever ashamed to call himself a sinner before God in the privacy of his own heart, so that he need be told not to be ashamed? And was there ever a need to explain to God the precise magnitude of our sins?

HOMILIES AGAINST THE ANOMOIANS AND ON THE CONSUBSTANTIALITY OF THE FATHER AND THE SON [*inter A. D.* 387/398]

As mentioned under the heading *Homilies against the Anomoians and on the Incomprehensible Nature of God*, the Migne text, following Montfaucon, offers in PG 48, 701-812 a single grouping of twelve homilies under the sole heading *Homiliae duodecim contra anomoeos de incomprehensibili*. Prior to Montfaucon's time this was not a customary grouping. The first five homilies were regarded as a series, and the other seven as isolated homilies. In more recent times it has become customary to divide the grouping into two series: the first, of the first five homilies, which is a legitimate and proper procedure; and the second, of the last seven, which is a mere convenience. Here I am following this same convenience of grouping the homilies 6 12 under a single heading, as given above. But this is purely for convenience, because most of the homilies in the grouping have little or nothing to do with that now customary heading.

Homilies 6 and 7 are to be dated in the year 387, while numbers 11 and 12 are generally assigned to Chrysostom's episcopal years in Constantinople, probably to the year 398 A. D. Numbers 8-10 are either undatable or of disputed date.

The titles of the seven homilies are 6) *On Saint Philogonius*; 7) *On the Homoousion*; 8) *On the Request of the Mother of the Sons of Zebedee*; 9) *On Lazarus Four Days Dead*; 10) *On the Prayers of Christ*; 11) *Against the Anomoians*; 12) *On the Divinity of Christ*. The Migne text is in PG 48, 747-812. A new edition of numbers 7-12 is being prepared by A. M. Malingrey.

1133

[7(2), 6]

These words do not signify the agony alone, but also the two wills that are in   330
opposition to each other, one of the Son and one of the Father. This is made clear when He says, "Not as I will, but as You will (1)." But they never admit this, and are always quoting us the saying, "I and the Father are one (2)." They assert that what was said about the power was said about the will; and they say that Father and Son have but one will. If then there is but one will of Father and Son, how is it that He says, "Only not as I will, but as You will?" Were this saying to be attributed to the Divinity it would result in a certain contradiction and it would give birth to numerous absurdities. But if it is attributed to the flesh the words will have such consistency that no complaint will be possible.

1134

[12(7), 4]

For not only does God produce creation but He even continues it and organizes it.   195
Speak, if you will, of Angels and Archangels and Virtues above, and, taking all creation   530

together, the visible and the invisible—it all enjoys His providence; and were it deprived of
that operation it would go to ruin and it would be destroyed and it would perish.

1. Matt. 26:39.
2. John 10:30.

THE PROOF THAT CHRIST IS GOD [*ca. A. D.* 387 *nisi forte A. D.* 381]

The usual Latin title *Against the Jews and Pagans that Christ is God* comes from a
less tactful age than our own. Neither does the usual Greek title contain so great a lack
of feeling as the Latin: *A Demonstration to Jews and Greeks that Christ is God, from the
Sayings concerning Him everywhere in the Prophets.*

The treatise occupies itself with proving Christ's divinity on the basis of the
fulfillment of prophecy; and to that end it investigates the Old Testament prophecies as
also Christ's own prophecies, and their fulfillment. Otto Bardenhewer dates the work ca.
387 A. D., but A. L. Williams in his *Adversus Iudaeos: A Bird's-Eye View of Christian
Apologiae until the Renaissance*, Cambridge 1935, pp. 135-138, dates it immediately
after Chrysostom's ordination to the diaconate, in 381 A. D.

Because of the abrupt apparent ending of the work, and because it after all says very
little about the Jews, it is suspected that the work, in the state in which we have it, is not
complete. The text is to be found in Migne, PG 48, 813-838.

1135

[11]

How, then, do you dare still to disbelieve, when you have received from [Christ] such   81
proof of His power, when you hear His words spoken before the events and see the
events happening in perfect accord with His words, with no discrepancy at all? Those
who first received the Bible (1) and who still preserve it bear witness to the fact that these
are not our fabrications, though they are our enemies and the offspring of those who did
the crucifying—they now keep and preserve the bible.

1. τὰ βιβλία.

HOMILIES ON PENANCE

The nine *Homilies on Penance* are a collection rather than a series. The authenticity of
four of these is at least questionable. No. 5 is probably a work of Germanus II. No.
7 belongs almost certainly to Severian of Gabala. No. 8 stands in considerable doubt; and
No. 9 is likewise doubtful, having been published by the Assemani's as a work of
Ephraim. I will cite passages from No. 9 anyway, because they are not infrequently
referred to in textbooks of theology. Moreover, it is my immediate impression that the
language of No. 9 is much more Chrysostom's than Ephraim's. I do not think the doubt of
Chrysostomic authenticity in the instance of No. 9 is very well founded.

About three hundred homilies falsely attributed to John Chrysostom have been printed
and there are still about six hundred more such spurious homilies in manuscript.

The text of the *Homilies on Penance* is in Migne 49, 277-350.

1136

[3, 4]

Have you sinned? Go into church and wipe out your sin. As often as you might fall   917
down in the marketplace, you pick yourself up again. So too, as often as you sin, repent   920

your sin. Do not despair. Even if you sin a second time, repent a second time. Do   919
not by indifference lose hope entirely of the good things prepared. Even if you are in
extreme old age and have sinned, go in, repent! For here there is a physician's office,
not a courtroom (1); not a place where punishment of sin is exacted, but where the
forgiveness of sin is granted. Tell your sin to God alone: "Before You alone have I
sinned, and I have done what is evil in Your sight (2)"; and your sin will be forgiven (3).

1137

[9]
  Do not look upon it as bread, do not regard it as wine; nor are these excreted into the   856
privy like the rest of foods. Perish the thought! But like wax brought into contact
with the fire, where nothing is lost and nothing is left over, so too the Mysteries are   878
thought to be consumed by the substance (4) of the body.

1138

[9]
  Since we know these things and are well aware of that terrible day and of that fire,   991
and have in mind those terrible torments, let us turn aside at last from the path on which   1032
we have strayed. For the hour will come when the theater of this world will be dissolved,
after which there will be no more contending for the prize, no more exertions to be
made after the end of this life, no more crowns to be merited after the collapse of this
theater. This is the time for repentance, that the time of judgment.

1. ἰατρεῖον . . . οὐ δικαστήριον.
2. Ps. 50[51]:6.
3. It seems to me that Chrysostom's frequent admonitions to confess *to God* and *to God alone* are but a way of emphasizing
   for the timid that in confessing to the priest they are in fact confessing to God, and that the priest's lips are as sealed as if
   he were not present at all. If he meant literally *to God alone*, why the admonition to come into the church to confess?
   Why so great an emphasis on place that we visualize, if not actually a confessional, at least a private corner of the church
   set aside for penance, the "physician's office," which is "not a courtroom," but a "place . . . where . . . forgiveness
   . . . is granted." See note 5 to § 1157 below.
4. τῇ . . . οὐσίᾳ. I take it that Chrysostom means that the whole of the substance (tangible material) in the Eucharistic
   Elements is corporeally assimilated into the body of the recipient. The whole problem, which has its source in the
   indecorousness of what normally happens to portions of the substance (material) of foods, is rather disgustingly prurient;
   but I suppose it was a problem for some. The scholastic view of the Eucharist largely obviates the problem, since it is
   held that the Eucharist (Real Presence) perdures only so long as the accidents of the species are recognizable; probably for
   only a few minutes after reception.

PANEGYRIC SERMONS

  Chrysostom's panegyric sermons are an interesting and valuable collection. They
include a course of seven *Homilies in Praise of Saint Paul*. These were translated into
Latin by Anianus of Celeda a decade or two after Chrysostom's death. Their translator
said of them that they do not simply portray the Apostle but bring him back from the
dead to be once again a living model of Christian perfection. Of special interest too are
the panegyrics on former bishops of Antioch: Ignatius, Babylas, Philogonius,
Eusthathius, and Meletius. An encomium of Diodore of Tarsus was delivered in 392
A. D. in Diodore's very presence.
  There are sermons also on Old Testament figures, more notably Job, Eleazar, and the
Maccabees and their mother; a panegyric *On All the Holy Martyrs*; and panegyrics on
individual martyrs, including Julian, Lucian, two on Roman, Barlaam, Pelagia,
Berenice, and Prosdoce.

The texts of the *Panegyric Sermons* are found in Migne, PG 50, where the genuine are distinguished from the spurious. The text of the short passage below from the *Panegyric on St. Lucian* is in Migne, PG 50, col. 522.

PANEGYRIC ON SAINT LUCIAN

1139

[2]

Do not be surprised that I call martyrdom a Baptism; for here too the Spirit comes in   833
great haste and there is a taking away of sins and a wonderful and marvelous cleansing
of the soul; and just as those being baptized are washed in water, so too those
being martyred are washed in their own blood.

HOMILIES ON THE INCIDENT OF THE STATUES [*A. D.* 387]

The twenty-one *Homilies on the Incident of the Statues* are perhaps the most famous of Chrysostom's works except for *The Priesthood*; and certainly they are among the very finest examples of his eloquence. They belong to the year 387 A. D., when John was official preacher in Antioch. John was still but recently ordained, and these wonderful discourses consolidated his reputation as a golden-mouthed orator.

Early in the year 387 A. D., in the last days of February or early in March, a popular sedition broke out in Antioch, the populace in general being exasperated by increased taxation. After better-minded citizens had laid their grievances before the prefect with no immediate and obvious success, a band of roisterers who probably paid no taxes to speak of anyway began to roam about the city performing indiscriminate acts of vandalism. They broke the windows and doors of the prefect's palace, and when repelled there they continued their pillage elsewhere in the city and ended by throwing down the statues of the Emperor Theodosius and the deceased Empress Flacilla, dragging them contemptuously through the city. The sedition was finally dispersed by a contingent of archers sent from the prefect.

With the rebellion put down, fear quickly replaced such untoward boldness as had been evidenced. Executions followed in considerable numbers, the people were on the verge of despair, many fleeing the city; and Theodosius was said to be so angered that he was considering the total destruction of the city.

Flavian, Bishop of Antioch, now went personally to Constantinople to intercede with Theodosius for his people and city, while Chrysostom remained at Antioch to quiet the people's fears, to ready them for the worst should it happen, and to prepare them for the possibility of a more violent and hasty journey into eternity than they might normally have been expected to enjoy. Hence, the *Homilies on the Incident of the Statues*, preached in March and April of 387 A. D.

Happy news finally came, two months after the sedition. Flavian returned to announce a successful embassy. The city was spared. He had spoken so eloquently on behalf of the people that Theodosius wept. It is likely that Chrysostom wrote Flavian's entreaty for him.

The Migne text of the *Homilies on the Incident of the Statues* is in PG 49, 15-222.

1143

[15, 1]

What can there be that is worse than hell? Yet nothing is more profitable than the   914
fear of it! for the fear of hell gains for us the crown of the kingdom. . . . Nothing

swallows up sins and makes virtue increase and abound as much as does a constant state (1) of fear.

1. φύσις.

BAPTISMAL CATECHESES [ca. A. D. 388-389]

Until the present century there was but little known remains of the catechetical instructions that Chrysostom must have delivered annually at Antioch from 386 to 397 A. D.

Migne (PG 49, 223-240) and the earlier editions included a pair of *Catecheses ad illuminandos*, belonging to Lent of 388 or 389 A. D. Fronto Ducaeus had included in an appendix in the second volume of his edition a Latin sermon *Ad neophytos*; but it was ignored by Sir Henry Savile, Dom Bernard de Montfaucon, and the Abbé Migne.

It was S. Haidacher who first noticed that the *Ad neophytos* of Fronto's edition was the same sermon as that from which passages were extant in St. Augustine's *Against Julian* (1, 6) of the year 421 A. D. Used so early, and probably in the Latin translation of the homilies of Chrysostom produced by the deacon Anianus of Celeda, its authenticity is well-attested. Haidacher published his findings in an article entitled *"Eine unbeachtete Rede des heiligen Chrysostomus an Neugetaufte,"* in the *Zeitschrift für katholische Theologie*, Vol. 28 (1904), pp. 168-186. That left us, then, with three authentic baptismal catecheses, two Greek and one in Latin translation.

Early in the present century, in 1909, A. Papadopoulos-Kerameus published for the first time a series of four baptismal instructions or catechetical sermons of Chrysostom, which were found in two tenth century Greek manuscripts, the *Moscow codex 216* and the *Saint Petersburg codex 76*. It is clear enough that these are Chrysostom's, and that they were delivered at Antioch in 388 or 389. Moreover, the first of these four is identical to the first of the two previously known *Catecheses ad illuminandos*, as found in Migne; and the fourth of the four is identical to the sermon previously known only in the Latin of Fronto Ducaeus' edition, the *Ad neophytos*, and from the Latin quotations (with a short Greek passage also) in Augustine's *Against Julian* 1, 6, as noted above. Papadopoulos-Kerameus' edition is in his *Varia Graeca sacra*, St. Petersburg, Russia, 1909, pp. xx xxv and 154-183. Now we had five of Chrysostom's authentic baptismal catecheses.

Furthermore, in 1955 A. Wenger discovered a series of eight baptismal catecheses of Chrysostom in Codex 6 of the Monastery of the Stavronikita (the Cross Triumphant) on Mount Athos. Wenger published the eight in 1957, along with a French translation, in his *Huit catéchèses baptismales inédites*, volume 50 in the series *Sources Chrétiennes*, Paris 1957. These lectures too seem to belong to 388 or 389 A. D. The third of Wenger's eight is identical to the fourth of Papadopoulos-Kerameus' four, which had in turn duplicated the *Ad neophytos* of Fronto's edition and the fragments extracted from Augustine's *Against Julian*.

It is seen, therefore, that we now have twelve of Chrysostom's *Baptismal Catecheses*. Only in this present instance will I depart from my policy of retaining the passage numbers of Rouët de Journel: his §§ 1228-1229 must become my §§ 1145a-b. I will take for the text of those two passages that of Augustine's *Contra Julianum*, a quite literal translation in fact; for I want to show also Augustine's valuable remarks on the passages.

From the First of the Two Catecheses ad illuminandos *in Migne or the First of the Four* Sermons to Candidates *in Papadopoulos-Kerameus; not in Wenger*

1144

[1, 3]

It is as if someone were to take a golden statue of a man which has long been tarnished   752
by time and by smoke and by dust and by corrosion and recast it, giving it back to
us perfectly cleansed and polished, when God takes this nature of ours, corroded with
the rust of sin and much dimmed by the smoke of our faults and deprived of the
beauty which was bestowed upon it by Him in the beginning, and casts it anew, throwing
it into the waters [of Baptism] as if in a smelting furnace. He pours out the grace of the
Spirit in place of fire, and then brings us forth renewed and refreshed and with a
brightness to rival the rays of the sun. The old man has been crushed and a new man,
more brilliant then the former, has been fashioned.

> *From the Second of the Two* Catecheses ad illuminandos *in Migne; not in
> Papadopoulos-Kerameus nor in Wenger*

1145

[2, 4]

The wonderful thing is not simply that God forgives our sins, but He does this without   917
even revealing them nor making them manifest and evident: He does not require
that we come forward publicly to tell out our faults. He but commands us to make our
explanation to Him alone, and to confess to Him. If some thieves or grave-robbers were
brought before civil judges and were told that if they would declare their errors they
would be free of punishment, they would agree to this in all haste, and would
think nothing of the shame in order to secure their safety. But in our circumstances there
is nothing of this sort. Rather, He both forgives the sin and does not require that it
be paraded before an audience. One thing only does He seek: that the person enjoying
this forgiveness learn the greatness of the gift he has received.

> *From the Fourth of the Four* Sermons to Candidates *in Papadopoulos-Kerameus or
> the Third of the* Huit catéchèses *in Wenger or the* Ad neophytos *in Fronto Ducaeus,
> quoted by Augustine in his* Contra Iulianum 1, 6

1145a

[*Apud Aug., Contra Iul*. 1, 6, 21]

Behold, they thoroughly enjoy the peacefulness of freedom who shortly before were   836
held captive. They are citizens of the Church who were wandering in error. They
have their lot in righteousness who were in the confusion of sin. For not only are they
free, but holy also; not only holy, but righteous too; not only righteous, but sons
also; not only sons, but heirs as well; not only heirs, but brothers even of Christ; not only   755
brothers of Christ, but also co-heirs; not only co-heirs, but His very members; not   756
only His members, but a temple too; not a temple only, but likewise the instruments of   750
the Spirit. You see how many are the benefits of Baptism, and some think its heavenly
grace consists only in the remission of sins; but we have enumerated ten honors.
For this reason we baptize even infants, though they are not defiled by sin [LEGE: though   835
they do not have sins]: so that there may be given to them holiness, righteousness,
adoption, inheritance, brotherhood with Christ, and that they may be His members.
[CONCERNING THIS PASSAGE, AUGUSTINE REMARKS IN HIS Contra Iulianum 1, 6, 22,
AFTER QUOTING THE PERTINENT LINE IN GREEK: "*You see that he (John Chrysostom)
certainly did not say, 'Infants are not defiled by sin,' or 'sins,' but, 'Not having sins.'*   614
*Understand 'of their own,' and there is no difficulty. 'But,' you will say, 'why did he
not add "of their own" himself?' Why else, I suppose, if not that he was speaking in a*

Catholic church and never supposed he would be understood in any other way,   105
when no one had raised such a question, and he could speak more unconcernedly
when you were not there to dispute the point (1)?"]

1145b

[*Apud Aug., Contra Iul.* 1, 6, 26]
   What John of Constantinople says, translated word for word, is this: "Christ came   614
once. He found our paternal note of hand, which Adam wrote. That man [Adam]
brought in the beginning of the debt. We increased the interest by our later sins." *Was he*
content to say: "the paternal note of hand," without adding "our?" He added
the "our" so that we might know that before we increased the interest by our later sins,
the debt of that paternal note of hand already pertained to us (2).

1. Julian of Eclanum had appealed to Chrysostom in support of Pelagianism and the denial of original sin. Julian quoted
Chrysostom's *Ad neophytos* as we have it above, "We baptize even infants, though they are not defiled by sin''; and he
took this to be a denial of original sin. Augustine has at hand not just the Latin translation of the *Ad neophytos*, but also
the original Greek; thus he can point out that Chrysostom did not put the matter in precisely the way the Latin translation
has it. What Chrysostom actually said was: "We baptize even infants, though they do not have sins." Augustine then
insists that the use of the plural *sins* rather than the singular *sin* makes it clear that Chrysostom was speaking of personal
sins. He then continues to exonerate Chrysostom and to deprive Julian of his source by quoting numerous other passages
from works of Chrysostom which do show him as affirming the existence of original sin. As we might well expect, of
course, Chrysostom's notion of original sin is not yet so clearly defined as is that of Augustine.
2. Augustine quotes also the Greek of the passage from Chrysostom: ἔρχεται ἅπαξ ὁ Χριστός, εὗρεν ἡμῶν χειρόγραφον
πατρῷον, ὅ τι ἔγραψεν ὁ Ἀδάμ, ἐκεῖνος τὴν ἀρχὴν εἰσήγαγεν τοῦ χρείους, ἡμεῖς τὸν δανεισμὸν νὐξήσαμεν
ταῖς μεταγενεστέραις ἁμαρτίαις.

HOMILIES ON HANNAH [*A. D.*387]

   There is no reason to suppose that Chrysostom wrote anything more extensive on the
Books of Samuel and Kings than that which is extant: the three *Homilies on David and*
Saul, belonging to the summer of 387 A. D. (Migne, PG 54, 675-708) and the five
Homilies on Hannah, the mother of Samuel.
   The five *Homilies on Hannah* belong to the Pentecost season of 387 A. D. The text of
the homilies is found in Migne, PG 54, 631-676.

1146

[1, 3]
   One way of coming to a knowledge of God is that which is provided by the whole of   131
creation; and another, no less significant, is that which is offered by conscience,   133
the whole of which we have expounded upon at great length, showing how you have a
self-taught knowledge of what is good and of what is not so good, and how conscience
urges all this upon you from within. Two teachers, then, are given you from the
beginning: creation and conscience. Neither of them has a voice to speak out; yet they
teach men in silence.

HOMILIES ON GENESIS, SECOND SERIES [*A. D.* 388]

   There are extant two series of Chrysostom's *Homilies on Genesis*. The first series
consists of only nine homilies. These, which were preached at Antioch in Lent of 386
A. D. shortly after John's ordination to the priesthood, are found in Migne, PG 54,
581-630.

The second series of *Homilies on Genesis* consists of sixty-seven homilies and comprises a complete commentary on that book. The sixty-seven homilies were assigned by Tillemont and de Montfaucon to the year 395. G. Rauschen's view prevails, however, that they were preached in the year 388 A. D. Where the two series deal with the same matters there are numerous passages literally identical. But if Chrysostom was going to crib some extensive passages of his sermons, he cannot have done better than to have stolen from himself.

The texts of the *Homilies on Genesis, Second Series* are found in Migne, PG 53-54.

1147

[2, 2]

To say that things which exist were gotten out of existing matter and not to confess   460
that the Creator of all things produced them out of what did not exist would be a sign   461
of extreme mental derangement.

1148

[4, 5]

If visible things are sufficient to teach us the greatness of the power of the Creator,   482
and if you then come to the invisible powers, and you strain your mind to the armies   488
of Angels, Archangels, Virtues above, Thrones, Dominations, Principalities, Powers,
Cherubim, Seraphim (1), what thought, what word can declare His indescribable
magnificence?

1149

[13, 1]

Do you see how all things were created by a word? But let us see what it says   509
afterwards about the creation of man: "And God shaped man (2)." See how, by means
of a condescension of terms employed for the sake of our weakness, it teaches at the
same time both the manner of creation and its diversity or variety, so that, speaking
in human terms, it indicates that man was shaped by the very hands of God, even as
another Prophet says: "Your hands created me and shaped me (3)."

1150

[15, 4]

Their intercourse took place after the transgression; until then they had behaved in   521
Paradise like angels, not burning with desire, not beset by other passions, not subject
to the necessities of nature, but, created entirely incorruptible and immortal, there   522
they had no need even for the protective covering of garments. "The two were naked,"   611
it says, "and were not ashamed (4)." For when sin and disobedience had not yet   612
entered upon the scene they were clothed with glory from above, which is why they
were not ashamed. But after their transgression of the command shame did enter in,
and the knowledge of their nakedness.

1151

[22, 1]

Is it not perfectly clear that anyone can, by his own choice, choose either wickedness   505
or virtue? For if this were not the case, and if such a faculty did not pertain to our   636
nature, it were not right that some be punished while others receive the reward of   700

virtue. But since everything depends, after grace from above, upon our own choice, so too are punishments prepared for sinners and recompense and reward for those who do right.

1152

[22, 2]

Would it not be utter insanity to say that angels sank so low as to have intercourse with women, and that incorporeal nature imitated the intercourse of corporeal beings? Did you not hear Christ say of the angelic essence (5), "In the resurrection they will neither marry nor give in marriage, but they will be like angles of God (6):" Nor is it ever possible for the incorporeal nature to experience that kind of desire.

483

1153

[25, 7]

God awaits occasions to show us His great liberality. Let us not by laziness, then, defraud ourselves of His gifts, but hasten and be eager to begin to take the path that leads back to virtue, so that, enjoying help from above, we may be strengthened to persevere to the end; for unless we are assisted (7) from above it is not possible for us to do right at any time.

650

671

1154

[30, 5]

Prayer is a powerful good. For if someone's speaking to a man about what is virtuous is seen to bear no insignificant fruit, how much greater weight of benefits will not he enjoy who engages in conversation with God? For prayer is, after all, conversation with God. . . . But is He unable, then, to present His gifts without our asking? It is for this reason that He waits: so that He may have occasion from us of justly making us worthy of His providential care.

120

1155

[42, 1]

That it is not because we are not able but because we are not willing that we are strangers to all His benefits is made perfectly clear by the fact that many men of the same race as ourselves are found to be shining examples of virtue. Such a one was the Patriarch [Abraham] himself, born before grace and before the law. By himself and by the knowledge that is inherent in our nature he came to so great a measure of virtue as to be able to deprive us of all our excuses. But perhaps some will say that this man enjoyed a great measure of God's solicitous care, and that the God of the universe showered His considerable providence in Abraham's regard. Yes, I agree. But if Abraham had not shown beforehand what was his own, He would not have enjoyed the things that are from the Master. Do not consider the latter only, therefore, but examine each case and learn how in every one of them proof was first given of personal virtue, and thus did they merit the help of God.

656

711

---

1. ἐπὶ τὰς τῶν ἀγγέλων στρατιάς, τῶν ἀρχαγγέλων, τῶν ἄνω δυνάμεων, τῶν θρόνων, τῶν κυριοτήτων, τῶν ἀρχῶν, τῶν ἐξουσιῶν, τῶν χερουβίμ, τῶν σεραφίμ. Perhaps ἄνω is supplied with δυνάμεων because the same term, δυνάμεις, occurs immediately above, where I translated "invisible *powers*." When it refers in a generic way to invisible created beings, δύναμις is a *power*; but as a member of a specific choir of angels, a δύναμις is a *Virtue*, if only because an ἐξουσία is a *Power*. In much the same way, *angel* with lower case initial is generic of the nine choirs, whereas *Angel* with upper case initial is specific of the first (lowest) choir.

2. Gen. 2:7.
3. Job 10:8.
4. Gen. 2:25.
5. τῆς τῶν ἀγγέλων οὐσίας.
6. Matt. 22:30; Mark 12:25; Luke 20:35.
7. μὴ τῆς ἄνωθεν ῥοπῆς ἀπολαύσαντας = not enjoying the influence from above.

HOMILIES ON THE BEGINNING OF THE ACTS OF THE APOSTLES [A. D. 388]

Besides a series of fifty-five *Homilies on the Acts of the Apostles* dating from 400 or 401 A. D., Chrysostom has left us also a course of four homilies *de mutatione nominum* on the changing of names of Paul and other biblical figures (PG 51, 113-156), and more to our present interest, a course of four *Homilies on the Beginning of the Acts of the Apostles*.

Both of these latter two series of four homilies were preached at Antioch soon after the Easter season of 388 A. D. The text of the four *Homilies on the Beginning of the Acts of the Apostles* is in Migne, PG 51, 61-112.

1156

[4, 8]

If Christ died and did not rise how is it that those in the account who fled from   84
impending danger while He was yet alive surrounded themselves with a thousand dangers
for His sake when He was dead? The others all fled, but Peter even denied Him three times
with an oath; and though he denied Him three times with an oath and was struck with fear
before an insignificant serving girl, after Christ's death he wanted to persuade us by his
very deeds that he had seen Him who had risen; and he changed so completely that he
scorned the ridicule of the whole assembled crowd and even went into the midst of the
Jews and said that the One who was crucified and buried had risen from the dead on the
third day and had ascended into heaven; and never did Peter show himself fearful again.
Whence did such courage come to him? Whence indeed, if not from his certitude of the
resurrection?

HOMILIES ON THE TREACHERY OF JUDAS

In the collection of *Homilies on the Treachery of Judas* are three sermons for Holy
Thursday. The first two, in Migne, PG 49, 373-392, are so similar to each other that
they are undoubtedly two recensions of the same work. What remains to be determined
is whether or not Chrysostom himself is responsible for both recensions, or whether a
later author is the redactor. The third such sermon, in Migne, PG 50, 715-720, is
generally regarded as spurious, or at least its authenticity is held gravely suspect.

The Holy Thursday homilies treat of the institution of the Eucharist, and the betrayal
of our Savior by Judas. The passage below is translated from the first of the pair in
Migne, PG 49 (col. 380).

1157

[1, 6]

Christ is present. The One who prepared that [Holy Thursday] table is the very One   896
who now prepares this [altar] table. For it is not a man who makes the sacrificial   856

gifts (1) become (2) the Body and Blood of Christ, but He that was crucified for us, Christ Himself. The priest (3) stands there carrying out the action (4), but the power and the grace is of God (5). "This is My Body (6)," he says. This statement transforms the gifts (7).

862

1. τὰ προκείμενα.
2. γενέσθαι.
3. ὁ ἱερεύς.
4. σχῆμα πληρῶν. The term σχῆμα means a figure, shape, appearance, posture, pretence. The idea here is that the priest is like a mime or an actor on the stage. But the reality of what is portrayed and acted out is accomplished by God.
5. It seems to me that Chrysostom's attitude here to the position of the priest in respect to the Eucharist,—that the priest is a silent performer, showing only what is actually being done by God,—is a key to understanding his frequent adjurations to confess our sins "to God" and "to God alone." See §§ 1132, 1136, and 1145 above, with their pertinent notes. Just as he says that we should confess to God or to God alone, so too does he say that the Eucharist is confected by God: but in the case of the Eucharist he certainly would not and does not dispense with the role of the priest, though he calls it a σχῆμα; and no more would he, I think, in the case of Penance.
6. Matt. 26:26.
7. τοῦτο τὸ ῥῆμα μεταρρυθμίζει τὰ προκείμενα.

HOMILIES ON THE GOSPEL OF JOHN [ca. A. D. 391]

The Suidas' mention of Chrysostom's having written a commentary on the Gospel of John is to be taken as referring to Chrysostom's course of eighty-eight exegetical *Homilies on the Gospel of John*.

The homilies on John are considerably shorter than most of his other homilies, and would have taken less than a half-hour for delivery. Probably they belong to the year 391 A. D.

It is interesting that in this series of homilies there is nothing said of John 7:53-8:11, the pericope of the woman taken in adultery. Nor, in fact, is this passage testified to anywhere in Chrysostom. There can be little doubt that it was absent from John's Gospel as known at this time in Antioch. Probably it does not belong to John's Gospel at all. The pericope is first attested in Latin Gospel manuscripts of the fourth century, and is found sometimes at the conclusion of John's Gospel (ch. 21), and sometimes at the end of chapter 21 in Luke's Gospel. From a remark in Eusebius' *History of the Church* 3, 39 it is clear that the same or a similar account of a woman taken in adultery was in the lost *Gospel of the Hebrews*, which same narrative was included also in Papias' lost *Explanation* (see § 95, above in Vol. 1).

Chrysostom's *Homilies on the Gospel of John* are in general of a somewhat more controversial character than his homilies on Matthew, a fact which is predictable enough if we but recall that it is John's Gospel which takes the divinity of Christ for its focal point, and that the Arian controversies were far from dead in Chrysostom's time.

Chrysostom uses the texts of John's Gospel to refute the radical Arians or Anomoians; and at the same time he develops his doctrine of condescension, something of which is to be seen already in his homilies against Anomoianism of a few years earlier: see §§ 1126 and 1128 above. Condescension is an attitude on God's part, according to which He in some way accommodates Himself to the capacities of creatures, angels or men, so that they may know Him even in the weak way that is commensurate with their capabilities. By this doctrine Chrysostom is able to explain the Scriptural statements of human frailties in Christ. It was largely these statements that the Arians had used as proofs against Christ's divinity; and it is by his doctrine of condescension that Chrysostom refutes their misinterpretations.

If the doctrine of condescension derives principally from a certain viewpoint or stance in respect to the incarnation, this cannot be wholly the case; for the Father too is condescending, and so must be the Holy Spirit (see §§ 1128-1129 above).

The text of the *Homilies on the Gospel of John* is in Migne, PG 59. The four volume edition of text and Italian translation in the series *Corona patrum Salesiana*, D. C. Tirone's *S. Giovanni Crisostomo, Le omilie su S. Giovanni Evangelista*, Turin 1944–1948, reprints the same text of de Montfaucon that is found in Migne.

1157a

[6, 1]

It is as if Christ were saying, "I am God and the genuine Son of God. I am of that   257
simple and blessed essence (1), and I need no one to bear testimony to Me. Even if   258
none should do so, I would not thereby be in any way diminished in nature. Yet,
because I am concerned for the salvation of the many, I have condescended (2)
to such humility as to commit the testimony of Me to a man (3)."

1158

[8, 1]

If He "enlightens every man who comes into the world (4)," how is it that there   724
are some who remain unenlightened? For not all have acknowledged the majesty of
Christ. How then does He enlighten every man? To such extent as in Him lies. And   695
if there are some who choose to close the eyes of their mind and do not want to receive   700
the rays of that light, their darkness comes not from the nature of the light, but from
their own wickedness in voluntarily depriving themselves of that gift.

1159

[10, 1]

Beloved, since God is loving toward men, and their Benefactor as well, He does   695
all things and so arranges that we may shine in virtue. And while He wills that we may
be well-pleasing to Him, He draws none by force or necessity; but by persuasion and
by benefiting them, He draws all who are willing and attracts them to Himself. That   684
is why some received Him when He came, and some did not (5). For He wants to have   700
no unwilling or coerced domestic, but all who are willing and who come of their own   701
choice, and who are grateful to Him for their service.

1159a

[11, 1]

I want to ask one favor of all of you before I turn to the words of the Gospel. Do not   31
refuse my request, for I ask nothing difficult or burdensome of you; nor do I ask that
which, if granted, will be advantageous to me alone who receive. Rather, it will be
advantageous to you also, who grant it, and perhaps even more so to you than to me.
What then do I ask of you? That each of you take in hand that part of the Gospels
which is to be read in your presence on the first day of the week or even on the
Sabbath; and before that day comes, sit down at home and read it through; consider
often and carefully its content, and examine all its parts well, noting what is clear,
what is confusing, what seems to assist the position of the adversaries but really does
not. And, in a word, when you have sounded every point, then go to hear it read. From
such zeal as this there will be no small benefit both to you and to me.

1159b

[11, 1]

He that was Son of God became Son of Man so that He might make sons of men   257
become children of God. . . . In no way did He diminish His own essence (6) by   313
this condescension, but He did thereby raise us, who had been sitting ever in darkness   375
and disgrace, to indescribable glory.

1160

[11, 1]

When you hear that "the Word was made flesh (7)," do not be disturbed nor   310
disheartened. . . . [2] Why does he use the expression "was made?" To stop the
mouths of heretics. For since there are some who are saying that the whole of the
Incarnation (8) was a phantasy and a show and an illusion he put down that "was   321
made" to take away their blasphemy beforehand, intending to show thereby not a   322
change of essence (9), perish the thought, but the assumption of true flesh. . . For
by union (10) and by conjunction (11) God the Word and the flesh are one, not in any   320
confused way, nor by an obliteration of essences (12), but by a certain union that is
indescribable and beyond understanding. . . . There was no possibility of raising 376
[our fallen nature] again, unless He that fashioned it in the beginning should stretch
forth His hand to it and remold it anew, by rebirth through water and the Spirit.

1161

[15, 1]

"I have multiplied visions and I have used similitudes in the hands of the Prophets   170
(13)"; that is to say, "I have condescended and have not appeared as I really am."   173
Since His Son was about to appear to us in true flesh, He prepared them from of old
to behold the essence (14) of God, insofar as it was possible for them to see Him.
But what God really is, not only have the Prophets not seen, but neither have the
angels nor the archangels seen. . . . The Son alone beholds Him, and the Holy   188
Spirit. . . . [2] "No one knows the Father except the Son (15)." What then? Are
we all in ignorance? Perish the thought! But no one knows Him as the Son knows   174
Him. Many have seen Him to the extent of the vision permitted them, but no one
has seen His essence; so too, all know God, but what His essence is no one knows,
except only the One begotten of Him. For by "knowledge" He means the exact notion
and comprehension such as the Father has in respect to His Son (16): "As the
Father knows Me, so do I know the Father (17)."

1162

[28, 2]

Someone will ask, "Are there no Christians who do evil, nor any pagans (18) living   651
in philosophy (19)?" I too know that there are Christians who do evil. But if there   654
are pagans who live upright lives, that I am not so sure of. Do not talk to me about those   655
who by nature are kindly and modest, for that is not virtue. Tell me rather of the man
who can withstand the great violence of his passions and still lead a regulated life (20).
That you cannot do. . . . But lest to any persons we seem to be contentious, we will
concede that among the pagans there are some who live uprightly. This in no way
contradicts my argument, for I spoke of what is general and not of what happens
but rarely.

1163

[31, 1]

"He that believes in the Son has everlasting life (21)." . . . . "Is it enough, then,   758
to believe in the Son," someone will say, "in order to have everlasting life?" By
no means! Listen to Christ declare this Himself when He says, "Not everyone who
says to Me, 'Lord! Lord!' shall enter into the kingdom of heaven (22)"; and the
blasphemy against the Spirit is alone sufficient to cast him into hell (23). But why
should I speak of a part of our teaching? For if a man believe rightly in the Father and   760
in the Son and in the Holy Spirit, but does not live rightly, his faith will avail
him nothing toward salvation.

1164

[34, 3]

Let us also imitate the [Samaritan] woman, and in the face of our own sins not be   916
ashamed because of men. Rather, as is proper, let us fear God who sees now what   917
we have done and who punishes later what we do not repent now. At present we do
the opposite of this. Instead of fearing Him who is to judge us, we shudder at those who
in no way hurt us, and we tremble at the shame which comes from them. . . . I
therefore exhort you, even if no one know our wicked deeds (24), let each of us enter
into his own conscience and set reason as judge over himself (25) and submit his
transgressions to the court (26). And if he does not want them to be paraded on that
fearful day, let him apply now the medicines of repentance and let him heal now his
wounds.

1165

[46, 1]

"No one can come to Me unless the Father, who sent Me, draw him (27)."   700
The Manicheans fairly leap upon this statement and say that nothing lies in our   656
power; yet the saying shows particularly that we are the masters of our will. Someone
will say, "If a man comes to Him, what need is there of drawing?" But this does
not take away our faculty of choice, but only shows our need of help, because it
points out that not just anyone may come at random, but he may come who is amply
supplied with assistance.

1166

[46, 3]

We have become one body, and "limbs of His flesh and of His bones (28)." Let   880
those who are initiated understand what I am saying (29). So that we may become this   810
not by love only (30) but even in every deed, let us be blended into that flesh. This   877
blending is effected by the Food which He has given, in His desire to demonstrate   878
to us the fond love (31) that He has for us. That is why He has commingled Himself
with us, and has kneaded up His body into us, so that we might subsist as a kind of unit
(32), like a body joined to a head.

1167

[63, 2]

In the Passion the Evangelists ascribe to Christ much that is human, thereby   313
showing the reality of the Incarnation (33). Matthew guarantees this by the agony and   349
the confusion and the perspiration, John by the sorrow. For if Christ had not been of
our nature, He would not have been overpowered by grief, once and again a second
time.

1168

[74, 1]

Christ says, "If anyone sees Me, he sees the Father (34)." If He were   257
of another essence (35) He would not say this. But if I may make use of an argument
of the crasser sort, no one who is ignorant of gold is able to discover the essence (36)
of gold in silver. For the nature (37) of one thing is not manifested in another.

1169

[86, 4]

Great is the dignity of priests. "Whose sins you forgive," He says, "they are   802
forgiven them (38)." . . . The things that are placed in the hands of the priest, it
belongs to God alone to give (39). . . . Neither angel nor archangel is able to do
anything in respect to what is given by God; rather, Father and Son and Holy Spirit   283
manage it all; but the priest lends his own tongue and presents his own hand. Nor
would it be just, if those who draw near in faith to the symbols of our salvation were   804
to be harmed by the wickedness of another (40).

1. τῆς οὐσίας.
2. κατέβην.
3. The man, of course, is John the Baptist.
4. John 1:9.
5. John 1:11.
6. τὴν . . . ἰδίαν φύσιν.
7. John 1:14.
8. τὰ τῆς οἰκονομίας ἅπαντα.
9. οὐ μεταβολὴν οὐσίας.
10. ἑνώσει.
11. συναφείᾳ.
12. οὐδὲ ἀφανισμοῦ τῶν οὐσιῶν.
13. Osee 12:10.
14. τὴν οὐσίαν.
15. Matt. 11:27.
16. περὶ τοῦ παιδός.
17. John 10:15.
18. Ἕλληνες.
19. By this time the word *philosophy* means *Christianity*, or *monasticism*, or *asceticism*, or at least *righteous living*.
20. φιλοσοφοῦντα.
21. John 3:36.
22. Matt. 7:21.
23. εἰς γέενναν.
24. κἂν μηδεὶς ἴδῃ τὰ ἡμέτερα.
25. καὶ καθίσαι ἑαυτῷ δικαστὴν τὸν λογισμόν.
26. καὶ εἰς μέσον ἄγειν τὰ πεπλημμελημένα.
27. John 6:44.
28. There can be little doubt that Chrysostom is quoting Eph. 5:30, but in a well-known variant reading (see Eberhard Nestle's New Testament) which is the standard reading of Jerome's Vulgate. Chrysostom's passage is: ἓν σῶμα γινόμεθα καὶ μέλη ἐκ τῆς σαρκὸς αὐτοῦ καὶ ἐκ τῶν ὀστέων αὐτοῦ.
29. The initiated are the baptized, who communicate. The statement is an oblique reference to the arcane discipline.
30. μὴ μόνον κατὰ τὴν ἀγάπην.
31. τὸν πόθον.
32. ἵνα ἕν τι ὑπάρξωμεν. The *we* that subsists as one is Christ and ourselves, Head and limbs (members).
33. τῆς οἰκονομίας.
34. John 14:9.
35. ἑτέρας οὐσίας.
36. τὴν οὐσίαν.
37. φύσις.
38. John 20:22.
39. This passage should be of value in the interpretation of other passages, such as §§ 1133 and 1136, where it is said that sins are confessed to God alone. It strengthens my apprehension that for Chrysostom one can speak to God alone even in the presence of the priest. For what is placed in the hands of the priest to do is done by God alone.

40. The efficacy of the sacraments does not depend upon the worthiness of the minister. If a priest, Chrysostom tells us in this statement, administers the sacraments while he is himself in a state of sin, the sacrilege is his and no guilt redounds to the recipient of the sacrament.

HOMILIES ON THE GOSPEL OF MATTHEW [*A. D.* 370]

The ninety *Homilies on the Gospel of Matthew* were delivered at Antioch, probably in the year 390 A. D. They constitute together the oldest extant complete commentary on the Gospel of Matthew.

The first twenty-five at least of the homilies were translated into Latin in the early fifth century by the deacon Anianus of Celeda. A fifth century Armenian translation was published in part by the Mechitarists of Venice in 1826. A Syriac version of the sixth century or earlier is extant in unpublished fragments; and likewise unpublished as yet are a tenth century Arabic translation and an eleventh century Georgian translation.

Some idea of the tremendous amount of work still to be done before we have a truly reliable and satisfactory critical edition of Chrysostom's works may be conjectured from the fact that Frederick Field's Cambridge edition (1839) of the three volumes of the *Homilies on the Gospel of Matthew* is regarded as the best edition of this work, though Field used no more than thirteen and perhaps only eleven of nearly two hundred extant manuscripts. Nairn's 1907 edition of *The Priesthood* is regarded as rather a marvel of scholarship; and Nairn used only about one half of the known manuscripts of that work.

Frederick Field's text of the *Homilies on the Gospel of Matthew*, as reprinted in Migne, PG 57-58, is used as the basis for the translations of the following excerpts.

1170

[1, 2(6)]

"The Evangelists, . . ." it may be said, "are in many places found to disagree   63
with each other." Yet, this very thing is a great proof of their truthfulness. For if
they had agreed exactly in all respects, even as to time and place and to the using of
the same words, none of our enemies would believe that they had not met together
and had not written what they wrote in accord with some human compact; for such
perfect agreement could not have come from candidness. But as it is, the discord
which seems to be present in little matters shields them from every suspicion and
clearly vindicates the character of the writers.

1171

[2, 2(3)]

Though He is Son of the unoriginate God, and genuine Son, He allowed Himself   755
to be called also Son of David so that He might make you a son of God. He allowed   754
a slave to become father to Him, so that He might make the Master Father to you, a
slave.

Do you see, then, immediately and from the initial words what kind of writings
the Gospels are? If you were in doubt about what concerns yourself, believe that too,
because of what concerns Him. For human reason would take it to be far more
difficult for God to become man than for a man to be reckoned a son of God. When,
therefore, you hear that the Son of God is Son of David and of Abraham, doubt no
more that even you, the son of Adam, shall be son of God. For He would not idly
and in vain so abase Himself had He not wanted to exalt us. He was born according to
flesh that you might be born according to spirit. He was born of a woman that you
might cease to be son of woman.

1172

[14, 4(6)]

Let us therefore take courage at His love of mankind and let us be diligent in showing   991
repentance before that day arrives which will preclude our benefiting from repentance.
Now everything depends on us; but then He alone who judges will be master of the
sentence (1). "Let us therefore come before His face in confession (2)," let us weep,
let us mourn. For if we should be able to call upon the Judge to forgive our sins before the day
appointed (3), it will not be necessary for us to go to trial at all. But if this is not done,   1020
He will hear us publicly in the presence of the world, and we shall have no longer
any hope of pardon.

1173

[25, 3(4)]

The best guard for the preserving of a benefit is remembrance of that benefit, and   897
perpetual thanksgiving (4). For this reason too the awesome mysteries, so filled with
our great salvation, which are celebrated at each synaxis (5), are called Eucharist
(6), because they are the anamnesis (7) of many benefits, and they exhibit the
summit of God's providence, and in every respect they prepare us to give thanks (8).

1174

[41, 3(5)]

"Blasphemy against the Spirit shall not be forgiven (9)," not even to those   903
who repent. But how can He say such a thing? For even this was forgiven to those
who repent. For many who said these things afterwards believed, and all was forgiven
them. But what does this saying of His mean? That this sin more than any other is
unpardonable. . . . What He says is this: "You say that you do not know Me.
But certainly you are not ignorant of the fact that to cast out devils and to effect
cures is a work of the Holy Spirit. It is not I alone, then, whom you do insult, but the
Holy Spirit too. And that is why your punishment cannot be averted by prayers,
neither here nor hereafter."

1175

[59, 1]

"It is necessary that scandals come (10)." . . . But when He speaks of its being   192
necessary He does not mean that the faculty of free will nor the ability of freely   193
choosing is taken away, nor that life is made subject to some kind of necessity through
its circumstances. He is only saying beforehand what will surely be. Luke sets forth
the same thing by means of another expression: "It is impossible that scandals
should not come (11)." . . . It is not that His prediction brings the scandals.   190
Away with such a notion! It is not because He foretold it that it happens; but because
it surely must happen He did foretell it. If those who introduce scandals had not
wanted to do such wickedness, the scandals would not have come; and if the
scandals were not going to come, He would not have foretold them.

1176

[62, 1]

"What, therefore, God has joined together, let man not put asunder (12)." See   977
the Teacher's wisdom! For when asked, "Is it lawful," He does not immediately   972
reply, "It is not lawful," lest they grumble and be disturbed. But before giving His

decision He makes it clear by His preparation what that decision must be, showing that this too is the ordinance of His Father, and that He does not enjoin these things in opposition to Moses, but as being quite in agreement with him. . . . But now He showed both by the style of creation and by the style of the lawgiving that one man ought cohabit always with one woman, and never be separated.

1177

[69, 2]

To be called and to be cleansed was a thing of grace. But when called and clothed   656
in clean garments, to continue to keep those garments clean pertained to the diligence   670
of those who were called. The calling itself was not from merit, but from grace.

1178

[77, 1]

"Of that day and that hour no one knows, neither the angels of heaven nor the   351
Son, except the Father (13)." By the saying, "Neither the angels," He stopped their
mouths, lest they seek to learn what even the angels did not know; and by the saying,
"Nor the Son," He forbids them not only to learn but even to inquire. . . . He refers
this knowledge to the Father both to make the matter more awesome and to preclude
their inquiring about it. If this is not the reason, and He really is ignorant of the
day and the hour, when will He come to know it? At the same time we do? And
who would say such a thing as that? The Son knows the Father clearly, just as
clearly as the Father knows the Son, and yet He does not know the day? . . .[2] . . .
He says, "When you do not expect it, He will come (14)," because He wants
them to be anxiously waiting, and constantly engaged in virtuous practice. What He
means is something like this: "If the generality of men (15) knew when they were to
die, they would strive earnestly [only] at that hour."

1179

[82, 4]

Let us therefore in all respects put our faith in God and contradict Him in nothing,   10
even if what is said seems to be contrary to our reasonings and to what we see.   558
Let His word be of superior authority to reason and sight. This too be our practice in
respect to the Mysteries (16), not looking only upon what is laid out before us, but
taking heed also of His words. For His word cannot deceive; but our senses are easily
cheated. His word has never failed; our senses err most of the time.

When the word says, "This is My Body (17)," be convinced of it and believe it,   851
and look at it with the eyes of the mind. For Christ did not give us something tangible,   852
but even in His tangible things all is intellectual. So too with Baptism: the gift is   857
bestowed through what is a tangible thing, water; but what is accomplished is   790
intellectually perceived: the rebirth and the renewal. If you were incorporeal He
would have given you those incorporeal gifts naked; but since the soul is intertwined
with the body, He hands over to you in tangible things that which is perceived
intellectually. How many now say, "I wish I could see His shape, His appearance, His
garments, His sandals." Only look! You see Him! You touch Him! You eat Him!

1180

[82, 5]

Think how indignant you are against the traitor, against those who crucified Him.   875

Take care, then, lest you too become guilty of the Body and Blood of Christ. They slaughtered His most holy body; but you, after such great benefits, receive Him into a filthy soul. For it was not enough for Him to be made Man, to be struck and to be slaughtered, but He even mingles Himself with us; and this not by faith only, but even in every deed He makes us His Body (18). How very pure, then, ought he not be, who enjoys the benefit of this Sacrifice (19)?

878

1. τῆς ψήφου γίνεται κύριος: *i. e.* will have control over the sentence.
2. ἐν ἐξομολογήσει. Ps. 94 [95]:2 in the Septuagint reading.
3. πρὸ τῆς κυρίας. The word ἡμέρα is frequently omitted in this idiomatic expression, so that ἡ κυρία already means *the appointed day*.
4. καὶ διηνεκὴς εὐχαριστία.
5. καθ᾽ ἑκάστην . . . σύναξιν. The *sýnaxis* is the *communion assembly*.
6. εὐχαριστία = thanksgiving.
7. ἀνάμνησις = commemoration or remembrance.
8. εὐχαριστεῖν. That is to say, *they prepare us to eucharist*.
9. Matt. 12:31.
10. Matt. 18:7.
11. Luke 17:1.
12. Matt. 19:6.
13. Matt. 24:36.
14. See Matt. 24:44.
15. οἱ πολλοί.
16. ἐπὶ τῶν μυστηρίων. This might be translated *in respect to the Sacrament*. But however it be worded, it is clear that the Eucharist is meant.
17. Matt. 26:26.
18. Chrysostom does not mean the mystical body of Christ that is the Church. He means that in receiving Communion our bodies are nourished and take increase from Christ's Body, so that His Body becomes our body, and our body therefore is His Body.
19. ταύτης . . . τῆς θυσίας.

HOMILIES ON THE EPISTLE TO THE ROMANS [*ca. A. D.* 391]

Chrysostom's commentary on Paul's Epistle to the Romans is entirely extant in thirty-two homilies, and is generally regarded as the finest surviving patristic commentary on that book. In these homilies on Romans, moreover, we find Chrysostom at his most eloquent.

Internal evidence leaves no doubt that the *Homilies on the Epistle to the Romans* belong to Chrysostom's Antiochian period, between 381 and 398 A. D. It is probable, moreover, that they were preached soon after the series on the Gospel of John, about the year 391 A. D.

St. Augustine quotes rather extensively from the tenth homily on Romans to demonstrate that Chrysostom cannot successfully be accused of having held Pelagian views on original sin.

Besides the three volume edition of the *Homilies on the Gospel of Matthew*, published at Cambridge in 1839, Frederick Field produced also a seven volume edition of Chrysostom's homilies on the Epistles of Paul, published at Oxford between 1845 and 1862. While the Migne edition reprinted Field's text for the homilies on Matthew, it ignored Field's text for the homilies on the Pauline Epistles, reprinting as elsewhere the text of de Montfaucon.

The Migne text of the Homilies on the Gospel of Matthew is in PG 60. Field's text is preferable, and is found in his volume 1.

1181

[1, 3]

"Through whom we have received grace and Apostleship for obedience unto   104
faith (1)." . . . He does not say "for questioning and reasoning," but "for obedience."   557
We were not sent, he says, to argue, but to give what was entrusted into our hands.   558
For when the Master makes some declaration, those who hear are not to bluster about
and be meddlesome about what is told them; they have only to accept it. It was for
this reason that the Apostles were sent: to tell what they had heard, not to add to it
anything of their own; and that we, for our part, should believe.

1182

[3, 2]

From the beginning God placed the knowledge of Himself in men, but the pagans (2)   135
awarded this knowledge to sticks and stones, doing wrong to the truth to such extent as
they were able. For really, the truth remained unharmed, its own glory being
immutable. And how, O Paul, is it plain that God put this knowledge in them?
"Because," he says, "what can be known of Him is manifested in them (3)." But
this is assertion, not proof. Only reason it out for me, and show me that the knowledge
of God was evident to them, and that they willfully turned aside from it. Whence, then,   134
was it plain? Did He send them a voice from above? Of course not! But He did
something that was better able to draw them to Him than a voice: He put creation   131
in front of them so that the wise and the simple, the Scythian and the barbarian,
having learned by vision the beauty of what they saw, might mount up to God.

1183

[8, 8]

Reverence, therefore, reverence this table, of which we are all communicants! Christ,   890
slain for us, the Sacrificial Victim (4) who is placed thereon!   895

1184

[10, 1]

What does this mean, "Because all have sinned (5)?" In that fall even those who   614
did not eat of the tree,—all did from that transgression (6) become mortal. . . . For   611
[Adam's sin in Paradise] was productive of that death in which we all participate. . . .
From this it is clear that it was not this sin, the sin of transgressing the Law, that ruined
everything, but that sin of Adam's disobedience. What is the proof of this? The fact
that even before the Law, all died. "Death reigned," he says, "from Adam to Moses,
even over those who had not sinned (7)." How did it reign? "In the likeness of
the transgression of Adam, who is a type of Him who was to come (8)." This too is
why Adam is a type of Christ: . . . That when a Jew would say to you, "How by   386
the righteous action of this one Man, Christ, was the world saved?" you might be able
to answer him, "How by the wrong-doing of one man, Adam, was the world condemned?"

1185

[10, 2]

We have been freed from punishment, we have put off all wickedness, and we   385
have been reborn from above (9), and we have risen again, with the old man buried,   376
and we have been redeemed, and we have been sanctified, and we have been given
adoption into sonship, and we have been justified, and we have been made brothers

of the Only-begotten, and we have been constituted joint heirs and concorporeal with Him and have been perfected in His flesh, and have been united to Him as a body to its head. All of this Paul calls an "abundance of grace (10)," showing that what we have received is not just a medicine to counteract the wound, but even health and comeliness and honor and glory and dignities going far beyond what were natural to us. And each of these was able by itself to do away with death; but when all of them seem to run together at the same time, there is not a vestige of it left, nor a shadow of it to be seen, so completely has it disappeared. . . . Christ paid out much more than the debt we owed, as much more as the boundless sea exceeds a little drop. . . . "For just as by the disobedience of one man the many were made sinners, so too by the obedience of One, the many will be made just (11)." . . . . What does the word "sinners" mean here? It seems to me that it means liable to punishment and condemned to death.

740

614

1186

[13, 8]
  Anyone who has the Spirit does not only belong to Christ, but He has Christ Himself; for wherever one Person (12) of the Trinity is present, the whole Trinity is present. The Trinity is undivided in Itself, and is united in Itself most precisely.

753
283

1187

[14, 6]
  What is it that has saved you? Your hoping in God alone, and your having faith in Him in regard to what He promised and did give. Beyond this there is nothing that you have contributed. If, therefore, it was this [hope with faith] that saved you, hold fast to it even now. It is certain that what provided you with such great blessings will not deceive you about the things that are to come. Since it found you dead and ruined and a prisoner and an enemy, and made you a friend and a son and a freedman and righteous and a joint-heir, and provided such great benefits as no man ever expected, how, after such liberal generosity and establishment of friendship, could it disappoint you in the future? . . . . What then is hope? Confidence in things to come.

580
582
758

757
755
756

1188

[18, 5]
  "If salvation is by grace (13)," someone will say, "why is it that we are not all saved?" Because you did not will it; for grace, even though it be grace, saves the willing, not those who are not willing and who turn away from it and who constantly fight against it and oppose themselves to it.

695
700

1. Rom. 1:5.
2. οἱ Ἕλληνες.
3. Rom. 1:19.
4. τὸ θῦμα.
5. Rom. 5:12, and Chrysostom with it: ἐφ' ᾧ πάντες ἥμαρτον. It is often pointed out in modern commentaries and in some not so modern that ἐφ' ᾧ does not mean *in whom*, but *because*. Chrysostom knew Greek too, and he never supposed it meant anything except because. He still refers the passage to original sin, and understands by the clause "because all have sinned" that what is meant is "because all have sinned [in Adam]." It is not just that all have sinned in sequence after Adam, but all have sinned in consequence of Adam.
   The modern tendency exhibited by a few authors to exclude from Rom. 5:12 any notion of original sin's passing from Adam to all of mankind is too much. All will now admit, I suppose, that Rom. 5:12 says (1) that through one man, Adam, sin made its entry into the world; and that (2) death came in consequence of sin; and that (3) in view of the causal relationship of sin to death, death is the lot of all men, (4) because all have sinned. The question remains, then, how to

interpret the final clause, "because all have sinned." The tendency of some to understand this final clause as referring solely to personal sin makes useless verbiage of the rest of the passage. Are we to understand that Adam is introduced merely as a historical reference to the first man who sinned? The final clause clearly calls for the interpretation "because all have sinned *in Adam*." It need not exclude personal sin, but it must include original sin.

It is probable, however, that even without the line beginning ἐφ' ᾧ and with only the first three points of the four noted above, Chrysostom and the Fathers at large would have seen Rom. 5:12 as referring to original sin. The mention of sin causing death, and death being therefore the lot of all men were enough; for it must be admitted that the Fathers in general do not easily distinguish between original sin and its effects. Thus, for Chrysostom, the very fact that men do die, even without the "because all have sinned," would point to original sin. Something of this is seen in the concluding lines of § 1185, where Chrysostom says that when Paul declares, "For the disobedience of one man the many were made sinners," sinners is to be so interpreted that the statement means, "By the disobedience of one man the many were made liable to punishment and condemned to death."

6. ἐξ ἐκείνου may otherwise mean "from that man"—but whether it points to the transgression or to Adam as the transgressor, the import is the same.
7. Rom. 5:14a.
8. Rom. 5:14b.
9. John 3:3.
10. Rom. 5:17.
11. Rom. 5:19.
12. μία τῆς τριάδος ὑπόστασις.
13. Rom. 11:6.

HOMILIES ON THE FIRST EPISTLE TO THE CORINTHIANS [*ca. A. D.* 392]

Chrysostom's course of forty-four homilies on First Corinthians was composed at Antioch, probably about the year 392 A. D. At any rate the series has in *Hom*. 7, 2 a reference to his sermon course on Matthew, and in *Hom*. 27, 2 a reference to the series on John's Gospel; so the course on First Corinthians must be later than those other two, which are usually assigned to *ca*. A. D. 390 and *ca*. A. D. 391.

In addition to the connected series of forty-four homilies on First Corinthians there is a set of three homilies on 1 Cor. 7:1ff. in Migne, PG 51, 207-242. A homily on 1 Cor. 15:28 escaped the earlier editions and was first published by S. Haidacher in the *Zeitschrift für katholische Theologie*, Vol. 31 (1907), pp. 141-171.

The text of the forty-four *Homilies on the First Epistle to the Corinthians* may be found in Migne, PG 61, or preferably, in volume 2 of Frederick Field's seven volume Oxford edition of Chrysostom's homilies on the Pauline Epistles.

1189

[8, 1(2)]

It may be that rulers are wicked and defiled, while those whom they rule are worthy   804
and modest; that laymen live in piety, while priests live in wickedness; but if everywhere grace required worthiness, there could neither then be Baptism nor Body of Christ nor the sacrifice priests offer. But as it is, God is accustomed to operate even through the unworthy, and the grace of Baptism is in no way hindered by the priest's [manner of] life.

1190

[19, 3(4)]

"But if the unbeliever departs, let him depart (1)." In this instance the matter is   976
no longer fornication. But what does it mean when he says, "If the unbeliever departs?" For example, if he commands you to offer sacrifice and to share with him in his impiousness for the sake of your marriage, or to leave, it is better that your marriage and not your religion be torn asunder (2).

1191

[24, 1]

"God is faithful; and He will not permit you to be tempted beyond your strength (3)."   657
There are, therefore, temptations which we have not the strength to bear. And   695
what are these? All, so to speak! For the strength is in God's hands, which strength we
draw down by our will. And so that you might learn well that it is not only those which
exceed our strength that we cannot easily withstand without God's help but those too which
belong to our being human, he added: "But with the temptation He will also give you a way
out, that you may be able to bear it (4)."

1192

[24, 1(3)]

"The cup of blessing which we bless, is it not communion of the Blood of   849
Christ (5)?" Very trustworthily and awesomely does he say it. For what he is saying   851
is this: "What is in the cup is that which flowed from His side, and we partake of it."
He called it a cup of blessing because when we hold it in our hands that is how we
praise Him in song, wondering and astonished at His indescribable Gift, blessing
Him because of His having poured out this very Gift so that we might not remain in
error; and not only for His having poured It out, but also for His sharing It with all
of us. "If therefore you desire blood," He says, "do not redden the platform of
idols with the slaughter of dumb beasts, but My altar of sacrifice (6) with My Blood."   890
What is more awesome than this? What, pray tell, more tenderly loving?   895

1193

[24, 2(3)]

In ancient times, because men were very imperfect, God did not scorn to receive the   892
blood which they were offering to idols. He did this to draw them away from those
idols; and this very thing again was because of His indescribable, tender affection.
But now He has transferred the priestly action to what is most awesome and magnificent.   890
He has changed the sacrifice itself, and instead of the butchering of dumb beasts,   895
He commands the offering up of Himself.

1194

[24, 2(4)]

"Because the Bread is one, we, the many, are in one Body (7)." "Why do I say   878
'communion?'" he says; "for we are that very Body." What is the Bread? The   851
Body of Christ! What do they become who are partakers therein? The Body of
Christ! Not many bodies, but one Body. For just as the bread, consisting of many   880
grains, is made one, and the grains are no longer evident, but still exist, though their
distinction is not apparent in their conjunction; so too are we conjoined to each
other and to Christ. For you are not nourished by one Body while someone else is
nourished by another Body; rather, all are nourished by the same Body.

1195

[24, 4(7)]

When you see [the Body of Christ] lying on the altar (8), say to yourself, "Because   849
of this Body I am no longer earth and ash, no longer a prisoner, but free. Because of   851
this Body I hope for heaven, and I hope to receive the good things that are in heaven,
immortal life, the lot of the angels, familiar conversation with Christ (9). This Body,

scourged and crucified, has not been fetched by death. . . . This is that Body which
was blood-stained, which was pierced by a lance, and from which gushed forth those
saving fountains, one of blood and the other of water, for all the world.'' . . .
This is the Body which He gave us, both to hold in reserve (10) and to eat, which was
appropriate to intense love; for those whom we kiss with abandon we often even bite
with our teeth.

1196

[28, 1]
  [Paul] says, "Let each one examine himself (11)," and then approach [to receive   917
Communion]. He does not command that one is to be examined by another, but
each is to examine himself, making the courtroom secret (12) and the trial unwitnessed.

1197

[32, 3(6)]
  Here [Paul] speaks of the tongues of angels (13) not as attributing a body to the   483
angels. What he is saying is something like this: "Even if I should so speak as angels   487
are accustomed to discourse with each other, without [love] I would be nothing but a
burden and an annoyance." So too where in another place he says, "To Him every
knee shall bend, of those who are in heaven and of those who are on earth and of those
who are in the subterranean regions (14)." He does not say this by way of attributing
knees and bones to the angels, perish the thought, but he wants to intimate their
intense worship by a figure of what is familiar to us. So here too he did speak of a tongue,
not referring to an organ of flesh, but as desiring to suggest in a manner known to us
the familiar conversation that they have with each other.

1198

[38, 2(3)]
  How could Christ have died for sinners if He Himself were in sin? Anyone who   345
would die on behalf of sinners ought himself be without sin; because if he too does   374
commit sin, how shall he die for other sinners? And if Christ died for the sins
of others, He died without having been a sinner Himself.

1199

[40, 1(2)]
  I want to speak openly [about the rite of Baptism]; but I dare not, because of the   810
uninitiate. These latter make explanation more difficult for us, compelling us either not
to speak openly or else to tell them the things that are not to be told (15).

1200

[42, 3(5)]
  I cling to your knees as I beseech you and entreat you that so long as we have this   991
tenuous grasp on life (16) we might be sorely pricked by what has been said, that
we might be converted and become better persons; that we may not, like that rich
man (17), lament to no purpose when we have gone hence, and continue in incurable
lamentation. For even if you have a father, even if you have a son, even if you have a
friend, even if you have any person at all who has ready speech with God, none of
these shall ever save you when you have been condemned by your own works. That

courtroom is of such a kind that it judges by actions alone, and in that place there   995
is no other way to be saved. . . . For if we have been remiss no just man will assist
us, no Prophet, no Apostle, no one at all.

1. 1 Cor. 7:15.
2. βέλτιον διασπασθῆναι τὸν γάμον καὶ μὴ τὴν εὐσέβειαν.
3. 1 Cor. 10:13a.
4. 1 Cor. 10:13b.
5. 1 Cor. 10:16.
6. θυσιαστήριον.
7. 1 Cor. 10:17.
8. προκείμενον.
9. τὴν μετὰ χριστοῦ ὁμιλίαν.
10. κατέχειν. I have translated this *to keep in reserve*. Certainly it seems to mean more than just to hold or touch. The usual
    meanings of κατέχειν include *to hold back, to restrain, to bridle, to detain, to gain possession of, to stay, to tarry, to
    have in possession, to occupy, to confine, to cover, to seize, to afflict, to master, to understand, to be inspired, to urge,
    to embezzle*, etc. Retention is a prominent note of several of these meanings; so one suspects that in the present
    Eucharistic context it means not just to hold in one's hand, but to keep in reserve, or to reserve (for worship).
11. See 1 Cor. 11:28.
12. ἀδημοσίευτον.
13. 1 Cor. 13:1.
14. Phil. 2:10.
15. τὰ ἀπόρρητα.
16. τὸ μικρὸν τοῦτο τῆς ζωῆς ἐφόδιον. Here the μικρὸν ἐφόδιον or *meager support* is simply the *tenuous grasp* we have
    on (of) life. Yet the term ἐφόδιον, meaning *provisions for a journey*, already meant Eucharistic Viaticum in Canon 13 of
    First Nicaea. See § 651s above.
17. Luke 16:19ff.

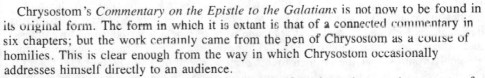

COMMENTARY ON THE EPISTLE TO THE GALATIANS [*inter A. D.* 393/397]

Chrysostom's *Commentary on the Epistle to the Galatians* is not now to be found in
its original form. The form in which it is extant is that of a connected commentary in
six chapters; but the work certainly came from the pen of Chrysostom as a course of
homilies. This is clear enough from the way in which Chrysostom occasionally
addresses himself directly to an audience.

When or by whom the work was given its present form is not known. As a course of
homilies it belongs to John's years at Antioch, that is, before 398 A. D., and after his
homilies on the Epistles to the Corinthians, that is, not before about 393 A. D.

The text of the *Commentary* is found in Migne, PG 61, 611-682; or better, in volume
4 of Frederick Field's Oxford edition.

1201

[2, 8]
We who were under sentence have been liberated by Christ; for all were dead, if   374
not in fact, at least by sentence. He delivered us when we were expecting the   380
blow. . . . The Sacrificial Victim was offered for all mankind (1), and was sufficient   386
to save all; but it is believers alone who enjoy the bounty thereof.

1. ὑπὲρ πάσης . . . τῆς φύσεως.

HOMILIES ON THE EPISTLE TO THE EPHESIANS [*inter A. D.* 392/397]

On the Epistle to the Ephesians Chrysostom composed a course of twenty-four homilies. Numerous points of internal evidence demonstrate clearly enough that the homilies on Ephesians belong to Chrysostom's Antiochian period. They can only be dated, however, as probably after 391 A. D. and certainly before 398 A. D.

The text of the *Homilies on the Epistle to the Ephesians* are found in Migne, PG 62, 9-176; generally a better text, however, is that of Frederick Field in volume 4 of the Oxford edition of 1845-1862.

1202

[1, 2]

"According to the good pleasure," [Paul] says, "of His will (1)," that is, because   200
of His earnestly willing it. This is as if one were to say, "His earnest desire." The
term "good pleasure" everywhere means the antecedent will (2); for there is also
another will. The first will, for example, is that those who have sinned should not   214
perish; but the second will is that those who have become wicked shall perish.
Certainly there is no necessity that He punish them; but He does will it. This same
thing is to be seen in Paul where he says, "I would that all men were even as
myself (3)"; and again, "I would that the younger [widows] marry, bear children (4)."
By "good pleasure," therefore, he means the first will, the earnest will, the will
in company with earnest desire, persuasion. . . . What he is saying is this: "He
earnestly longs for, He earnestly desires our salvation."

1203

[1, 3]

He that praises and marvels at the grace tendered himself will be the more   752
attentive and the more earnest. "With which He has made us full of grace (5),"   757
[Paul] says. He does not say, "With which he has favored (6) us, but "With which
He has made us full of grace." That is to say, He has not only delivered us from sins, but
has made us lovable (7). Just as if someone were to take a leper consumed by illness
and disease, and by age and poverty and hunger, and were to turn him suddenly into
a comely youth surpassing all men by his beauty, shedding a bright sunbeam from his
cheeks, yes, shaming the dazzling beams of the sun with the sparkle of his eyes;
and then were to set him down in the flower of his age, and on top of that, array him
in purple and a diadem and all the royal regalia. That is how God has decked out our
soul, how beautiful and desirable and lovable He has made it.

1204

[4, 2]

"For by grace," [Paul] says, "you have been saved (8)." But lest the greatness   656
of the benefits inflate you, see how he brings you down: "By grace you have been
saved," he says, "through faith." And then again, lest a violence be done free will (9),   700
after he has added what pertains to us he takes it away again when he says, "and that
not of ourselves (10)." The faith, he means, is not from ourselves; for if He had not   555
come, if He had not called, how should we be able to believe? "For how shall they
believe," [Paul] says, "unless they do hear (11)?" Thus the work of faith is not ours.
"It is the gift," he says, "of God (12)."

1. Eph. 1:5.
2. τὸ θέλημα . . . τὸ προηγούμενον.
3. 1 Cor. 7:7.
4. 1 Tim. 5:14.
5. ἐχαρίτωσεν ἡμᾶς. This is usually translated *He has favored us*, and certainly that is a correct translation; but Chrysostom chooses another possible meaning for his exegesis, and so must we: *He has made us graceful* or *has made us full of grace*. A participial form (κεχαριτωμένη) from the same verb (χαριτόω) as ἐχαρίτωσεν is found in the *Hail, full of grace* or *Hail, highly favored one* of Luke 1:28, and our familiar prayer which incorporates that passage: *Hail, Mary, [thou that hast been made] full of grace!*
6. ἐχαρίσατο, which is a form of the verb χαρίζομαι.
7. ἐπεράστους.
8. Eph. 2:8a.
9. τὸ αὐτεξούσιον.
10. Eph. 2:8b.
11. Rom. 10:14.
12. Eph. 2:8b.

HOMILIES ON THE EPISTLE TO THE PHILIPPIANS [*inter A. D.* 398/404]

Chrysostom Baur held, with no great success, that John's course of fifteen *Homilies on the Epistle to the Philippians* belongs to its author's Antiochian period. There is, however, quite sufficient internal evidence to assign it to the years of Chrysostom's episcopate, and therefore to his years in Constantinople, 398-404 A. D. Closer than that we dare not venture.

The text of the homily course on Philippians is found in Migne, PG 62, 177-298, and in volume 5 of Frederick Field's Oxford edition.

1205

[1, 1]

[In the greeting of the Epistle to the Philippians, Paul addresses himself:]   406
"To the co-bishops and deacons (1)." What does this mean? Were there plural   952
bishops of one city? Certainly not! It is the presbyters that [Paul] calls by this title;
for these titles were then interchangeable, and the bishop is even called a deacon. That is
why, when writing to Timothy, he says, "Fulfill your diaconate (2)," although
Timothy was then a bishop. That he was in fact a bishop is clear when Paul says   958
to him, "Lay hands on no man lightly (3)," and again, "Which was given you with   961
the laying on of hands of the presbytery (4)"; and presbyters would not have   953
ordained (5) a bishop.

1206

[3, 4]

Weep for the unbelievers! Weep for those who differ not a whit from them,   1030
those who go hence without illumination (6), without the seal (7)! These truly deserve   831
our lamentation, our tears. They are outside the royal city (8) with those who have
been found guilty, with the condemned. "Amen, I tell you, if anyone is not born of
water and the Spirit, he shall not enter into the kingdom of heaven (9)." Weep for
those who die in their wealth, and who with all their wealth prepared no consolation
for their own souls, who had the power to wash away their sins and did not will to
do it. . . . . Let us weep for them, let us assist them to the extant of our ability,   1001
let us think of some assistance for them, small as it may be, yet let us somehow

assist them. But how, and in what way? By praying for them and by entreating
others to pray for them, by constantly giving alms to the poor on their behalf. . . .

Not in vain was it decreed by the Apostles that in the awesome Mysteries   897
remembrance should be made of the departed. They knew that here there was much
gain for them, much benefit. For when the entire people stands with hands uplifted,
a priestly assembly (10), and that awesome sacrificial Victim is laid out, how, when
we are calling upon God, should we not succeed in their defense? But this is done for
those who have departed in the faith, while even the catechumens are not reckoned as
worthy of this consolation, but are deprived of every means of assistance except one.
And what is that? We may give alms to the poor on their behalf.

1. Phil 1:1. A fair number of New Testament manuscripts and late patristic works bear witness, as Chrysostom does, to the
    reading συνεπισκόποις where σὺν ἐπισκόποις is to be preferred. The first is *co-bishops*; the second *with [the]*
    bishops. On the textual evidence and in the light of history we must read in Paul *with the bishops*. But since it is
    Chrysostom and not Paul whom I am translating, I must take the word as Chrysostom saw it, and render it *co-bishops*.
    But knowing that the reading should be *with the bishops* does not at all annul the problem, for the term is, in any case, in
    the plural, and we have never known more than one bishop to a city. Perhaps Chrysostom's explanation deserves
    considerable more attention than it has ever been given.
2. 2 Tim. 4:5. διακονία = *diaconate* or *ministry*.
3. 1 Tim. 5:22.
4. 1 Tim. 4:14.
5. ἐχειροτόνησαν.
6. Illumination = Baptism. See St. Clement of Alexandria, § 407 with its pertinent note.
7. The seal, of course, is Confirmation; but it must not be argued that Chrysostom makes Confirmation a Sacrament
    necessary for salvation. For him Confirmation is inseparable from Baptism and is simply the crown on the baptismal rite.
8. βασιλείων. The term βασίλειον in the singular were the palace; but in plural it is the royal city.
9. John 3:5.
10. πλήρωμα ἱερατικόν.

HOMILIES ON THE SECOND EPISTLE TO TIMOTHY [*inter A. D.* 393/397]

Photius said that Chrysostom gave more eloquent sermons when he was a priest at
Antioch than he did later as Bishop of Constantinople. The remark is reasonable enough,
when we consider that cathedral preacher was his chief if not only assignment in
Antioch, whereas his many duties as Bishop of Constantinople would have prevented his
giving his preaching the same preparation that he could budget to it in Antioch.

Montfaucon had a tendency, because of Photius' remark, to fix all of Chrysostom's
more eloquent preaching at Antioch, and so too the ten *Homilies on the Second Epistle*
to Timothy.

Probably de Montfaucon's dating was correct in this instance, but for the wrong
reasons. Polished style alone is not sufficient for a proper dating of the homilies. But at
any rate, there is adequate enough evidence of the internal sort, and that apart from
style, to assign these homilies to Antioch, and therefore, before 398 A. D. Probably
they belong after 392 A. D., because the period through 392 is already rather well
accounted.

The text of the ten homilies is found in Migne, PG 62, 599-662, and in volume 6 of
Frederick Field's Oxford edition.

1207

[2, 4]

The oblation is the same even if some common person (1) offer it, even if Paul offer   866
it, even if Peter offer it. It is the same which Christ gave to His disciples, and which

now the priests do. The latter oblation is not inferior to the former, because it is not
men who sanctify even the latter, but the same [Christ] who sanctified the former.   896
For just as the words which God spoke are the same as those which now the   862
priest says, so too is the oblation the same, and the Baptism, as that which He gave.
Thus the whole is of faith. The Spirit immediately leaped upon Cornelius (2), because   656
Cornelius had previously done what was his part and had contributed his faith.

   This too, therefore, is His Body, as well as that. Anyone who thinks that the one   851
is inferior to the other does not know that Christ is present even now and that even
now He is working.

1. It is clear a few words further on that Chrysostom has no thought of the sacrifice being offered by anyone who is not
   a priest. His *common person* or *chance individual* is simply the ordinary unlauded parish priest. Such a priest's Mass
   is the same as that of St. Peter or St. Paul, and indeed, the same as that of Christ Himself; for Christ is the High Priest of
   every Mass.
2. Acts 10:44.

EXPLANATIONS OF THE PSALMS [*ca. A. D.* 396]

   A series of homilies on fifty-eight of the Psalms, 4-12, 43-49, 108-117, 119-150 in
the Vulgate numbering, has come down to us under the title *Explanations of the Psalms*.
Perhaps they were never preached; but they do represent Chrysostom at his best. Probably
they belong to his last years in Antioch and we cannot be far wrong in dating them to.
A. D. 396.
   It has often been said that these homilies or explanations are all that is left of a complete
commentary on the Psalms; but there is really no reason to suppose that the work was
ever any more extensive than it is in the form in which it is extant. There are, of course,
on other Psalm passages many other isolated homilies or fragments of homilies preserved
under Chrysostom's name, some genuine and some spurious.
   In his exegesis of the Psalms Chrysostom does not confine himself to the Septuagint
reading as he does in other Old Testament exegetical works, but refers often to the
Hebrew and Syriac, and to the Greek of Symmachus, Aquila, and Theodotion.
   The text of the *Explanations of the Psalms* is in Migne, PG 55.

                                    1208
[On Ps. 44: No. 2]
   "Grace is poured out upon Your lips (1)." Do you perceive that this statement is   341
about the Incarnation (2)? But what is this grace? That by which He teaches, that   388
by which He works miracles. Here grace means that which came into the flesh:
"He upon whom," it says, "you will see the Spirit descending like a dove and
abiding on Him, this is He who will baptize (3). For all grace is poured out in that
Temple (4); the Spirit does not give that Temple a measure only: "For of His
fullness have we received (5)." That Temple has received grace entire. . . . There
indeed is grace entire; the grace that is in men is small, but still it is a droplet from that
grace.

1. Ps. 44[45]:3.
2. περὶ τῆς οἰκονομίας. The *economy* or *divine plan* has come to mean, very baldly, Christ's Incarnation.
3. See John 1:33.
4. The Temple of which Chrysostom speaks is the incarnational Body of Christ, in which Godhead tabernacled.
5. John 1:16.

HOMILIES ON THE SECOND EPISTLE TO THE THESSALONIANS
[*inter A. D.* 398/404]

Besides eleven homilies on First Thessalonians Chrysostom wrote also a course of five homilies on Second Thessalonians. Both series belong to his episcopal years in Constantinople, between 398 and 404.

The text of the homilies on the two Epistles to the Thessalonians is found in Migne, PG 62, 391-500, and in volume 5 of Frederick Field's Oxford edition.

1213
[4, 2]

"Therefore, brethren, stand fast and hold the traditions which you have been   100
taught, whether by word or by our letter (1)." From this it is clear that they did not hand down everything by letter, but there was much also that was not written. Like that which was written, the unwritten too is worthy of belief. So let us regard the tradition of the Church also as worthy of belief. Is it a tradition? Seek no further.

1. 2 Thess. 2:15.

HOMILIES ON THE EPISTLE TO THE HEBREWS [*ca. A. D.* 403]

Chrysostom's series of thirty-four *Homilies on the Epistle to the Hebrews* belongs to his last years in Constantinople. It was published only after John's death, and from stenographic notes taken down by an Antiochian priest named Constantine.

The text of these homilies is not in a very reliable state. That in volume 7 of Frederick Field's Oxford edition is usually regarded as much superior to that of the earlier editions and to that in Migne, PG 63, 9-236.

1217
[3, 2(4)]

This is the office (1) of angels: to minister to God for our salvation. To do all for   492
the salvation of the brethren, therefore, is an angelic work; or rather, it is the work of Christ Himself: for He saves us as Master, they as servants.

1218
[5, 1(2)]

Neither is there any other cause of the Incarnation (2) except this alone: He saw   360
us bowed down to the ground, perishing, tyrannized by death; and He had mercy.   374
"To make reconciliation," [Paul] says, "for the sins of the people, so that He might be a merciful and faithful High Priest (3)." But what does "faithful" mean? True, able; for the only faithful High Priest is the Son, able to deliver from their sins those whose High Priest He is.

1219

[12, 3(5)]
　Everything depends upon God, but not so as to hinder our free will (4). "But if it   700
depends on God," someone will say, "why does He blame us?" That is why I said,   690
"not so as to hinder our free will." It depends upon us and upon Him. We first must
choose the good, and when we have chosen, then does He provide that which is
His part. He does not anticipate our choice, lest violence be done to our free will.
But when we have chosen, then great is the assistance He provides us. . . . Our part
is to chose beforehand and to will; God's part to perfect and to bring to an end. Since,   656
then, the greater part is God's, [Paul] speaks after the fashion of men and says that the
whole of it is God's. For an example of what I mean, we see a house well built,
and we say that it is all due to the architect; but certainly it is not all due to him, but
also to the workmen, the owner, . . . and many others. Yet, because the architect
contributed the greater part, we say that it is all his doing. . . .
　Even should you run, even should you strive earnestly, he says (5), do not suppose   650
that the good result is yours. For if you had not crucial help from above, all were in
vain. It is perfectly clear, however, that with that help you will achieve what you
earnestly strive for, so long as you also run, and so long as you will it.

1220

[16, 4(9)]
　It is not right to say, "I am not able"; for that is to accuse the Creator. If He make   652
us in disability and then command us, it were an accusation against Himself. [4(10)]   723
"How is it, then," someone will say, "that many are not able?" It is because they do
not will it. "Why do they not will it?" Because they are indolent. If all were willing,
all too would be able. . . . We have God working with us and acting in conjunction   690
with us. Let us but choose, let us apply ourselves to the task at hand, let us only be   695
serious about it, let us keep it in mind, and everything else will follow.

1221

[17, 2(4)]
　"So also was Christ offered once (6)." By whom was He offered? Quite evidently,   380
by Himself. Here [Paul] shows that Christ was not Priest only, but also Victim and   382
Sacrifice. Therein do we find the reason for the words *was offered*. "He was offered
once," [Paul] says, "to take away the sins of many (7)." Why does he say *of many*   386
and not *of all*? Because not all have believed. He did indeed die for all, for the
salvation of all, which was His part. . . . But He did not take away the sins of
all men, because they did not will it.

1222

[17, 3(6)]
　What then? Do we not offer daily? Yes, we offer, but making remembrance (8) .   890
of His death; and this remembrance is one and not many. How is it one and not many?   891
Because this Sacrifice is offered once, like that in the Holy of Holies. This Sacrifice   892
is a type of that, and this remembrance a type of that. We offer always the same,   895
not one sheep now and another tomorrow, but the same thing always. Thus there
is one Sacrifice. By this reasoning, since the Sacrifice is offered everywhere, are
there, then, a multiplicity of Christs? By no means! Christ is one everywhere. He is   859
complete here, complete there, one Body. And just as He is one Body and not
many though offered everywhere, so too is there one Sacrifice.

1223

[21, 2(4)]

"Faith is the substance (9) of things hoped for, the evidence of things that are not   560
seen. For in this the elders had testimony borne to them (10)." Wowee (11)! What   567
an expression he uses! He says, "evidence of things that are not seen!" It is usual to
speak of evidence in regard to things that are very plainly seen. Faith, he says, is the
seeing of things that are not plain. It brings the things that are not seen to the same
full assurance that is had with things that are seen. Neither is it possible to
disbelieve in things that are seen, nor again is it possible for there to be faith unless
one is as fully persuaded about things invisible as he is about things most clearly
seen.

Since the objects of hope seem to be unsubstantial (12), faith favors them with   582
substance (13); or rather, it does not so favor them, but it is their substance (14). For
example, the resurrection has not come, nor does it exist substantially (15), but hope makes
it subsist (16) in our soul. That is [what Paul means when he says] "the substance of things
hoped for."

1224

[28, 2(4)]

It was in [Christ's] power not to suffer, had He so willed. "For He did no sin, nor   350
was deceit found in His mouth (17)." So too He says in the Gospels, "The prince of   345
the world is coming, and he has nothing on Me (18)." If He had wished, therefore, He
need not have come to the cross. "I have the power," He says, "to lay down my soul, and I
have the power to take it up again (19)." If then, He that had no necessity of being
crucified was crucified for our sake, how much more, then, ought we bear all things nobly?

1. λειτουργία.
2. τῆς οἰκονομίας.
3. See Heb. 2:17.
4. αὐτεξούσιον.
5. See Rom. 9:16.
6. Heb. 9:28a.
7. Heb. 9:28b.
8. ἀνάμνησιν ποιούμενοι.
9. ὑπόστασις.
10. Heb. 11:1-2.
11. If Chrysostom had not said it, would I tell you he did? *Wow* and the intensive *wowee* are apparently a part of the
vocabulary of the (almost) universal human language, like *mama* and *papa*. The word Chrysostom uses is βαβαί,
transliterated *babaí*, and pronounced *vavéh*; and it is an exclamation indicative of curious and pleasant surprise. What
else can it be but *wow*! or *wowee*!?
12. ἀνυπόστατα.
13. ὑπόστασιν.
14. οὐσία.
15. οὐδέ ἐστιν ἐν ὑποστάσει.
16. ὑπίστησιν.
17. Is. 53:9 and 1 Peter 2:22.
18. John 14:30. Chrysostom quotes the second clause as καὶ οὐκ ἔχει ἐν ἐμοὶ οὐδέν. I suppose it means *he has nothing to
do with Me*, or *he has nothing to hold over Me*; but literally, it is *he has nothing on Me*.
19. John 10:18.

FRAGMENTS

As might be expected with a writer and preacher of such widespread popularity and
authority as Chrysostom, an enormous number of fragments of his writings and homilies

are found as quotations in other authors. I doubt that any satisfactory collection or catalogue of such fragments has ever been made; and in any case, large numbers of these fragments are to be found in still unpublished manuscripts in the oriental patristic languages. Often the source of the fragments can be identified; and again many times it cannot.

1228-1229

[For the fragments of one of Chrysostom's BAPTISMAL CATECHESES (HOMILIA AD NEOPHYTOS) *found in St. Augustine's* CONTRA IULIANUM 1, 6 *and given in Rouët de Journel as nos. 1228 and 1229, see above §§ 1145a and 1145b. The entire homily is extant, as noted above in the introduction to the* BAPTISMAL CATECHESES *where also my reason for taking the passages from Augustine's quoting of them is given.]*

1230

[A fragment in Photius (Migne, PG 103, 112) lists among the "crimes" charged to Chrysostom at the Synod of The Oak:]

Sixth, that he gave a license to sinners by teaching: "If you sin again, repent again; and as often as you sin, come to me and I will heal you (1)."   908

1. The charge has the ring of truth to it. But there could be no such charge, nor any basis for such, against a man who does not know that sins are confessed not just to God or to God alone but also to a priest. This passage should be of value in considering the statements of Chrysostom in §§ 1131, 1132, 1136, 1145, and 1169. See those places with their pertinent notes. For those who still prefer to believe that the practice of sacramental confession was foreign to Chrysostom, the anecdotes of Socrates and Sozomen at §§ 2163a-b below, telling of the abolition of the office of Presbyter Penitentiary and of sacramental confession in the time of Nectarius, Chrysostom's immediate predecessor at Constantinople, will explain why the practice could be foreign to Chrysostom.

APOSTOLIC CONSTITUTIONS [ca. A. D. 400]

The so-called *Apostolic Constitutions* or *Constitutions of the Holy Apostles by Clement* is an interesting work with a curious history. In eight books, it is, as Altaner notes, the largest extant collection of legislative and liturgical material of so early a date. The work pretends (6, 18, 11) to be of Apostolic origin, written out and sent around to all bishops and priests by St. Clement of Rome. In that respect it is a forgery of the grosser and more impious sort. Here the use of Clement's name is not merely a congenial literary device. It was done with deliberate intent to deceive.

The work may be divided into three parts, embracing books 1-6, book 7, and book 8. The first part, books 1 through 6, is a revision of a work called the *Didascalia of the Twelve Apostles*, which latter work originated in Syria in the period *ca.* A. D. 200-250. Mostly the *Apostolic Constitutions* in this part simply brings the *Didascalia* up to date on more recent legal and liturgical matters. For example the *Didascalia* prescribes fasting in Holy Week, whereas the *Constitutions* extends this to a Lent of forty days.

Part two, the whole of book 7, can be divided into two sections. Section one (ch. 1-32) is an enlargement and paraphrase of the *Didache*. Section two (ch. 33-49) is a collection of prayers of praise and thanksgiving (ch. 33-38); instruction on the teaching of catechumens and administration of baptism (ch. 39-45); a catalogue of the bishops consecrated by the Apostles (ch. 46), which list shows a knowledge of the *Pseudo-Clementines* and of Eusebius' *History of the Church*; and morning, evening, and meal prayers (ch. 47-49). The morning prayer in ch. 47 is the *Greater Doxology*, the

Gloria of the Roman Mass; and the meal prayer in ch. 49 is almost verbally identical to that in the pseudo-Athanasian *De virginitate* 12 (Migne, PG 28, 265).

The third and most valuable part of the work is the final book 8. In this there are three sections, the first dealing with charisms (ch. 1-2), the second with ordinations and blessings (ch. 3-26), and the third, with legal prescriptions (ch. 27-47), the final chapter 47 constituting what is generally treated as a separate work but which seems also to be the work of the Pseudo-Clement, the eighty-five so-called *Apostolic Canons* (§§ 1237-1239 below). Chapters 6-15 contain the entire so-called Clementine Liturgy, the oldest extant complete text of a Mass.

The work in its present form cannot be earlier than the year 341 A. D., because twenty of the eight-five *Apostolic Canons* are extracted bodily from the Canons of the Synod of Antioch of that year. It is probable that the work was put in its present form about the year 400 A. D.

Otto Bardenhewer was of a mind that the techniques, knowledge, doctrines and peculiarities of the Pseudo-Clement are such that we may with considerable probability identify him with the Pseudo-Ignatius who was responsible for the longer recension of the Ignatian Letters. However that may be, the Pseudo-Clement is probably from Syria, and he has Arian tendencies. His use of Clement's name is not a mere literary pleasantry, a participation in a genre that was never meant to deceive. Unlike so many other pseudepigraphers, he expected and intended to mislead his audience and did so deliberately. He continues his deception even into his canon of Scripture (see below, § 1239), where he includes two Epistles of Clement (one genuine and one so-called, both accounted for in volume one of the present work), as well as the very work he was fabricating, the *Apostolic Constitutions*.

Except for book 8, chapter 47, the so-called *Apostolic Canons*, the *Apostolic Constitutions* was condemned by the Quinisext Council of Constantinople, called the Council in Trullo or Trullanum (the Trullanum being a meeting hall in the Imperial Palace at Constantinople), in 692 A. D., as "falsified by heretics." The date of the Council in Trullo, incidentally, is usually chosen by historians as marking the end of the ancient period of Church History.

The text of the *Apostolic Constitutions* in Migne (PG 1) and Mansi (Vol. 1) is not at all reliable. The edition of F. X. Funk in his two volume *Didascalia et Constitutiones apostolorum*, Vol. 1 Paderborn 1905, is still standard.

1231

[3, 16, 1]

Appoint, [O Bishop], a female deacon (1) faithful and holy, for the ministerings of   957
women. For sometimes it is not possible to send a male deacon into certain houses of
women, because of unbelievers. Send a female deacon, because of the thoughts of the
petty. [2] A female deacon is of use to us also in many other situations. First of all,   954
in the baptizing (2) of women, a [male] deacon will touch only their forehead with
the holy oil, and afterwards the female deacon herself anoints them; for it is not
necessary for the women to be gazed upon by men.

1232

[5, 7, 19]

God created man when the latter did not yet exist, from different elements (3),   509
giving Him his soul from what did not exist. Now He will restore for souls already   506
existing their bodies that have been dissolved. For the resurrection is of those who   1011
lie dead, not of the not existing. [20] He created the first bodies from things not existing
and fashioned them from their different elements; here, however, He raises up the dead,

giving them life. He forms man in the womb from a little seed, and in him He fashions
the soul that did not exist. . . . So too He raises up from the dead all men even as
He caused them to exist.

1012

1233

[7, 22, 2]

First you will anoint with holy oil (4), then you will baptize with water, and
finally you will seal with myron (5), so that the chrism (6) may be a partaking of the
Holy Spirit, the water a symbol of death, and the myron a seal of the articles of
agreement (7).

840
798
898

1234

[8, 5, 7: *Invocation in the Ordination of Bishops*]

Grant to him, almighty Master, through Your Christ, possession (8) of the Holy
Spirit, so that he may have, according to Your mandate, the power to remit sins,
to confer orders (9) according to Your precept, and to dissolve every bond, according
to the power which You gave to Your Apostles.

900
960
440

1235

[8, 27, 2]

A bishop is to be ordained by three bishops or two; and if anyone be ordained by
one bishop, he and the one ordaining are to be deposed. [3] But if necessity compel him
to be ordained by one bishop because of the inability, there being persecution or
some other such cause, of more than one to be present, let the vote of several
bishops be taken in reference to ordaining.

961

1236

[8, 28, 2]

A bishop gives the blessing, he does not receive it. He imposes hands, he ordains,
he offers the Sacrifice (10). He receives a blessing from bishops, but never from
presbyters. He deposes every cleric deserving of deposition, except a bishop, whom
alone he cannot depose. [3] A presbyter gives the blessing, he does not receive it;
he receives a blessing from a bishop and from a fellow-presbyter, and he likewise
gives it to a fellow-presbyter. He imposes hands; he does not ordain; he does not
depose, but he excommunicates (11) underlings if they are deserving of such
penalty. [4] A deacon does not bless. He does not bestow blessing, but he receives
it from bishop and presbyter. He does not baptize; he does not offer the Sacrifice.
When a bishop or a presbyter offers the Sacrifice, he distributes to the laity, not as
a priest, but as one who is ministering to priests (12). [5] The other clerics are never
permitted to do the work of the deacon. [6] A deaconess (13) does not bless, but
neither does she perform anything else that is done by presbyters and deacons; but
she guards the doors, and greatly assists (14) the presbyters, for the sake of decorum,
when they are baptizing women. [7] A deacon excommunicates a subdeacon, a
lector, a cantor, and a deaconess, if there be necessity of such action and there be
no presbyter present. [8] A subdeacon (15) is not permitted to excommunicate,
and certainly it is not permitted to a lector, nor a cantor, nor a deaconess, to
excommunicate, whether cleric or layman; for they are the inferiors of deacons (16).

952
953
792
960
965

954
828
868

956
957

955
956

951

1. The word form used here and throughout the present passage for deaconess is ἡ διάκονος, simply the word deacon made feminine by the feminine form of the article. This is the same form that St. Paul uses in respect to Phoebe, the διάκονος of the Church at Cenchrae, in Rom. 16:1, where I am in doubt as to whether it should be translated *deaconess* or *servant*. Other passages in the present work know the term διακόνισσα.
2. φωτίζεσθαι.
3. ἐκ διαφόρων.
4. ἐλαίῳ ἁγίῳ. This indicates olive oil, τὸ ἔλαιον.
5. μύρῳ. The term τὸ μύρον indicates a sweet smelling oil, in Church usage largely a mixture of olive oil and balsam (balm), still called myron in the Eastern Church but answering to chrism in the West.
6. χρῖσμα was, in classical usage, a thicker ungent than myron; but here it is obviously synonymous with ἔλαιον, the (holy) oil. Probably we would do no wrong in the present instance were we to translate χρῖσμα as chrismation.
7. σφραγὶς τῶν συνθηκῶν.
8. τὴν μετουσίαν also means *participation* and *communion*.
9. διδόναι κλήρους.
10. χειροθετεῖ, χειροτονεῖ, προσφέρει.
11. ἀφορίζει.
12. ὡς διακονούμενος ἱερεῦσιν. As one who is *deaconing* to priests, if you will: as one who assists the priests by his service.
13. διακόνισσα.
14. καὶ ἐξυπηρετεῖσθαι.
15. ὑποδιάκονον.
16. ὑπερέται γάρ εἰσιν διακόνων. The implication is that they are assistants to deacons.

APOSTOLIC CANONS [*ca. A. D.* 400]

This work constitutes the forty-seventh chapter of book eight of the so-called *Apostolic Constitutions*, treated immediately above.

Apparently the Pseudo-Clement of the *Apostolic Constitutions* is responsible also for this collection of *Apostolic Canons*, which he compiled and appended to the former work. The *Apostolic Canons* deal mostly with the ordination, duties, and conduct of the clergy, and in form they resemble conciliar canons of the period. In fact the first twenty of the eighty-five *Apostolic Canons* are taken almost verbatim from the canons of the Council of Antioch of 341.

Canon 85 of the *Apostolic Canons* is a list of the canonical books of Scripture. It includes in the Old Testament canon some but not all of the deuterocanonical Scriptures; and of Maccabees it specifies three books. The New Testament canon omits the Apocalypse, which is not surprising in a Syrian canon of this period. The author of the work pretends that this list of canons, along with the constitutions, is of Apostolic authority, and that it is being written down by Clement, who then sent it around to all the bishops and priests of the world. So it is not surprising either that he includes in his New Testament canon the *Letter of Clement to the Corinthians*, and the so-called *Second Letter of Clement to the Corinthians*; but in addition to these he has even the amazing gall to add also the "*Constitutions* addressed to you bishops by me, Clement, in eight books." The Acts of the Apostles, moreover, he designates the "Acts of Us Apostles."

As noted with the *Apostolic Constitutions*, of which the *Apostolic Canons* forms a part, the text tradition in Mansi is not at all reliable. And Migne, while he prints a poor text of the *Constitutions*, does not have the *Canons* at all. F. X. Funk's text in Volume 1 of his *Didascalia et Constitutiones apostolorum*, Paderborn 1905, is still regarded as standard.

1237

[1]
A bishop is to be ordained by two or three bishops, a presbyter by one bishop, as also a deacon and the rest of the clerics.
                                                                                                                        961
                                                                                                                        960

1238

[39]
The presbyters and the deacons are to perform no ministerial action without the   953
permission (1) of the bishop; for it is he to whom the people of the Lord have been
committed and from whom an accounting for their souls will be demanded.

1239

[85]
The books to be held in reverence and regarded as holy by all of you, clergy and   41
laity, are, of the Old Testament: Five of Moses, Genesis, Exodus, Leviticus, Numbers,
Deuteronomy; one of Jesus, son of Nave; one of Judges; one of Ruth; four of Kingdoms;
two of Chronicles of the Book of Days; two of Esdras; one of Esther; three of Maccabees;
one of Job; one Psalter; three of Solomon, Proverbs, Ecclesiastes, and the Canticle of
Canticles. Of the Twelve Prophets, one book. One of Isaias, one of Jeremias, one of
Ezechiel, one of Daniel. Apart from these, you ought to teach your children the Wisdom of
the most learned Sirach.
In ours, that is, the New Testament, there are four Gospels: Matthew, Mark, Luke,   42
and John; fourteen Epistles of Paul, two Epistles of Peter, three of John, one of
James, one of Jude. Two Epistles of Clement; and the *Constitutions* in eight books
addressed to you bishops through me, Clement, which are not to be divulged to   810
all because of the secret things in them; and the Acts of us Apostles.

1. ἄνευ γνώμης. It is difficult to distinguish in this concept *without the knowledge, against the will,* and *contrary to the
   mind,* any one of which is probably a better *translation* than *without the permission*; but *without the permission,* after all,
   is really what is meant.

THE SACRAMENTARY OF SERAPION [*ca. A. D.* 350]

Serapion, Bishop of Thmuis in Egypt, was previously mentioned in volume one of the
present work, at page 334, in connexion with letters addressed to him about the year
360 A. D. by Athanasius of Alexandria.
An eleventh century manuscript discovered in the Mount Athos laura by A.
Dimitrijewsky constitutes the unique example of a *Euchologion* (Sacramentary or
Missal) ascribed to Serapion of Thmuis. This *Euchologion*, in Greek, consists of some
thirty prayers. It is certainly of Egyptian origin, and dates from about the year 350 A. D.,
with an earlier date to be preferred to a later one. Of its thirty prayers the first and
the fifteenth are ascribed specifically in their headings to Serapion; and the rest, in view
of their style and content, are certainly by the same author. Eighteen of the thirty prayers
are of a Eucharistic character, seven concern Baptism and Confirmation, three are for
ordinations, one is for the blessing of the holy oils, and one is for funerals.
An appended *Letter concerning Father and Son* is not in Serapion's style as witnessed
by the *Euchologion* and by his treatise *Against the Manicheans.* The *Letter* is a
somewhat clumsy defense of Nicene doctrine.
The Liturgy or Mass represented in the *Euchologion* has much in common with the
so-called Liturgy of St. Mark; but it also exhibits numerous peculiarities attributable to
Serapion. A prayer for the union of the Church, drawn from the *Didache* 9, 4 (§ 6) is
interposed between the consecration of the Bread and that of the Wine; there is an
epiclesis calling down the Logos upon the species; and there seems in all to be no
inconsiderable influence of Gnosticism upon the Liturgy.
The text of the *Euchologion* was first published by its discoverer, A. Dimitrijewsky,

Ein Euchologium aus dem 4. Jahrhundert verfasst von Sarapion, Bischof von Thmuis, Kiev 1894. Unaware of this edition, G. Wobbermin published the text again in 1898 in the series *Texte und Untersuchungen*, vol. 18, part 3b. F. E. Brightman restored the prayers to their proper sequence in his edition, published serially in the *Journal of Theological Studies*, London, Vol. 1 (1900), pp. 88-113 and 247-277. Johannes Quasten's edition in his *Monumenta eucharistica et liturgica vetustissima*, volume 7 in the series *Florilegium patristicum*, Bonn 1935, pp. 48-67, is solely of the Eucharistic prayers. The edition of F. X. Funk in his *Didascalia et Constitutiones apostolorum*, Vol. 2, Paderborn 1905, pp. 158-195, is generally regarded as the standard text.

ANAPHORA or PRAYER OF THE EUCHARISTIC SACRIFICE

1239a

[13, 1]

It is right and proper to praise, laud, and glorify You, the Father increate (1) of   250
the Only-begotten Jesus Christ. We praise You, God increate, who are unsearchable,   251
indescribable, inconceivable by any created being (2). We praise You, who are   173
known by the Only-begotten Son, You that are proclaimed, explained, and made known by
Him to created nature (3). We praise You who know the Son and reveal (4) to the saints
His glory; You who are known through Your begotten Word and are seen and are described
to the saints. We praise You, Father invisible, Bestower of immortality.

[2] You are the Fount of life, the Fount of light, the Fount of all grace and of all
truth (5), lover of mankind and lover of the poor, who are reconciled to all and who
draw all to Yourself (6) through the sojourning of Your beloved Son. Let us pray:
Make us living men; give us the Spirit of Light, that we may know You as the One
who is true, and Him whom You have sent, Jesus Christ (7). Give us Your Holy   290
Spirit, so that we may be able to proclaim and explain Your indescribable mysteries.
May the Lord Jesus and the Holy Spirit be on our lips and may You be lauded by us.

[3] For You are above every Principality and Power and Virtue and Domination
and every Name that is named not only in the present age but in that to come (8).   488
Assisting You are thousands of thousands and myriads of myriads (9) of Angels,
Archangels, Thrones, Dominations, Principalities and Powers (10). Assisting You
are two most honored six-winged Seraphim, with two wings covering their face, with
two their feet, and flying with two (11), the while they cry "Holy!" Accept therewith
our hallowing too, as we say, "Holy, holy, holy Lord Sabaoth (12), heaven and
earth is full of Your glory (13)." Heaven is full, and full is the earth, with Your
magnificent glory, Lord of Virtues (14). Full also is this Sacrifice, with Your strength   890
and Your communion (15); for to You we offer this living Sacrifice (16), this unbloody   891
oblation.

[4] To You we offer this bread, the likeness (17) of the Body of the Only-begotten.   853
This bread is the likeness of His holy Body because the Lord Jesus Christ, on the
night on which He was betrayed, took bread and broke and gave to His disciples,
saying, "Take and eat, this is My Body, which is being broken for you (18),   852
unto the remission of sins." On this account too do we offer the Bread, to bring
ourselves into the likeness of His death (19); and we pray: Reconcile us all, O God
of truth, and be gracious to us. And just as this Bread was scattered over the   880
mountains and when collected was made one, so too gather Your holy Church   420
from every nation and every country and every city and village and house and make
it one living Catholic Church (20).

We offer also the cup, the likeness of His Blood, because the Lord Jesus Christ
took the cup after He had eaten, and He said to His disciples, "Take, drink, this is

the new covenant, which is My Blood which is being poured out for you unto the
remission of sins (21).'' For this reason too we offer the chalice, to benefit ourselves
by the likeness of His Blood. O God of truth, may Your Holy Logos come upon this
Bread, that the Bread may become the Body of the Logos, and on this Cup, that
the Cup may become the Blood of the Truth. And make all who communicate
receive the remedy of life, to cure every illness and to strengthen every progress and
virtue; not unto condemnation, O God of truth, nor unto disgrace and reproach!

[5] For we invoke (22) You, the Increate, through Your Only-begotten in the   897
Holy Spirit. Be merciful to this people, let it be deserving of progress, let the angels   480
be present among the people, sent for the destruction of evil and for the security of   492
Your Church. We beseech You also on behalf of all the departed, of whom also this is
the commemoration (23):—*after the mentioning of their names*:—Sanctify these souls,
for You know them all; sanctify all who have fallen asleep in the Lord (24) and   1001
count them all among the ranks of Your saints and give them a place and abode
(25) in Your kingdom. Accept also the thanksgiving of Your people (26) and bless
those who offer the oblations and the Thanksgivings (27), and bestow health and
integrity and festivity and every progress of soul and body on the whole of this
Your people through Your Only-begotten Jesus Christ in the Holy Spirit, as it was
and is and will be in generations of generations and unto the whole expanse of the
ages of ages. Amen.

PRAYER OVER THE CHRISM WITH WHICH THE BAPTIZED ARE ANOINTED

1240

[25, 1]
God of powers, aid of every soul that turns to You and comes under Your   840
powerful hand in Your Only-begotten, we beseech You, that through Your divine   841
and invisible power of our Lord and Savior Jesus Christ, You may effect in this
chrism a divine and heavenly operation, [2] so that those baptized and anointed in   125
the tracing with it of the sign of the saving cross of the Only-begotten, through
which cross Satan and every adverse power is turned aside and conquered, as if
reborn and renewed through the bath of regeneration, may be made participants in   836
the gift of the Holy Spirit, and confirmed (28) by this seal, may remain firm and   846
immovable (29), unharmed and inviolate. . . .   798

PRAYER OVER THE OIL OF THE SICK OR OVER BREAD OR OVER WATER

1241

[29, 1]
We beseech You, Savior of all men, You that have all virtue and power, Father   940
of our Lord and Savior Jesus Christ, and we pray that You send from
heaven the healing power of the Only-begotten upon this oil, so that for those
(who are anointed *or* who partake of these creatures of Yours), it may be effective   811
for the casting out of every disease and every bodily infirmity (30), for an antidote
against every demon, for escape from every unclean spirit, for the expulsion of
every evil spirit, for the banishing of every fever and chill and every weakness, for
good grace and remission of sins, for a remedy unto life and deliverance, for health
and integrity of soul, of body, and of spirit (31), for perfect vigor.   504

1. ἀγένητος. I suspect that ἀγένητος (increate) should be read ἀγέννητος (unbegotten).
2. πάσῃ γενητῇ ὑποστάσει.
3. τῇ γενητῇ φύσει.
4. See Matt. 10:27 and Luke 10:22, where, however, it is the Son who gives the revelation, seemingly about the Father. This passage of Scripture is quoted in antiquity in many confused and confusing ways.
5. See John 1:14.
6. See John 12:32.
7. See John 17:3.
8. Eph. 1:21.
9. See Deut. 17:10 in the Septuagint version.
10. Col. 1:16.
11. Is. 6:2.
12. See note 123 on page 370 of Vol. 1 of the present work.
13. Is. 6:3.
14. See 2 Peter 1:17. Dependence here, however, is dubious.
15. τῆς σῆς μεταλήψεως.
16. See Rom. 12:1.
17. τὸ ὁμοίωμα.
18. 1 Cor. 11:23-24.
19. Rom. 6:5.
20. See the *Didache* 9, 4 (§ 6 above).
21. 1 Cor. 11:25 and Matt. 26:27-28.
22. ἐπεκαλεσάμεθα.
23. ἡ ἀνάμνησις.
24. Apoc. 14:13.
25. John 14:2.
26. That is, receive their Eucharisting: δέξαι δὲ καὶ τὴν εὐχαριστίαν τοῦ λαοῦ.
27. That is, those who are the celebrants of the Eucharist: καὶ εὐλόγησον τοὺς προσενεγκόντας τὰ πρόσφορα καὶ τὰς εὐχαριστίας.
28. ἀσφαλισθέντες.
29. 1 Cor. 15:58.
30. Matt. 4:23; 9:35; 10:1.
31. ψυχῆς, σώματος, πνεύματος reflects the trichotomy, the threefold division of man: body, soul and spirit.

GNOSTIC WRITINGS [*saec*. 2⁰/7⁰]

Gnosticism in general is a religious philosophy, or more accurately, an uncountable number of religious philosophies; and again in general, the common element found in all the various religious philosophies which pass as Gnosticism is the pretense to a hidden and esoteric knowledge, to secret revelation. No precise definition of Gnosticism can be given because Gnosticism is a term broadly applied not to a single system but to a very large number of esoteric religious philosophies.

In its broader sense Gnosticism includes in its family pagan Hermeticism and the Hermetic writings; the anti-Christian and anti-Jewish Mandaeism of Iraq, which pretends to have John the Baptist for its founder; Manicheism, which seems to be an agglomerate drawing upon Christianity, the Iranian religions, perhaps even Buddhism, and whose founder Mani or Manes was crucified in Persia in 273 A. D.; and even certain movements originating in Judaism.

In its narrower sense, with which we are concerned, Gnosticism, the so-called Christian Gnosticism, embraces again an uncounted number of pseudo-Christian sects dating from the second century to the seventh, and sometimes with remote origins in pre-Christian times. The term Gnosticism was first applied to these sects by the Fathers and Writers of the second and third century.

Until comparatively modern times we had little knowledge of Gnosticism except that which could be gleaned from the Christian opponents of Gnosticism, especially St. Irenaeus in his *Adversus haereses* and the other authors of similar works. It is always somewhat dangerous and suspect at best to judge any movement solely by the remarks and descriptions of its opponents. Original Gnostic writings began to come to light, however, in the latter part of the eighteenth century; and with the publication of a few Gnostic works at the end of the nineteenth century, it became evident that the Fathers had not been too severe at all in their judgments.

In 1946 a whole library of Gnostic works was found at Chenoboskion, the modern Nag-Hammadi. The Chenoboskion find consists of thirteen codices containing fifty-one works; and not all of the Chenoboskion writings have been published even now.

The Fathers regarded Gnosticism in the various forms in which they encountered it as Christian heresy or heresies. With the publication about a century ago of actual Gnostic writings, it has been made clear that the Fathers dignified Gnosticism too much by regarding it even as Christian heresy. Gnosticism in its various forms is for the most part, and except perhaps for some of its milder forms, not Christian heresy at all, but an utterly alien religious philosophy managing to pass itself off as Christian by simply drawing somewhat upon Christian terminology, disguising itself with an overlay of "Christian" words.

How empty of any real Christianity Gnostic systems can be will be evident in the case of those Gnostics whose writings included the fantastic *Books of Ieou* and the *Pistis Sophia*, selections from which are given below.

THE FIRST BOOK OF IEOU: THE BOOK OF THE GREAT WORD OF MYSTERY [*saec.* 3⁰]

Among the manuscripts collected in Egypt by the celebrated Scottish explorer James Bruce is one which he discovered in 1769 and which passed into the possession of the Bodleian Library at Oxford in 1842, where it is now known simply as Bruce Codex 96 or the Codex Brucianus.

The Bruce Codex contains three works, all in a somewhat fragmentary condition: the first and second *Books of Ieou*, referred to in the *Pistis Sophia*; and an anonymous treatise, probably of a Sethian sect.

The language of the *Books of Ieou* is the Sahidic dialect of Coptic, showing some influence also of the Subachmimic dialect. It is generally presumed that the *Books of Ieou* are translations into Coptic from a lost Greek original; but I think there is no real evidence for such an assumption except for the presence of the usual mishmash of Greek loan words; and that might be accounted for in other ways.

The German translation of the whole content of the Bruce Codex, with the Greek loan words clearly indicated, the work of Carl Schmidt and Walter Till, is found in the Berlin Corpus, *Die griechischen christlichen Schriftsteller der ersten Jahrhunderte*, Vol. 45 (13), subseries *Koptisch-gnostische Schriften*, Vol. 1, 3rd edition, Berlin 1962. It is from this very literal German edition in comparison with the old but latest and standard edition of the Coptic text in Carl Schmidt's *Gnostische Schriften in koptischer Sprache aus dem Codex Brucianus*, in the series *Texte und Untersuchungen*, Vol. 8, Leipzig 1892, that I have translated the following selections.

1241a

[1]

This is the book of the recognitions of the invisible God, recognitions by means of   68
the hidden mysteries which, for the elect generation, point out the way to refreshment in
the life of the Father; to the arrival of the Savior, the Redeemer of souls who will accept for
themselves the word of life which is higher than all life; to the knowledge of Jesus, the one
who lives, who, through the Father, has come forth from the light-eon into the perfection

of the Pleroma; to the teaching besides which there is none other, which Jesus, the one who lives, taught His Apostles when He said: "This is the teaching in which all knowledge dwells."

Jesus, the one who lives, began to speak to His Apostles: "Blessed is he that has crucified the world and has not allowed the world to crucify him."

The Apostles answered in one voice and said: "Lord, teach us how to crucify the world so that it cannot crucify us, causing us to perish and lose our lives."

Jesus, the one who lives, answered and said, "He that has crucified the world is the same that has found My word and has carried it out in accord with the will of Him who sent Me."

[2] The Apostles answered and said: "Speak to us, Lord, so that we might hear You. We have followed You with all our heart, we have left father and mother, we have left vineyards and fields, we have left possessions, we have left the majesty of the king and have followed You, so that You might teach us the life of Your Father who sent You."

Jesus, the one who lives, answered and said: "The life of My Father is this: that from the generation of the mind you take your soul and it stops being earthly and becomes rational through that which I tell you in the metaphor of My word, so that you may fulfill it and be saved from the Archon of this Eon and his snares, which have no end. You, however, are My disciples; hasten, then, to take My word carefully to yourselves so that you may know it, so that the Archon of this Eon, the same who found nothing subject to his command in Me, will be unable to contend with you, and so that you yourselves, O My Apostles, may fulfill My word in respect to Me, that I Myself may make you free, and that you may be saved by a freedom in which there is no blemish. Just as the Spirit of the Paraclete is safe, so too will you be made safe through the freedom of the Spirit of the Holy Paraclete."

1241b

[4]

Jesus, the one who lives, answered and said: "Everyone who wears My virginity   68
and My [. . .] and My garment without having understood Me and without having known Me, since he is blaspheming My name, I have [let him go to] ruin; and he has become again an earthly child because he has not known My word accurately, the word which the Father has spoken so that I myself might teach it to those who will know Me in the perfection of the Pleroma of Him who sent Me."

The Apostles answered and said: "O Lord Jesus, You that are the one who lives, teach us perfection and it will be enough for us."

And He said: "The word that I Myself give you [. . . MAJOR LACUNA . . .].

[5] He emanated Him, being of this stamp (1):

This is the True God. In this stamp He will set Him up as head; He will be called Ieou. Afterwards My Father will move Him to bring forth other emanations, so that they may fill up these places. This is His name in regard to the treasures which are outside of here. He will be called by this name, Ioeiaôthôuikhôlmiô, which means True God. He will set Him up in this stamp as head over the treasures which are outside of here. This is the stamp of the treasures over which He will set Him as head; and this is the way the treasures are emanated, since He is their head. This is the stamp in which He really is, before He was moved to bring forth emanations (2):

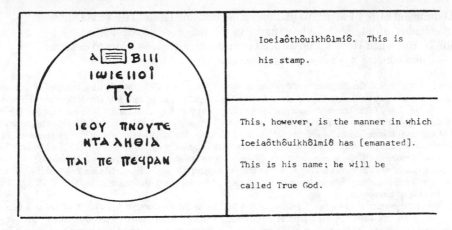

Ioeiaôthôuikhôlmiô. This is

his stamp.

This, however, is the manner in which

Ioeiaôthôuikhôlmiô has [emanated].

This is his name; he will be

called True God.

Afterwards He is called Ieou because He will be Father of a host of emanations, and at My Father's command, a host of emanations will come forth from Him; and they themselves will become fathers of treasures. I want to set a host over them as heads; and they will be called Ieou. The True God, nevertheless, since He is an emanation of My Father, will become Father of all Ieou's which the True God will emanate at the command of My Father. He that will be head over them will move them; a host of emanations will come forth from all Ieou's at the command of My Father, when He will move them; and they will fill up all treasures and will be called orders of the light-treasures. Myriads of myriads will originate from them.

This, now, is the stamp in which the True God is found, when He will be set up as head over the treasures and before He has brought forth emanations, because My Father has not yet moved Him to emanate and to bring forth. This is His stamp which just now I have discussed.

On the other hand, this is His stamp when He will bring forth emanations. This is the stamp of the True God, as He really is:

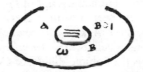

The three strokes which are there are the voices which, when He is commanded, He will emit from Himself to praise the Father, so that He may Himself bring forth emanations and may Himself emanate.

This is His stamp, as He is:

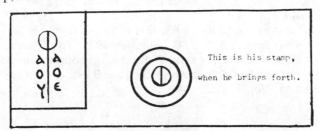

This is his stamp,

when he brings forth.

Thus is the True God found, when He will emanate emanations, when He is moved by My Father, by the command of My Father, to bring forth emanations and set them up as heads over the treasures. There will come forth from them a host, and they will fill up all treasures at the command of My Father, so that they may become Gods. The True God will be called Ieou the Father of all Ieou's, whose name in the language of My Father is Ioeiaôthôuikhôlmiô. But when He is set up as head over the treasures, in order to emanate them, his stamp is this which I have just now discussed.

1. There are apparently ten letters in the diagram of the stamp or *tupos*, one of which is entirely illegible, and several of which are uncertain. Numbering the letters from 1 to 10 from left to right, it can be said that five letters are perfectly clear: 1 = *Hori*, 3 = *He*, 7 = *TI* (the standard monogram), 8 = *Tau*, and 9 = *Kappa*. 2 cannot be read at all; but since it stands directly before a *He*, it can only be a vowel (if this is intended as a word, and if the rules of Coptic orthography are followed!); and of the several possibilities, a simple mathematical likelihood belongs to *Ou*, which is most frequent before *He*. 6 is undoubtedly an O, and probably *Ô*, I think, rather than *Ou*. 4 is possibly a *Kappa* turned 180°. 5 might be a *Shai* turned 90°; but I think it more likely that it represents a monogram (not standard to Coptic in any of its dialects) of *Ei* and *Iota*; for though not standard to Coptic, something very like this is frequent enough in ligatured Greek. 10, if it is the left half of a *Hêta*, may be a *spiritus asper*. My inclination, then is to read the legend of the stamp as *HOUKEiOTiTKH*. I will leave to another the task of interpreting it.
2. As to the inscription in the stamp, the first two lines apparently belong to the mystery; at any rate, they are still such to me. I take the *Tu* just above the center of the stamp as abbreviating the term *tupos*, which I translate *stamp*, though it might as easily be translated *type*. The inscription in the lower half of the stamp is standard Coptic, and reads *Ieou pnoute ñtalêthia pai pe pefran* and is to be translated: *Ieou, the True God, this is His name*.

PISTIS SOPHIA or THE FAITH WISDOM [saec. 3⁰]

The work called *Tpistis sophia*, which is to be translated *The Faith Wisdom* or perhaps *The Faithful Wisdom*, has sometimes been classified as an apocryphal gospel—*The Gospel of Pistis Sophia*—but that really gives it far too great a dignity. This fantastic work is not Christian at all. Like the *Books of Ieou* it is a Barbelo-Gnostic writing, and there is far more of Egyptian paganism in it than there is of Christianity.

Tpistis sophia is extant in a single manuscript in a somewhat fragmentary condition. The manuscript is of the fourth century; the work itself belongs to the latter half of the third century. It is not quite so old as the *Books of Ieou*, which are mentioned in *Tpistis sophia*.

The first known owner of the sole manuscript of *Tpistis sophia* was Dr. A. Askew, a London physician of the late eighteenth century: hence its title *Codex Askewianus*. In 1785, a few years after the death of Askew, the manuscript was purchased by the British Museum, where it is now catalogued as *MS. Additional* 5114.

The language of the work is the Sahidic dialect of Coptic. Scholars still argue whether it is pure Sahidic, or Sahidic influenced by another dialect; and if the latter, whether the influencing dialect is Subachmimic, Achmimic, or Fayumic. Carl Schmidt, with a considerable but by no means unanimous following, believed that the work is a translation from a lost Greek original. Like the *Books of Ieou*, however, the *Pistis Sophia* is so peculiarly Egyptian in its underlying notions that I am inclined to regard it as an original work in Coptic.

The latest and best edition of the Coptic text of *Tpistis sophia* is Carl Schmidt's *Pistis Sophia* in the series *Coptica*, Vol. 2, Copenhagen 1925. The selections below are translated from Schmidt and Till's German version, in comparison with the Coptic, in the same volume of the Berlin Corpus in which the *Books of Ieou* are found: Vol. 45 (13), Coptic section, Vol. 1, Berlin 1962.

1241c

[136]

It happened that when our Lord Jesus was crucified and was raised from the dead on the third day, when His disciples gathered about Him they besought Him and said: 68

"Our Lord, have mercy on us, for we have left father and mother and the whole world and have followed You."

Then Jesus stood with His disciples by the water of the ocean and called out this prayer, in which He said:

"Hear Me, My Father, Thou Father of all Fatherhood, Thou unending Light, Aeêiouô, Iaô, Aôi, Ôia, PSinôther, THernôps, Nôpsiter, Zagourê, Pagourê, Nethmomaôth, Nepsiomaôth, Marakhakhtha, THôbarrabau, THarnakhakhan, Zorokothora, Ieou, Sabaôth (1)."

While Jesus said this, Thomas, Andrew, James, and Simon the Cananean were standing on the West with their faces turned to the East; Philip and Bartholomew, however, were on the South [with their faces] turned to the North; the other disciples, however, men and women, were standing behind Jesus. Jesus, however, was standing at the altar of sacrifice.

And Jesus called out, the while He turned to the four corners of the world with His disciples, who were all clothed in linen garments, and said: "Iaô, Iaô, Iaô. This is its meaning: Iôta, because the All has gone forth; Alpha, because it will come back again; Ô-mega, because the perfection of all perfections will take place."

1241d

[137]

Jesus continued and said: "Listen now, while I tell you the mystery [of the Archons]. It happened that when Ieou bound them, He drew a force from the Great Invisible and bound it to that which is called Kronos. And He drew forth another force, Ipsantakhounkhainkhoukheôkh, which is one of the three thrice-powerful gods, and bound it to Ares. Again He drew another force from Pistis, the Sophia, the daughter of Barbelo (?), and bound it to Aphrodite. . . . Orimuth corresponds to Kronos, Munichunaphôr corresponds to Ares, Tarpetanuph corresponds to Hermes, Chôsi corresponds to Aphrodite, Chônbal corresponds to Zeus; these are their imperishable names (3)."

68

1. ⲇⲉⲏⲓⲟⲩⲱ· ⲓⲁⲱ· ⲁⲱⲓ· ⲱⲓⲁ· ⲯⲓⲛⲱⲑⲉⲣ· ⲑⲉⲣⲛⲱⲯ· ⲛⲱⲯⲓⲧⲉⲣ· ⲭⲁⲅⲟⲩⲣⲏ· ⲡⲁⲅⲟⲩⲣⲏ· ⲛⲉⲑⲙⲟⲙⲁⲱⲑ· ⲛⲉⲯⲓⲟⲙⲁⲱⲑ· ⲙⲁⲣⲁⲭⲁⲭⲑⲁ· ⲑⲱⲃⲁⲣⲣⲁⲃⲁⲩ· ⲑⲁⲣⲛⲁⲭⲁⲭⲁⲛ· ⲍⲟⲣⲟⲕⲟⲑⲟⲣⲁ· ⲓ̈ⲉⲟⲩ· ⲥⲁⲃⲁⲱⲑ. Apparently these are magical names of the Father of Jesus. See E. A. Wallis Budge, *The Gods of the Egyptians*, Vol. 1, 1904 (reprinted 1969), p. 280.

2. Barbelo is the female father.

3. These are the names of the five planets, Egyptian and Greek, corresponding in the same order to Saturn, Mars, Mercury, Venus, and Jupiter.

ST. OPTATUS OF MILEVIS [ca. A. D. 320–ca. A. D. 385]

The Donatists were the logical heirs of the anabaptist sacramental practice of St. Cyprian of Carthage. The Donatist schism began about the year 312 A. D., with its immediate antecedents going back to about 303 A. D. It lasted for just a hundred years, and confined itself always to Africa.

When Caecilian was consecrated Bishop of Carthage in 311 or 312 A. D., a rich widow, Lucilla by name, who had a personal spite against him, succeeded in her design of having a considerable part of the Carthaginian clergy refuse to recognize the validity of his consecration on the grounds of the unworthiness of the consecrating bishops, Felix of Aptunga in particular being accused of having surrendered the books of Scripture during the Diocletian persecution—a charge which was subsequently found to be false. The dissident party chose a lector, one Majorinus, as bishop; and he was consecrated by Donatus of Casae Nigrae, to be identified with Donatus the Great, who gave his name to the schism.

It was only in the latter days of the schism that both parties called forth their best advocates: Parmenian writing on behalf of the Donatists, and Optatus of Milevis for the Catholic side. Little is known about St. Optatus except from his own writing against Parmenian. Bishop of Milevis in Numidian Africa, presumably he was born about the year 320, and lived to about 385 A. D. P. Monceaux, in his *Histoire littéraire de l'Afrique chrétienne*, Vol. 5, pp. 245-246, finds evidence in Optatus' work to show that he was "a good man, had an engaging disposition, and was certainly no fool." He was, moreover, "sincere, honorable, practical, and a man of simple faith."

THE SCHISM OF THE DONATISTS [*ca. A. D.* 367]

Parmenian's work in defense of the Donatists, entitled *Against the Church of the Apostates (Adversus ecclesiam traditorum)*, had appeared already in 363. St. Optatus' refutation, labeled simply *libri Optati* in the manuscripts but called in modern times *Contra Parmenianum* or *De schismate Donatistarum*, was begun about 367 A. D. He wrote it in six books. A seventh book was added, perhaps by Optatus himself or perhaps by a continuator, probably about the year 385 A. D. It was Optatus who first gave clear expression to the principle that the Sacraments confer their grace *ex opere operato*, when he wrote in book 5 chapter 4: The Sacraments are holy of themselves and not on account of men (see § 1242a, below). The Migne edition, PL 11, 883-1103, reprinting that of Andrew Gallandi, is superseded by the edition of C. Ziwsa in the Vienna Corpus (CSEL), Vol. 26 (1893).

Besides the work against Parmenian, it is possible that a few sermons of Optatus have survived. (See the notes in A. Hamman's *Supplementum* to Migne, Vol. 1, cols. 287-300).

1242

[2, 2]

You cannot deny that you are aware that in the city of Rome the episcopal chair   432
was given first to Peter; the chair in which Peter sat, the same who was head—that   420
is why he is also called Cephas (1)—of all the Apostles; the one chair in which unity
is maintained by all. Neither do other Apostles proceed individually on their own;   434
and anyone who would set up another chair in opposition to that single chair would,   410
by that very fact, be a schismatic and a sinner. [3] It was Peter, then, who first
occupied that chair, the foremost of his endowed gifts. He was succeeded by Linus,
Linus was succeeded by Clement, Clement by Anencletus, Anencletus by Evaristus,
Evaristus by Eleutherus, Eleutherus by Xystus, Xystus by Telesphorus, Telesphorus
by Hyginus, Hyginus by Anicetus, Anicetus by Pius, Pius by Soter, Soter by
Alexander, Alexander by Victor, Victor by Zephyrinus, Zephyrinus by Callistus,
Callistus by Urban, Urban by Pontianus, Pontianus by Anterus, Anterus by Fabian,
Fabian by Cornelius, Cornelius by Lucius, Lucius by Stephen, Stephen by Xystus,
Xystus by Dionysius, Dionysius by Felix, Felix by Marcellinus, Marcellinus
by Eusebius, Eusebius by Melchiades, Melchiades by Sylvester, Sylvester by Mark,
Mark by Julius, Julius by Liberius, Liberius by Damasus, Damasus by Siricius, our   422
present incumbent (2). . . . I but ask you to recall the origins of your chair, you
who wish to claim for yourselves the title of holy Church.

1242a

[5, 4]

There is no man who is baptizing always and everywhere. Some were engaged in   800
this work in times past, others engage in it now, others still will engage in it in   803
the future. The workers can be changed but the Sacraments cannot be changed. If,   820
then, you can see that all who are baptizing are workers, not lords, and that the
Sacraments are holy of themselves and not by reason of men (3), what is it that you
claim so urgently for yourselves? What is it that you insist God excludes from His
gifts? Admit that it is God who controls what is His own.   802

1. Optatus seems to suggest that Cephas means head, whereas it means rock. One wonders if he either is confusing or has inherited a confusion of the semitic roots *kp* (ךפ), referring to rock, and *qp* (ףפ), referring to head. On the other hand, when the Lord told Simon that his new name was Cephas (rock, or peter), He also told him that it was on him that He was founding His Church, *i.e.*, that Peter, the rock, was to be its foundation and head; so it may be only that there is a kind of anacoluthon in Optatus' thought and manner of expression. Louis Du Pin suggested (Paris edition, 1700) that Optatus thought that Cephas derived from the Greek κεφαλή, meaning head. François Baudoin, another of the classic commentators, had already suggested in his 1563 edition that the whole interjected phrase *unde et Cephas appellatus est* might be a marginal gloss that had crept across the page and into the text.
2. *hodie qui noster est socius.* Besides the predictable Linus-Cletus-Clement problem, which is still insoluble, there are several evident shortcomings in Optatus' list. He has transposed the proper positions of Alexander (who followed Evaristus) and Eleutherus (who followed Soter). Pius should precede, not follow, Anicetus. He has omitted Eutychian and Caius who should have been placed, in that order, between Felix and Marcellinus; and he has omitted Marcellus after Marcellinus. Siricius, "who is our companion today", was Bishop of Rome from 384 to 399 A. D., which latter fact is one of the reasons for supposing that Optatus made a second edition of his work about 385 A. D., when the seventh book also was added.
3. *et sacramenta per se esse sancta, non per homines.* Historically this is the first clear expression of the theological principle that the sacraments produce their effect *ex opere operato.*

ST. PACIAN OF BARCELONA [† *inter A. D.* 379-392]

St. Pacian was the father of the Pretorian Prefect Dexter to whom St. Jerome dedicated his *De viris illustribus*. He was already dead when Jerome added him to his catalog (392 A. D.); but still flourishing in the time of Theodosius, whose reign began in 379 A. D. Jerome notes that Pacian bore the burden of the episcopacy at Barcelona in the Pyrenees, and comments on his simple eloquence and personal integrity, saying also that his life was even more illustrious than his words.

Pacian's authentic remains consists of three letters to an otherwise unknown Novatianist named Sympronian, and two sermons: one on Penance and one on Baptism.

Pacian is not an especially original thinker but his writings have no small importance as an early testimony in the area of baptismal theology and penitential practice. His style is truly delightful, and it is unfortunate that his writings are not more readily accessible and more widely read.

Otto Bardenhewer noted already in 1923 that R. Kauer was preparing an edition of the works of St. Pacian for the Vienna Corpus. That edition has not appeared, and the Migne edition, reprinting Gallandi of 1770 which was itself a reworking of Jean de Tillet's edition (the *editio princeps*) of 1538, may still be regarded as the standard.

THREE LETTERS TO THE NOVATIANIST SYMPRONIAN [*inter ca. A. D.* 375-392]

The grouping of the three letters as a single work is, of course, quite artificial; but it is convenient, and the letters all deal with the same subject matter: the defense of

Catholicism and its penitential doctrine as opposed to Novatianism and its refusal to grant forgiveness for sins committed after Baptism. The three letters seem to be grouped in their correct chronological order. The first must date, in view of its mention of Apollinarism, from after about 375 A. D. In its chapter four is found the celebrated line: *Christianus mihi nomen est, Catholicus vero cognomen.*

The Migne edition is in PL 13, 1051-1082.

1243

[1, 4]

Christian is my name, and Catholic my surname. The one designates me, while the other makes me specific. Thus am I attested and set apart. . . . When we are called Catholics it is by this appellation that our people are kept apart from any heretical name.   421

1244

[1, 6]

Certainly God never threatens the repentant; rather, He pardons the penitent.   900
You will say that it is God alone who can do this. True enough; but it is likewise true
that He does it through His priests, who exercise His power. What else can it mean   925
when He says to His Apostles: "Whatever you shall bind on earth shall be bound
in heaven; and whatever you shall loose on earth shall be loosed in heaven?" (1)
Why should he say this if He were not permitting men to bind and to loose? Why,
if He were permitting this to the Apostles alone? Were that the case, He would   820
likewise be permitting them alone to baptize, them alone to Confer the Holy Spirit, them   840
alone to cleanse the pagans of their sins; for all of these things are commissioned not to
others but to the Apostles. But if the loosing of bonds and the power of the Sacrament   440
is given to anyone in that place, either the whole is passed on to us from the form
and power of the Apostles, or nothing of it can be imparted to us by whatever   828
decrees. . . . . If, then, the power both of Baptism and Confirmation (2), greater   843
by far than charisms, is passed on to the bishops, so too is the right of binding
and of loosing.

1245

[3, 12]

"Whatever you shall loose on earth shall be loosed also in heaven." (3) . . .   901
"Whatever you shall loose," He says; and He excepts absolutely nothing. "Whatever,"
He says: whether it be great or whether it be small.

1. Matt. 16:19; John 20:23.
2. *et lavacri et chrismatis potestas.*
3. Matt. 16:19; John 20:23.

SERMON EXHORTING TO PENANCE [*ante A. D.* 392]

Although called a *libellus* in its Latin title, the *Sermon Exhorting to Penance* is a sermon actually prepared for oral delivery; and Pacian shows in this work as well as in his only other extant sermon, the one on Baptism, that he had a very fine hortatory style and a good pastoral sense.

The Migne text, still standard, is in PL 13, 1081-1090.

1245a

[4]

After the passion of the Lord the Apostles . . . sent out a letter . . . to Gentile   902
believers: . . . "It seemed proper to the Holy Spirit and to us to lay no greater burden
upon you than this: It is necessary for you to abstain from meat sacrificed to idols (1)
and from blood and from fornication. You will do well to observe these things.
Farewell (2)." This is the whole conclusion of the New Testament. The Holy Spirit
overlooked many things, but He bound us to these things under pain of capital
danger (3). Other sins are remedied by compensatory works of supererogation (4);
but these three crimes are to be feared like the breath of the basilisk (5), like a cup
of poison, like a deadly arrow; for they do not merely weaken the soul but snatch it quite
away. Stinginess is redeemed by generosity; insult by apology, severity by
agreeableness, harshness by gentleness, fickleness by seriousness, perversity by
honesty; and for whatever else, amends are made by practice of the opposite.
But what can he do who was contemptuous of God? What shall the murderer (6)
do? What remedy shall the fornicator find? . . . These are capital sins, brethren,   633
these are mortal (7). [6] Someone may say: Are we then about to perish? . . . Are
we to die in our sins? . . . I appeal first to you brethren who refuse penance for your
acknowledged crimes: you, I say, who are timid after your impudence, who are
bashful after your sins, who were not ashamed to sin but now are ashamed to confess.   916

1245b

[11]

Remember that confession (8) extinguishes hell (9) for you. And you may guess the   918
intensity of hell from what is visible. Some of its chimneys boil away the greatest
mountains by its subterranean fires. Etna in Sicily and Vesuvius in the Campania burn
with unflagging balls of fire; and they will test us, sear us, devour us in an eternity
of judgment, nor will they be finished after any number of ages.

1. *ut abstineatis vos ab idolothytis.*
2. Acts 15:28-29.
3. *capitalis periculi conditione legavit.*
4. *Reliqua peccata meliorum operum compensatione curantur.*
5. Far more deadly even than the dreaded Gaboon viper, the basilisk kills merely by looking at his victim or by breathing on
   him. Unlike the Gaboon viper, however, the basilisk is a legendary reptile, and consequently is of no danger except to
   legendary persons.
6. *sanguinarius.* Pacian interprets the *abstineatis vos a . . . sanguine* of Acts 15:29 as a prohibition of murder, the shedding
   of blood.
7. *Ista sunt capitalia, fratres, ista mortalia.*
8. *exomologesis.*
9. *gehennan.*

SERMON ON BAPTISM [*ante A. D.* 392]

The general remarks about the text in our heading to the *Three Letters to the Novatianist
Sympronian* and in the heading to the *Sermon Exhorting to Penance* may be applied
also to the present *Sermon on Baptism*. The Migne text is in PL 13, 1089-1094.

1245c

[2]

After Adam sinned, as I noted before, when the Lord said, "You are earth, and to   611
earth you shall return (1)," Adam was condemned to death. This condemnation   614

passed on to the whole race. For all sinned, already by their sharing in that nature (2), as the Apostle says: "For through one man sin made its entry, and through sin death, and thus it came down to all men, because (3) all have sinned."

1245d

[6]

Someone will say to me: But the sin of Adam deservedly passed on to his posterity,   614
because they were begotten of him: but how are we to be begotten of Christ, so that
we can be saved through Him? Do not think of these things in a carnal fashion.
You have already seen how we are begotten by Christ our Parent. In these last   312
times Christ took a soul and with it flesh from Mary: this flesh came to prepare   311
salvation, this flesh was not left in the lower regions, this flesh He conjoined to His   370
spirit and made His own. And these are the nuptials of the Lord, so that like that   972
great Sacrament they might become two in one flesh, Christ and the Church (4).   402
From these nuptials a Christian people is born, when the Spirit of the Lord comes upon
that people.

1. Gen. 3:19.
2. *ipsa iam urgente natura*, more literally, *already by a burdening nature itself*.
3. *in quo*. St. Pacian does not seem to refer the *in quo* to Adam; at least not in any grammatical way. He correctly
understands that *in quo*, rendering the Greek ἐφ' ᾧ, has the sense of *because*. His manner of quoting the celebrated
passage (Rom. 5:12) is: *Quia per unum hominem peccatum introivit, et per delictum mors, et sic in omnes homines
devenit, in quo omnes peccaverunt*. Yet it is clear enough in this same passage that he does regard the sin of Adam as
having been passed on to all his progeny.
4. Eph. 5:32.

FAUSTINUS [fl. ca. A. D. 380]

To know Faustinus we must first make the acquaintance of St. Lucifer of Cagliari.
Bishop of that Church in Sardinia, Lucifer was one of the West's most adamant
defenders of the orthodox Nicene doctrine. When the unfortunate Council of Milan
condemned St. Athanasius, Lucifer refused to be a party to such treachery against that
great man, and for his intransigence he was sent into exile in the East in 355 A. D. To
this point he was a most honorable man.

When Arianism was finally carried to its logical and abominable conclusion in
Anomoianism, a term meant to express the view that the Father and the Son are unlike
in all things, the Nicene party saw the absolute necessity of closing ranks and
retrenching; and a kind of peace was effected between themselves, *i.e.*, the
Homoousians, and those whom they had formerly regarded as enemies of the faith, the
Homoiousians. It was admitted that many of the latter were perfectly orthodox in their
thinking, but used only an unorthodox terminology; and in the face of the real enemy in
genuine Arianism, the Nicene men were able to abandon their quarrel with the
Homoiousians, a quarrel which had in the course of time truly become no more than an
argument over words. In short, a man might now still cling to the term homoiousios; but
if he understood it in the same sense in which the Nicene men understood the term
homoousios, the latter would accept him into their communion.

At this point Lucifer, a homoousian, ought to have yielded; but he would not. He
became in fact a schismatic. His followers are known as Luciferians, and they continued
in his schism for about twenty years after his death, *i.e.*, until about 390 A. D.   Lucifer
was inflexible, but a good man for all of that; and in his native Sardinia he is called a
saint, enjoys a local cult, and is given the honors of the altar.

The Faustinus with whom we are presently concerned was a priest in Rome and a

Luciferian. He is best remembered as co-author with another Luciferian priest, one Marcellinus, of a petition to the Emperors Valentinian II, Theodosius I and Arcadius to protect the Luciferians against their Catholic persecutors. Of that work, well-received by the Emperors and generally called the *Libellus precum Faustini et Marcellini presbyterorum*, O. Guenther's excellent critical edition is to be found in Vol. 35, part 1, pp. 5-44 of the *Corpus Vindobonensis* (CSEL).

THE TRINITY [*ca. A. D.* 380]

Faustinus is sole author of the *De Trinitate* or *De fide contra Arianos*; and he shows himself a much better theologian than Lucifer, whose language is often hilariously intemperate, and who was, for all his zeal, hardly more than a pamphleteer. (Lucifer is of some importance linguistically, however, because the language in which he wrote was common street Latin.) Faustinus' work on the Trinity is in seven short books, the seventh being devoted to the theology of the Holy Spirit in refutation of the homoiousian and pneumatomachian Macedonians. The work never uses the term Macedonian, however, a fact which led A. Wilmart to date the work as early as *ca*. 380 A. D. His reasoning seems quite valid; for it is soon after 380 that the term Macedonian becomes common enough in literature.

Wilmart was preparing a critical edition of the *De Trinitate* already in 1908; but the work never appeared (like so many of the good things that Wilmart was preparing), and the edition of Andreas Gallandi, reprinted in Migne, PL 11, 37-80, remained the standard until it was superseded in 1967 by M. Simonetti's edition in *Corpus Christianorum*, Vol. 69, pp. 295-353.

1246

[50 (*al*. 7, 3)]

Since the Lord commands that the nations be baptized "in the name of the Father and of the Son and of the Holy Spirit (1)," it is most evident that the Holy Spirit is not a creature. Either He is of that very companionship in which He is one with the Father and the Son, or the Lord would have been commanding what He never did, that someone be baptized in the name of a creature. The divine power would be much derogated from if, along with the confession of the divine name, a like confession were made also of a creature. It is quite proper that but one name is spoken of when it is said: "In the *name* of the Father and of the Son and of the Holy Spirit," so that faith is posited in one principal authority of the perfect and indivisible Trinity.

234
268

1. Matt. 28:19.

ST. AMBROSE OF MILAN [*ca. A. D.* 333 *aut ca. A. D.* 339–*A. D.* 397]

The best evidence for dating Ambrose's birth is his letter no. 59 to Severus in which he states that he is now fifty-three years of age and is suffering from barbarian outbreaks and the calamities of wartime. Some regard the latter as a reference to the war of 387 A. D. with Maximus the Usurper, and date his birth in 333; others regard it as a reference to the war of 393 A. D. with Eugene the Usurper, and date his birth accordingly in 339 or 340. The latter dating seems to have the better part of the argument at the present time; but the matter is by no means closed.

Born at Treves, Ambrose was the son of the Pretorian Prefect of Gaul. His father died young, and Ambrose's widowed mother returned to Rome with her three children. Ambrose's sister Marcellina took the veil of a consecrated virgin in Rome, and his brother Satyrus followed in his father's footsteps, both in occupying a high civil post and in dying young.

Ambrose was trained both in rhetoric and in the legal profession; and about the year 370 A. D. he was made Consul of Liguria and Emilia, with his official residence in Milan.

The Bishop of Milan, Auxentius, was an Arian; and when he died the election of his successor witnessed considerable violence between the Arian and the Catholic parties. Ambrose intervened, only to find himself the unexpected choice of both parties. Although only a catechumen at the time, he finally yielded to their pressure and was consecrated Bishop of Milan on December 7, 374, just a week after his Baptism.

St. Ambrose was an exemplary bishop both in his public and in his private life. In his dogmatic and scriptural writings it is true that he shows no great originality, depending heavily upon his Greek predecessors; but in his moral and ascetical writings his thought is quite independent, and it is here that he is at his best. Apart from these works, which are of extraordinary importance for pastoral theology and which mark him as perhaps the most brilliant mind of his time, he is remembered particularly for having succeeded in preventing the restoration of the statue of the goddess of victory to the senate chambers, a pagan altar which Gratian had removed in 382 A. D.; and for having successfully ordered the Emperor Theodosius to do public penance after his massacre, in consequence of a revolt, of 7000 people at Thessalonica in 390 A. D.

On a popular level Ambrose is best remembered as the author of hymns, several of which are recited in the Liturgy of the Hours; and he has given his name to the style of plainsong, Ambrosian Chant, preserved in the liturgy of the Milanese or Ambrosian Rite.

As he lay dying in his bed on a porch, several of Ambrose's deacons, standing at a distance, were whispering about who might succeed him at Milan. When the name Simplician was mentioned, Ambrose, as if taking part in a discussion which he ought not to have been able to hear at all at so great a distance, called out in a loud voice, "Old, but good! Old, but good! Old, but good!" Simplician did in fact succeed him, Ambrose dying in the year 397 A. D.

Paulinus, a deacon and Ambrose's intimate friend and secretary, wrote, at the behest of St. Augustine, his *Life of Ambrose* twenty-five years after the saint's death. He recalls a number of miraculous events of Ambrose's last days and immediately subsequent to his death, to some of which he was himself the eyewitness.

LETTERS

The corpus of Ambrose's letters contains 91 entries, not a few of which are of considerable importance for a history of his times. Preparation of an edition for the Vienna Corpus (CSEL) was begun about thirty years ago. It was finally decided to release the parts that were ready; and about one half of the letters appeared in 1968 in Otto Faller's edition in Volume 82 of the Vienna Corpus. For the letters which have not yet appeared in the Vienna Corpus we must still rely on Migne's reprint of the Maurist edition of J. Du Frisch and N. le Nourry, in Pl 16, 875-1286. J. R. Palanque, however, in the chapter *"Essai de chronologie Ambrosienne"* in his *Saint Ambroise et l'empire romain*, Paris 1933, pp. 480-556, has improved the Maurist dating of the letters in a number of instances; and where he differs with the Maurists, we offer the dates established by Palanque. The numbering of the letters in the following selections is according to the Maurists; and for those letters which have to date appeared in the Vienna Corpus, the numbering of the Faller edition is given in parenthesis as *al*.

LETTER OF AMBROSE TO CONSTANTIUS, A BISHOP. A. D. 379.

1247

[2, 16]

Each of our merits will hang in the balance, and it is often inclined to this side or   770
that by the superior weight either of our good works or of our degenerate crimes. If
evil deeds turn the scale, alas for me! But if good, then pardon is at hand. No one is free of
sin; but where good works prevail, sins are lightened, overshadowed, and covered up. On
the day of judgment either our works will assist us or they will plunge us into the abyss, as
if dragged down by a millstone.

LETTER OF AMBROSE TO THE EMPEROR VALENTINIAN II. A. D. 384.

1248

[18, 7]

[The city of Rome herself declares:] "Your sacrifice is a ritual of being sprinkled   558
with the blood of slaughtered beasts. What do you seek in the dead beasts? Utterances   560
of God? Come and become acquainted on earth with the heavenly army. We live here, but
our military service is there. May God Himself who fashioned me teach me the mystery of
heaven, not a man who is ignorant even of himself. Whom shall we believe about God,
more than God Himself? How should I be able to believe in you, who admit you do not
know what you worship?"

LETTER OF AMBROSE TO VIGILIUS, A BISHOP. A. D. 385.

1249

[19, 7]

But there is hardly anything more serious than to be joined in marriage to a stranger (1),   972
where the instigations both of lustful appetite and of disharmony and the shameful crimes
of sacrilege are welded together. For if marriage itself needs to be sanctified by the priestly
veil and blessing, how is it possible to speak of a marriage where there is no agreement in
faith?

LETTER OF AMBROSE TO THE EMPEROR VALENTINIAN II, A. D. 386.

1250

[21, 14]

This [denial of the divinity of Christ] was written in the Council of Rimini, and I am   452
right when I shiver at the thought of that Council. I follow the teaching of the Council of
Nicaea, from which neither death nor the sword shall ever be able to separate me.

LETTER OF AMBROSE TO SIMPLICIAN, A PRIEST. ca. A. D. 386.

1251

[37 (al. 7), 23]

The Apostle taught me, however, that beyond freedom itself there is a freedom to   591
serve. "For though I was free," he says, "I made myself the servant of all, so that   590

I might gain the more (2)." What is there beyond freedom, except to have the Spirit of grace, to have love? For freedom makes one free in relation to men; but love makes one a friend in relation to God (3).

LETTER OF AMBROSE TO HIS SISTER MARCELLINA. A. D. 388.

1252

[41, 7]

[The devil] dragged the human race into a perpetual captivity by the heavy debt of   374
inherited liability (4) which the author of the debt transmitted to his posterity as   383
their inherited debt (5). The Lord Jesus came and offered His death in place of the   386
death of all, and poured out His blood in place of the blood of everyone.

SYNODAL LETTER OF AMBROSE, SABINUS, BASSIAN, AND OTHERS TO POPE SIRICIUS. ca. A. D. 389.

1252a

[42, 1]

We recognized in the letter of your holiness the vigilance of the good shepherd.   435
You faithfully watch over the gate entrusted to you, and with pious solicitude you guard
Christ's sheepfold (6), you that are worthy to have the Lord's sheep hear and follow
you. Since you know the sheep of Christ you will easily catch the wolves and
confront them like a wary shepherd, lest they disperse the Lord's flock by their
constant lack of faith and their bestial howling.

1253

[42, 3]

They pretend to honor marriage; but what praise can be given marriage if there is no   972
glory in virginity? Neither do we deny that marriage has been sanctified by Christ,
since the divine word says: "The two shall become one flesh (7)" and one spirit. But
we are born before we are brought to our goal, and the mystery of the divine operation   968
is much more excellent than the remedy for human weakness. It is quite right   983
that a good wife be praised, but even better that a pious virgin be preferred.   984

LETTER OF AMBROSE TO SABINUS, A BISHOP. ca. A. D. 390.

1254

[48, (al. 32), 5]

Just as in the form of God, He lacked nothing of the divine nature and its fullness, so   257
too in the form of man there was nothing lacking in Him, by the absence of which
He might have been judged an imperfect man; for He came to save the whole man.
It would not have been fitting for One who accomplished a perfect work in others   310
to allow anything imperfect in Himself. If something was lacking in His humanity,   314
He did not redeem the whole man; and if He did not redeem the whole man, He
was a deceiver when He declared that He had come to save the whole man. But
He did not deceive, because "It is not possible for God to lie (8)." Because He came,   370
therefore, to save and redeem the whole man, it follows that He took upon Himself the
whole man, and that His humanity was perfect.

1255

[48 (*al*. 32), 6]

Our opinion [*in the passage immediately above, no. 1254*], as you may recall,   107
is such. If the words are in any way disturbing they do no harm to faith; for a mind
which does not doubt covers over a doubtful word and protects the faith from a lapse.

LETTER OF AMBROSE TO HORONTIAN, A PRIEST. *ca. A. D. 387.*

1256

[70, (*al*. 18), 23]

"Who is a God like You, taking away sins and transferring impiousness (9)?"   751
You harbor no memory of Your indignation. It is as if You plunge all our iniquities
into the sea just as you made plumb bobs of the Egyptians (10). It is Your will to
restore us to mercy, which you bestow as a twofold favor, forgiving sins and
putting them out of mind. . . . For the words "taking away sins" mean the   931
remission thereof; and those sins are so fully taken away that it is as if they never
existed, there being no memory of them. But the words "transferring impiousness"
mean that by our confessing of our failings and by our covering them over with the
fruit of good works they are charged to the author of guilt and the instigator of sin.
For what else does he do that confesses his fault, but prove that he was beguiled
by the cunning malice of the spiritual wickedness opposing him?

LETTER OF AMBROSE TO CONSTANTIUS, A BISHOP. [undatable].

1257

[72, 8]

We have been redeemed not by perishable things, not by silver and gold, but by   374
the precious blood of our Lord Jesus Christ (11). . . . The price of our gaining of   384
freedom was the blood of the Lord Jesus, which was necessarily paid out to him
to whom we were sold by our sins (12).

1. *I.e.*, to one who is not of the faith.
2. 1 Cor. 9:19.
3. It is generally considered that the Simplician to whom this letter is addressed is the same who succeeded Ambrose in the
   see of Milan.
4. *obnoxiae hereditatis gravi fenore.*
5. *quod obaeratus auctor ad posteros de fenerata successione transmiserat.*
6. John 10:7 *ff.*
7. Matt. 19:5.
8. Heb. 6:18.
9. Micheas 7:18. Ambrose reads the passage: *"Quis Deus sicut tu, auferens peccata et transferens impietates."* The
   transferens is important to his interpretation of the passage, which requires the translation *transferring*.
10. *sicut Aegyptium plumbum.*
11. See 1 Peter 1:18-19.
12. The passage reflects the untenable theological view, shared by Origen (§ 508 above) and Pope St. Gregory the Great
    (§ 2311 below), that the price of our redemption was paid to Satan. This was not an uncommon view in antiquity, and no
    doubt derives from a misplaced logic working upon too etymologically literal an understanding of the term *redeem*,
    meaning to buy back.

COMMENTARIES ON TWELVE OF DAVID'S PSALMS [*inter ca. A. D. 381-397*].

The *Enarrationes in duodecim Psalmos Davidicos* or *Explanatio in duodecim Psalmos*
is just as artificial a grouping as is the collection of *Letters*; but it is convenient to treat

 them as a single work, and we continue to do so. The Psalms commentated are nos. 1, 35-40, 43, 45, 47-48, and 61. The commentary on Ps. 1 may have been written as early as 381 A. D. and certainly not after 390. Those on Ps. 45, 47-48 and 61 were written about the year 390. The commentaries on Ps. 35-40 might qualify in fact as a separate and single work. They have a certain cohesiveness with each other in their style. As a group they were completed after Sept. 6, 393, when Theodosius won the victory over Eugene the Usurper. The commentary on no. 43 was written in the year 397.

The Maurist text, reprinted by Migne in PL 14, 921-1180, as well as the edition of the Ballerini brothers, have been superseded by Otto Faller's edition in Vol. 64 of the Vienna Corpus (CSEL).

1258

[36, 26]

The Egyptian people were plunged into the Red Sea, but the Hebrew people went   1032
over. Moses passed through; but Pharao was cast down headlong, because the
heavier weight of his sins plunged him downwards. In the same way do sacrileges
cast down headlong into the lake of burning fire those who fling their proud insults
in the face of God.

1259

[37, 57]

[The sinner] not only confesses his sins, but he even enumerates them and admits   918
his guilt (1); for he does not want to conceal his faults (2). For just as fevers are not   920
able to be assuaged when they are deep seated, but offer a hope of cessation when   919
they break, so too the illness of sins burns on while it is hidden, but disappears when
it shows itself in confessions.

1260

[38, 25]

We saw the Prince of Priests coming to us, we saw and heard Him offering His   896
blood for us. We follow, inasmuch as we are able, being priests; and we offer the   866
sacrifice on behalf of the people. And even if we are of but little merit, still, in the   862
sacrifice, we are honorable. For even if Christ is not now seen as the one who   867
offers the sacrifice, nevertheless it is He Himself that is offered in sacrifice here on   890
earth when the Body of Christ is offered. Indeed, to offer Himself He is made   895
visible in us, He whose word makes holy the sacrifice that is offered.

1261

[40, 30]

It is to Peter himself that He says: "You are Peter, and upon this rock I will build   423
My Church (3)." Where Peter is, there is the Church. And where the Church, no   430
death is there, but life eternal.

1262

[43, 19]

A name, therefore, is the peculiarity of anything, by which it is able to be understood.   140
I am of the opinion that Moses, when he asked: "What is Your name?" (4),   256

wanted to know what is peculiar to God, and to know something special about Him.   257
God, knowing what was on his mind, did not, therefore, tell him His name but His
occupation. That is, He expresses a thing, not an appellative, when He says:
"I am who am" (5); for there is nothing more peculiar to God than always to exist.
Those, therefore, who deny that Christ is coeternal with the Father may be considered
as denying that Christ is God, whose property it is always to exist and at no time not
to have existed.

1263

[43, 71]

If you but consider that the just man can only barely be saved, you will truly   657
understand that his footsteps too do sometimes falter, and God can be seen as the   638
author of their faltering; for He often allows even the just to be tempted, so that
the learned may the better be tested by temptations. Who indeed is so strong that
he can never be moved by temptation, unless the Lord be his help and come to his
assistance?

1. *Non solum confitetur peccata sua, sed etiam enumerat et accusat.*
2. *delicta sua.*
3. Matt. 16:18.
4. Exodus 3:13.
5. Exodus 3:14.

THE FAITH [A. D. 378-380]

The earliest of St. Ambrose's dogmatic writings, the five books of the *De fide* were
dedicated *ad Gratianum Augustum*. Books 1 and 2 were written about the month of
September in the year 378; and books 3 to 5 near the end of the year 380. The work
constitutes a defense of the divinity of the Son in the face of radical Arianism.

The Maurist edition reprinted in Migne, PL 16, 527-698 was superseded in 1962
with the appearance of Otto Faller's edition in Vol. 78 of the Vienna Corpus (CSEL).

1264

[1, 2, 16]

Certainly to avoid the possibility of error, let us heed what the Holy Scriptures   260
tell us about the Son, for our better understanding. He is called the Word, He is   261
called the Son, He is called the Power of God, and He is called also the Wisdom of   257
God. The Word, because He is immaculate; the Power, because He is perfect; Son,   281
because He is begotten of the Father; Wisdom, because He is one with the Father, one in
eternity and one in divinity. Not that the Father is identical with Him that is the Son,
for between Father and Son there is the explicit distinction involved in generation.
The Son is God from God, Everlasting from Everlasting, Fullness from Fullness. [17]
These are not bare names, but signs of operative power; for in the Father there is
fullness of divinity, and fullness of divinity is likewise in the Son,—not different (1),
but one divinity. Neither is that confused which is one, nor multiplex, that which is
not different (2).

1265

[1, 5, 42]

[The Arians] employ their poison full strength in dialectical disputation, which   16
philosophers define as having no power to build up and as consisting only of a studied

effort to destroy. God does not deign to save His people by means of dialectics:
the kingdom of God is in the simplicity of faith, not in contentious words (3).

1266

[1, 16, 106]

God is of a simple nature, not conjoined nor composite. Nothing can be added 151
to Him; He has in His nature only what is divine: filling up everything, never Himself 154
confused with anything; penetrating everything, never Himself being penetrated;
everywhere complete, and present at the same time in heaven, on earth, and in the
farthest reaches of the sea; incomprehensible to the sight, uninterpretable to prophetic 173
utterance, inestimable to the mind, to be pursued by faith, to be worshiped by 180
religion. Whatever could be conceived as more religious, whatever more excellent
in beauty, whatever more sublime in power, this, you may be sure, belongs to God.

1267

[2, 7, 56]

As a man, then, [Christ] doubts, as a man He is troubled. His strength is not 332
troubled, not troubled His divinity; but His soul is troubled; troubled in consequence 322
of His assumption of human fragility. And because He took a soul, He therefore 349
took also the affections of the soul (4); for God, by the very fact of His being God,
would not have been able to be troubled or to die. . . . [58] When we read, therefore,
that the Lord of majesty was crucified, let us not suppose that He was crucified in 334
His majesty; but because it is Jesus Christ who was crucified, the same who is God
and the same who is man, God by His divinity and man by His taking of flesh, it
is said that the Lord of majesty was crucified.

1268

[3, 11, 87]

A priest must offer something in sacrifice and according to the Law he must enter 382
the holy place through blood. Therefore, because God had repudiated the blood of
bulls and of rams, it was necessary for this Priest, as you have read, to enter into the
holy of holies, penetrating the heights of heaven, by means of His own blood, so that
He might become an eternal oblation for our sins. Priest and Victim, therefore, are
one and the same. But the priesthood and the sacrifice are a duty of the human
condition; for like a lamb He was led to the slaughter, and He is a priest according to
the order of Melchisedech.

1269

[4, 8, 91]

The substance of the distinct, incomprehensible, and unutterable Trinity is 237
somehow indistinct. For we accept that there is a distinction and not a confusion of 238
Father and of Son and of Holy Spirit; a distinction, but not a separation; a distinction, 239
but not a plurality. In the divine and amazing mystery we accept that there is an
everlastingly permanent Father, an everlastingly permanent Son, an everlastingly
permanent Holy Spirit; not two Fathers, not two Sons, not two Spirits. . . . The
distinction we know, the secrets we do not know; the causes we do not discuss, the
outward signs we preserve (5).

1270

[4, 10, 124]

"My flesh is truly food and My blood is truly drink (6)." You hear Him speak of   850
His flesh, you hear Him speak of His blood, you know the sacred signs (7) of the   849
Lord's death; and do you worry about His divinity? Hear His words when He says:
"A spirit has not flesh and bones (8)." As often as we receive the sacramental
elements (9) which through the mystery of the sacred prayer are transformed (10)   864
into the flesh and blood of the Lord, we proclaim the death of the Lord (11).   856

1271

[4, 10, 132]

[The Arians] think that they must posit the objection of His having said: "I live   257
on account of the Father (12)." Certainly if they refer the saying to His divinity,
the Son lives on account of the Father, because the Son is from the Father; on account
of the Father, because He is of one substance with the Father; on account of the
Father, because He is the Word given forth from the heart of the Father (13); because 252
He proceeds from the Father, because He is generated in the paternal bowels (14),
because the Father is the source (15) of the Son, because the Father is the root (16)
of the Son.

1272

[5, 6, 83]

Finally, speaking of the Father, He says, ". . . to those for whom it has been   191
prepared (17)," thus showing that the Father too is not wont to attend simply
to requests but to merits; for "God is not one to respect persons (18)." So too the   213
Apostle says: "Whom He foreknew, He predestined (19)"; for He did not predestine
them before He foreknew them, but He foreknew the merits of those whose reward
He predestined.

1273

[5, 7, 90]

Can men be loved by the Father as the Son is, in whom the Father was well-pleased?   755
He is well-pleasing in Himself, we through Him. Those in whom the Father sees
His own Son according to His own likeness, He admits through His Son to the
favor of sons, so that inasmuch as we are conformed by likeness, we can be called
to adoption through the generation of the Son (20). The eternal love that is of God's
nature is one thing, while that which is of grace is another.

1274

[5, 12, 150]

We are of Christ's kingdom beforehand; but afterwards, of the Father's kingdom.   388
For it is written: "No one comes to the Father except through Me (21)." While
still on the way, I am of Christ; but when I shall have arrived, I am of the Father;
yet everywhere through Christ and everywhere under Christ.

1. *non discrepans*.
2. *indifferens*.
3. See 1 Cor. 4:20.
4. *animae passiones*.
5. *sacramenta servamus*.

6. John 6:56.
7. *sacramenta*.
8. Luke 24:39.
9. *sacramenta*.
10. *transfigurantur*.
11. See 1 Cor. 11:26.
12. John 6:58.
13. See Ps. 44[45]:1.
14. *ex paterno . . . utero*.
15. *fons*.
16. *radix*.
17. Matt. 20:23.
18. Acts 10:34.
19. Rom. 8:29.
20. *I. e.*, we are loved by the Father insofar as we are in the likeness of the Father and thereby remind the Father of the Son, who is in the Father's likeness; and thus, ultimately because of the Father's having generated the Son, we become sons of the Father by His adopting us. The eternal love of the Father for the Son is of the divine nature; His loving us is a grace given us.
21. John 14:6.

THE DEATH OF HIS BROTHER SATYRUS [*A. D.* 378]

In his earlier years St. Ambrose's brother Satyrus, like Ambrose himself, practiced law and held public office. When Ambrose was made Bishop of Milan, however, Satyrus resigned his office and devoted himself entirely to the management of Ambrose's secular affairs in order to free the latter for a full-time attention to his episcopal duties.

Ambrose was very close to his brother and when Satyrus died in February of the year 378 A. D. Ambrose delivered a very beautiful discourse at the funeral, and a week later gave another discourse on the resurrection. The text tradition has combined these two discourses into a single work under the title *Two Books of St. Ambrose on the Death of His Brother Satyrus*, or the *De excessu fratris sui Satyri*. The text in Migne, PL 16, 1289-1354, has been superseded since 1955 by Otto Faller's edition in the Vienna Corpus (CSEL), Vol. 73, pp. 207-325.

1275

[2, 46]

The world was redeemed by the death of one Man. It was possible for Christ not   350
to have died, had He not willed to do so. But He did not regard death as something   386
to be shunned, as if it were ignoble, nor did He think He could rescue us any better
than by His dying. Thus His death became life for all.

1276

[2, 87]

If earth and heaven are renewed, why should we doubt that man can be renewed,   1011
when it is on his account that earth and heaven were made? If the treacherous man is
preserved for punishment why should not the just man be continued for glory? If the worm
of sinners does not die how shall the flesh of just men perish? For the resurrection, as the
very etymology (1) of the word tells us, is this: that what has fallen should rise up again;
that what has died should be made to live again. [88] And this is the course and fundament
of justice, that, since actions are common both to body and to soul,—for what the soul
pondered the body effected,—both shall come to the judgment and both shall either be
given over to punishment or be preserved for glory.

1277

[2, 89]

There is, if I do not err, just and ample reason; but I do not demand a reason of Christ.   557
If I am convinced by reason, I am rejecting faith. Abraham believed God; and we
believe, so that we who are the heirs of his race may likewise be the heirs of his faith.

1. *sonus*.

PARADISE [*ca. A. D.* 375]

The work entitled *Paradise* or *De paradiso* is, if not the earliest, certainly one of the
earlier of St. Ambrose's writings, dating most probably from within a few months or a
year of his having been made bishop. It is an elegant little work deserving of closer
study. The text in Migne (PL 14, 275-314) was superseded already in 1897 by Karl
Schenkl's edition in the Vienna Corpus (CSEL, Vol. 32, part 1).

1278

[10, 48]

Nor is it a matter of indifference that the woman was not formed of the same clay   510
from which Adam was made, but was made from the rib of Adam himself, so that we
might know that the flesh of man and woman is of but one nature, and that there   511
is but one source of the human race. Therefore at the beginning it is not two that are
made, man and woman, nor two men, nor two women, but first man is made, and then
woman from him. For God willed to settle one nature upon mankind, and starting
from the one origin of this creature, He snatched away the possibility of numerous
and disparate natures.

CAIN AND ABEL [*ca. A. D.* 375]

Tradition divides the work entitled *De Cain et Abel* into two books; but the division
is quite inept and can hardly stem from Ambrose hmself. The work itself is undoubtedly
authentic; but the division into two books is retained only to avoid confusing the numeration
of the usual citations. It is one of Ambrose's earlier writings, to be dated only a few months
after his *De paradiso*.

The text in Migne (PL 14, 315-360) has long since been superseded by Karl Schenkl's
edition in the Vienna Corpus (CSEL, Vol. 32, part 1).

1279

[2, 3, 11]

He saw that the sufferers could not be saved without a remedy and for that reason He   200
brought medicine to the ill, He brought strength and health to all, so that whoever   215
should perish must ascribe to himself the causes of his own death, since such a one did
not want to be cured although he had the remedy by which death could have been
evaded. The clear mercy of Christ, however, is preached in every instance: by the   388
fact that those who perish do perish by their own negligence, while those who are saved
are made free by Christ's purpose, "who wills that all men be saved and come to
a knowledge of the truth." (1)

1. 1 Tim. 2:4.

THE HOLY SPIRIT [*A. D.* 381]

The three books on *The Holy Spirit*, the *De Spiritu Sancto*, were written in the early months of the year 381, completed before Easter of that year.

There can be little or no doubt that it is Ambrose whom St. Jerome calls "a jackdaw decked in another bird's plumage," and whom Jerome, in view of the present work, accuses of writing "bad things in Latin taken from good things in Greek." Rufinus, of course, defends Ambrose; and the whole of the affair provides another chapter to the Punch-and-Judy history of Jerome and Rufinus.

A less prejudiced critique of Ambrose's present work can be had from the pen of St. Augustine, who, with no personal interest in the matter, says in his treatment of *Christian Instruction* (4,21): "When treating of the profound subject of the Holy Spirit, and in showing that the Holy Spirit is equal with the Father and the Son, St. Ambrose makes use of a simple style of discourse; for his subject required not so much the embellishments of language as proofs to move the minds of his readers."

The Migne text (PL 16, 703-816) has been superseded by Otto Faller's edition of 1964 in the Vienna Corpus, CSEL, Vol. 79, pp. 1-222.

1280

[Prol. 18]

Damasus did not cleanse, Peter did not cleanse, Ambrose did not cleanse, Gregory did not cleanse; for the ministries are ours but the Sacraments are Yours. No, it belongs not to human powers to confer things that are divine. That, Lord, is Your function and the Father's.   802

1281

[1, 3, 42]

(Baptism) is complete if you confess Father, Son, and Holy Spirit. If you deny one,   826
you undermine the whole. If you mention but One in words, whether Father or Son
or Holy Spirit, while in faith you deny neither Father nor Son nor Holy Spirit,   803
the Sacrament of faith is complete (1); and in the same way, even if you say Father
and Son and Spirit, but you lessen the power either of Father or Son or Holy Spirit,
the whole mystery is empty.

1282

[1, 6, 77]

If there is any grace in the water, it is not from the nature of water but from the   800
presence of the Holy Spirit. . . . [79] We were sealed, therefore, with the Spirit   285
by God. For just as we die in Christ in order to be born again, so too we are sealed   750
with the Spirit so that we may be able to possess His splendor and image and grace,
which is indeed our spiritual seal. For although it is in our body that we are visibly   798
sealed, it is truly in our heart that we are sealed, so that the Holy Spirit may imprint
on us the likeness of His heavenly image.

1283

[1, 6, 80]

Who would dare to say that the Holy Spirit is separated (2) from the Father and   267
Christ, when it is through Him that we attain to the image and likeness of God, and
through Him that, as the Apostle Peter says, we become "partakers of the divine   754
nature (3)"?

1284

[1, 15, 152]

Know, then, that just as the Father is the Fount of Life, so too, there are many who   273
have stated that the Son is designated as the Fount of Life. It is said, for example,
that with You, Almighty God, Your Son is the Fount of Life, that is, the Fount of
the Holy Spirit. For the Spirit is life, just as the Lord says: "The words which I have
spoken to you are Spirit and life (4)''; because where the Spirit is, there is life; and
where there is life, there too the Holy Spirit.

1285

[3, 11, 79]

By the term footstool (5) the earth is to be understood; and by the earth the Flesh   342
of Christ, which also today we adore in the mysteries, and which the Apostles, as we
said above, adored in the Lord Jesus. For Christ is not divided but one; and neither   323
is His birth from the Virgin denied when He is adored as Son of God. Since, therefore,
the mystery (6) of the Incarnation is to be adored, and the Incarnation is the work   267
of the Spirit, . . . it can scarcely be doubted that the Holy Spirit too is to be adored
when (7) He that, according to the flesh, was born of the Holy Spirit is to be adored.
[80] And let no one divert this to the Virgin Mary: Mary was the temple of God, not   121
the God of the temple. And therefore He alone is to be adored, who was working in
the temple.

1286

[3, 6, 112]

How could it be that (the Holy Spirit) would not have all that pertains to God, seeing   268
that He is named along with Father and Son when priests baptize, is invoked in the
oblations, is proclaimed along with Father and Son by the seraphim in the heavens,
dwells with Father and Son in the saints, is poured out upon the just, and is given
as the source of inspiration in the prophets? So too all divine Scripture is called   20
θεόπνευστος (8), because of the fact that God inspires what the Spirit has spoken (9).

1287

[3, 18, 137]

Note well that it is through the Holy Spirit that sins are forgiven (10). Men make use   900
of their ministry in the forgiveness of sins (11), but they are not exercising any
power that is theirs by right. It is not in their own name, but in the name of the Father
and of the Son and of the Holy Spirit that they forgive sins (12). They ask and the   927
divinity forgives (13). The ministration is of man, but the gift bestowed is from the
Power on high.

1. St. Ambrose is not professing that in general Baptism in the name of Jesus alone is valid. His statement is in explanation
   of Acts 19:5 and similar passages which speak of Baptism in the name of Jesus. He is in fact at pains to show that even
   when Scripture speaks of Baptism in the name of Jesus, it is truly a Trinitarian Baptism of which it speaks.
2. *discretum*.
3. 2 Peter 1:4.
4. John 6:64.
5. *scabellum*: see Is. 66:1, wherein God says: "Heaven is My throne, My footstool the earth." A *scabellum*, besides being
   a footstool, is also a musical instrument played with the foot; but the Hebrew הֲדֹם רַגְלָי, literally *a (foot)stool for my
   feet*, does not share this ambiguity.
6. *sacramentum*.
7. Not *cum* but *quando*, suggesting time rather than consequence; i. e., the term *when* does not mean *since* or *because*, but
   whenever, its implication being *always*.

8. = divinely inspired.
9. See 2 Tim. 3:16.
10. *peccata donantur*.
11. *remissionem peccatorum*.
12. *peccata dimittunt*.
13. *divinitas donat*.

THE MYSTERY OF THE LORD'S INCARNATION [*A. D.* 382]

The title of the work *De incarnationis dominicae sacramento* exhibits St. Ambrose's use of the term *sacramentum* which we are inclined to translate *mystery*. The usage presents no problem; in fact, it gives us some insight into the development of theological terminology, providing us with a better understanding of the meaning of our own term mystery, by helping us to concretize the latter.

The writing of the work can be dated as belonging to the early months of the year 382. Delivered as a lecture and forming but a single book, the work is usually distinguished in two parts. Paragraphs 1 to 78 are in refutation of the Apollinarist notion that the Incarnate Lord had not a rational soul, its place being supplied by the divine Verbum. Paragraphs 79 to 116 are in refutation of Eunomianism, replying to the difficulty proposed by the court of the Emperor Gratian, as to how one who is both begotten and unbegotten can be of one nature and substance. The very statement of the problem, of course, involves a simple misstatement of orthodox doctrine. As Incarnate God, the begotten and unbegotten, though one person, has two natures.

The Migne edition (PL 16, 817-846) is now superseded (1964) by Otto Faller's edition in CSEL, Vol. 79, pp. 223-281.

1288

[5, 35]

There are not enough hours in the day for me to recite even the names of all the various sects of heretics. But what is contrary to all of them is the general belief that Christ is the Son of God, eternally from the Father, and born of the Virgin Mary. . . . Since God must ever be eternal, He receives the mysteries (1) of the Incarnation not as divided but as one: for both are one, and He is one in both, that is, in His divinity and in His body. He is not one from the Father and another from the Virgin, but the same in one way from the Father and in a different way from the Virgin. [36] Generation is not prejudicial to generation, nor flesh to divinity. . . . [37] For that reason too He died in accord with His reception of our nature; and He did not die, in accord with the substance of eternal life. He suffered in accord with His reception of a body, so that His having truly received a body might be believed; and He did not suffer, in accord with the Word's divinity which could not be acted upon from without (2), and to which all pain is foreign (3).

322
324

332

310

1289

[6, 54]

Therefore He accepted from us what it were proper for Him to offer for us in order to redeem us by means of what is oùrs. . . . The sacrifice is of ours, the reward is of His own; and you will find many things in Him both in accord with nature and beyond nature. According to the condition of the body He was in the womb, He nursed at His mother's breast, He lay in the manger; but superior to that condition, the Virgin conceived and the Virgin bore, so that you might believe that He was God who

322
332
314

781

restored nature, though He was man who, in accord with nature, was born of a   782
human being. . . . [56] You have learned, therefore, that He offered in sacrifice   380
what was of ours. What reason was there for the Incarnation, except that flesh, which
had sinned, might be by flesh redeemed? It was what sinned, therefore, that has
been redeemed.

1. *sacramenta.*
2. *et non patiebatur secundum Verbi impassibilem divinitatem.*
3. *quod totius exsors doloris est.*

EXPLANATION OF DAVID THE PROPHET [*A. D.* 383/389]

The *Apologia prophetae David ad Theodosium Augustum*, based upon sermons, can
only be dated as after the death of the Emperor Gratian (August of 383 A. D.), referred
to in 6, 27, and before the composition of the *Commentary on Luke* (A. D. 389), which in
3, 38 refers to the present work. The theme of the *Explanation* is that David, who was both
adulterer and murderer, obtained full pardon and forgiveness of God by reason of his open
confession, his penance, and his zeal for God's house.

A work entitled *Apologia David altera* in the editions is not a genuine continuation of
the present work, and is to be regarded as totally spurious.

The Migne edition (PL 14, 851-884) has been superseded since 1897 by Karl
Schenkl's edition in the Vienna Corpus: CSEL, Vol. 32, part 2, pp. 297-355.

1290

[1, 11, 56]
Before we are born we are infected with the contagion, and before we see the light   614
of day we experience the injury of our origin. In iniquity we are conceived (1)—   615
he does not say whether the wickedness is of our parents or our own—and in sins each
one's mother gives him life. Nor with this did he state whether his mother gave birth
to him in her own sins or whether the sins of which he speaks pertain in some way
to being born. But consider and see what is meant. No conception is without iniquity,
since there are no parents who have not fallen. And if there is no infant who is even
one day without sin, much less can the conceptions of a mother's womb be without
sin. We are conceived, therefore, in the sin of our parents, and it is in their sins that
we are born (2).

1290a

[1, 5, 20]
(Our Lord Jesus) was truly rich in the wealth of His majesty and in the fullness of   488
true divinity. He was served in untiring solicitude by the Angels and Archangels,
Virtues and Powers and Principalities, Thrones and Dominations, Cherubim and
Seraphim.

1. See Ps. 50[51]:7.
2. The passage is frequently cited in reference to the doctrine of original sin. Certainly no thorough treatment of the latter
teaching can ignore the present passage; but it is equally clear that if the present passage is to be related at all to original
sin, here the emphasis is upon concupiscence, as if that were itself the essence of original sin. The notion of original sin
expressed in the passage which Rouët de Journel offers as § 1291 is clearer and much more to the point: "We all sinned
in the first man, and by the succession of nature's guilt there is a succession passed on from one to all. . . . Adam,
therefore, is in each of us. It is in him that the human condition failed in its duty; for through one man sin was transmitted
to all." Unfortunately the passage is of little use to the student of Ambrose, since it is from the spurious *Apologia David
altera* (2, 12, 71).

PENANCE [*A. D.* 387/390]

The two books *De paenitentia* are directed toward refutation of the Novatianist heresy which had its beginnings at Rome in 251 A. D. Originally Novatianism had admitted the Church's power to forgive sins, but had forbidden her the right to exercise that power on the grounds that to do so were scandalous. By Ambrose's time Novatianism was allowing that the Church might properly forgive sins of lesser gravity, but not grave sins. Ambrose, of course, defends the Church's right to forgive all sins.

Otto Faller dates the work between the years 387 and the beginning of 390 A. D. Faller's edition (1955) in the Vienna Corpus, CSEL Vol. 73, pp. 117-206, supersedes Migne's text in PL 16, 465-524.

1292

[1, 1, 4]

What is there more severe than the practice of [the Novatianists], who proclaim a   586
penance which they will not grant? By denying forgiveness they remove the incentive
to repentance. For no one could do penance properly if he did not hope for
forgiveness.

1293

[1, 2, 7]

For those to whom [the right of binding and of loosing] has been given, it is   900
plain that either both are allowed, or it is clear that neither is allowed. Both are   803
allowed to the Church, neither is allowed to heresy. For this right has been granted
to priests only.   925

1294

[1, 3, 10]

[The Novatianists] claim that, having excepted the more grave sins, they can   901
grant forgiveness for the less weighty. But this was not the teaching of Novatian, the
author of your error, who thought that no one should be admitted to penance
(1). . . . God, however, makes no distinction. He promised His mercy to all, and   925
granted to His priests the license of forgiving sins without any exception.

1295

[1, 8, 36]

Why, then, do you impose hands and believe it to be the effect of the blessing   792
if perchance some sick person recovers? Why do you presume that any can be cleansed   940
by you from the filth of the devil? Why do you baptize, if it is not allowed that
sins be forgiven through men? In baptism too there is forgiveness of all sins; what   836
is the difference whether priests claim this power is given them to be exercised   925
in Penance or at the font (2)? The mystery is the same in both.

1296

[1, 15, 80]

For he is purged as if by certain works of the whole people, and is washed in the   936
tears of the multitude; by the prayers and tears of the multitude he is redeemed from
sin, and is cleansed in the inner man. For Christ granted to His Church that one

should be redeemed through all, just as His Church was found worthy of the coming of the Lord Jesus so that all might be redeemed through one.

1297

[2, 2, 12]
   Things that are impossible with men are possible with God. God is able, whenever   900
He wills, to forgive us our sins, even those we think cannot be forgiven. Thus
it is possible for God to give us what to us seems impossible to obtain. Now, it   820
seemed impossible that sin should be washed away in water. . . . But what was
impossible was made possible by God, who gave us so great a grace. It seemed
likewise impossible for sins to be forgiven through penance; yet Christ granted
even this to His Apostles, and by His Apostles it has been transmitted to the   925
offices of priests. That has been made possible, therefore, which seemed to be
impossible.

1298

[2, 3, 19]
   It is most evident from the preaching of the Lord that we have been commanded to   901
restore the grace of the heavenly Sacrament to those guilty even of the most   916
grave crime, if, with their whole heart and by an open confession of their sin, they
do penance. It is certain, therefore, that you have no excuse for remaining in
your sins.

1299

[2, 6, 40]
   If you wish to be justified, confess your sin (3). For a shamefaced confession of   916
sins (4) breaks the bond of your crimes. [41] You see what God, your God, demands of
you: that you keep in mind the grace you have received and that you do not boast
as if you had not received it (5). You see by what a promise of forgiveness He draws
you to confession (6).

1300

[2, 10, 95]
   Rightly are they reproved (7) who think that they can do penance repeatedly (8);   907
for they are making a farce of Christ (9). Indeed, if they truly did penance, they
would take no thought of repeating it afterwards. For just as there is one Baptism,
so too is there one Penance, which, however, is done publicly; for it is necessary
to repent of daily sin; this latter, however, is of lesser faults, the former of the   633
more grave (10).

1. *qui nemini paenitentiam dandam putavit.*
2. *per lavacrum.*
3. *fatere delictum tuum.*
4. *verecunda confessio peccatorum.*
5. See Ps. 49[50]:7 and 1 Cor. 4:7.
6. *ad confitendum.*
7. *Merito reprehenduntur*, as in the Migne text. Faller prefers the reading which joins *merito* to the preceding sentence, and
    has *repperiuntur* rather than *reprehenduntur*.
8. *qui saepius agendam paenitentiam putant.*
9. *Qui (al. quia) luxuriantur in Christo.* See 1 Tim. 5:11.
10. St. Ambrose seems to confirm what we have long suspected: that when the Fathers pronounce the Sacrament of Penance

non-iterable, they are referring to the public aspects of the Sacrament. There are sources enough to show that in practice the private reception of the Sacrament was repeatable. Origen (§ 485a above), before the middle of the third century, already gave advice on the selection of a regular confessor. I think we can safely assume that, theoretically, sacramental confession with public penance was available only once, and that for grave sin. Again theoretically, frequent sacramental penance was available and encouraged for lesser sins. But we may also assume that the stress on the latter's being for less grave sin was largely therapeutic; *i.e.*, by stressing that repeated penance was for less grave sin, it was intended to convey the notion that there should never be reason to have to confess grave sin a second time. If someone had already received the "one" Sacrament of Penance, and afterwards had occasion to confess secret grave sins even repeatedly, doubtless he would have been given absolution. And if his sins were not secret but public, he might even be admitted a second time to the "one" Sacrament of Penance, *i.e.*, to the sacrament administered in certain conditions of publicity.

COMMENTARY ON THE GOSPEL OF LUKE [*ca. A. D.* 389]

The *Expositio evangelii secundum Lucam*, like so many of St. Ambrose's writings, has its basis in his homilies. The work has been variously dated from 387 to 389 A. D. Probably Heinrich Schenkl is closest to the truth when he suggests that the homilies on which the ten books of the Commentary are based were delivered from 385 to 389 A. D., while the Commentary itself, as a unified work, belongs to the year 389.

The first two of the ten books depend heavily upon Origen, and both Augustine and Jerome were quite critical of the work. Later ages have been kinder to Ambrose than were many of his contemporaries, and the *Commentary on the Gospel of Luke* has long been regarded as one of his richest works.

Karl Schenkl edited the various works of Ambrose in Vol. 32, parts 1 and 2, of the Vienna Corpus, both parts appearing in 1897. With his death a third part, CSEL Vol. 32, part 4, embracing the *Expositio evangelli secundum Lucam*, was edited by his son, Heinrich Schenkl. The work appeared in 1902, and supersedes the text of the Migne edition (PL 15, 1587-1850) as well as that of the Ballerini edition. A more recent edition (1955), relying heavily on the work of Schenkl, is that of M. Adriaen in Vol. 14, pp. 1-400, of the *Corpus Christianorum*.

1301

[2, 83]

The Lord was baptized, not to be cleansed Himself but to cleanse the waters, so   801
that those waters, cleansed by the flesh of Christ which knew no sin, might have   820
the power of Baptism. Whoever comes, therefore, to the washing (1) of Christ   836
lays aside his sins.

1302

[2, 84]

Fear the Lord and be confident in the Lord (2). "The Lord will station His angels   650
around those who fear Him, and He will deliver them (3)." You see indeed,
then, how the strength of the Lord is cooperative in human endeavors, so that no one
can build without the Lord, no one can preserve without the Lord, no one can
undertake anything without the Lord.

1303

[4, 71]

[Divine generation] is a thing the full nature of which the human mind is incapable   551
of understanding by any investigative process; by faith, however, it is grasped in its
fullness. For even if I am not permitted to know how He was born, neither am I

permitted to be ignorant of the fact that He was born. The course of His generation I
do not know, but the Author of His generation I do know. We were not present   558
when the Son of God was born of the Father; but we were present when the Son   560
said He was from the Father. If we do not believe God, whom then should we
believe? For everything that we believe, we believe either through seeing or through
hearing. Sight often errs, hearing demands belief. Or does it make a difference who
it is that makes the assertion? If good men state something, we would think it wrong
not to believe. God asserts, the Son proves (4).

1304

[6, 101]
    You see how all things are in the one name of Christ. It is the same Christ who   566
was born of the Virgin, who worked wonders among the people, who died for our
sins, and who rose from the dead. If you were to take away but one of these things
you would take away your salvation. Even the heretics appear to have Christ, for
none of them denies the name of Christ; yet, anyone who does not confess all that
pertains to Christ does in fact deny Christ.

1305

[7, 156]
    Just as those who pay money absolve a debt, nor are they free of the name of debtor   923
until the whole amount, even to the last penny, is absolved by some kind of payment,
so too by the compensation of love and of other virtuous actions, or by some kind   913
of satisfaction, the penalty of sin is removed.

1306

[7, 205]
    That gnashing is not of bodily teeth, nor is that perpetual fire made up of physical   1015
flames, nor is the worm a bodily one. These things are spoken of, however, because,
just as worms are born of massive overeating and fevers, so too, if anyone does not boil
away his sins, . . . he will be burned up in his own fire and devoured by his own
worms. Whence also Isaias says: "Walk in the light of your fire, and the flame which
you have ignited (5)." It is a fire which the gloominess of sins generates. It is a worm
insofar as irrational sins of the soul stab at mind and heart and eat the guts out of your
conscience (6).

1306a

[7, 234]
    Adam was brought into being; and we were all brought into being in him. Adam   614
perished and in him all perished (7).

1307

[8, 2]
    If every marriage is from God it is not licit to dissolve any marriage. How,   976
then, does the Apostle say: "If the unbeliever departs, let him depart (8)"? What is
remarkable in this saying is that, far from intending Christians to find in it an excuse
for divorce, he shows that not every marriage is in fact from God; for Christians,
in God's tribunal (9), cannot be joined to pagans, when the law forbids it.   980

1308

[8, 5]

You dismiss your wife, therefore, as if by right and without being charged with
wrongdoing; and you suppose it is proper for you to do so because no human law
forbids it; but divine law forbids it. Anyone who obeys men ought to stand in awe of
God. Hear the law of the Lord, which even they who propose our laws must obey:
"What God has joined together let no man put asunder (10)."

974
981

1309

[10, 60]

When He says: "Not My will but Thine be done (11)," He is referring to His
own human will, while the Father's is the will of the Godhead. The will of the Man
is temporal, but that of the Godhead is eternal. The will of the Father is not one
thing and the will of the Son another; for there is but one will where there is one
Godhead.

330

1310

[10, 88]

Peter was sorrowful and he wept because, being a man, he had strayed. I do not
find that he said anything; but I do find that he wept. I read about his tears, but I do
not read about any satisfaction. But what cannot be defended can be washed away.
Tears wash clean the fault which he would have blushed to confess in words. . . .
[89] Those are good tears which cleanse from guilt.

911
760

1. *lavacrum*.
2. *Time Dominum et praesume de Domino*.
3. Ps. 33[34]:8.
4. *Deus asserit, probat Filius*.
5. Is. 50:11.
6. The present passage with its ambiguous if not downright dubious remarks on the nature of hell is one of the passages in which St. Ambrose shows an unfortunate dependence upon Origen. See § 463 above.
7. This passage is quoted by St. Augustine in the *Opus imperfectum contra Iulianum*. See § 2007 below.
8. 1 Cor. 7:15.
9. *Dei iudicio*.
10. Matt. 19:6.
11. Luke 22:42.

SERMON AGAINST AUXENTIUS [*A. D.* 386]

The Empress Mother Justina was a convinced Arian; but while Gratian was Emperor
she had little influence. When Gratian was murdered in 383 A. D., however, he was
succeeded by his brother Valentinian II, who was then only twelve years of age. With
Valentinian, Justina was able to exercise a much greater influence than was hers when
Gratian ruled.

At the encouragement of Justina, Valentinian II had an Arian and Gothic disciple of
Wulfilas, Mercurinus by name, made bishop of Milan in opposition to Ambrose. Upon
coming to Milan Mercurinus changed his name to Auxentius, in memory of the Arian
predecessor of Ambrose in that see. A law was decreed ordering that various churches of
Milan be turned over to the Arians, while Ambrose himself was ordered to quit the city.

The populace supported Ambrose with great fidelity and no small amount of public
demonstrating; and ultimately the Arian attempt was brought to naught. On Palm

Sunday in the Portian Basilica outside the city walls, one of the churches which
Ambrose had been ordered to surrender, and amid civil demonstrations of passive
resistance on the part of the Milanese and while imperial soldiery surrounded the
Church, Ambrose preached his powerful *Sermon against Auxentius*. He was fearless,
and with the general support of the people he was able to prevail over the imperial court.
The laws advantaging the Arians were henceforth set aside.

The text of the *Sermo contra Auxentium* is traditionally found in the corpus of
Ambrose's letters, immediately after Letter no. 21, a letter to Valentinian II concerning
the same matter. The text in Migne, PL 16, 1007-1018, still serves as the standard.

1311

[35]

The tribute that belongs to Caesar is not to be denied. The Church, however, is   411
God's, and it must not be pledged to Caesar; for God's temple cannot be a right of
Caesar. [36] That this is said with sentiments of respect for the emperor no man
can deny. And what is there more full of respect than that the emperor be styled a
son of the Church? And when he is called such, he is called such without sin,
because it is a compliment to be called such. For the emperor is in the Church, not
over the Church; and far from refusing the Church's help, a good emperor seeks it.

COMMENTARY ON PSALM 118 [inter A. D. 387-388]

The *Expositio in psalmum 118* is treated in the text tradition as a work separate and
distinct from Ambrose's *Enarrationes in duodecim psalmos Davidicos*. Like the latter,
however, it is probably made up of more or less unrelated homilies, or at least
it is based on such.

Psalm 118 [119] is composed of twenty-two groups of eight verses, each such octet
beginning with a successive letter of the twenty-two letters of the Hebrew alphabet.
Ambrose's commentary is in twenty-two chapters or *sermones*, each dealing with
the matter of one such octet. Each begins with an explanation, largely fanciful, of the
meaning of the pertinent Hebrew letter.

The Migne text in PL 15, 1197-1526, has been superseded since 1913 by M. Petschenig's
edition in the Vienna Corpus, CSEL Vol. 62.

1312

[3, 2]

"Reward Your servant . . . (1)." [3] It is neither strange nor arrogant if David asks   583
his Lord God for a reward for his heavy labors. It is the prerogative of faith and of   584
justice to lay claim to the reward of God's favor. It is on this score that Peter is reproved;
for when he was walking on the water his human feelings caused his doubt to be
greater than the confidence inspired by his apostolic authority. In the gospel too we
are taught to have faith and not to draw back from doing those things which are   556
above a man. . . . It is not insolent arrogance but an innocent conscience which   585
seeks a reward from Him whom you serve. Despair belongs to the crass sluggard;
hope, however, is an incentive to labor.

1313

[8, 57]

The earth, therefore, is full of the mercy of the Lord; for the forgiveness of sins   724 is given to all. The sun is commanded to rise over all; and indeed, this sun does in fact rise daily over all. That mystic Sun of Justice, however, has risen for all, comes to all, suffered for all and rose again for all. He suffered so that He might take away the sin of the world. If, however, anyone does not believe in Christ, he but cheats himself of this general benefit.

386

1314

[22, 30]

Come, then, and search out Your sheep, not through Your servants or hired men, but do it Yourself. Lift me up bodily and in the flesh, which is fallen in Adam. Lift me up not from Sara but from Mary, a Virgin not only undefiled but a Virgin whom grace has made inviolate, free of every stain of sin (2).

786

1. Ps. 118[119]:17.
2. *ut incorrupta sit virgo, sed virgo per gratiam ab omni integra labe peccati.*

HEXAMERON [*post. A. D.* 389]

The *Hexameron* or *Exaemeron in libris sex* is a series of nine sermons on the six days of creation, preached during a Holy Week. Internal evidence indicates that the sermons can hardly have been prepared before the year 389 A. D. Unfortunately a closer dating of the work is not presently possible.

The work is organized in six books, headed "first day", "second day", etc. For the first, third, and fifth days there are two sermons each, one given in the morning and the other in the afternoon.

Although the work shows considerable dependence upon St. Basil's nine sermons on the hexameron, it is not a naked dependence, and the treatment of the material is such that it becomes entirely Ambrose's own. And while Basil showed a considerable curiosity about matters of natural history, Ambrose omits all such and is concerned only with what pertains to eternal life.

The Migne text, PL 14, 123-274, is entirely superseded by Karl Schenkl's edition of 1897 in the Vienna Corpus, CSEL Vol. 32, part 1, pp. 1-261.

1315

[1, 4, 16]

Heaven and earth is the sum total of visible things, which seem not only to be ordered to the embellishment of this world but even to the disclosure of invisible things, providing, as it were, an argument for those things which are not seen, as the prophetic utterance announces: "The heavens tell the glory of God, and the firmament proclaims the works of His hands (1)." The Apostle likewise states much the same thing, though in other words, when he says: "His invisible attributes (2) are known through the things which He made (3)." We easily recognize Him as the Author of the Angels, Dominations, and Powers:—He that by the authority of His command made so beautiful a world as this to come into being out of nothing (4), when before it did not exist, and who gave substance, whether directly or in cause, to those things which before did not exist (5).

131

480
488

461

509

1316

[1, 5, 19]

The world was made, therefore, and that which before did not exist began to be.

461

In the beginning, however, there was the Word of God, and the Word always was.   256
But even the Angels, the Dominations, and the Powers had a beginning of their   480
being at some time, although they were already in existence when this world was   488
made. For "all things were created and established, things visible and invisible,   481
whether Thrones or Dominations or Principalities or Powers (6)."   460

1317

[2, 1, 2]

If there were increated matter God would seem to lack the power of creating   468
matter, and have borrowed for His work that which was already at hand. But if   461
such matter were disordered, how remarkable it is that matter coeternal with God
would not have been able to confer beauty and order upon itself, seeing that it
did not receive its substance from a creator but possessed it timelessly itself. It
is a greater thing, therefore, that the Fashioner of all things provided the material
with which He worked, than it would be if He had simply put material in order.
He provided the matter which enabled Him to do His fashioning; and He put
that matter in order, giving it the shape which renders beautiful that which He
provided.

1317a

[6, 7, 40]

But let us consider the course of our own creation. He says: "Let Us make man   232
to our image and to our likeness (7)." Who says this? Is it not God, who made you?   467
And what is God, flesh or spirit? Certainly not flesh, He is spirit, to which flesh
can have no likeness; for spirit is incorporeal and invisible, while flesh is bounded
and seen. To whom does He say it? Certainly not to Himself, for He does not say
"Let Me make" but "Let Us make". Nor to the Angels, for they are ministers;
and servants can have no partnership in the operation of the master, nor works with
their author. It is the Son to whom He speaks, even if the Jews will not have it
and the Arians fight against it. . . . [41] . . . [And it is the Son] who is the   256
image of God the Father, the Son who always is and who was in the beginning.   257
Indeed, it is this Image who says: "Philip, whoever sees Me sees also the Father (8)."   264

1318

[6, 7, 42]

That soul is painted by God, that soul which has in itself the steadying grace   740
of virtues and the splendor of piety. That soul is well-painted, in which the likeness
of the divine operation is reflected. That soul is well-painted, in which there is the
splendor of glory and the image of the substance of the Father. In accord with this
image, which shines forth, the picture is a priceless one. Adam, before his sin,   520
was just such an image; but when he fell, he lost the image of the heavenly and   610
took on the image of the terrestrial.

1319

[6, 8, 46]

I ask, therefore, whether it seems to you that justification is granted in accord   750
with the body or in accord with the soul; and you may answer. But you cannot doubt,
since justice, whence the term justification is derived, certainly pertains to the
mind and not the body. You are a portrait, O man, a portrait painted by your Lord

God. Yours is a good artist and painter. Do not deface the good picture, which
reflects not deceit but truth, which expresses not guile but grace (9).

1. Ps. 18[19]:2.
2. *invisibilia eius*.
3. Rom. 1:20.
4. *ex nihilo fecit esse*.
5. *et non exstantibus aut rebus aut causis donavit habere substantiam*.
6. Col. 1:16.
7. Gen. 1:26. If in the next few lines Ambrose seems to imply that man cannot be in God's image, he shortly distinguishes (see § 1318 and § 1319 below) in view of man's being both flesh and spirit.
8. John 14:9.
9. *Noli bonam delere picturam, non fuco sed veritate fulgentem, non cera expressam sed gratia*. There is a careful byplay in the terms which my poor rhetoric cannot reproduce. *Fucus* means not only deceit; it is also a red pigment which might be used in painting; and further, it is a naturally red beeswax. *Cera*, which I render *guile*, really means *wax*. But it does, in various idiomatic expressions, also mean guile, as is evident from the English term *sincere*, from the Latin *sine cera*: literally, *without wax*. A literal translation (and others are possible) of the passage in question might be: Do not deface the good picture, resplendent not in red beeswax but in truth, formed not in wax but in grace.

THE DUTIES OF THE CLERGY [*ca. A. D.* 391]

In the three books of his *De officiis ministrorum* or *The Duties of the Clergy* St.
Ambrose takes the three books of Cicero's *De officiis* and converts their ideals from
the pagan and Stoic to the Christian. There is really a very close correspondence between
the two works, even in numerous lesser details. Cicero, for example, dedicated his *De
officiis* to his son Marcus, then a student in Athens; Ambrose dedicates his work of the
same title to his sons, the clerics who serve the Church.

A means to date the work with any precision is lacking; but the books may be
assigned with some probability to the era *ca.* A. D. 391. The work has not yet
appeared in the Vienna Corpus, and the Maurist edition as reprinted in Migne (PL 16,
23-184) remains the standard, unless one prefer the Ballerini, Vol. 4, pp. 21-184.

1319a

[1, 15, 57]

Why do sinners have an abundance of wealth and riches, and feast constantly and   771
sumptuously, knowing no pain or sorrow, while the just are in want and are
punished by the loss of spouse or children? The parable in the Gospel (1) must
supply the answer. The rich man was clothed in purple and fine linen and gave
great banquets every day; but the poor man, full of sores, gathered the crumbs
from his table. After the death of each of them, however, the poor man took his
rest in the bosom of Abraham, while the rich man was in torment. Is it not evident
from this that rewards and punishments according to merits await us after death?

1320

[3, 2, 11]

Moreover the same words frequently mean something different. In one sense   177
we call God good; man in another. In one sense we say God is just; man in   153
another. . . . For the form of perfection is twofold; in one way partially, in another
way the totality; in one way here, in another way there; in one way according to a man's
capability, in another way according to the perfection that belongs to the future. God,
however, is just through all, wise above all, perfect in all (2).

1. See Luke 16:19ff.
2. *iustus per omnia, sapiens super omnia, perfectus in omnibus*.

ABRAHAM [*A. D.* 387]

The two books on *Abraham*, or *De Abraham libri duo*, were separate in their origins, but already united as a single work by Ambrose himself. The first book, directed to catechumens and assembled from catechetical homilies, portrays Abraham as the ideal of the righteous man who is dependent upon God. The accounts in Genesis are presented according to a perfectly literal understanding. The second book has its origins in sermons to the already baptized, and seeks to uncover a deeper and allegorical meaning·in the texts.

As a unified work, *Abraham* may be assigned to the year 387 A. D. The Migne text (PL 14, 419-500) has been superseded since 1897 by Karl Schenkl's edition in the Vienna Corpus, CSEL Vol. 32, part 1, pp. 499-638.

1321

[1, 3, 21]

It is good that faith should precede reason, lest we seem to demand reasons from 562
our Lord God in the same way that we might demand them of a man. How 558
unworthy it were that we should believe the human testimonies of another, and not 10
believe the utterances of God Himself!

1322

[1, 7, 59]

No one is permitted to know a woman other than his wife. The marital right is 977
given you for this reason: lest you fall into the snare and sin with a strange woman. 974
"If you are bound to a wife do not seek a divorce (1)"; for you are not permitted, while your wife lives, to marry another. To seek another when you have your own is a crime of adultery and all the more grave because you are trying to invest your sin with legal authority (2).

1323

[2, 11, 79]

The Church was redeemed at the price of Christ's blood. Jew or Greek, it makes 831
no difference; but if he has believed, he must circumcise himself from his sins so that he can be saved; . . . . for no one ascends into the kingdom of heaven except through the Sacrament of Baptism (3).

1324

[2, 11, 84]

"Unless a man be born again of water and the Holy Spirit, he cannot enter 831
the kingdom of God (4)." No one is excepted: not the infant, not the one prevented 834
by some necessity. They may, however, have an undisclosed exemption from 835
punishments; but I do not know whether they can have the honor of the kingdom (5).

1. 1 Cor. 7:27.
2. To divorce and remarry is more gravely sinful than to live in concubinage; for the former is concubinage with the added hypocrisy of pretending to legalize what is contrary to divine law. Henry C. Lea complained much in his *History of Sacerdotal Celibacy* that the Catholic Church is much harder on a priest who attempts marriage in a formal manner than on one who lives in concubinage, *i.e.*, without the supposed benefit of law. He is correct in his facts, but not in his complaining of them; for he does not understand the reason for such an attitude on the part of the Church. The priest who keeps a mistress is guilty of a moral fault; but the priest who attempts marriage is at fault both morally and doctrinally.

Obviously, however, the greater gravity of the latter instance should provide no comfort to the former; nor does any right thinking person suppose otherwise.

3. *per sacramentum baptismatis*.

4. John 3:5.

5. The present sentence makes it clear that when St. Ambrose says in the preceding "no one is excepted," he means that the Scriptural utterance expresses no exception; he does not know whether or not some logical exception, *e.g.*, state of infancy or actual impossibility or non-culpable ignorance, may have been presumed and left unexpressed.

DEATH AS A BLESSING [*ca. A. D.* 388/390]

In a treatise *Isaac and the Soul* Ambrose regards the marriage of Isaac and Rebecca as a foreshadowing of the union of Christ with the human soul, drawing also upon the Canticle of Canticles as typifying this same union.

In *De bono mortis* or *Death as a Blessing* Ambrose continues his development of the ideas introduced in *Isaac and the Soul* and shows that physical death is not a thing to be feared but is actually a blessing for humanity, a good thing to be desired.

The Maurist text in Migne (PL 14, 539-568) is superseded by Karl Schenkl's edition in the CSEL (1897), Vol. 32, part 1, pp. 701-753.

1325

[4, 15]

If we meditate on the fact that God did not make death, but only after man fell   611
into the disgrace of guilt and deception did God decree the sentence that earth should
return to earth, we shall discover that death is the end of sin; and if we were to live   991
longer our guilt would only be the greater (1).

1. *ne, quo esset vita diuturnior, eo fieret culpa numerosior*.

THE VIRGINS [*A. D.* 377]

For anyone who has but a general interest in Ambrose there is likely to be some confusion over his several works on the states of virginity and widowhood, so we will list these works all together here in full title and chronological order:

    a) *De virginibus ad Marcellinam sororem suam libri tres* (*A. D.* 377);

    b) *De viduis liber unus* (*A. D.* 377/378);

    c) *De virginitate liber unus* (*ca. A. D.* 378);

    d) *De institutione virginis et sanctae Mariae virginitate perpetua ad Eusebium liber unus* (*A. D.* 391/392);

    e) *Exhortatio virginitatis liber unus* (*A. D.* 393).

And in addition to the above, also to be reckoned with is a spurious work preserved among the writings of Ambrose and frequently cited as his, entitled *De lapsu virginis consecratae*. It deals with the concrete case of a consecrated virgin named Susanna, who broke her vow, sinned with a lector, and murdered the child she conceived. Several modern authors have attributed this last named work to Nicetas of Remesiana, a city of Jugoslavia now known as Bela Palanka. This latter attribution too, however, seems to be anything but certain.

The first of these works, *The Virgins*, in three books and written for Ambrose's sister Marcellina, was written in 377 and is apparently the earliest of Ambrose's writings. The first book treats of the dignity of virginity. The second book sets forth various examples:

the Mother of God, St. Thecla, and a martyred virgin of Antioch. The opening lines of book three supply the information that Marcellina had received the veil of virginity at the hands of Pope Liberius, presumably in the year 353 or 354 A. D. It is the earliest mention of a public profession of vows. The Maurist text in Migne (PL 16, 187-232) has been superseded by the edition of Otto Faller in Vol. 31 of B. Geyer's and J. Zellinger's *Florilegium patristicum*, Bonn 1933.

1325a

[2, 2, 6]

Mary's life should be for you a pictorial image of virginity. Her life is like a   785
mirror reflecting the face of chastity and the form of virtue. Therein you may find a model
for your own life, . . . showing what to improve, what to imitate, what to hold fast to.

THE WIDOWS [*A. D.* 377/378]

Written shortly after the three books *De virginibus ad Marcellinam* the much briefer *De viduis*, like most of Ambrose's writings, has its basis in his preaching. The main point of *The Widows* is the superiority of widowhood over a second marriage.
The Maurist text in Migne, PL 16, 233-262, is still the standard.

1325b

[11, 68]

What we suggest by way of counsel we do not command as a precept. We do not   979
so much bind the widow as encourage her. We do not prohibit second marriages, but
neither do we recommend them. Consideration of weakness is one thing, the grace of
chastity another. Again I say, we do not prohibit second marriages, but neither do we
approve a multiplicity of marriages. What is permitted is not necessarily expedient. "All
things may be lawful for me," says the Apostle, "but not all are expedient (1)." To drink
wine is lawful, but for the most part it is unseemly (2).

1. 1 Cor. 6:12.
2. *Et vinum bibere licet, sed plurimum non decet*. Or does he mean that too much is unseemly?

VIRGINITY [*ca. A. D.* 378]

Written shortly after his *De viduis*, Ambrose's *De virginitate* quite possibly belongs to the year 378 A. D. Most certainly it is compiled from his own preaching, as is indicated clearly in several passages in the work itself, phrases such as "you have just heard in the reading", or "as you heard the Lord saying this morning".
Ambrose found himself accused of being too strong in his encouraging of young girls to a life of virginity, and the *De virginitate* is his explanation and defense of his position.
The text of the Migne edition, PL 16, 265-302, remains the standard.

1325c

[3, 14]

Only consider for a moment that it was the virgins who merited to witness the Lord's   984
resurrection even ahead of the Apostles.

1325d

[4, 17]

Then, as I said before, the Lord himself repeated the same words: "Woman,   252
why do you weep? Whom do you seek (1)?" . . . "Why do you weep?" That   256
is to say, you are the cause of your own weeping, you are the author of your
own lamentation, because you are disbelieving of Christ. Believe, and you will
see Him. Christ is present, nor is He ever absent to those who seek Him. . . . [18]
"Whom do you seek?" That is to say, do you not see that Christ is present? Do you
not see that Christ is the strength of God, that Christ is the wisdom of God, that   261
Christ is holiness, that Christ is chastity, that Christ is integrity, that Christ is born   781
of a Virgin, that Christ is from the Father and with the Father and in the Father always,
begotten not made, never unworthy but always beloved, true God of Godhead true?

1. John 20:13.

THE CONSECRATION OF A VIRGIN AND THE PERPETUAL VIRGINITY OF MARY [A. D. 391/392]

The treatise *De institutione virginis et sanctae Mariae virginitate perpetua ad Eusebium liber unus* was addressed to a certain Eusebius of Bologna, probably a nobleman of that city and not the bishop, shortly after Ambrose had given the veil of virginity to Eusebius' niece.

The standard edition is still that in Migne, PL 16, 305-334.

1326

[6, 41]

Neither does it make any difference that the Scripture says: "Joseph took his wife and   973
went into Egypt (1)"; for any woman espoused to a man is given the name of wife.
It is from the time that a marriage begins that the marital terminology is employed. It is
not the deflowering of virginity (2) that makes a marriage, but the marital contract
(3). It is when the girl accepts the yoke that the marriage begins, not when she comes to
know her husband physically (4).

1327

[8, 52]

Who is this gate (5), if not Mary? Is it not closed because she is a virgin? Mary is the   782
gate through which Christ entered this world, when He was brought forth in the
virginal birth (6) and the manner of His birth did not break the seals of virginity (7).

1. Matt. 1:24; 2:14.
2. *defloratio virginitatis*.
3. *pactio coniugalis*.
4. *Denique cum iungitur puella, coniugium est, non cum virili admixtione cognoscitur*.
5. See Ezech. 44:1ff.
6. *virginali fusus est partu*.
7. *et genitalia virginitatis claustra non solvit*.

EXHORTATION TO VIRGINITY [*A. D.* 393]

After discovering the relics of the martyrs Vitalis and Agricola at Bologna in 393 A. D., Ambrose journeyed on to Florence where he dedicated the basilica of St. Lawrence built by a pious widow named Juliana. Later that same year he expanded the discourse which he had delivered at the dedication of the basilica and published it under the title *Exhortatio virginitatis*.

The standard text is still that of Migne, PL 16, 335-364.

1327a

[4, 20]

Only think, my daughters, if you wish to marry, how much is lacking if you are   984 without a father. You have no valuable dowry; and even if you had such in abundance you would only be paying a high price for servitude. Who will not be contemptuous of those who have no father? To whom will you fly for refuge? Where will you seek help against the injuries inflicted by your husband? How great are the misfortunes peculiar to marriage! How many and how severe its humiliations! How numerous its chains!

SYMPATHY AT THE DEATH OF VALENTINIAN [*A. D.* 392]

Valentinian II, only twenty years of age, was assassinated at Vienne on May 15, 392, by the Frankish General Arbogast. The body was brought to Milan and interred only at the end of July or at the beginning of August. Only two days before his death Valentinian had sent messengers to Ambrose to deliver his request for Baptism. Ambrose was already in the Alps when news came to him that the emperor was dead. In the discourse *De obitu Valentiniani consolatio* which Ambrose delivered on the occasion of Valentinian's burial he speaks from the heart, words of praise for the dead emperor and words of sympathy and consolation for the living. And if some were disturbed because Valentinian had died without the forms of Baptism Ambrose explains that in the desire for it, Valentinian had the Sacrament itself.

The text in Migne, PL 16, 1357-1384, has been superseded by Otto Faller's edition in the Vienna Corpus, Vol. 73 (1955), pp. 329-367.

1328

[51]

But I hear you lamenting because he had not received the sacraments of Baptism (1).   832 Tell me, what else could we have, except the will to it, the asking for it? He too had just now this desire; and after he came into Italy it was begun, and a short time ago he signified that he wished to be baptized by me. Did he, then, not have the grace which he desired? Did he not have what he eagerly sought? Certainly, because he sought it, he received it. What else does it mean: "Whatever just man shall be overtaken by death, his soul shall be at rest (2)"?

1. *sacramenta baptismatis*.
2. Wis. 4:7.

THE MYSTERIES [*A. D*. 390-391]

The authenticity of the treatise *De mysteriis* has been contested, but on insufficient grounds. The ancients acknowledged it as a genuine work of Ambrose; and in the last thirty years or so of our own time it has had sufficient defenders—Otto Faller, Jerome Frank, Bernard Botte, and R. H. Connolly among others—that by this time it is very nearly universally accepted as genuine.

The text in Migne (PL 16, 389-410) is superseded as standard by Otto Faller's edition in the Vienna Corpus, CSEL Vol. 73 (1955), pp. 80-116.

1329

[3, 8]

What did you see? Water certainly, but not water only; the levites (1) ministering there, the high priest (2) asking questions and consecrating. . . . Believe, then, in the presence there of the Godhead. If you believe in His operation, can you disbelieve in His presence? Whence comes this operation, if it is not preceded by His presence?

791
800

1330

[4, 20]

You have read, therefore, that the three witnesses in Baptism are one: water, blood, and the Spirit (3): and if you withdraw any one of these, the Sacrament of Baptism is not valid (4). For what is water without the cross of Christ? A common element with no sacramental effect. Nor on the other hand is there any mystery of regeneration without water: for "unless a man be born again of water and the Spirit, he cannot enter the kingdom of God (5)." Even a catechumen believes in the cross of the Lord Jesus, by which also he is signed; but unless he be baptized in the name of the Father and of the Son and of the Holy Spirit, he cannot receive the remission of sins nor be recipient of the gift of spiritual grace.

826
235
822

831

1331

[6, 32]

Peter was clean, but he still had to wash his feet (6); for he was in sin by a succession from the first man, when the serpent tripped him and persuaded him to err. Therefore Peter's feet were washed to take away his hereditary sins (7); for our own are taken away by Baptism.

809
836

1332

[7, 42]

You have received the spiritual sign (8), the spirit of wisdom and understanding, the spirit of counsel and fortitude, the spirit of knowledge and piety, the spirit of holy fear: now keep what you have received. God the Father signed you, Christ the Lord confirmed you, and the Spirit gave a pledge in your hearts.

840
798
548

1333

[9, 50]

Perhaps you may be saying: I see something else; how can you assure me that I am receiving the Body of Christ? It but remains for us to prove it. And how many are the examples we might use! Let us prove that this is not what nature has shaped it to be,

851

but what the blessing has consecrated; for the power of the blessing is greater than   864
that of nature, because by the blessing even nature itself is changed.   856

1334

[9, 58]
    Christ is in that Sacrament, because it is the Body of Christ; yet, it is not on that   851
account corporeal food, but spiritual. Whence also His Apostle says of the type: "For   857
our fathers ate spiritual food and drank spiritual drink (9)." For the body of God is a
spiritual body.

1. *levitas, i.e.,* the deacons.
2. *summum sacerdotem, i.e.,* the bishop.
3. See 1 John 5:8.
4. *non stat baptismatis sacramentum.*
5. John 3:5.
6. *sed plantam lavare debebat.* In classical Latin *planta,* whether or not qualified by *pedis,* is the sole of the foot. The
   term *planta* is used again in the final sentence of the present passage. It is an unusual word, but Ambrose employs it to
   complete a rhetorical device. What we have translated "when the serpent tripped him" is *quando eum supplantavit serpens,"*
   the word *supplantare* deriving from *sub + planta,* under foot, the verb meaning, in Cicero's usage, *to throw a person
   down by tripping up his heels.*
7. *hereditaria peccata.* I suppose a dozen tentative explanations might be advanced in an attempt to save Ambrose from the
   unfortunate consequences of this remark. But does he really need our help? It must be admitted, first of all, that he
   seems not to have had a very clear notion of original sin, and his very term *hereditary sins* is rather unfortunate. And if in
   this instance he says that Baptism remits personal sins while the *lotio pedum* takes away original sin it is probably only
   an overenthusiastic explanation of the *lotio pedum;* and in *Abraham* 2, 11, 84 (§ 1324 above) he does know the
   necessity of Baptism even for infants.
8. *signaculum spiritale.*
9. 1 Cor. 10:2-4.

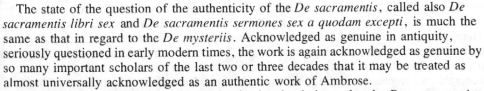

THE SACRAMENTS [A. D. 390-391]

    The state of the question of the authenticity of the *De sacramentis,* called also *De
sacramentis libri sex* and *De sacramentis sermones sex a quodam excepti,* is much the
same as that in regard to the *De mysteriis.* Acknowledged as genuine in antiquity,
seriously questioned in early modern times, the work is again acknowledged as genuine by
so many important scholars of the last two or three decades that it may be treated as
almost universally acknowledged as an authentic work of Ambrose.

    Otto Faller has rightly pointed out what is already obvious, that the *De sacramentis*
consists not of *libri sex* but of *sermones sex.* Faller suggests, moreover, that the
De sacramentis as we have it is either Ambrose's own draft of his catechetical lectures,
written down beforehand for his own use, or a private shorthand copy taken by an
unknown person while Ambrose preached, and afterwards transcribed, or a copy taken
down by a secretary and then written out for Ambrose's own use—and with any of these
three possibilities the work was then published soon after Ambrose's death. Faller
dates the work, along with the *De mysteriis,* as belonging to the years 390-391 A. D.

    Otto Faller's edition in CSEL Vol. 73 (1955), pp. 15-85 supersedes the Maurist
text in Migne (PL 16, 417-462).

1335a

[1, 2, 5]
    When he questioned you [at Baptism]: "Do you renounce the devil and his works?"   836
what did you answer? "I do so renounce!" "Do you renounce the world and its

delights?'' what did you answer? ''I do so renounce!'' Keep your answer in mind and never go back on the promises of the word you have pledged (1).

1336

[3, 1, 7]

In Baptism all guilt is washed away. Guilt thereby disappears; but because Adam   836
was tripped up by the devil (2), whose venom spilled out on Adam's feet, you therefore   809
wash feet, so that in that part for which the serpent lurks the assistance of sanctification
may be especially prominent, and he may not trip you up (3) again. You wash feet,
therefore, so as to wash away the poisons of the serpent.

1337

[3, 2, 8]

[Baptism] is followed by a spiritual signing (4), as you have heard in the reading   840
today; for after the font it but remains to perfect the work, when, at the invocation of the 798
priest the Holy Spirit is poured out, the spirit of wisdom and understanding, the   548
spirit of counsel and fortitude, the spirit of knowledge and piety, the spirit of holy
fear: seven powers, as it were, of the Spirit (5).

1338

[4, 4, 13]

Who, then, is the author of the Sacraments if not the Lord Jesus? Those Sacraments   801
came from heaven; for every counsel is from heaven.

1339

[4, 4, 14]

You may perhaps say: ''My bread is ordinary.'' But that bread is bread before the   856
words of the Sacraments; where the consecration has entered in, the bread becomes
the flesh of Christ. And let us add this: How can what is bread be the Body of Christ?
By the consecration. The consecration takes place by certain words; but whose words?   862
Those of the Lord Jesus. Like all the rest of the things said beforehand, they are
said by the priest; praises are referred to God, prayer of petition is offered for the people, 866
for kings, for other persons; but when the time comes for the confection of the   897
venerable Sacrament, then the priest uses not his own words but the words of Christ.   802
Therefore it is the word of Christ that confects this Sacrament (6).

1340

[4, 5, 23]

Before it be consecrated it is bread; but where the words of Christ come in, it is the   860
Body of Christ. Finally, hear Him saying: ''All of you take and eat of this; for this   862
is My Body (7).'' And before the words of Christ the chalice is full of wine and water;   856
but where the words of Christ have been operative it is made the Blood of Christ,   852
which redeems the people.   861

1. *Quando te interrogavit: "Abrenuntias diabolo et operibus eius?" quid respondisti? "Abrenuntio." "Abrenuntias saeculo et voluptatibus eius?" quid respondisti? "Abrenuntio." Memor esto sermonis tui, et numquam tibi excidat tuae series cautionis.*
2. *Adam supplantatus a diabolo est.*
3. *supplantare te.* Note the similarity of this terminology and that of the footnote immediately preceding to the terminology in the *De mysteriis,* § 1331 above.

4. *spiritale signaculum*. The same terminology is found in the *De mysteriis*, § 1332 above.
5. The enumeration of the seven gifts is precisely as found in Ambrose's *De mysteriis*, § 1332 above, even in respect to the inconsequential connectives. Both passages read: *"spiritum sapientiae et intellectus, spiritum consilii atque virtutis, spiritum cognitionis atque pietatis, spiritum sancti timoris."* The Vulgate reading of Is. 11:2-3 is *spiritus sapientiae et intellectus, spiritus consilii et fortitudinis, spiritus scientiae et pietatis; . . . spiritus timoris Domini.*
6. Lest there be any misunderstanding, I beg to point out that in this final sentence the word of Christ is not the *Verbum Christus quod est* but the *sermo Christi*.
7. Luke 22:19.

THE AMBROSIASTER [*fl. inter A. D.* 366-384]

A work entitled *Commentaries on Thirteen Pauline Epistles* (Hebrews is absent) was falsely attributed in antiquity to Ambrose and is preserved in the tradition of his works. It was Erasmus of Rotterdam who gave its unknown author the name Ambrosiaster, that is, the Pseudo-Ambrose.

The work originated in Rome in the time of Pope Damasus (A. D. 366-384) and can be dated no more closely. A part of the manuscript tradition attributes the Commentary on Romans to an otherwise unspecified Hilary, probably believed to be Hilary of Poitiers. Attempts have been made to identify the Ambrosiaster with the Luciferian Deacon Hilary, with the political figure Decimius Hilarian Hilary, and with the Jew Isaac, a convert who later returned to Judaism and made slanderous accusations against Pope Damasus. In considering the Jew Isaac as Hilary and the Ambrosiaster, the conjecture is made that at his baptism he took the name Gaudentius, a translation of Isaac, and used Hilary as a pseudonym in his writings; for if something is *hilarius* it causes one to be *gaudens*.

A Pseudo-Augustinian collection of 127 *Quaestiones veteris et novi testamenti* is probably the work of the Ambrosiaster, and some ascribe also to him a version of the same work having 151 questions. The Jew Isaac is known as the author of a *Fides Isaatis ex Iudaeo* in a Paris manuscript of the eighth or ninth century, published by J. Sirmond in 1630 and again by H. Zeuschner in 1909.

COMMENTARIES ON THIRTEEN PAULINE EPISTLES [*inter A. D.* 366-384]

In Migne the *Commentaria in tredecim epistulas Beati Pauli* is found among Ambrose's writings (PL 17, 45-508). Migne's text is now superseded, however, by the edition of Henry Joseph Vogels *(Commentarius in epistulas Paulinas)*, CSEL Vol. 81, part 1 (1966), Romans; part 2 (1968), 1st and 2nd Corinthians; and part 3 (1969), the rest of the Pauline epistles without Hebrews.

1341

[In Rom. 5:12]
"In whom"—that is, in Adam—"all have sinned (1)." And he said "in whom",   614
using the masculine form, when he was speaking of a woman, because the reference
was not to a specific individual but to the race (2). It is clear, therefore, that all
have sinned in Adam, *en masse* as it were (3); for when he himself was corrupted by
sin, all whom he begot were born under sin. On his account, then, all are sinners,
because we are all from him. He lost God's favor when he strayed.

1341a

[In I Cor. 7:11]

"A wife is not to separate from her husband; but if she has separated she is to remain   974
unmarried." This admonition of the Apostle is that if she separated because of the   975
wicked behavior of her husband she is to remain unmarried, or else be reconciled
to her husband. And if, he says, she is not able to remain continent because she does not
wish to struggle against the flesh, she is to be reconciled to her husband. For it is not
permitted that a woman marry, if she divorced her husband because of fornication
or apostasy or if he sought to use his wife in an illicitly lascivious manner. . . .
If, then, a man apostatize or seek a perverted use of his wife, the woman can neither
marry nor return to him.

Neither can a man divorce his wife; [for he says]: "A man is not to divorce his wife."
It presumes of course: "except for cause of fornication (4)." And therefore he
does not subjoin what he says when speaking of a woman: "but if she has separated,
she is to remain so"; for it is permissible for a man to marry a wife, if he has divorced a
sinful wife, because a man is not bound by the law as a woman is; for man is head
over woman (5).

1341b

[In I Cor. 7:15]

"But if an unbeliever departs, let him depart." He protects the designs of religion   976
by his prior assertion that Christians may not forsake their spouses. But if an unbeliever
departs out of hatred for God, the believer will not be guilty of having dissolved the
marriage; for the honor of God is greater than that of matrimony (6). "For a brother or
sister is not subject to bondage (7) in a case of this kind." That is, there is no
reverence owed to a marriage with a person who has a horror for the Author of marriage.
For that which is without devotion to God is not a ratified marriage (8), and that is why it
is not a sin for one who has been dismissed on account of God to enter upon a
marriage with another. For contemptuousness of the Creator dissolves the bond of
matrimony (9) for the one who has been forsaken, nor is he to be accused if he has joined
himself to another. But the departing disbeliever is recognized as sinning both against
God and against marriage, because he would not remain in a marriage under
devotion to God. He has no faith to preserve the marriage, if he goes away so that he
will not hear that the Author of marriage is the God of the Christians.

1342

[In 2 Cor. 5:21]

"For our sakes He made Him, who knew no sin, to be sin." He says God the Father   345
made His Son, Christ, to be sin; and that Christ knew no sin, that is, He had never   383
committed a sin. He was made not of some different kind; but made incarnate, He was
made sin. . . . Since all flesh is under sin, when made flesh He was made sin.
And since He was sacrificed for sins, it is not improper to say that He was made sin; for in
law, the victim that is offered up for sins is denominated sin.

1342a

[In Eph. 5:31]

"For this reason shall a man leave father and mother and cleave to his wife and   972
they shall be two in one flesh." To commend this unity he supplies an example of unity.
Just as a man and a woman are one in nature so Christ and the Church are recognized

as one through faith. [32] "This is a great mystery—I mean in reference to Christ and the Church." He means that the great sign (10) of this mystery is in the unity of man and woman. . . . Just as a man forsakes his parents and cleaves to his wife, so too he forsakes every error and cleaves to the Church and subjects himself to her Head, which is Christ.

1343

[In 1 Tim. 2:4]

God "wills all men to be saved"; but that is if they come to Him. For He does not will that they be saved who do not want to be saved. He wills that they be saved if they themselves also will it. Thus, He that gave the law to all excludes no one from salvation. Similarly, does not a physician make it publicly known that he desires to cure everyone, so that the sick will come to him? It would not truly be salvation if it were given to someone who did not want it.

200

1. The *in quo* of the passage renders the Greek ἐφ' ᾧ. The Latin is barely capable of being translated in the sense of *because*; but it is difficult to translate the Greek in any other way. St. Augustine is usually blamed for initiating the "in whom" interpretation, referring the *in quo* to Adam. But the Ambrosiaster is certainly older than Augustine, who, in fact, quotes this very passage, attributing it to St. Hilary (Aug., *Contra duas epistolas Pelagianorum* 4, 4, 7). Altaner notes that the Ambrosiaster may be regarded (against W. Mundle) as "a precursor of the Augustinian view of the doctrine of grace and original sin" (*Patrology*, 2nd English ed., 1961, p. 458).
2. The Ambrosiaster seems to regard the sin primarily as Eve's, though he refers its hereditary effects to Adam. Throughout he looks upon womankind with a considerably jaundiced eye, a failing genuine enough in his case, but not nearly so general among the Fathers and Writers as is popularly supposed.
3. *omnes in Adam peccasse quasi in massa*. This is perhaps the origin of Augustine's idea of mankind being, after the sin of Adam, a *massa damnata*.
4. See Matt. 5:32.
5. See 1 Cor. 11:3. In the case of divorce on grounds of adultery, the Ambrosiaster says that the law forbidding remarriage obliges the woman, however innocent, but that the innocent man is not bound by this law, because man is superior to woman. Note, however, that the genuine male chauvinism of the passage is not in St. Paul but in the Ambrosiaster's misconstruction of Paul. Nevertheless, it would be interesting to investigate any evidence there may be as to how widespread this strange notion may have been, especially in view of the extraordinary influence wielded by the Ambrosiaster in general in the late Middle Ages.
6. *maior enim causa Dei est quam matrimonii*.
7. *servituti subiectus*.
8. *non enim ratum est matrimonium, quod sine Dei devotione est*.
9. *Contumelia enim creatoris solvit ius matrimonii*.
10. *sacramentum*.

RUFINUS [ca A. D. 345-410]

Tyrannius Rufinus, generally specified as "of Aquileia", was born about the year 345 A. D. in the North Italian village of Concordia, a few miles to the west of Aquileia. He died shortly after Alaric's sack of Rome in 410 and was buried in Sicily.

As a youth in Rome he was a fellow student of Jerome, who had come there from Stridon in Dalmatia. There began the friendship—more than friendship, for Jerome loved him deeply—that was to end in such shockingly vituperative disaster that it saddened and scandalized the whole Christian world.

Upon hearing that Rufinus was coming from over the sea and was on his way to the holy places, Jerome had written to him: "Never did sailor tempest-tossed so look for harbor: never did parched field so thirst for rain: never did mother on the curving shore keep so anxious watch for her son. . . . There is no way of buying love. Friendship that can end was never true" (Jerome, *Epistula ad Rufinum* 3, 2, 6—Helen Waddell's translation in *The Desert Fathers*, p. 57).

But the friendship did end; and with a bang so loud that Augustine shuddered and warned Jerome that if he continued his attacks on Rufinus never again could any man have a friend whom he would not dread as a future foe (Augustine, *Epistula ad Hieronymum* 110, 6, 7). In a quarrel, Jerome knew no moderation. Not only did he not cease his attacks, he carried them beyond the grave. Rufinus was dead, and Jerome knew it when he said of him: "Cato without, Nero within!" (Jerome, *Epistula ad Rusticum* 125, 18). And Rufinus was scarcely cold in his grave when Jerome, who had once loved him hysterically, showed that his hatred was no less hysterical when he wrote: "The scorpion now lies buried in Sicilian soil between Enceladus and Porphyrion, and the many-headed hydra has at last ceased from hissing against me. So an opportunity is vouchsafed me of expounding the Bible instead of having to counter the vicious attacks of heretics" (*Praef. ad Comm. in Ezech.* [PL 25, 16]—in J. N. D. Kelly's *Rufinus: A Commentary on the Apostle's Creed*, p. 93, n. 9).

The cause of their quarrel is not now so important as the quarrel itself. Both had been accused of being Origenists. Jerome set out to prove that Origen was a heretic and that he himself was not. His technique was to translate Origen in such a way as to emphasize and magnify anything suspect. Rufinus at the same time made no denial, but began to publish translations of Origen in an attempt to prove him orthodox, glossing over as much as possible anything suspect and rendering all in the best light possible. We are indebted to both for having preserved the largest part of what little remains of Origen's writings; but at the same time, keeping in mind the techniques they employed in translating and the purposes they had in mind in publishing their translations, it is often difficult to decide just what Origen did say.

And to Jerome we are indebted for vituperative sarcasm that has left us, the ages having filtered away his malice, a rather charming picture of Rufinus. He had a funny walk that reminded Jerome of a turtle. And he called him Piggy because when he talked his phrases were punctuated by little grunts and snorts. And when Grunnius lectured, he had first to line up his books in a row on the lectern before him. And when he had an especially clever remark to make, he always tipped his hand by his nervous habit of frowning away his smile and cracking his knuckles. All of this, as Helen Waddell so aptly remarks, might have passed as amicable clowning on Jerome's part: except that that is when Jerome stabbed out his vicious "Cato without, Nero within!"

EXPLANATION OF THE APOSTLES' CREED [*inter A. D.* 401-404]

Rufinus recounts that after Pentecost and before setting out individually on their missionary journies the Apostles gathered together to settle on a common form for their preaching of the faith. Each contributed the clause he considered fitting; and they decided to call it a *symbol*, because σύμβολον in Greek means both *a*) a *token* or *watchword*—and this symbol should be the test of the true faith; and *b*) a *collection*—referring to the peculiar manner of its joint authorship through all the Apostles.

He further supposed that this pristine Apostles' Creed had been variously corrupted in various places, but was kept in its purest form in the Church of Rome. The creed on which he comments, then, is effectively our Apostles' Creed. The precise form of it on which he comments is the baptismal creed of Aquileia; but he was at great pains throughout to show in what respects the Aquileian form of what was for him quite literally the Apostles' Creed differed from the more authentic form used at Rome. Thus he reports quite accurately the text of the Aquileian baptismal creed and of the Roman baptismal creed.

The idea that the so-called Apostles' Creed was a joint effort of the Apostles was once

quite widespread and is occasionally encountered even today on a popular level. There
are creeds extant which specify by the Apostles' names the specific clause which each
contributed. It was the humanist Lorenzo Valla († 1457) who first denied effectively the
direct apostolic origin of the so-called Apostles' Creed.

Rufinus' *Expositio symboli* was written most probably between the years 401 and 404
A. D. The text in Migne (PL 21, 335-386) reprints that of Dominic Vallarsi and is
entirely superseded by the edition of Manlius Simonetti in the *Corpus Christianorum*,
Vol. 20 (1961), pp. 133-182.

1343a

[1]
I am neither much inclined nor am I well-equipped for writing, most faithful Pope   436
Lawrence (1); for I know well the danger of exposing my poor talents to the
criticism of the many. In your letter, however, you are so rash, if I may say it, as to
order me by Christ's Sacraments, which we hold in the greatest reverence, to write
something for you on the faith as presented in the content and structure of the
Creed. . . . We shall attempt, therefore, to restore and emphasize the simplicity of the
words of the Apostles.

1344

[35 (*al.* 37)]
Handed down in the Old Testament, first of all there are the five books of Moses: 41
Genesis, Exodus, Leviticus, Numbers, and Deuteronomy. After these is Jesus Nave,
and Judges together with Ruth. After these the four books of Kingdoms, which
the Hebrews count as two; Paralipomenon, which is called the Book of Days; and two of
Esdras, which they reckon as one; and Esther. Of the prophets there is Isaias,
Jeremias, Ezechiel, and Daniel; and then one book of twelve prophets. Job also and the
Psalms of David are separate books. And there are three of Solomon handed down
in the Churches: Proverbs, Ecclesiastes, and the Canticle of Canticles. And with these
they conclude the number of the books of the Old Testament. Of the New, however,   42
there are the four Gospels: Matthew, Mark, Luke and John. The Acts of the
Apostles, recounted by Luke. Of the Apostle Paul there are fourteen Epistles; of the
Apostle Peter, two Epistles; of James, the Apostle and brother of the Lord, one; of
Jude, one; of John, three; and the Apocalypse of John. These are the writings which the
Fathers included in the Canon and on which they desired to base the assertions
of our faith. [36] At the same time, however, let it be known that there are other books
which most call ecclesiastical rather than canonical. These are: Wisdom, attributed
to Solomon; and another Wisdom, attributed to the son of Sirach. Among Latin-speaking
people this latter is called by the generic term Ecclesiasticus, a term designating
not the author of the little book but the character of its writing. Of the same kind is the
little book of Tobias and Judith, and the books of Maccabees. In the New
Testament there is the little book called the Book of the Shepherd, or Hermas; and that
called the Two Ways; and (2) the Judgment according to Peter. The Fathers desired
that all of these be read in church, but that no appeal be made to the authority
of these books as confirming the faith. Other writings, which they called apocryphal,
they did not want read in church.

1. *Papa Laurenti*. Lawrence, presumably a bishop, has not been identified. The term *Pope* was not yet restricted to the
   Bishop of Rome. See §§ 568a, 570b, and 651 above in Vol. 1.
2. *vel*. St. Jerome knew an apocryphal work called *Iudicium* which was ascribed to St. Peter. One would like to translate the
   connective *vel* in its usual equivalent to *or*; but the *Two Ways* is almost certainly the *Didache*, and it is impossible to
   believe that Rufinus could have confused any work by or concerning Peter (the title may be *The Judgment of Peter*) with

the *Didache*. In late Latin *vel* can sometimes be synonymous with *et*; hence, we translate it *and* in the present instance. Moreover, if Rufinus had meant *or*, since in that case the context would have demanded the conjunctive rather than the disjunctive *or*, he ought to have said *aut* or *seu*. High on my list of things to do on a rainy Tuesday: read Rufinus, making notes on each instance of his use of the word *vel*, in order to get a better insight into his meaning in the present instance.

ST. JEROME [*ca. A. D.* 347–*A. D.* 419 *aut* 420]

Eusebius Hieronymus, our St. Jerome, was born about the year 347 A. D. at Stridon in Dalmatia. The precise location of Stridon (or Strido) has not yet been determined. In Dalmatia, possibly it was somewhat to the north, in the region of Aquileia and Emona (the modern Ljubljana), or it may have been more southerly, in the frontier regions between Dalmatia, Croatia, and Bosnia, at Grahovo Polje.

He came to Rome very early (perhaps already in 354) to begin his education, where Aelius Donatus the famous grammarian was among his teachers, and Rufinus of Aquileia (*q.v.*) his fellow student.

From Rome he went to Gaul where he associated himself with a group of monks at Treves, and then to Aquileia where he continued to practice the ascetical life.

In 373 or 374 he set out rather impulsively for Jerusalem but was obliged by ill health to break off his journey and remain at Antioch. Here he attended the lectures of Apollinaris of Laodicea and gained a thorough knowledge of Greek. From 375 to 378 he lived as a hermit to the east of Antioch in the desert of Chalcis. It was here that he mastered Hebrew and earned the admiration of his contemporaries as the unique trilingual scholar.

Ordained to the priesthood in 379 A. D. by Paulinus of Antioch, he soon afterwards journeyed on to Constantinople where he was on good terms with Gregory of Nazianz and Gregory of Nyssa, and became an ardent admirer of the exegesis of Origen. His earliest translations of Origen may be dated in this period.

In 382 at the invitation of Pope Damasus he attended the Roman synod intended to heal the Antiochian schism, and stayed on at Rome as the secretary and confidant of Damasus. It was Damasus who commissioned Jerome's revision and retranslation of the Latin Scriptures; and though Damasus died two years later Jerome's scriptural studies and his translating of the Bible continued for thirty-five years until his own death. Generally speaking Jerome's Vulgate Bible was not well-received in his own time, a fact which may be attributed in part to widespread personal enmities against Jerome and in part to a common apprehension that the open admission that the Latin translation *(Vetus Itala)* then in use was not already perfect in every respect would be the source of general scandal.

In Rome Jerome led an ascetical circle composed largely of women and which included several ladies of the Roman aristocracy. His somewhat imprudent relationship with these ladies, Paula and her daughters Blesilla, Paulina, and Julia Eustochium, along with their friends Marcella, Principia, Asella, Lea, Furia, Titania, Marcellina, Felicitas and Fabiola—they met in Marcella's house on the Aventine to pray and to sing the Psalms in Hebrew—along with Jerome's sharp castigations of the loose-living Roman clergy contributed much to his unpopularity with that same clergy; and when his protector Damasus died Jerome shortly (385 A. D.) left for the Holy Land and Bethlehem. There he remained for thirty-five years until his death.

Paula and Julia Eustochium followed him to Bethlehem and built three convents for women and a monastery for men. Jerome presided over the monastery, Paula and Julia Eustochium successively over the convents.

Jerome's life was never peaceful and his last years involved him in the so-called First Origenist Controversy against John of Jerusalem and against Rufinus. And then there was the Pelagian controversy, the polemics against Jovinian and Vigilantius, and dangers from the migrating tribes of Huns, Isaurians and Saracens.

The faults of Jerome's character and temperament were many and obvious. He was a great scholar and a saint, however, not because of his tempestuous irascibility, his bitter sarcasm and self-conscious arrogance, but in spite of these things. He died at Bethlehem on September 30 in 419 or 420 A. D.; and we should be not at all surprised if Jerome, upon arriving at the heavenly portals, immediately involved St. Peter in a caustic argument over Origen and the latter's orthodoxy or lack thereof. Should that have been the case, the only thing certain is that Jerome will have accounted himself the winner with the right to audit Peter's books.

The Migne edition of Jerome's works in PL 22-30 reprints the eleven volume Verona edition of Dominic Vallarsi of 1734-1742. It is gradually being superseded by editions in the Vienna Corpus (Vols. 54-56, 59) and in the *Corpus Christianorum* (Vols. 72-78 with 73 A, 75 A-76 A).

LETTERS

The corpus of Jerome's letters (including letters to him as well as from him) as given by Vallarsi and Migne embraces 150 entries. It is now recognized that the last three are not genuine; indeed, no. 148 is to be attributed to Pelagius. I. Hilberg's edition of the letters in the Vienna Corpus, Vols. 54-56 (1910-1918), has added four items, making a total of 154 entries.

Among the spuria in Migne's Volume 30 are another 53 letters. Of these it is now recognized that part of no. 18 is authentic, only the final section from *Pelicani cum suos a serpente filios occisos* being a spurious addition. Furthermore, letters 22 23 and 26 29 from this same section of spuria are now recognized as authentic works of Jerome; only they are not letters but homilies.

I. Hilberg's Vienna Corpus edition embracing 154 letters is presently regarded as the standard.

LETTER OF JEROME TO HELIODORUS. *Inter A. D.* 374/379.

1345

[14, 8]

Far be it from me to speak adversely of any of these clergy who, in succession from   951
the Apostles, confect by their sacred word the Body of Christ, and through whose   866
efforts also it is that we are Christians; and who, having the keys of the kingdom of   900
heaven, in a certain way act as judges prior to the day of judgment, and who keep the
Bride of Christ in modest chastity (1). But the situation of monks, as I have often
suggested, is one thing, and that of clerics is another. Clerics feed the sheep. I am fed.
They live off the altar. If I bring not my gift to the altar, I am, as it were, an unfruitful tree
and the axe is laid to my root.

LETTER OF JEROME TO POPE DAMASUS. *Inter A. D.* 374/379.

1346

[15, 2]

I follow no leader but Christ and join in communion with none but Your Blessedness,   435
that is, with the chair of Peter. I know that this is the rock on which the Church has
been built. Whoever eats the Lamb outside this house is profane. Anyone who is not in   417

the ark of Noah will perish when the flood prevails. . . . I do not know Vitalis,
Meletius I reject, and I ignore Paulinus (2).

LETTER OF JEROME TO POPE DAMASUS. *Inter A. D.* 374/379.

1346a

[16, 2]

The Church here is split into three parts, each eager to seize me for its own. . . .   435
Meanwhile I keep crying: "He that is joined to the chair of Peter is accepted by me!"
Meletius, Vitalis, and Paulinus each claims to be loyal to you, which I could believe did
only one make the claim. As it is, either two of them are lying, or else all three.
Therefore I implore Your Blessedness by the cross of the Lord, by the necessary glory of
our faith, the Passion of Christ,—that as you follow the Apostles in dignity may
you follow them also in worth,— . . . tell me by letter with whom it is that I should
communicate in Syria. Despise not a soul for whom Christ died!

LETTER OF JEROME TO MARCELLA. *Inter A. D.* 382/385.

1347

[27, 1]

I might, with perfect right, treat my detractors with contempt: for it is useless to play   25
the lyre for an ass (3). . . . But let them have this for my response: I am not so
dull-witted nor of such crass ignorance—qualities which they take for holiness and
call themselves disciples of fishermen, as if men were made holy by a lack of
knowledge—I am not, I say it again, so ignorant as to suppose that any of the Lord's
words are either in need of correction or not divinely inspired. But the Latin codices   28
are proved to be faulty by the discrepancies which they all exhibit among themselves;
and it was my desire to restore them to the form of the Greek original, from which
my detractors do not deny that they have been translated.

LETTER OF JEROME TO POPE DAMASUS. *Inter A. D.* 382/384.

1348

[36, 15]

You ask why a just man would have been ignorant of something and would have   351
done something contrary to his own will (4). To this the final answer can only be
that no man, save Him only who deigned to assume flesh for our salvation, can have
full knowledge and a complete grasp of the truth.

LETTER OF JEROME TO PAMMACHIUS. *A. D.* 392 *aut* 393.

1349

[48, 9]

My calumniator ought to blush for saying that I condemn first marriages when he   983
reads: "I do not condemn digamists, not even trigamists, and if I may use such a word,   979
not even octogamists (5)." It is one thing not to condemn, another to commend;
one thing to grant forgiveness, another to praise as virtuous. If, however, it seemed hard
of me to say, "Whatever is equally permissible must be weighed in the same kind of
balance," no one, I think, will judge me harsh and rigorous, when he reads that   984
the places prepared for virgins and married persons are different from those prepared
for trigamists, octogamists, and penitents.

1350

[48, 21]

Tell me how Jesus entered through closed doors (6) . . . and I will explain how   964
Saint Mary can be both Mother and Virgin. A Mother before she married, she
remained a Virgin after bearing her Son (7). Therefore, as I started to say, the Virgin
Christ and the Virgin Mary have dedicated in themselves the principles of virginity
for both sexes. The Apostles were either virgins or remained continent after their
marriages. Those persons chosen to be bishops, presbyters, or deacons (8) are either   952
virgins or widowers; or certainly, having once received the priesthood (9), they
remain forever chaste (10).

LETTER OF JEROME TO NEPOTIAN. A. D. 394.

1350a

[52, 5]

It is on account of the Greek word κλῆρος, which means in English *lot* or   951
inheritance (11), that the clergy are so called, either because they are of the lot of the
Lord or because the Lord is Himself their lot or portion. And he that is the Lord's
portion or who has the Lord for his portion must so conduct himself that he both
possesses the Lord and is possessed by the Lord. . . . Rarely, if ever, should the foot
of a woman cross your threshold.

LETTER OF JEROME TO AMANDUS. Ante A. D. 398 (?).

1351

[55, 3]

Joined to your letter and inquiry I find another short paper bearing the following   974
request: "Ask him"—meaning me—"whether a woman who has left a husband who
was an adulterer and a sodomite, and who has herself been compelled to be married
to another (12), can, without doing penance, be in communion with the Church (13),
while he that she first left is still living." . . . Tell that sister who asks us about her   975
state, not our judgment but the Apostle's: ". . . The woman who has a husband,
so long as the husband lives, is bound by law. But if her husband is dead, she is set free
of the law of her husband. Therefore, so long as her husband lives, she will be an
adulteress if she marry another husband (Rom. 7:2-3)."

Do not tell me about the violence of a ravisher, about the persuasiveness of a
mother, about the authority of a father, about the influence of relatives, about the
intrigues and insolence of servants, or about household losses. So long as a husband
lives, be he adulterer, be he sodomite, be he addicted to every kind of vice, if
she left him on account of his crimes he is her husband still and she may not take another.

LETTER OF JEROME TO OCEANUS. A. D. 399.

1352

[77, 3]

The laws of Caesar are one thing, Christ's another. The Papian (14) commands one   974
thing, our Paul another. Their laws allow men to give free rein to their lack of   981
chastity, condemning only rape and adultery, and unrestrained lust is allowed in brothels
and with slave girls, as if it were social status rather than licentiousness that determined
guilt. With us, however, what is unlawful for women is equally unlawful for men;
and since both are in a like servitude to God, both are reckoned as of equal status (15).

LETTER OF JEROME TO PAMMACHIUS AND OCEANUS. A. D. 401.

1353

[84, 2]

They charge me with having praised Origen. Unless I am mistaken there are only   1015
two places in which I have done so: the short preface to the *Homilies on the Canticle of
Canticles* (addressed to Damasus), and the prologue to the *Book of Hebrew Names* (16).
But what is said in those passages of the dogmas of the Church? What of Father, Son, and
Holy Spirit? What of the resurrection of the flesh? What of the condition and substance of
the soul? It is a question of simple interpretation, and I have merely praised his learning.
There is nothing there that concerns either faith or dogmas. Morals only are dealt with, and
his clear exposition dispels the mist of allegory. I praised the commentator, not the
dogmatist; his brilliance, not his faith; the philosopher, not the Apostle. If they want to
know my judgment of Origen, let them read my *Commentaries on Ecclesiastes* (17); let
them examine my three volumes on the Epistle to the Ephesians (18), and they will see that
I have always opposed his doctrines. . . . [3] If you will believe me, I have never been
an Origenist; but if you will not believe that of me, then believe that I have now ceased
to be one.

LETTER OF JEROME TO HEDIBIA. *Post A. D.* 406.

1354

[120, 9]

The glory of the Savior is the yoke of our triumph. He is crucified as man that He   332
may be glorified as God. . . . We say this not as if we believed that His godhead   324
and His humanity were so utterly distinct that we would be reckoning two persons
in one Son of God, whereby we would be blamed for a new heresy; rather, the
Son of God and the Son of Man is one and the same person.

LETTER OF JEROME TO AGERUCHIA. A. D. 409.

1354a

[123, 9]

What then? Do we condemn second marriages? Not at all; but we praise   979
first marriages. Do we expel digamists from the Church? Far from it; but we urge the
once-married to continence.

1354b

[123, 10]

Many years ago when I was helping Damasus, bishop of the city of Rome, with   979
his ecclesiastical papers, and had to reply to the queries of councils east and west, I saw a
married couple who were both of them sprung from the very lowest class of people. The
man had already buried twenty wives and the woman had had twenty-two husbands. And
now, as each thought, they were joined to each other in their final marriage. Men and
women alike were filled with the greatest curiosity to see which of these clods would bury
the other. The husband won. . . . And what shall we say to such a woman? Surely, just

what the Lord said to the Samaritan woman: "You have had twenty-two husbands and he that now buries you is not your husband" (19).

LETTER OF JEROME TO CTESIPHON. A. D. 415.

1355

[133, 1]

What the Greeks call πάθη and what we call passions,—for example, vexation   727
and gladness, hope and fear, two of which relate to the present and two to the future,—[the Pelagians] assert can be expelled completely from our minds; and they say that every root and fiber of vice can be removed from a man by meditation on virtue and the constant practice of virtue.

1355a

[133, 6]

It is not enough for me that God has given me grace once, but He must give it   712
always. I ask, that I may receive; and when I have received, I ask again. I am covetous   711
of receiving God's bounty. He is never slow in giving, nor am I ever weary of receiving. The more I drink, the more thirsty I become.

1356

[133, 7]

Listen, I ask you, only listen to [Pelagius'] profanation. "If," he says, "if I   727
want to bend my finger, move my hand, sit, stand, walk, run, spit (20), use two little fingers to blow my nose (21), empty my bowels (22), or urinate (23), is it always necessary for me to have God's help?" Listen, you blasphemous ingrate, and hear the preaching of the Apostle: "If you are eating, if you are drinking, or if you are doing anything else, do all in the name of God" (24).

LETTER OF JEROME TO EVANGELUS. [Date not determined].

1357

[146, 1]

I hear that a certain one has fallen into such insanity that he ranks deacons before   953
presbyters, that is, before bishops. For when the Apostle teaches that presbyters are   954
the same as bishops, must not a mere server of tables and of widows be insane when he arrogantly sets himself over those by whose prayers the Body and Blood of Christ   866
is confected? Do you ask for proof [that priests (presbyters) and bishops are the same]? . . . In the Acts of the Apostles, Paul speaks thus to the priests (25) of a   406
single church: "Take heed to yourselves and to the whole flock, in which the Holy Spirit has stationed you as bishops, to rule the Lord's Church which He acquired by His own blood" (26). And lest any should argue contentiously that there were   441
a multiplicity of bishops in one church, listen also to another testimony which clearly proves that a bishop and a presbyter are the same. "For this reason have I left you in Crete, that you might correct whatever needs correcting and establish presbyters in all the cities, just as I have appointed you to do" (27). . . . When afterwards one was chosen to preside over the others, this was done to remedy

schism, lest anyone rend the church of Christ by drawing it to himself. For even at Alexandria from the time of Mark the Evangelist up to the bishops Heraclas and Dionysius the presbyters have always named as bishop one chosen from among their own number and set in a more exalted position, just as an army elects its commander, or as the deacons elect one of themselves known for his diligence and call him archdeacon (28). What, after all, can a bishop do, ordination excepted, that a presbyter cannot do?   960

1. *sobria castitate*. Is it *modest chastity*, in the sense of *chaste modesty*, or *moderate chastity*, which is hardly chaste at all? One suspects that Jerome's sarcasm is again to be reckoned with. At any rate the phrase seems to have two handles and Jerome must have had a firm grip on both.
2. The three claimants to the See of Antioch. It is Paulinus whom Rome will shortly recognize and by whom Jerome will be ordained a priest (379 A. D.).
3. *Asino quippe lyra superflue canit*.
4. See Gen. 27:23, wherein Isaac, intending to bless Esau, is deceived and gives his blessing to Jacob.
5. The passage is from St. Jerome's *Against Jovinian* (§ 1378a, below). A digamist is one who enters a second marriage after the first spouse is dead; trigamist and octogamist are to be understood similarly. Certainly St. Jerome does not condone bigamy, the action of one who gets a second spouse while the first still lives.
6. John 20:19.
7. *Virgo post partum, mater ante quam nupta*.
8. *Episcopi, presbyteri, diaconi*.
9. *sacerdotium*.
10. *in aeternum pudici*.
11. *Si enim* κλῆρος *Graece*, sors *Latine appellatur*.
12. *et alio per vim accepto*.
13. *possit absque poenitentia communicare ecclesiae*.
14. I suspect that the reading *Papianum* is after all the correct one. W. H. Fremantle, translating Jerome's letters for the Second Series of *A Select Library of the Nicene and Post-Nicene Fathers*, read *Papinianum* and explained that Papinianus was a reknowned Roman jurist in the time of Marcus Aurelius and Septimius Severus, executed by Caracalla; all of which is true, but not much to the point. There is also a jurist S. Papirius, known for his legal compilation called the *ius civile Papirianum*; but still not to the point. For if Jerome refers to the law in a general way it is only preliminary to his specific concern which is the law on marriage and in respect to divorce: permitted or not. Christ's law does not permit divorce; Caesar's does. Jerome's point is best exemplified if we read *Papianum* as an adjective of Papius or Papia. And the consul Papius, with his co-consul Poppaeus, was, in the time of Augustus, responsible for a law intended to reform the divorce process, but still allowing an immense laxity, amounting practically to divorce upon request. The law is known as the *lex Papia Poppaea*; it is this *law Papia Poppaea* that Jerome calls *the Papian*.
15. *et eadem servitus pari condicione censetur*. In antiquity civil law in regard to marital conduct was more demanding of women than of men. If a married man had relations with an unmarried woman, it was fornication and of no great consequence. For a married woman to have relations with an unmarried man was adultery; and at least by statute it was severely punished. The logic of this, of course, finds its place purely in considerations of progeny and inheritance.
16. The *Homilies on the Canticle of Canticles* referred to is Jerome's translated edition (A. D. 385-387) of Origen's work of that title. The *Book of Hebrew Names* is Jerome's own work, a glossary explaining the meaning of Old Testament proper names, written in A. D. 388 and having all the shortcomings that might be expected in such a work originating at so early a time.
17. See below, § 1373.
18. See below, § 1370.
19. See John 4:18.
20. *sputa iacere*.
21. *duobus digitulis narium purgamenta decutere*.
22. *relevare alvum*.
23. *urinam digerere*.
24. 1 Cor. 10:31.
25. *sacerdotes*. We have continued our practice of translating *presbyter* as presbyter, rather than interpret whether it means bishop (early usage) or priest (later usage). In Jerome it is clear enough that a presbyter is a priest; and in passage § 1350 above he speaks of *episcopi, presbyteri, et diaconi*. (When he uses the term *sacerdos*, it refers sometimes to a priest, sometimes to a bishop. And compare *sacerdotium* in the present passage, which seems to be a generic term for the estate of any of the major orders, with the *sacerdos* of § 1360, who is a bishop.) In the present Letter to Evangelus, Jerome is arguing that there is no difference between a presbyter (a priest) and a bishop, except that the latter can ordain whereas the former cannot. His position can probably be reduced to this, that the difference between priesthood and episcopate is not one of orders and powers, but one merely of jurisdiction and faculties.
26. Acts 20:28.
27. Titus 1:5.
28. *archidiaconum*.

DIALOGUE BETWEEN A LUCIFERIAN AND AN ORTHODOX
CHRISTIAN [*A. D.* 379 *si non* 382]

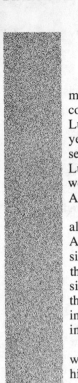

Lucifer of Cagliari in Sardinia is a sad figure, an innocent victim of the Arian madness. He was staunchly orthodox and refused to subscribe to Athanasius' condemnation even when Liberius of Rome did so subscribe in order to save himself. Lucifer withstood the Emperor Constantius to his face and as a consequence he spent six years (355-361 A. D.) in exile. When Julian succeeded Constantius in 361 A. D. and, to serve his own devious ends, allowed all the exiled bishops to return to their sees, Lucifer, instead of going back to Sardinia or to attend the Council called at Alexandria, went up to Antioch and consecrated Paulinus, thus adding more fuel to the fire of the Antiochian schism.

Lucifer's point of difference with orthodoxy was simply that he would not agree to allow converted Arian bishops to remain as bishops in the Catholic Church, although Athanasius himself, in the council at Alexandria, agreed to do so. It was pointed out that since Lucifer admitted the validity of Arian baptism, he ought to concede validity to their orders. The argument is really a *non sequitur*; but what is even more basic, it simply is not *ad rem*; for Lucifer did not deny the validity of their orders, but only that they could decorously be allowed to exercise those orders after having been so intimately involved in such fundamental heresy. His position is not without merit, and is in any case quite understandable of one who had suffered so much from Arianism.

Regarded as a schismatic, Lucifer died in his see of Cagliari in Sardinia in 371 A. D. without having been reconciled to the Orthodox position. It is doubtful, however, that his so-called schism had any distinct organization in his own lifetime, and Luciferianism was a dead issue within about thirty years after his death.

Jerome's *Dialogue against the Luciferians* or *Dialogue between a Luciferian and an Orthodox Christian*—the *Dialogus contra Luciferianos* or *Altercatio Luciferiani et Orthodoxi*—was written either at Rome in 382 A. D. or, according to some, at Antioch in 379 A. D. Rome and 382 seems to carry the better part of the argument, but the question is by no means settled.

The standard edition is still Migne's Vallarsi in Pl 23, 155-182.

1358

[8]
Luciferian Christian: . . . Do you not know that the imposition of hands after 840
Baptism for an invocation of the Holy Spirit is the custom of the Churches? Do you 403
demand to know where it is written? In the Acts of the Apostles. And even if it had not the 100
authority of Scripture the consent of the whole world in this matter would confer on
it the force of precept. For there are many other observances in the Church which, though
due to tradition, have acquired the authority of the written law, as for instance the
practice of dipping the head three times in the baptismal font, and then, on going out, of
tasting a mixture of milk and honey which signifies infancy; and again, of not
worshipping on bended knee nor fasting on Sunday and on all the days of Pentecost
(1); and there are many other unwritten practices the observance of which is vindicated
by reason.

1359

[9]
Orthodox Christian: I do not deny that it is the practice of the Churches in the case of 828
those who, living far from the larger cities, have been baptized by the presbyters
and deacons, for the bishop to come to them to invoke the Holy Spirit upon them by 843

the imposition of his hand. . . . The well-being of a church depends upon the dignity   792
of its chief priest (2); and if some extraordinary and unique power is not accorded him,   953
there will be as many schisms effected in the Churches as there are priests. That
is why without chrism and a command from the bishop neither presbyter nor deacon
can have the right to baptize (3). Yet we know that frequently, when necessity demands   829
it, even the laity are permitted to baptize (4). For whoever has received is able
to give.

1360

[11]
   Orthodox Christian: If a [heretical] person who baptizes someone into his faith   830
can have no injurious effect on the one baptized, then he that ordains a priest in that belief   803
does not defile the one ordained (5).   962

1360a

[19]
   Orthodox Christian: . . . The whole world groaned when, to its astonishment, it   90
discovered that it was Arian. . . . The little ship of the Apostles was in peril,
driven by the winds and with her sides buffeted by the waves. There was now no hope.
But the Lord awoke, He commanded the storm, the beast (6) died, and there was calm
once again. Let me speak more clearly. All the bishops who had been banished
from their proper sees were, by the clemency of the new emperor (7), returned to their
own churches.

1. If the Luciferian means that this was not written law he errs; for what he describes is specified in the twentieth canon of Nicaea (§ 651z above). See also Tertullian, § 367 above in Vol. 1.
2. *Ecclesiae salus in summi sacerdotis dignitate pendet.*
3. *Inde venit, ut sine chrismate et episcopi iussione neque presbyter neque diaconus ius habeant baptizandi.* Chrism here, no doubt, stands for ordination. Without ordination (chrismate) and mandated faculty (iussione), neither priest nor deacon has a right to function as such.
4. *Quod frequenter, si tamen necessitas cogit, scimus etiam licere laicis.*
5. *Si in fide sua baptizato baptizans nocere non potuit, et in fide sua sacerdotem constitutum constituens non inquinavit.*
6. Constantius had succeeded in exiling virtually all orthodox bishops, supplanting them with Arians. St. Basil the Great in Caesarea stands forth as one of the notable exceptions. Constantius died in 361 A. D.
7. Julian the Apostate recalled all the exiled bishops; and if it was an act of clemency which greatly benefited the Church, certainly his motives were otherwise. New bishops, Arians, had been appointed in those sees, and bringing back the old bishops was expected to keep everything at sixes and sevens.

AGAINST HELVIDIUS: THE PERPETUAL VIRGINITY OF THE BLESSED VIRGIN MARY [ca. A. D. 383]

   Helvidius was a contemporary of St. Jerome and, if Gennadius of Marseilles is correct, a disciple of the Arian bishop Auxentius, the same who held the see of Milan prior to Ambrose's accession.

   With but little training in eloquence and less in theology, Helvidius was an opponent of monasticism and of virginity as a way of life; and in contemning virginity he found it expedient to deny the perpetual virginity of Mary, maintaining that after the birth of our Savior Mary came together with Joseph and that the persons whom the Gospel calls the brothers of the Lord were the children of this union. Helvidius' book on this subject was the source of major scandal in Rome and among the ascetics gathered about Jerome.

   The writing itself which Helvidius produced is not extant; but from Jerome's

references to it we can be certain that Helvidius had appealed to the authority of Tertullian and Victorinus of Pettau as supporting his views. Jerome counters that Helvidius has misinterpreted Victorinus; and as for Tertullian, "he simply was not a man of the Church."

Jerome's great vituperative gifts are at their best in his *De perpetua virginitate Beatae Mariae adversus Helvidium*, written about the year 383 A. D.; and what he begins with the rapier he finishes off with the broad axe. For anyone who can see the humor in verbal mayhem the present work is an unprecedented delight.

The standard edition remains at present that of the Migne Patrology, PL 23, 183-206.

1361

[19 (*al*. 21)]

We believe that God was born of a virgin, because we read it (1). We do not believe   781
that Mary was married after she brought forth her Son, because we do not read it.   783
Nor do we say this in order to condemn marriage: for virginity itself is the fruit of   983
marriage. . . . You say that Mary did not remain a virgin. As for myself, I claim that   973
Joseph himself was a virgin, through Mary, so that a Virgin Son might be born of a
virginal wedlock.

1361a

[22 (*al*. 24)]

We have played the rhetorician and have carried ourselves somewhat after the manner   984
of platform orators. But it was you, Helvidius, who made us do it; for though the
Gospel shines today in fullest splendor you would have it that virgins and married
women share an equal glory. And since I know that you, having been bested by the truth,
will resort to disparagement of my life and to bad-mouthing my character,—little
ladies generally act in this fashion; and, when their masters have bested them, they sit in
the corner and wish them evil,—I only tell you in advance that your railings will
redound to my glory, when you lacerate me with the same mouth you used in your
detraction of Mary. The Lord's servant and the Lord's Mother will have each an equal
portion of your canine eloquence (2).

1. The import, of course, is that we read it in the Scriptures; and as much can be gathered from the prior context of the passage.
2. *caninam facundiam*.

COMMENTARIES ON THE EPISTLE TO THE GALATIANS [*A. D.* 386 *aut* 387]

It was shortly after his coming to Bethlehem, in 386 or 387 therefore, that Jerome wrote his commentaries on four of the Pauline Epistles: Philemon, Galatians, Ephesians, and Titus, in that order. He undertook the work at the request of Paula and Julia Eustochium, and intended to comment on all the Pauline Epistles, though only the four mentioned were actually written.

A commentary on all the Pauline Epistles handed down under Jerome's name (Migne, PL 30, 645-902) is entirely spurious, a sixth century reworking of an otherwise lost commentary by Pelagius.

The standard edition of Jerome's *In Epistulam ad Galatas commentarii* is Migne's Vallarsi, PL 26, 307-438.

1362

[2, 3, 11]

But since in the Law no one is justified before God, it is evident that the just man lives   760
by faith (1). . . . It should be noted that he does not say that a man, a person,
lives by faith, lest it be thought that he is contemning good works. Rather, he says the
just man lives by faith. He implies thereby that whoever would be faithful and would
conduct his life according to the faith can in no other way arrive at the faith or live
in it except first he be a just man of pure life, coming up to the faith as it were by certain
degrees.

1363

[3, 5, 22]

The fruit of the Spirit, however, is love, joy, peace, patience, kindness, goodness,   592
faith, modesty, continence, against which there is no law (2). And what other one
of the fruits of the Spirit ought to be given the primary place, if not love, without which
the other virtues are not rightly virtues at all, and from which all other good things
come?

1364

[3, 6, 10]

While we have time, therefore, let us do good to all, especially, however, to those of   991
the household of the faith (3). The time for sowing, as we have said, is the present
time, and in the life we now lead. In this life we can sow what we will; but when this life
is over, the time for works is at an end. Whence also the Savior says: "Work while
it is yet day; the night will come when none shall be able to work (4)."

1. Gal. 3:11.
2. Gal. 5:22-23.
3. Gal. 6:10.
4. See John 9:4.

COMMENTARIES ON THE EPISTLE TO THE EPHESIANS [*A. D.* 386 *aut* 387]

See above, our introduction to the *Commentaries on the Epistle to the Galatians*.
The standard edition of Jerome's *In Epistulam ad Ephesios commentarii* can still be
reckoned as Migne's Vallarsi, PL 26, 439-554. A better edition will be welcomed
at any time.

1365

[1, 1, 7]

The flesh and blood of Christ is understood in two ways; there is either the spiritual   850
and divine way, by which He Himself said: "My flesh is truly food, and my blood is truly   857
drink (1)"; and "Unless you shall have eaten my flesh and drunk my blood you
shall not have eternal life (2)." Or else there is the flesh and blood which was crucified
and which was poured out by the soldier's lance.

1366

[1, 1, 11]

In whom also we have been called by lot, predestined according to the plan of Him that   158

works all things according to the counsel of His will (3). . . . Let it be noted that
this προορισμὸς and πρόϑεσις, that is, *predestination* and *plan*, are taken
together as that in reference to which God works all things according to the counsel of
His will. Not that all things that come to pass in the world are brought about by the
will and counsel of God, for that were to impute evil to God; but that all things that He   469
does in His counsel He does also in His will, so that they are done with the full reason and
by the power of the one doing them. . . . *He desires all men to be saved and to*   200
come to an acknowledgement of the truth (4). But because no one is saved without his own   212
willing it (for we have free choice), He wants us to desire the good, so that, when
we shall have willed it, then He too will Himself will that His counsel be fulfilled in us.

1367
[2, 3, 14]
   In Exodus the Lord says: "I am who I am"; and: "Tell this to the children of   140
Israel: 'Who Is sent me to you (5).'" . . . God, who always is, has no beginning (6)   141
from outside Himself, and He is His own origin and the cause of His own substance;   156
nor can He be understood as having anything that supports Him from without.

1368
[2, 4, 5]
   The Lord is one and God is one, because the domination of the Father and of the   237
Son is one divinity. Moreover the faith too is said to be one, because we believe
likewise in Father and in Son and in Holy Spirit. And there is one Baptism, for it is in one 826
and the same way that we are baptized in the Father and in the Son and in the Holy
Spirit. And we are dipped three times so that the one Sacrament of the Trinity may   825
be made apparent (7). And we are not baptized in the *names* of the Father and of the Son
and of the Holy Spirit, but in *one* name, which one name we know to be God.

1369
[2, 4, 10]
   The Son of God descended, therefore, into the lower regions of the earth (8), and   390
ascended above all the heavens, not so much to fulfill the Law and the Prophets as
for the sake of certain other hidden arrangements (9) which were known to Him
alone with the Father. Neither can we know how the blood of Christ can have been   371
useful to the angels and to those who were in the lower world (10); we can know
nothing except that it was in fact useful.

1370
[3, 5, 6]
   There are many who say there are no future punishments for sins nor any torments   1033
extrinsically applied, but that sin itself and the consciousness of guilt serve as   1015
punishment, while the worm in the heart does not die, and a fire is kindled in the mind,   1032
much like a fever, which does not torment the ailing person externally but punishes even
bodies by its seizures, without the application of any torments that might be brought
to bear from without. These arguments and fraudulent fancies are but inane and
empty words having the semblance of a certain eloquence of speech but serving only to
delude sinners; and if they give them credence they only add to the burden of eternal
punishment which they will carry with them.

1. John 6:56.
2. John 6:54.

3. Eph. 1:11.
4. 1 Tim. 2:4.
5. Ex. 3:14.
6. *principium*.
7. *ut Trinitatis unum appareat sacramentum*.
8. *in inferiora terrae*.
9. *occultas dispensationes*.
10. *in inferno*.

COMMENTARIES ON THE EPISTLE TO TITUS [*A. D.* 386 *aut* 387]

See above, our introduction to Jerome's *Commentaries on the Epistle to the Galatians*. The standard edition of the *In Epistulam ad Titum commentarii* remains Migne's Vallarsi, PL 26, 555-600.

1371

[1, 5]

For a bishop, since he is God's steward, must be blameless (1). A presbyter and 953
a bishop are the same; and before the urging of the devil gave rise to factionalism
in religion, so much so that it was being said among the people, "I am of Paul, I of
Apollo, I of Cephas (2)," the churches were governed by a joint council of the
presbyters (3). After it was seen that each, when he was baptized, thought that he now 406
belonged to the one baptizing and not to Christ, it was decreed throughout the world 441
that one chosen from among the presbyters should be placed over the others, and the total
care of the church should pertain to him. Thus were the seeds of schisms destroyed.
If it be supposed that it is merely our opinion and without scriptural support that
bishop and presbyter are one (4), the latter term speaking of age (5) while the former is
the name given an office (6), examine again the words the Apostle addressed to the
Philippians: "Paul and Timothy, servants of Jesus Christ, to all the saints in Christ
Jesus who are at Philippi with the bishops and the deacons, grace to you, and peace
(7)," etc. Now Philippi is but one city in Macedonia, and certainly in one city
there could not have been numerous bishops. It is simply that at that time the same
persons were called either bishops or presbyters (8).

1371a

[3, 10]

Heretics bring sentence upon themselves since they by their own choice withdraw 415
from the Church, a withdrawal which, since they are aware of it, constitutes damnation.
Between heresy and schism there is this distinction to be made, that heresy involves
perverse doctrine, while schism separates one from the Church on account of
disagreement with the bishop (9).

1. Titus 1:7.
2. 1 Cor. 1:12.
3. *communi presbyterorum consilio*.
4. Here again, it must be supposed that in Jerome's language *presbyter* is the usual term for priest; and he is not so much
   explaining that the presbyters are bishops, but that bishops and priests are equal in orders. This is, of course, a grand
   oversimplification; but properly explained, the position is not at all without merit.
5. πρέσβυς = old. πρεσβύτερος is the comparative degree, older, or, as a noun, elder.
6. ἐπισκοπέω = to look over, to inspect, to guard. ἐπίσκοπος, therefore, is the guardian or overseer.
7. Phil. 1:1-2.

8. Again, if we are to have a clear notion of what Jerome is driving at, it is important to remember that for Jerome presbyter = priest. He does not mean to prove simply that the scriptural presbyters are bishops, but that the scriptures used the terms priest and bishop indiscriminately. For Jerome, there is no difference in the sacramental orders of priest and bishop. He maintains that in the beginning all priests were bishops; in the course of time it became expedient to elect one of the group superior; and that in common usage the term *episcopus* came to be restricted to this superior while the term *presbyter* came to be fixed upon the rest.

9. *episcopalem dissensionem*.

PREFACE TO THE THREE SOLOMONIC BOOKS [*ca. A. D.* 398]

In the autumn of 386 A. D., soon after his arrival in Bethlehem, Jerome began his revision of the then common Latin text of the Old Testament. He had not yet completed his work of revision when he decided instead to retranslate the whole of the Old Testament from the original tongues, that is, those books of which the original language was either Hebrew or Aramaic. This work he began in 391 with the books of Samuel and Kings, followed by the sixteen prophetic books, Psalms in 392, Job about 393, Esdras, Nehemias, and Paralipomenon between 394 and 396.

After a long illness he took the work up again in 398 with the three books of Solomon (Proverbs, Ecclesiastes, and Canticle of Canticles), to which he provides the present *Praefatio in libros Salomonis*. Between 398 and 405 he completed his Old Testament with the Pentateuch and the books of Josue, Judges, Ruth, Esther, Tobias, and Judith.

Jerome did not translate Baruch, Jesus Sirach, Wisdom, and Maccabees, nor the deuterocanonical parts of Esther. But apparently he did send copies of Sirach and Wisdom in an older Latin translation, along with his translations of the three Solomonic books, to Chromatius and Heliodorus, to whom he dedicates his translations of those latter three books, Proverbs, Ecclesiastes and the Canticle of Canticles. The passage which we are about to cite (§ 1372) from his *Preface* is concerned largely with Sirach and Wisdom.

The *Praefatio in libros Salomonis* is to be found in Migne, PL 28, 1241-1244.

1372

There is also the book of Jesus, son of Sirach, which is termed παvάρετος (1); 41
and another book, Wisdom, attributed to Solomon, is a ψευδεπίγραφος (2).
The former of these, known in Hebrew (3), the Jews do not call Ecclesiasticus, as among
Latin speaking people; but it is referred to as Parables. It is grouped with Ecclesiastes and
the Canticle of Canticles, since it displays a likeness to Solomon both in format and
in content. The second was never known in Hebrew, for its very style bespeaks
Greek eloquence; and some of the older authors affirm that it is a work of Philo the Jew.
Just as the Church reads Judith and Tobias and the Books of Maccabees, but does not
accept them as belonging among the canonical Scriptures, so too let her read these two
volumes for the edification of the people but not for the purpose of confirming the
authority of the Church's teachings (4).

1. The term παvάρετος, meaning *all-virtuous*, has been applied, sometimes much in the manner of a title, to Ecclesiasticus (Sirach) and also to Wisdom. The former is also termed Wisdom of Sirach, while the latter is called Wisdom of Solomon. Furthermore, Jerome notes that among the Jews Sirach is called Parables, the same title that is given in Hebrew to the book which we call Proverbs.

2. The term *pseudepigraphal* means falsely ascribed, *i.e.*, its attribution of authorship is false. Current usage, however, is somewhat at variance with the root meaning; and in comparatively modern times it may be said in general (and without perfect accuracy!) that the books which Protestant scholarship terms apocryphal are the ones Catholic scholars have termed deuterocanonical; while the books Protestants term pseudepigraphal are, by Catholics, called apocryphal. Most

recently, however, the term pseudepigraphal seems to be generally falling out of use, in favor of the term apocryphal. In his use of the term, Jerome simply means that Solomon did not in fact write the book called Wisdom of Solomon.
3. Hebrew Sirach was unknown after the 10th century until some fragments of it began to come to light towards the end of the 19th century.
4. *non ad auctoritatem ecclesiasticorum dogmatum confirmandum.*

COMMENTARY ON ECCLESIASTES [*ca. A. D.* 388/389]

Jerome himself tells us that he wrote his *In Ecclesiasten commentarius* five years after the death of Paula's daughter Blesilla, hence, about the year 388 or 389 A. D. He also states that his commentary is based on the Hebrew, the original text, that is to say, on his own translation thereof. It is not necessary to suppose, however, that he had already made his connected translation of the whole work as such from Hebrew; for that he probably did not do until about the year 398, when he sent his translation of Ecclesiastes to Chromatius and Heliodorus (see introduction to the *Preface to the Three Solomonic Books*, immediately preceding). And in any case, the readings frequently differ considerably from the Clementine Vulgate.

Migne's Vallarsi (PL 23, 1009-1116) is now superseded by P. Antin's edition in the *Corpus Christianorum*, Vol. 72 (1959), pp. 249-361.

1373

[1, 15]

A perverse one will not be able to be ornamented, and the impairment will not be able   1014
to be counted (1). . . . It can also be understood thus: There is so great a
wickedness in this world that it is really changed about and can scarcely return
to its pristine state of good, nor can it anymore find it easy to receive
again the order and perfection in which it was first created. Otherwise,
integrity would be restored to everything through penance and only the devil
would persist in his error. . . . Finally, so great is the number of seducers
and of those whom they snatch away out of God's flock that such a
computation were simply beyond comprehension.

1374

[9, 1]

This have I taken to heart, that I might consider all things: that the just and wise,   762
with their works, are in the hand of the Lord. Man recognizes neither love nor hatred: all
is before them (2). . . . The meaning is this: I have given my heart to reflection,
desiring to know whom God would love and whom He would hate. And I
found indeed that the works of the just are in the hand of God, but whether
they be loved by God or not they cannot know and they waver in uncertainty.

1375

[10, 11]

If the serpent, the devil, bites someone secretly, he infects that person   916
with the venom of sin. And if the one who has been bitten keeps silence and   920
does not do penance, and does not want to confess his wound to his
brother and to his master, then his brother and his master, who have the word
that will cure him (3), cannot very well assist him. For if the sick man is

ashamed to confess his wound to the physician, medicine will not cure that to which it is not applied.

1. Eccl. 1:15, reading: *Perversus non poterit adornari et imminutio non poterit numerari*. The Vulgate reading is: *Perversi difficile corriguntur, et stultorum infinitus est numerus* (The perverse are difficult to correct, and the number of fools is infinite). I make a literal rendering of the Hebrew: The crooked cannot be made straight and the defective cannot be counted.
2. Eccl. 9:1. Again, however, the reading differs considerably from the Vulgate; nor is it an entirely literal rendering of the Hebrew.
3. *qui linguam habent ad curandum*.

COMMENTARIES ON MICHEAS [*ca. A. D.* 391]

Jerome's *In Michaeam commentarii*, along with his commentaries on Nahum, Habacuc, Sophonias, and Aggeus were written most probably in 391 A. D.; certainly before 393, for in 392 he already speaks in the past tense of his having written these works.

The Vallarsi edition of the *Commentaries on Micheas*, reprinted in Migne (PL 25, 1151-1230), has been entirely reworked by M. Adriaen, whose edition, superseding Migne's Vallarsi entirely, appears, along with the commentaries on Osee, Joel, Amos, Abdias and Jonas, in the series *Corpus Christianorum*, Vol. 76 (1969), pp. 421-524.

1376

[2, 5, 2]

There are some who assert that in almost all citations (1) taken from the Old 27
Testament some sort of error has been made; either the order is changed, or the words, and where the meaning itself is different, that the Apostles or the Evangelists have not taken their testimonies after direct consultation with the book itself but that they relied on memory which is always subject to error (2).

1. *testimoniis*.
2. Jerome is pointing out that the quotation of Micheas 5:2 (5:1 in the Hebrew and in the Septuagint) as found in Matthew 2:6 differs considerably in its actual wording from what is found in the Hebrew, and neither does it correspond to the Septuagint reading, which also differs from the Hebrew. While verbally the differences are considerable, however, there is really very little difference in their actual meaning; and this in spite of the fact that both the Hebrew and the Septuagint agree that Bethlehem is the least place among the thousands of Juda, while the text in Matthew says that Bethlehem is in no way the least among these thousands. Even in those direct contradictions the meaning is really the same, to wit: Bethlehem is now a place of no importance; but she shall be known everywhere because the great leader of Israel is to come forth from her.

COMMENTARIES ON HABACUC [*ca. A. D.* 391]

What we said immediately above in introducing the *Commentaries on Micheas* applies also to Habacuc. The Migne text (PL 25, 1273-1338) of the *In Habacuc commentarii* is likewise superseded by M. Adriaen's reworking of the Vallarsi, in *Corpus Christianorum*, Vol. 76A (1970), pp. 579-654.

1377

[1, 1, 14]

Just as the providence of God looks to mankind and even to individuals, so   195
too we can recognize in other animals a certain general plan and order and
course of events. For example, how a vast number of fish is born and lives in the
water, how reptiles and quadrupeds come forth on the land and by what
foods they are nourished. Besides, it is absurd to lower the majesty of God   189
to this: that He would know at any particular moment how many gnats
are born, or how many die, how great a multitude of bugs and fleas and flies are
on the earth, how many fish swimming in the water, and which of the
weaker must fall prey to the stronger. Let us not be such idiotic worshipers of
God that, while we extend his power down even to such minutiae, we are
injurious to ourselves, holding that the same providence guides both the
rational creatures and the irrational (1).

1. This whole passage has generally been understood as indicating that Jerome supposed God's majesty
 prevented His having a knowledge of such contemptible and useless information as how many fleas exist, etc.
 I am really not certain that Jerome is quite that proud. It seems to me that Jerome is not denying to God
 such a knowledge, but only that his majesty comes into the matter at all. He seems to be making a distinction
 which commentators have usually missed—perhaps for the reason that no one except Jerome makes such a
 distinction: the divine providence which cares for men is something different than whatever it is in
 God that cares for irrational creatures. I do not like such a distinction; but I do think it is there in Jerome; and it
 still invests its author with a considerable pride; but far less than the pride which declares that God numbers
 the hairs of a man's head but has no time for the fleas nesting therein.

AGAINST JOVINIAN [ca. A. D. 393]

Little is known of Jovinian, a renegade monk of Rome, except what is apparent
through Jerome's treatise against him, *Adversus Iovinianum*, dating from about
393 A. D. From Jerome's refutations it may be concluded that Jovinian
denied that virginity is a higher estate than matrimony; that fasting is any better
than thankful eating; that a person baptized with the Spirit as well as with
water can anymore sin; that there is any distinction of gravity in sinning; that
there is any distinction of degree in eschatological rewards and punishments; and
that the Blessed Mother was a virgin *in partu*.

Jovinian died prior to the year 406; for in that year Jerome wrote his *Adversus
Vigilantium*, in which he sarcastically suggests that in Vigilantius the corrupt
mind of Jovinian has been reborn, though Jovinian "at a table full of pheasants
and swine's flesh not so much breathed out as belched out his life's breath."

Migne's Vallarsi is still the standard edition (PL 23, 211-338).

1378

[1, 13]

"If, however, you have married a wife, you have not sinned (1)." It is one   983
thing not to sin, quite another to do well. "And if a virgin has married, she   982
has not sinned (2)." Not that virgin, however, who has once and for all
dedicated herself to the worship of God; for if one of these has married she
shall have damnation because she has nullified her first faith.

1378a

[1, 15]

The first Adam was married once, the second not at all (3). Let those who   979

approve digamy show us the third and twice-married Adam whom they
are following. It is true that Paul allowed second marriages; and by the same
token (4) he also allowed third and fourth marriages, and as often more as a
husband died. The Apostle was forced to choose many things he did not
want. . . . Where one marriage is exceeded it matters not if it be a second or a
third, because monogamy is already breached. "All things are lawful, but
not all are expedient (5)." I do not condemn digamists, not even trigamists, and
if I may use such a word, not even octogamists. I will go even further
and say that I welcome even penitent pimps. Whatever is equally permissible
must be weighed on the same kind of balance.

1379

[1, 26]

If [Jovinian] should obstinately contend that John was not a virgin, while we   984
have maintained that his virginity was the reason for the special love [which
our Savior had for him], let him explain, if John was not a virgin, just
what was the reason he was loved more than the other Apostles. "But," you   430
will say, "it was on Peter that the Church was founded" (6). Well, in another
place (7) the same is accorded to all the Apostles, and all receive the keys of
the kingdom of heaven, the strength of the Church depends equally on
all of them; but one among the twelve is chosen to be their head in order to   420
remove any occasion for division (8). But why was not John chosen, who was a   410
virgin? Because deference was paid to age, for Peter was the elder (9), lest
one who was a youth, hardly more than a boy, be set over men of advanced
age (10).

1380

[2, 3]

God created us with free will, and we are not forced by necessity either to   505
virtue or to vice. Otherwise, where there were necessity there would be   775
no crown. Just as with good works, it is God who brings them to perfection,
depending not so much on him that wills nor on him that runs as on God
who pities and assists him to reach the goal (11); so too with wickedness and
sin, the seed that prompts us is our own, while its germination and
maturation belongs to the devil.

1381

[2, 25]

At the Passion of Christ all wavered, all alike were made unprofitable; there   634
was none who did good, not even one (12). But do you dare to say that
Peter and the other Apostles, who fled, denied Him to the same extent as
Caiphas did, and the Pharisees, and the people who cried out, "Crucify Him!
crucify Him!" (13)? And if I may be silent about the Apostles, does the
guilt of Annas and Caiphas and of Judas the traitor seem to you to be the same
as that of Pilate who was compelled against his will to sentence the Lord?

1382

[2, 30]

There are venial sins and there are mortal sins (14). It is one thing to owe ten   633

thousand talents, another to owe but a farthing (15). We shall have to
give an accounting for an idle word no less than for adultery. But to be made to
blush and to be tortured are not the same thing; not the same thing to grow
red in the face and to be in agony for a long time. . . . If we entreat for
lesser sins we are granted pardon; but if for greater sins, it is difficult to obtain
our request. There is a great difference between one sin and another.

929

1383

[2, 32]
   It is our task, according to our different virtues, to prepare for ourselves
different rewards. [33] . . . If we were all going to be equal in heaven it would
be useless for us to humble ourselves here in order to have a greater place
there. . . . [34] Why should virgins persevere? Why should widows toil?
Why should married women be continent? Let us all sin, and after we repent
we shall be the same as the Apostles are!

770
1046

1. 1 Cor. 7:28.
2. *Ibid.*
3. *Primus Adam monogamus, secundus agamus.*
4. *eadem lege.*
5. 1 Cor. 6:12.
6. See Matt. 16:18.
7. See Matt. 18:18 and John 20:22-23.
8. *schismatis tollatur occasio.*
9. *senior erat.*
10. *progressae aetatis hominibus praeferretur.*
11. See Rom. 9:16.
12. See Ps. 13[14]:4 and its repetitious twin Ps. 52[53]:4.
13. John 19:6.
14. *Sunt peccata levia, sunt gravia.*
15. *quadrantem.* Farthing has always seemed to be a particularly apt translation for *quadrans*, when no
   specific amount is implied. Both are minor coins; and while the *quadrans* is the fourth part of an *as*, the farthing
   is the fourth part of a penny.

COMMENTARIES ON JONAS [*ca. A. D.* 394]

   Jerome eventually completed commentaries on all of the twelve minor
prophets. The commentaries on Nahum, Micheas, Sophonias, Aggeus and
Habacuc, as we have seen, were written *ca.* A. D. 391. About the year 394 Jerome
took up the series again and added Jonas and Abdias.
   Migne's reprint of Vallarsi's edition of the *In Ionam commentarii* (PL 25,
1117-1152) is superseded by M. Adriaen's edition in the *Corpus Christianorum*,
Vol. 76 (1969), pp. 377-419.

1384

[3, 6]
   If all rational creatures are equal, and by their own free will are, in view of
their virtues or of their vices, either raised up to the heights or plunged down
to the depths, and after the lengthy passage of infinite ages there will be a
restitution of all things (1) and but a single dignity for all the soldiers, how
far apart will a virgin be from a whore? What difference between the Mother of

1034

1014

the Lord and—it is impious even to say it—the victims of public
licentiousness? Will Gabriel and the devil be the same? The Apostles and the
demons the same? The Prophets and pseudo-prophets the same? Martyrs
and their persecutors the same?

1. Jerome is describing the Origenist theory of the final apokatastasis.

AGAINST JOHN OF JERUSALEM [ca. A. D. 397]

Jerome's treatise *Contra Ioannem Hierosolymitanum*, in the form of a letter to
Pammachius, is another episode in his continuing refutation of Origenism.
John, Bishop of Jerusalem, was accused of holding Origenist doctrine by
Epiphanius of Salamis; and when Jerome needed priestly ministrations for his
monasteries around Bethlehem, and did not want to be in any way dependent
upon John, Epiphanius solved his problem by ordaining Jerome's own
brother Paulinian.

The ordination of Paulinian is interesting. He did not want to be anything but
a simple monk and his humility regarded the clerical estate as too great a
burden for his capacities. Epiphanius had founded a monastery at Ad in the
diocese of Eleutheropolis, the town which Acts 9:32, 35 knows as Lydda, about
thirty miles to the northwest of Jerusalem; and it was there that Paulinian was a
monk. Probably neither Epiphanius nor John could rightly claim jurisdiction in
the monastery; but both did. Epiphanius had Paulinian gagged so that he
could not adjure him in the name of Christ to desist, and ordained him deacon.
Assured that the worst was over, Paulinian then consented to exercise his new
order immediately; and as soon as that Mass was over, Paulinian was seized
again, bound and gagged, and ordained to the priesthood.

Through all these proceedings one is somewhat inclined to side with John
of Jerusalem, who found the whole affair quite irregular. Nevertheless,
while John tried to center his differences with Jerome on the affair of Paulinian,
while giving assurance of his own faith in the Trinity and ignoring the Origenist
accusations which were the basic point at issue, it is probably true that he
did have at least certain Origenist leanings.

The Migne reprint of Vallarsi's edition (PL 23, 355-396) is still the standard.

1385

[22]

Whence did Cain and Abel, the first offspring of the first human beings,   506
have their souls? and the whole human race afterwards, what do you suppose   508
is the origin of their souls? Was it from propagation (1), like the brute
animals, in such a way that just as body comes from body so too soul is
generated from soul? . . . But certainly . . . God is engaged daily in
making souls; God, for whom to will is to have done and who never ceases to
be the Creator.

1. *ex traduce*. A tradux is the shoot of a vine, prepared for transplanting. The opinion Jerome is describing and
rejecting is called traducianism, long since condemned as heresy.

COMMENTARIES ON THE GOSPEL OF MATTHEW [*A. D.* 398]

It was Eusebius of Cremona who asked Jerome, in the spring of 398, to write the *In evangelium Matthaei commentarii*; and he wanted it done in two weeks. In sending the completed work, Jerome said in his preface that the time had been much too short to write an adequate exposition, so he had produced only a brief and preliminary treatise without reference to previous authors. He "reserved the perfect work for a future day" (*Preface*, lines 107-108); and that day, of course, never came.

The Migne reprint of Vallarsi (PL 26, 115-218) is now superseded by the edition of D. Hurst and M. Adriaen in the *Corpus Christianorum*, Vol. 77 (1969).

1386

[3, 16, 19]

We read in Leviticus (1) about lepers, where they are ordered to show themselves 　　900
to the priests, and if they have leprosy, then they are to be declared unclean by the 　　920
priest. It is not that the priests make them lepers and unclean; rather, it is the priests
who separate the leper from one who is not a leper, and they can distinguish the
clean from the unclean. Just as in the Old Testament (2) the priest makes the leper 　　925
clean or unclean, so in the New Testament (3) the bishop and presbyter binds 　　918
or looses not those who are innocent or guilty, but by reason of their office, when
they have heard various kinds of sins, they know who is to be bound and who
loosed (4).

1387

[3, 18, 10]

So great is the dignity of souls that each one has from the beginning of his 　　492
birth an angel delegated to guard him. 　　493

1388

[3, 19, 9]

Wherever there is fornication and a suspicion of fornication a wife is freely 　　974
dismissed. And because it is always possible that someone may calumniate the innocent
and, for the sake of a second joining in marriage, act in criminal fashion against
the first, it is commanded that when the first wife is dismissed a second may not be
taken while the first still lives.

1389

[4, 24, 36]

The Apostle writes about the Savior: "In whom are hidden all the treasures of 　　351
wisdom and knowledge (5)." All the treasures, therefore, of wisdom and knowledge
are in Christ; but they are hidden. Why hidden? After the resurrection when He was
asked by the Apostles about the day, He gave a very plain reply: "It is not for
you to know the times or moments upon which the Father, by His own authority, has
decided (6)." When He says, "It is not for you to know," He shows that He
Himself does know, but that it is not expedient for the Apostles to know, so that
always uncertain of the coming of the Judge, they may live daily as if they were
to be judged perhaps on that very day (7).

1390

[4, 26, 26]

After the type had been fulfilled by the passover celebration (8) and He had eaten   849
the flesh of the lamb with His Apostles, He takes bread which strengthens the   893
heart of man, and goes on to the true Sacrament of the passover (9), so that
just as Melchisedech, the priest of the Most High God, in prefiguring Him, made
bread and wine an offering, He too makes Himself manifest in the reality of His own
Body and Blood (10).

1. See Lev. 13:2 and 14:2.
2. *ibi*.
3. *hic*.
4. The whole passage is rather ill-expressed and filled with anacolutha. In fact, the whole of the *In evangelium Matthaei commentarii* bears the marks of Jerome's extreme haste in writing it. But be that as it may, the point Jerome is making would seem to be that in the Old Testament when one suspecting leprosy showed himself to the priests, the priest did not make him either a leper or clean, but simply told him which he was. In the New Testament, when a penitent confesses, the priest does not make him a grave sinner or an innocent person, but tells him which he is and binds or looses him accordingly. It is still muddled; but Jerome's thought is muddled, and to unmuddle it might do violence to what he has in mind. The usual point that is made of such comparision is that in the Old Testament the priest did not free one from leprosy, but only gave a declaratory judgment that the person was already cured. In the New, priests do not simply tell the penitent that God has already forgiven him, but, by the words of absolution which they pronounce, they actually effect the forgiveness. See W. A. Jurgens, *The Priesthood: A Translation of the Peri Hierosynes of St. John Chrysostom*, New York 1955, p. 117, note 83.
5. Col. 2:3.
6. Acts 1:7.
7. *quasi die alia iudicandi sint*. I suspect a colloquial usage of *alius*. Translated literally the clause is: *as if they were to be judged on another day*; but certainly that is not what the passage means. No doubt the *die alia* indicates a vague and unspecified day, to come at any time; some day; hence, *perhaps on that very day*.
8. *Postquam typicum pascha fuerat impletum*.
9. *et ad verum paschae transgreditur sacramentum*. The term *transgredior* really means to pass over—but to so translate would create a pun which is not in the Latin.
10. *ipse quoque in veritate sui corporis et sanguinis repraesentaret*.

SHORT COMMENTARIES ON THE PSALMS [ante A. D. 392] and
TREATISES OR HOMILIES ON THE PSALMS [ca. A. D. 401 et postea]

A work called the *Breviarium in psalmos* (PL 26, 821-1270), though handed down under Jerome's name, was suspected already by Vallarsi of being unauthentic. At the end of the last century Germain Morin concluded to the satisfaction of scholars that the *Breviarium* drew heavily upon two genuine Hieronymian sources, the *Commentarioli in psalmos* or *Short Commentaries on the Psalms*, written before the year 392, the work being noted in Jerome's *De viris illustribus*; and the *Tractatus sive homiliae in psalmos*, begun probably about 401 A. D. Until Morin's time the *Tractatus* had lain unnoticed in manuscripts, and the *Commentarioli*, known as a title, was thought to be lost.

Morin rediscovered several manuscripts of the *Commentarioli* (and was thus able to identify passages drawn therefrom for the *Breviarium*). His edition of the *Commentarioli* was published for the first time in the *Anecdota Maredsolana* 3, 1, in 1895. An only slightly reworked second edition of Morin was prepared and published by the editors of the *Corpus Christianorum*, in their volume 72 (1959), pp. 163-245; and this may be taken as the present standard edition. The Morin text is reprinted also in Adalbert Hamman's *Supplementum* to the Migne Patrology, Vol. 2 (1960), cols. 9-75.

The *Tractatus sive homiliae in psalmos* remained unpublished and unsuspected until Morin brought them again to the light of day. In 1897 he published fifty-nine such homilies or treatises (along with ten others on Mark and ten also on other biblical texts) in the *Anecdota Maredsolana* 3, 2. In 1903 he added fourteen more to the number of homilies on the Psalms and two others on Isaias (*Anecdota Maredsolana* 3, 3). Both collections, that of 1897 and that of 1903, are reprinted with minor emendations in the *Corpus Christianorum*, Vol. 78 (1958). The Vallarsi-Migne editions of Jerome are supplemented also in this instance by Hamman's work as noted above; but especially in the case of the *Tractatus sive homiliae* the *Corpus Christianorum* printing will be found much easier to use than Hamman's *Supplementum*.

1392

[TREATISE ON PSALM 95 (96): *Corpus Christianorum* 78, 154 or *Morin* 3, 2, 138]

Ours and every other race of men knows God naturally. There are no peoples   130
who do not recognize their Creator naturally. Granted that sticks and stones are worshipped, still those who so worship recognize that there is something greater than themselves, and even in their error they show (1) that they have wisdom, that is, they show that there is no race of people which does not recognize God naturally. The pagans worship idols, that is, sticks and stones; but when they have a dispute and when an oath is sworn among them, they do not say, "These stones see," or "These sticks see," but, "God sees, God hears."

1393

[COMMENTARY ON PSALM 138 (139): *Corpus Christianorum* 72, 242 or *Morin* 3, 1, 95].

How should I be able to understand what You are, when in You are all things,   173
and there is nothing that can escape You, and Your Spirit is everywhere? From which   266
we recognize that God is the One who is everywhere in His entirety.

1. Not *iudicant* as in Rouët de Journel, but *indicant*.

APOLOGY AGAINST THE BOOKS OF RUFINUS [*A. D.* 401]

I have already treated enough of the quarrel between Jerome and Rufinus in the general introduction to each of these men (see Rufinus especially); and there is no need to enter into it again at any length.

In the spring of 397 A. D., shortly after Theophilus of Alexandria had succeeded in effecting a wary truce between Jerome and Rufinus, the latter began his translation of Origen's *The Fundamental Doctrines* (see Vol. 1, p. 190 above). In the preface to his translation Rufinus mentioned Jerome as the model of his scholarship, probably intending only to compliment Jerome and to appease him the more.

But when Jerome received a copy of the work through the good offices of his friends Pammachius and Oceanus, he was quite incensed both at what he regarded as a falsified translation and at the fact that his own name should be in any way associated with the work. He pretended, in fact, that Rufinus had praised him not in earnest but only to make a mockery of him. He now made his own translation of *The Fundamental Doctrines*, which he forwarded to Pammachius and Oceanus along with a lengthy letter which, though it never names Rufinus, clearly accuses him of falsification and heresy.

Rufinus saw the letter only much later, and in as evil a mood as he could muster, wrote his *Apologiae in Hieronymum libri duo*. To this Jerome countered in 401 A. D.

with the work which claims our present interest, the most bitter and vitriolic of all his writings, and perhaps the most unjustified: his *Apologiae adversus libros Rufini libri duo*; and when Rufinus wrote him privately suggesting that if he did not desist from his attacks, he would find himself in a court of law defending himself against charges of libel, and at the same time threatening to reveal certain of Jerome's youthful indiscretions, Jerome added, in 402 A. D., a third book, the *Liber tertius vel ultima responsio adversus scripta Rufini*.

The standard text is still Migne's Vallarsi, PL 23, 397-492.

1394

[1, 23]

Just as he alone who is chief of Angels is called an Archangel, so too Principalities   488
and Powers and Dominations would not be called such unless they had some subjects   953
inferior to them in rank. . . . Just as among men an order of dignity is perceived by reason of the kind of work in which they engage, and while bishop and presbyter and every rank in the Church has its own order, all remain men, so too among angels there are different merits while all continue in their angelic dignity. Neither do angels become men, nor do men change back into angels.

1395

[2, 4]

That soul which Jesus took, did it exist before He was born of Mary? Or in the   312
virginal origin in which He was begotten of the Holy Spirit was it created simultaneously   507
with the body? Or was it created immediately and sent down from heaven when the   508
body was already shaped in the womb? Of these three views, I wish to know which one you   506
hold. If it existed before He was born of Mary, it was active in some way when it was not yet the soul of Jesus, and because of the merits of its virtues it was afterwards made His soul. If it had its beginning from a shoot (1), then the condition of human souls, which we acknowledge to be eternal (2), is one with that of the souls of brute animals, which are dissolved with their bodies. But if the soul is created and sent down at the same time that the body is formed, simply admit it and relieve our scruple.

1. *Si cepit ex traduce*. That is, as a natural offspring from the soul of Mary. But Jerome is really only toying with Rufinus throughout, taunting him with the uncertainties of Origen. See the final paragraph of § 446 above.
2. *aeternas*. Though that which is eternal properly has neither beginning nor end; but Jerome is using the term in its looser sense, applied to that which has no end, though it does have a beginning.

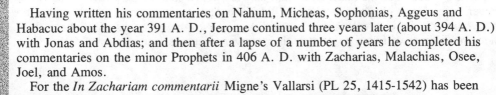

COMMENTARIES ON ZACHARIAS [*A. D.* 406]

Having written his commentaries on Nahum, Micheas, Sophonias, Aggeus and Habacuc about the year 391 A. D., Jerome continued three years later (about 394 A. D.) with Jonas and Abdias; and then after a lapse of a number of years he completed his commentaries on the minor Prophets in 406 A. D. with Zacharias, Malachias, Osee, Joel, and Amos.

For the *In Zachariam commentarii* Migne's Vallarsi (PL 25, 1415-1542) has been entirely superseded by Mark Adriaen's reworking of Vallarsi in the *Corpus Christianorum*, Vol. 76A (1970), pp. 747-900. We will not have occasion to quote from all the commentaries on the minor Prophets, but let it now be noted that Adriaen's edition in Vols. 76 and 76A of the Corpus Christianorum is complete with all twelve, in a total of 1050 pages.

1395a

[3, 14, 8]

"If anyone drink of the water which I will give him, it shall become in him a   822
fountain of water living and springing up unto life everlasting (1)*"*; and again: 823
"Whoever believes in me, as Scripture has said, 'From his belly shall flow
rivers of living water (2)*.'"* For just as one who drinks of His teaching shall
have within himself a living fountain, so too, one who believes in Him shall have,
according to what is contained in the words of the Scriptures, rivers of living water flowing
from his belly. Many refer the living waters to those who thirst, that is, at Easter and
Pentecost, when what is written is fulfilled: "Wash, be clean" (3).

1. John 4:13-14.
2. John 7:38. It seems not to be any single passage of the Old Testament that the Scripture itself quotes, but the substance of
   several passages: Ezech. 36:25; 47:1-12; Is. 44:3; Joel 3:18; Zach. 13:1, 14:8, and no doubt others.
3. Is. 1:16. Jerome is referring to Easter and Pentecost as the proper liturgical seasons for the administration of Baptism.

AGAINST VIGILANTIUS [*A. D.* 406]

Vigilantius was a priest of Calagurris in Aquitaine. He had visited Jerome in
Bethlehem in the year 395 A. D., bringing with him a letter of introduction from
Paulinus of Nola; and on his return he informed Paulinus that Jerome was a
dyed-in-the-wool Origenist! This did nothing to endear him to Jerome nor to dispose
Jerome the better for their greater confrontation still to come.

About the year 404 A. D. a priest of Gaul, one Riparius, sent Jerome, for refutation,
a treatise by Vigilantius which constituted an attack on the practices of venerating relics,
of keeping vigils, of sending alms to Jerusalem, and of observing clerical celibacy.

Jerome ground his teeth for about two years and then sat down to write his *Contra
Vigilantium* in a single night. It is not one of his gentler efforts. Jerome excelled in the
dubious art of argumentation *ad personam*. He was perfectly capable of using the length
of a man's nose to disprove the validity of his theological opinions. Vigilantius opposed
the practice of keeping vigil at the tombs of the saints; and he had the misfortune of
bearing a name which means "one who keeps watch". Jerome suggests that he ought
instead have been called Dormitantius, *i.e.*, "one who prefers to sleep."

The standard edition is Migne's Vallarsi, PL 23, 339-352.

1396

[6]

You say in your book that while we live we are able to pray for each other, but   122
afterwards when we have died, the prayer of no person for another can be heard; and this is
especially clear since the martyrs, though they cry vengeance for their own blood, have
never been able to obtain their request. But if the Apostles and martyrs while still in the
body can pray for others, at a time when they ought still be solicitous about themselves,
how much more will they do so after their crowns, victories, and triumphs?

THE GALEATIC OR HELMETED PROLOGUE [*A. D.* 391]

Jerome began his translation of the Old Testament from the Hebrew in 391 A. D.,
with the Books of Samuel and Kings. The preface which he wrote to these books and
published most probably in that same year is variously termed the *Praefatio in libros*

Samuel et Malachim, the *Praefatio in librum Regum*, the *Praefatio in libro Regum*, and, since it stands really as a preface to his continuing translation of the Old Testament, the *Prologus Scripturarum*. It is perhaps best known, however, as the *Prologus galeatus* or *Principium galeatum*, *i.e.*, the helmeted prologue, from a phrase which Jerome himself uses within the work.

The *Galeatic or Helmeted Prologue* provides us with Jerome's notion of what constitutes the canon of the Old Testament.

The standard edition remains at present Migne's Vallarsi, PL 28, 547-558.

1397

[*Prol. gal.*]

Just as there are twenty-two letters by which we can write in Hebrew anything we 41 say, . . . so too there are twenty-two books. . . . The first . . . we call Genesis. The second . . . is called Exodus. The third . . . Leviticus. The fourth . . . we call Numbers. The fifth . . . is called Deuteronomy. These are the five books of Moses which they call . . . the Law.

The second group is made up of the Prophets; and they begin with Jesus son of Nave. . . . Then . . . there is the Book of Judges, in which they include Ruth, which relates a history which took place in the time of the Judges. The third is Samuel, which we call First and Second Books of Kingdoms. The fourth, . . . Kings, which contains in one volume the Third and Fourth Books of Kingdoms. It is much better to say . . . Kings than . . . Kingdoms. For the author does not describe the kingdoms of many nations, but that of the one Israelite people, composed of twelve tribes. The fifth, Isaias. The sixth, Jeremias. The seventh, Ezechiel. The eighth book is of the Twelve Prophets. . . .

The third group consists of the ʹΑγιόγραφα (1). The first book begins at Job. The second at David, which they divide into five parts, comprised in the one volume of Psalms. The third, having three books, is Solomon: Proverbs, . . . Ecclesiastes, . . . and the Canticle of Canticles. The sixth is Daniel. The seventh, . . . Words of Days, which we can more significantly call a χρονικὸν of the whole divine history. We call this work Παραλειπομένων, and it has a First and a Second Book. The eighth is Esdras, which is divided into two books by Greeks and Latins alike. The ninth is Esther.

Thus there are in the Old Law twenty-two books: five of Moses, eight of Prophets, and nine of Hagiography. . . .

This prologue to the Scriptures may serve as a kind of helmeted prologue to all the books which we shall turn from Hebrew into Latin (2); and thus we may be certain that whatever is not among these is to be placed among the ἀπόκρυφα. Therefore the Wisdom, commonly ascribed to Solomon; and the Book of Jesus son of Sirach; and Judith, and Tobias, and the Shepherd (3) are not in the canon. Of Maccabees, I have found the First Book in Hebrew, but the Second is Greek, which is demonstrated by its very φράσει (4).

1. The term *Hagiographa* means *Sacred Writings*.
2. *His prologus Scripturarum, quasi galeatum principium omnibus libris, quos de Hebraeo vertimus in Latinum.*
3. *I.e., The Shepherd* of Hermas. See above, Vol. 1, pp. 32-37.
4. The term may be rendered *phraseology* or *style*.

COMMENTARIES ON ISAIAS [*inter A. D.* 408-410]

Soon after completing his commentaries on the twelve Minor Prophets, about the year 407, Jerome turned to the exegesis of Daniel; and with that completed, he occupied himself intermittently between the end of 408 and the beginning of the year 410 A. D. with writing his *In Isaiam commentarii*.

He had given some thought to such a work in earlier years. Already in 381 he had written his Letter 18 to Damasus from Constantinople, a letter which constitutes what he now calls a "short and hasty treatise" dealing with the vision of the Seraphim and the burning coal in Isaias 6. A second time he had taken up Isaias for exegesis, when, in 397, he wrote a historical exposition of the ten visions of Isaias in chapters 13-23 of the scriptural book.

This latter work, dedicated to a Bishop Amabilis in Gaul, has not been preserved as a separate work; but now Jerome included it as Book Five in the eighteen books of his *Commentaries on Isaias*, so we have it intact anyway.

Migne's Vallarsi edition of the *Commentaries on Isaias* (PL 24, 17-678) is now entirely superseded by Mark Adriaen's edition in the *Corpus Christianorum*, Vols. 73 and 73A, both published in 1963.

1398

[1, 1, 10]

A man, therefore, cannot see the face of God. But the angels, even those of 170
the least in the Church, always see the face of God (1). And: "Now we see 172
in a mirror and enigmatically, but then we shall see face to face (2)"; when
from men we shall progress to angels (3) and we shall be able to say with the
Apostle: "But we all, with faces unveiled, mirroring the glory of the Lord,
are being transformed into His very image, from glory to glory, as if by
the Spirit of the Lord (4)." It is granted to no creature to see the face of the Lord,
because of the peculiarities of the creature's own nature; but though God is
believed to be invisible, then He will be able to be discerned by the mind.

1399

[3, 6, 8]

When, however, it is said of the person of God, "for Us," and that in the 233
plural, it is to be taken in that same sense in which we read in Genesis, "Let Us
make man to Our image and likeness (5)," as indicating the mystery of the
Trinity (6). For just as in the Gospel we read the Lord's saying, "I and the
Father, we are one (7)," and we refer the *one* to their nature and the *we are* to
their diversity of Persons, so too, when the Lord gives an order the Trinity
commands.

1400

[3, 7, 15]

He shall eat butter and honey, so that He may know to reject the evil and to choose 779
the good. . . . Do not marvel at the novelty of the thing, if a Virgin gives
birth to God, who has such great power that, about to be born after so long a 236
time, when called upon He now sets you free. For this is He that saw Abraham 310
and spoke with Moses. Let me say what is even more remarkable, lest
you think that He is about to be born only as a phantasm: He uses the food of
infancy, He eats butter and milk. And after so long a time the Evangelist
is able to bear witness about Him: "The Boy, however, advanced in wisdom
and age and grace with God and men (8)"; and this is said in order to attest
the truth of His human body. But even before He begins to eat bread and
when He is still fed with butter and honey He shall have judgment of good and
evil, so that, rejecting the evil, He can choose the good. Not that He did
this, either rejecting or choosing; but that He knew to reject and choose, so that

by these words we may know that His infancy with its human body is in
no way prejudicial to divine wisdom.

1401

[14, 53, 5]

"But He was wounded for our iniquities (9),"—and in the Psalm He says,   374
"They have pierced My hands and feet (10)"—so that He might cure our   383
wounds by His own wound; and "He was bruised," or enfeebled, "for our
crimes (11)," so that, having been reviled for us, He might spare us from being
reviled.

1402

[18, 66, 24]

Their worm shall not die and their fire shall not be extinguished (12). . . .If anyone   1014
wants these punishments someday to end, granted it be after a very long time,
and to have an end to these torments, let them make use of these testimonies:
'When the full number of the Gentiles shall have entered, then all Israel shall be   1033
saved (13).'' . . . Just as we believe there are eternal torments for the devil and all
the nay-sayers and impious persons who say in their heart: "There is no God (14),"
so too, for sinners and impious persons who are, nevertheless, Christians, whose   1036
works are to be tried in the fire and purged, we think that the sentence of the Judge   1034
will be tempered and blended with clemency (15).

1. See Matt. 18:10. It seems clear that the *Angeli . . . minimorum in ecclesia* are guardian angels.
2. 1 Cor. 13:12.
3. No doubt when Jerome says: *"Quando de hominibus in angelos profecerimus"*, he is speaking figuratively, to indicate that we shall enjoy certain angelic privileges. See above, § 1394.
4. 2 Cor. 3:18.
5. Gen. 1:26.
6. *ut sacramentum indicet Trinitatis.*
7. John 10:30. We have given a literal translation at the expense of English usage, in order to better illustrate Jerome's argument.
8. Luke 2:52.
9. Is. 53:5.
10. Ps. 21 [22]:18.
11. Is. 53:5.
12. Is. 66:24.
13. Rom 11:25. Jerome also cites Gal. 3:22; Mich. 7:9; Is. 12:1; Is. 7:4 in the Septuagint reading; and Ps. 30[31]:20.
14. Ps. 13[14]:1 or 52[53]:2.
15. For one so adamantly opposed to Origen's theology, it is remarkable how much of that theology Jerome himself retained.

DIALOGUE AGAINST THE PELAGIANS [*A. D.* 415]

Jerome's *Dialogus adversus Pelagianos*, in three books, is the last of his polemical
writings, belonging to the year 415. In its dialogue form Atticus is the Catholic
protagonist while Critobulus represents the Pelagian view.

Pelagius had come in person to Palestine. On July 30, 415, he had to defend himself
before a synod in Jerusalem, and in December of the same year, at Diospolis. He was
accepted into communion by John of Jerusalem.

In some respects Jerome's *Dialogue against the Pelagians* is the finest of his
polemical works. It is comparatively free of the invective, vituperation, and

argumentation *ad personam* that mark so much of his other writings. In other respects, however, it is one of Jerome's weakest works; and the reason for these characteristics is to be found for the most part in Jerome himself. If he now writes in a calmer and more staid manner, it is because he did not find himself personally and emotionally involved in the controversy. Furthermore, if he adopts a kindly attitude, it is very likely because he has certain Pelagian leanings himself which prevent him from realizing the full import of the Pelagian heresy.

Pelagius puts man's destiny entirely in his own hands. Now, that may be a gross oversimplification, but it is the way his doctrine is generally represented. He held that man can live entirely without sin, and that it is easy to lead a moral life. To his statement that men can live without sin, he would not have added what his opponents attributed to him, "without the grace of God." But the problem is really one of prevenient grace; and Pelagianism denies the necessity of this initial help of God to start a man on the path of righteousness, and it involves problems in the theology of original sin.

It is generally considered that Jerome's anti-Pelagian writings are much less effective than Augustine's. No doubt this is true. Augustine can be typified as an absolute predestinationist, while Jerome is often termed a synergist, this latter term indicating that he sees a man's salvation as a work accomplished jointly by God and the man himself. Sometimes Jerome seems to have no idea of prevenient grace himself, as in the present work (§ 1404a) when he says: "It is our part to seek, His to grant what we ask; ours to make a beginning, His to bring it to completion; ours to offer what we can, His to finish what we cannot." Yet he is aware in other passages that we cannot even do penance unless God first converts us (his *Letter to Demetrias* 130, 12, in which he says: "It is ours to will or not to will; and even this faculty that is ours is not ours, except by the mercy of God.").

Jerome is not a Pelagian; but it is probably true that he has certain Pelagian tendencies and sympathies. This, of course, must account in considerable measure for the staid and decorous approach that he takes in his *Dialogue against the Pelagians* in comparison to the wicked temper and animus that he displays in all his other polemical writings. If the work had been written a year later, after the Pelagians burned his monasteries and put his very life in danger, so that he had to seek safety by barricading himself in a tower,—the Pelagians did not think his *Dialogue* was nearly so decorous and conciliatory as we do,—we might expect, Jerome being what he was, that the tone of the work would be somewhat different.

The standard edition is Migne's reprint of Vallarsi in PL 23, 495-590.

1403

[1, 3]

Critobulus: If we must rely on God's help in every single action that we   531
perform, will it then be impossible for us to shape a pen for writing, and
polish it when it has been shaped, and put our hand to forming letters with it;
or to be silent, to speak, to sit, to stand, to walk, to run, to eat, to fast, to weep,
to laugh, and to do other things of such kind, unless God help us?

Atticus: As I see it, it is clearly impossible.

1404

[2, 16]

Atticus: The Savior is comforted in His agony by an angel (1), and my   657
Critobulus, having the power of free will, does not need the help of God! The
Savior prayed so earnestly that drops of that blood gushed forth, which He

was about to pour out completely in His Passion. "Why do you sleep?" He says. "Rise up and pray that you do not enter into temptation! (2)" According to your view He ought to have said: "Why do you sleep? Rise up and struggle, for you have free will, and once that power has been given you by the Lord, you need the help of no one else. For if you do this, you will not enter into temptation!"

1404a

[3, 1]

Atticus: This much you must know, that Baptism forgives past sins, but it does not safeguard future justice, which is preserved by labor and industry and diligence, and depends always and above all on the mercy of God. It is our part to seek, His to grant what we ask; ours to make a beginning, His to bring it to completion; ours to offer what we can, His to finish what we cannot.

836

659

1405

[3, 6]

Atticus: Marcion asks this, and all the heretical dogs (3) who tear apart the Old Testament and who are wont to construct a syllogism of this sort: Either God knew that man, whom He placed in paradise, was going to transgress His command, or He did not know it. If God knew it, man is not at fault for being unable to avoid God's foreknowledge, but the fault is God's, who so created man that man could not obviate God's foreknowledge. And if God did not know it, then, when you take away His foreknowledge you likewise deny His divinity. By such logic as this God will be at fault for having chosen Saul, who, afterwards, was to become a most impious king. And the Savior will be held guilty either of ignorance or of injustice for having said in the Gospel: "Have I not chosen the twelve of you as Apostles? And one of you is a devil! (4)" Ask Him why He chose the traitor Judas; why He committed the coffers (5) to him when He knew that Judas was a thief. Do you want to hear the reason? God judges the present, not the future. Nor does He condemn him who, He knows by reason of His foreknowledge, will afterwards become such as is displeasing to Him. So great is His goodness and so indescribable His clemency that He chooses him who, He sees, is presently good, and who, He knows, will turn out bad, giving him the power of conversion and repentance. . . . It is not because God knew the future that Adam sinned; but God foreknew, as God, that Adam would do this of his own will.

191

193

190

723

192

1406

[3, 12]

Critobulus: Granted that no one has been able to avoid all sin in boyhood, adolescence, and youth. But can you deny that many just and holy men, after their faults, have devoted themselves wholeheartedly to virtues, and that by these virtues they were free of sin?

Atticus: That is what I told you in the first place: we have this power to sin or not to sin, to turn our hand to good or to evil; and thus free will is preserved. But this is limited by time and human weakness; to continue perpetually in a state of sinlessness is reserved to God alone, and to Him who

613

636

657

was Word made flesh but was not subject to sin and to the injury done the   345
flesh. Nor will you ever convince me that because I can do something for a short
time I can do it continuously. Can I fast, keep vigil, walk, read, sing psalms,
sit, and sleep forever?

1. See Luke 22:43. Jerome indicates that the verse in question is found in some codices, Greek and Latin,
   but absent in others.
2. Luke 22:46.
3. *omnes haereticorum canes*.
4. John 6:71.
5. *loculos*.

COMMENTARIES ON JEREMIAS [*A. D.* 415 *et postea*]

Jerome began his *In Ieremiam commentarii* in the year 415. He had commented
on chapters 1-32 of Jeremias in six books dedicated to the priest Eusebius of
Cremona when he interrupted the work to take up the defense of orthodoxy
against Pelagianism; and in the troubles that were initiated by the burning of his
monasteries in 416, he never found time to continue on Jeremias. He died
in 419 or 420 with this work still incomplete.

Migne's Vallarsi (PL 24, 679-900) was superseded already in 1913 by Siegfried
Reiter's edition in the Vienna Corpus (CSEL), Vol. 59. With only such changes
as indicated by his own pages of addenda and corrigenda in the Vienna
Corpus edition, Reiter's work is now reprinted in the *Corpus Christianorum*, Vol.
74, 1960.

1407

[4, 15, 2]
After the captivity which took place under Vespasian and Titus and   1016
afterwards under Hadrian, the ruins of Jerusalem are to remain until the end
of time (1), although the Jews themselves think a gold and jewel-bedecked
Jerusalem is to be restored and that there will again be victims and sacrifices
and marriages of the saints and a kingdom in the lands of the Lord and Savior.
[3] Granted that we cannot accept this, neither, however, do we dare to
condemn it, because so many men of the Church and martyrs said the same
(2).

1408

[5, 36, 5]
"Perhaps," He says, "they may hear and be converted (3)." The uncertainty   190
of the word "perhaps" cannot pertain to the majesty of the Lord, but it is
spoken on account of our condition, so that the free will of man may be
preserved, lest it be supposed that in view of His foreknowledge there is, as it
were, a kind of necessity either of doing something or of not doing it.

1409

[5, 60, 1]
"And Ananias the prophet took the chain"—or *furca* (4), which in Hebrew is   26
called a *muthoth* (5)—"from the neck of Jeremias the prophet and broke

it (6)." . . . [2] The Septuagint . . . does not translate the term prophet in
connexion with Ananias, lest perhaps it seem to call him a prophet who
was not a prophet. Occasionally in the Holy Scriptures terms are used in
accord with what the opinion of the times would employ, and not in accord
with what is really the truth of the matter.

1. *usque ad consummationem saeculi.*
2. *multi ecclesiasticorum virorum et martyres ista dixerunt.*
3. Jer. 26:3.
4. A *furca* was a kind of yoke put over the neck for punishment of a slave. It had two prongs to which the
   unfortunate victim's arms could be tied.
5. *Muthoth* is Jerome's transliteration, who regularly gives the construct in such situations, and who, furthermore,
   admits that he has great difficulty with pronunciation. The term should be read: *moṭâ*.
6. Jer. 28:10.

TREATISES OR HOMILIES ON THE GOSPEL OF MARK [*A. D.* ?]

At the end of the last century, while investigating the problems of authenticity
in the various Hieronymian collections of homilies and treatises on the
Psalms, Germain Morin discovered, along with numerous other homilies of
Jerome, what he was able to put together as a collection of ten homilies of St.
Jerome on the Gospel of Mark, Jerome's *Tractatus in Marci Evangelium.* For this
group of ten homilies, which cannot be satisfactorily dated, Morin found three
manuscripts of the first, never before published. The other nine had previously
been published in Volume 2, pp. 263-271 of the Erasmian edition of the
works of Chrysostom, Venice, 1549.

Morin's collection of the ten *Tractatus* was first published in 1897 in the
Anecdota Maredsolana 3, 2. The second edition of Morin's text is in the *Corpus
Christianorum*, Vol. 78 (1958), pp. 449-500. The collection is reprinted also in
Adalbert Hamman's *Supplementum* to the Migne Patrology, Vol. 2 (1960), cols.
125-171.

1410

[10, 13, 32]

Of the Son it is said: "Of that day and hour no one knows, except the   351
Father; not the angels in heaven and not the Son (1)." If we receive Baptism   826
equally in the Father, Son, and Holy Spirit, we must believe there is one name
for Father, Son, and Holy Spirit, which is God. If God is one, how can
there be a diversity of knowledge in one divinity? What is greater, to be God
or to know all things? If He is God, how does He not know? . . . In the
Apostle we read about Christ: "In whom are hidden all the treasures of wisdom
and knowledge (2)." See what He says: "*all* the treasures of wisdom and
knowledge." Not that some are and some are not: but *all* the treasures of
wisdom and knowledge; but they are *hidden.* So what is in Him is not lacking
to Him, even though it be hidden from us. But if all the treasures of wisdom
and knowledge are hidden in Christ, we must ask why they are hidden.
If we men were to know the day of judgment, which is the subject of the
statement, and that the day of judgment is to come after two thousand years,
knowing that it is so far in the future, we would only become more negligent.
We would say, "What difference does it make to me if the day of judgment
is to come after two thousand years?" When it is said that the Son does

not know the day of judgment, it is so stated for our sake, so we do not know when the day of judgment is to come. Finally, see what follows that statement: "Take care, watch and pray; for you do not know when that time will come" (3).

1. Mark 13:32.
2. Col. 2:3.
3. Mark 13:33.

PELAGIUS [*fl ca. A. D.* 412]

Pelagius, called the Archheretic, and the dates neither of whose birth nor death can be established, was very likely a native of Ireland, or if not, at least, as his name indicates, of the Isles. He came to Rome about the year 384 and remained there as an ascetic and monk until 410. Having fled to Carthage along with his disciple Caelestius before the Visigoths entered Rome, it was in 411 at Carthage that his teachings met their first opposition; and it was in 412 that Augustine first began to write against him.

Excommunicated at a Council of Carthage in 411, Pelagius took refuge in the East, where in 415 Jerome took up his pen against him; but in the East he enjoyed the confidence of various bishops, John of Jerusalem among them. The Pelagian doctrines were condemned in councils at Carthage and at Milevis in 416, by Pope Innocent I in 417, and after some vacillation, by Pope Zosimus in 418. Finally Pelagianism was condemned in canons 1 and 4 of the Ecumenical Council of Ephesus in 431 (see below, § 2141b and § 2141c). Pelagius disappears from history after 418, and has long since been presumed dead.

The basic principle of Pelagianism is the affirmation of the self-sufficiency of man's free will. Pelagius asserted that by relying solely on his own powers a man can always will and do what is good. Pelagianism involves further a denial of original sin, a denial of the absolute necessity of Baptism, and presents a total distortion of the theology of grace. Insofar as his moral conduct is concerned, it must be admitted that he led a life of exemplary virtue.

Pelagius' writings were quite numerous. But few of them have been preserved in full and under his own name. In the 1940's G. de Plinval was able to attribute nineteen minor works to Pelagius, garnering them largely from published works falsely attributed to Jerome, Fastidius, Paulinus of Nola and others. A well-organized conspectus of the literary remains of Pelagius, showing the results of the extensive investigations of Germain Morin, Alexander Souter, and George de Plinval, can be found in Adalbert Hamman's *Supplementum* to Migne, Vol. 1 (1959), cols. 1101-1570, which also is now the most convenient source for all the writings more recently attributed to Pelagius, with references for finding the works not actually printed there.

LETTER OF PELAGIUS TO DEMETRIAS

The *Epistula ad Demetriadem seu liber de institutione virginis* is an undoubtedly authentic writing of Pelagius. The lady Demetrias to whom the letter is addressed is the same who was in correspondence also with Jerome (*Ep*. 130) and Augustine (*Ep*. 150). The text of this letter is found twice in Migne: in PL 30, 15-45, with Jerome's writings; and in PL 33, 1099-1120, with the writings of Augustine. Even in Migne, however, it is attributed to Pelagius in its heading.

1411

[3]
   For God, desiring to endow the rational creature with the function of voluntary goodness   725
and the power of free will, and by implanting in man the possibility of both, makes   727
it man's special character that he wills, so that he is naturally capable both of good and of
evil, and he may be inclined to the willing of either. . . . For how many philosophers
have we ourselves heard and read and even seen, who are chaste, patient, modest,
generous, abstemious and kind, while at the same time they reject the honors and delights
of the world and are lovers of justice no less than of knowledge? Whence comes this, I ask,
to men not acquainted with God, by which they are pleasing to God? Whence this
goodness, if not from a goodness theirs by nature? And since those virtues which I
mentioned can be seen to be present either all in one man or individually in various
individuals, and since the nature of all men is one, by their own example they demonstrate
to each other that it is possible for all those virtues to be present in all men, which can be
found either all in one (1) or individually in individuals. And if even without God, men can
demonstrate so thoroughly that they have been made by God, only think what Christians
are able to do, whose nature and life is so much the better equipped through Christ, and
who are assisted also by the help of divine grace. . . . [4] For there is, I say, in our
minds, a certain natural — if I may so term it—sanctity, which, presiding as it were in the
recesses of the mind, exercises its judgment over what is good and what is evil.

1412

[8]
   But certainly we do not so defend the goodness of nature that we would say it is   725
not able to do evil, when we profess that it is capable of good and of evil. Rather,
we vindicate it against injuries of such a kind that, by its having been corrupted, we
would seem to be impelled to the evil; for we can do neither good nor evil without
willing it, and we have always a freedom to do one of two things, since we are
always able to do otherwise. . . . If, as we have said, even before the Law and   726
long before the coming of our Lord and Savior there were those who are reported to have
lived in a just and holy manner, how much the more, after the enlightenment of His
coming, is it to be believed that we are capable of it; and we who have been strengthened
by the grace of Christ and reborn into a better humanity, who have been expiated for and
cleansed by His blood, and who have been urged on toward perfect justice by His example,
how much better ought we be than were those who lived prior to the Law, better even than
those who were under the Law, saying with the Apostle: "Sin shall no longer have
dominion over you; for you are not under the Law, but under grace" (2).

1. I have amended the reading *omnia in omnibus* to *omnia in uno*. The sense of the passage demands this change; and since
   the phrase *omnia in omnibus* occurs in the clause immediately preceding, its repetition were an easy scribal error for
   omnia in uno. So that the reader may judge for himself, we give the entire sentence in Latin: *Et cum ista, quae dixi, vel*
   omnia in uno vel singula in singulis haberi videamus, cum omnium natura una sit, exemplo suo sibi invicem ostendunt
   omnia in omnibus esse posse, quae vel omnia in omnibus [read: *uno*] *vel singula in singulis inveniantur.*
2. Rom. 6:14.

FREE WILL [*ca. A. D.* 416]

   Pelagius' work entitled *De libero arbitrio*, in four books, is known only from several
fragments. In addition to the fragments in Migne, two newly discovered fragments were
published by Alexander Souter in the *Proceedings of the British Academy*, Vol. 2
(1905-1906), pp. 437-439. These were quickly followed by another fragment from
Souter, published in the *Journal of Theological Studies*, Vol. 12 (1911), pp. 32-35.

These three fragments made clear what had long been suspected: Pelagius wrote his *Free Will* in response to Jerome's *Dialogue against the Pelagians*. Since Jerome wrote in 415, Pelagius' work may be conveniently dated as *ca* A. D. 416. The three above mentioned fragments are reprinted in Hamman's *Supplementum* to Migne, Vol. 1 (1959), cols. 1539-1543.

A more important fragment from book 3 of the work has long been known, preserved by reason of its having been quoted by Augustine in his *De gratia Christi* 4, 5. The text of the fragments from that work can be found in Migne PL 48, 611-615; or, for the presently pertinent fragment alone, in PL 44, 362; or better, at the aforementioned place in Augustine's *De gratia Christi* in the Vienna Corpus edition, CSEL Vol. 42 (1902), p. 127.

1413

[Frag. from Book 3, in Aug., *The Grace of Christ* 4, 5]

We distinguish those three elements and set them down in a definite order. In the | 725
first place we put being able; in the second, choosing; in the third, the actuality of being | 726
(1). We locate the being able in nature, choosing in will, and being in effect. The | 727
first, which is to be able, pertains properly to God, who grants this to His creature. The other two, which are choosing and being, are in reference to man, because they stem from the source of the choosing. Therefore, in desiring and doing good, the praise belongs to man; or rather, both to man and to God, who gives man the possibility of his own willing and working, and who always assists that same possibility by the help of His grace. But that man is *able* to choose the good and carry it out belongs to God alone.

1. *Primo loco posse statuimus, secundo velle, tertio esse.*

FRAGMENTS FROM UNDETERMINED WORKS OF PELAGIUS

S. Hellmann, in the section *Sedulius Scotus* in L. Traube's *Quellen und Untersuchungen zur lateinischen Philologie des Mittelalters* 1, 1, Munich 1906, p. 99, n. 2, offers two fragments attributed to Pelagius in a 12th century *Codex Cusano* C 14 (now 37). The fragments are reprinted by Hamman in his *Supplementum* Vol. 1, col. 1570. They have absolutely nothing to do with our present objectives, but are much too delightful to be allowed to molder away unheeded; so, lest the remainder of this page be left blank, the passages are as follows.

1413a

[*Pelagius*]

The term contention is not used except in reference to the defense of falsehood; constancy in regard to truth, however, is called assertion.

1413b

[*Pelagius*]

Verbosity is said to be present when vain things are discussed; when, however, truth is stated, in however a copious manner, the term verbosity cannot be used.

CAELESTIUS [† *ca. A. D.* 429]

Caelestius, probably of Italian origin, is found at Rome about the year 405, where he is a firm disciple of Pelagius. With the latter he went to Carthage in 410, remaining there when Pelagius went on to Palestine. Adjudged a heretic in the African synods of 411 and 412, he went to Ephesus where he was ordained to the priesthood, and then on to Constantinople. In 417 and 418 he was back in Rome, where he shared in the condemnations of Pelagius by Pope Innocent I in the former year and Pope Zosimus in the latter. In 418, following the condemnation by Zosimus, Caelestius was obliged by imperial edict to leave Rome and return to Constantinople; and it is probably in the latter place that he died. No trace of him is found after the year 429 A. D. Of his not inconsiderable writings only fragments are preserved.

FRAGMENT IN JEROME'S LETTER 133

The following fragment of an unspecified writing of Caelestius is preserved as a quotation in Jerome's *Letter to Ctesiphon* 133, 5, the letter itself dating from 415 A. D. (Other excerpts from Jerome's letter are found above, at § 1355, § 1355a, and § 1356.) The best source for the text of the present fragment will be the third volume of I. Hilberg's Vienna Corpus edition of Jerome's letters, Vol. 56 (1918). In regard to Caelestius, see also the passage from Marius Mercator, § 2019 below.

1414

[133, 5]
This man [*Caelestius*] . . . *theorizes thus*: "If I do nothing without the help of   725
God, and if in all my individual actions all that I do is attributed to Him, then it is not I
who labor, but rather God's help that shall be crowned in me. And it is in vain that   770
He gives me a power of choice which I cannot employ unless He assists me at every turn.
For a will that needs the support of another is not a will at all. But God has given me free
will, and it is not free at all unless I do what I will."

JULIAN OF ECLANUM [† *ca. A. D.* 454]

When Pope Zosimus promulgated his decision against Pelagianism in 418 a letter went out to all the bishops of the world requiring their assent in the matter. Julian, Bishop of Eclanum in Apulia, headed a group of eighteen bishops who refused; and from that time he assumed leadership of the Pelagian party. He was expelled from his see by Pope Zosimus and was exiled by the civil authority. With no permament domicile, we find him about the year 420 enjoying the hospitality of Theodore of Mopsuestia; and in the late 420's he tarried for a long time with Nestorius in Constantinople.

Pelagianism was a rather well-developed system, and it owes its synthesis largely to Julian. As with Pelagius and Caelestius, however, his rather extensive writings are for the most part extant only in fragmentary condition.

EIGHT BOOKS TO FLORUS [*A. D.* 421 *aut* 422]

In 419 Julian had written his *Libri quattuor ad Turbantium*, a criticism of the first of the two books of Augustine's *De nuptiis et concupiscentia*. Several fragments of these

Four Books to Turbantius are preserved in Augustine's first *Contra Iulianum*. Julian followed his *Four Books to Turbantius* with a criticism of the second of Augustine's two books *De nuptiis et concupiscentia* in 421 or 422 in his *Libri octo ad Florum*.

Turbantius and Florus were, like Julian himself, Italian bishops in exile because of their Pelagianism. Almost the whole of the first six books of the *Eight Books to Florus* can be reconstructed from Augustine's second and unfinished work against Julian, the *Contra Iulianum opus imperfectum*. It is in this latter unfinished work that Augustine says of Julian: "In disputation most loquacious, in contention most calumnious, in profession most fallacious."

The best source for the fragments of the *Eight Books to Florus* is Michaela Zelzer's edition of the *Opus imperfectum* based on work initiated by Ernest Kalinka, published in the Vienna Corpus, CSEL Vol. 85, part 1, 1974. That volume, however, covers only the first three books of Augustine's *Opus imperfectum*, and the Migne edition (PL 45, 1049-1068) must still be used for books four through six.

1415

[1, 78]

Julian: Liberty of choice, by which man is emancipated from God, consists in the possibility of committing sin and the possibility of refraining from sin.   725

1416

[5, 41]

Julian: The will cannot subsist except in a movement of the mind, no one compelling.   725
If, however, someone compels, certainly it is a movement; but it is not will, the strength of which is fulfilled in the second part of that definition, that is, no one compelling.

INDEX OF SCRIPTURAL REFERENCES AND CITATIONS

The reference numbers are to the consecutive numbering of the text passages rather than to pages, whether the Scripture reference be pertinent to the passage itself or to its accompanying notes. Passages which require Septuagint consultation are marked *Sept.*; and in these the numbering is that of the Septuagint. Passages 1-910u are in Vol. 1; 911-1416 are in Vol. 2; and 1417-2390 are in Vol. 3.

DOCTRINAL INDEX

In the following index points of doctrine are numbered consecutively. After each doctrinal statement appear the numbers of the passages of THE FAITH OF THE EARLY FATHERS which have some bearing upon that doctrinal statement. The passage itself will usually be found to be an affirmation of the doctrinal statement; but in some instances it will be found to be in contradiction to it. In the latter case the passage number is enclosed in parentheses. The Fathers and the early Christian Writers do not agree with each other with a precise mathematical unanimity, nor could it be expected that they would. And in any case we must stress that an isolated patristic text is in no instance to be regarded as a ''proof'' of a particular doctrine. Dogmas are not ''proved'' by patristic statements but by the infallible teaching instruments of the Church. The value of the Fathers and Writers is this: that in the aggregate they demonstrate what the Church did and does yet believe and teach. In the aggregate they provide a witness to the content of Tradition, that Tradition which itself is a vehicle of revelation.

Passage numbers 1-910u are to be found in Vol. 1; 911-1416 in Vol. 2; and 1417-2390 in Vol. 3.

NATURAL RELIGION

1. The concept of religion:
    631   635   1603   1743   2236   2377   2378
2. Man has a natural tendency toward religion [see also 130].
    270   275   1841

REVEALED RELIGION

REVELATION

10. Revelation deserves the assent of reason [see also 558].
    173   354a   455   562   818b   1179   1321
11. In the present order revelation is for us a moral necessity.
    334   629   1557   1746
12. Miracles are possible.
    1697   1773
13. Miracles provide an external criterion of revelation [see also 82].
    133b   1784   1819
14. Miracles do not of themselves, however, suffice to confirm the truth of doctrine.
    638
15. Prophecy provides another external criterion of revelation [see also 81].
    57   61   175   276a   530   626   1497   1615
16. There are also internal criteria of revelation: sentiments of the soul.
    1265   1557   1593   1822

SACRED SCRIPTURE

INSPIRATION

20. The Sacred Scriptures, written under the inspiration of the Holy Spirit, have God for their author [see also 50].
    22   26b   122b   123   126   149   185   203   328b   390a   400   404   447a   468a   483   577   976
    1045   1078   1089a   1286   1479   1588   2158   2167   2302
21. Inspiration consists in the action of God's using the intellect and will of the sacred writer after the fashion of an instrument.
    122b   149   162   163   175   179   388   910a   1609   1766   2302
22. The primary object of such inspiration is the things that concern salvation.
    149   818b   1045   1479   1687   1709   2096
23. Nevertheless inspiration extends to all parts of Sacred Scripture and in some sense even to the words themselves.
    483   979   2158
24. But inspiration does not carry with it the revelation of those things to be written which the writer was able, with divine help, to know in a natural way.
    1612   1767
25. No error can be found in the Sacred Scriptures.
    22   138   203   390a   400   480   1106   1347   1417   1421   1597   1612

26. Every assertion made by the sacred writer is true according to the meaning which he wished to express and did express.
    1409   1610a   1611   1804
27. Bearing in mind that every assertion made by the sacred writer is true according to the meaning which he wished to express and did express, the presence of apparent errors in Scripture in regard to history and the sciences can be explained.
    138   1376   1421   1687   2096
28. With the possible exception of the Septuagint the versions of Sacred Scripture are not inspired.
    1347   1421   1597
29. Some of the Fathers believed that the Septuagint version was made under inspiration.
    149a   819
30. In regard to the several senses of Scripture:
    447a   469   480   1588
31. The reading of the Scriptures is recommended also to the laity.
    1159a

CANONICITY

40. The sole criterion of canonicity is Catholic Tradition, which has its basis in Apostolic Tradition.
    341   745s   819   1584   1607   1896
41. The Tridentine canon of the Old Testament is founded in Catholic Tradition.
    190   484   745t   791   819   882   910t   1020   1078   1239   1344   1372   1397   1585   2015b
    2167   2373
42. So also is the Tridentine canon of the New Testament founded in Catholic Tradition.
    94   95   211   268   341   439-440   479a?   503   538   652   652b   653   656   745t   791   819   910t
    1020   1078   1239   1344   1585   2015b   2167   2373

THE OLD LAW

50. God is the Author of the Law, both the Old and the New [see also 20].
    185   230   276a   410a   421a   445   680   1093   1567   1895   2205
51. The purpose of the Old Law was to prepare for the coming of Christ [see also 300].
    61   134b   188   303a   834a   1093   1599   1600   1602   1897   2205
52. The Old Law, therefore, is abrogated by the revelation of the New Law.
    45   46   96   133a   134a   1599   1602   1897   2205

THE GOSPEL

60. Gospel: meaning of the word. The single and fourfold gospel:
    5   7a   9   20   31   57   60   61   81a   112   128   195   208   215   238   288   427   1825   2291
61. The authenticity and historicity of the four Gospels was acknowledged in Christian antiquity.
    129   141   143   199a   208   214   215   268   339   341   439-440   474   503   538   1597   2152
62. The witnesses who affirm the genuinity of the four Gospels are worthy of belief.
    (201)   212   (261)   264
63. The four Gospels contain true histories.
    60   195   264   268   519   619   666   1170   1615   1784
64. The authenticity and historicity of the Gospel of Matthew:
    1   5   7a   10   95   143   167   208   214   339   341   439-440   503   538   1606
65. The authenticity and historicity of the Gospel of Mark:
    13   24   31   95   208   214   268   339   341   439-440   503   538   651bb   652
66. The authenticity and historicity of the Gospel of Luke:
    1   63   143   195   208   214   217   268   339   341   439-440   503   538
67. The Gospel of John is also authentic and historic, although it takes a spiritual approach to history.
    182   208   214   264   268   339   341   439-440   503   538   1825
68. The genuinity of the four Gospels is confirmed from the apocryphal gospels.
    474   1241a-d
69. The genuinity of the four Gospels is confirmed also from the manner in which the heretics of antiquity made use of them.
    195   214   339   340   341   474   2152

DIVINE ORIGIN OF CHRISTIANITY

80. Jesus Christ came into the world as a divine legate [see also 302 and 310].
    47   51   54b   290   405   520   1746   2077

81. The predictions of the Prophets fulfilled in Christ prove His mission divine [*see also* 15 *and* 300].
    61 122 125 127 222 468a 638 1135 1470 1615

82. The divine character of Christ's mission is proved also by His miracles [*see also* 13].
    109 122 189 618 619 1031 1032 1094 1784 1819

83. Christ's predictions of the future, which have been fulfilled, prove his mission divine.
    116 654

84. The Resurrection of Christ is proved by arguments that are certain.
    13 47 51 63 129 665 818a 1156 1471

85. The wonderful spread of Christianity along with its continued endurance serve to prove its divine origin [*see also* 404 *and* 405].
    274 279 282 320a 369 555-556 621 1614 1783 1784

86. The virtues of Christians when compared to the vices of the pagans argue to the divine origin of Christianity and its teachings.
    97 112 186 271 273 274 280 281 283 285 2167a 2167d

87. The change in moral values which comes with conversion argues to the divine origin of Christianity and its teachings.
    118 263 276 369 621 661a

88. Martyrdom is a testimony to the truth of the Christian religion.
    11 63 144 243 285 640 1465

89. The internal character of Christian doctrine argues to its divine origin.
    118 192 276a 405

90. The Church's doctrine is in no way determined by popularity.
    1360a

TRADITION

100. Sacred Tradition is a true source of revelation.
    192 198 242 291 295 371 (818b) 917 954 1098 1213 1358 1419 1419a 1581 1631
    1899 2168 2172 2390

101. Sacred Tradition completes Sacred Scripture through its authentic interpretation thereof.
    242 291 443 1098 1419a 2168

102. Apostolic Tradition has always been acknowledged as the rule of faith.
    74 94 190a 191 192 209 210 211 212 213 257 264 293 296 298 329 341 394
    443 445 785 898 1043 1107 1623 1705 2142

103. There was a progressive revelation until the death of the Apostles.
    239 2329

104. Since the death of the Apostles it has not been possible for the body of revelation either to be augmented or diminished.
    2 213 226 242 288 289 293 785 972 1181 2169 2173

105. Nevertheless the proposition that there is a certain progress in dogma is not in every sense to be rejected.
    226 328a 371 444 1145a 1765 2173 2174

106. Unanimity of the Fathers in matters of faith and morals provides certitude.
    1898 1899 1900 2004 2142 2168 2175

107. As private teachers, however, the Fathers can err.
    190a 1255 1623 2175

RELIGION AND CULT

120. Among the acts of religion there is prayer [*see also* 712].
    26a 55 79 281b 557a 1154 2001

121. The saints in heaven are worthy objects of worship, which worship, however, is not the same as that given to God.
    81 572 1109 1285 1603 2378

122. There is a communion of saints by which the souls of the just dead, knowing us and our needs, pray for us.
    852 1396 1513 1603 1770 1935

123. Christian tradition bears witness to the honoring of relics.
    70 81 1738 2148 2294a 2295a

124. The honoring of sacred images is lawful and pious.
    952 2095 2377

125. The cross of our Lord is to be held in honor, whether it be a question of its actual relics, or images of it, or the sign of the cross made by the motion of the hand.
    367 751a 824 954 1240 1815 1844 2233c

THE ONE GOD

EXISTENCE OF GOD

130. The existence of God is able to be known with certainty by the natural light of reason.
197 228 269 270 275 287 331 334 416 455 645 662 888 984 1130 1392 1593 1693

131. Man is able to arrive at a knowledge of God from a consideration of the order in the visible world.
152 172 198 228 269 332 515 624 662 746 747 959 984 987 1050 1117 1146 1182 1315 1508 1841 2137 2338

132. Man is able to arrive at a knowledge of God from a consideration of the government of providence.
110 172 269 987 1032 1557

133. Man is able to arrive at a knowledge of God from the dictates of conscience.
411 1146 1557 2315

134. Positive revelation is not necessary in order to arrive at a natural knowledge of God.
(227) 269 1182 1508

135. There is a certain natural knowledge of God's existence innate in men [see also 2].
130 270 332 403 425 662 987 1182 1841 2093 2137 2338

136. On the direct perception of God in this life:
1545

137. The existence of God is provable a posteriori.
334 1596 2339

ESSENCE OF GOD

140. The essence of God is existence itself, whence His proper name, Yahweh [see also 174].
729 786 857 877 993 1015 1046 1262 1367 1489 1493 1591a 1596 1649 1669 2098 2345

141. God is existence, of Himself and independently.
754 860 861 932 991 993 1367 1489

ATTRIBUTES OF GOD

150. The divine attributes are really the same as the divine substance (essence).
192a 199b 229 1481 1664 1666 1669 1670 1676 1748

151. God is utterly simple and admits of no composition whatever.
199b 321 424 451 754 756 786 822a 911 923 1041 1066 1122 1128 1266 1660 1669 2066 2067 2081

152. God is spirit.
111 152 164 277 374 451 452 822b 894 1066 1105 1128 2050 2081 2094 2351

153. God has every perfection in an infinite degree.
229 423 815 1042 1320 1712 2081 2341

154. God is immeasurable and is present everywhere.
85 177 234a 424 608 754 815 860 893 894 899 1070 1105 1266 2119 2156 2304 2353

155. God is completely unchangeable.
111 132 814 815 1046 1493 1663 1758 2264

156. God is eternal.
110 152 161 164 206 321 331 608 628 814 822a 860 899 1015 1367 1481 2264

157. God is one and unique.
45 191 194 196 199a 203 205 274a 275 290 322 328a 331 397 445 515 608 1089a 1551 2236 2341

158. God is all-powerful.
111 171 194 205 323 325 402 424 628 651f 815 822a 910a 1089a 1366 1711 1741

KNOWLEDGE ABOUT GOD

170. No creature can of its unaided nature see God.
236 270 451 452 747 891 986 1075 1106 1123 1125 1126 1127 1128 1161 1398 1653 2150 2212

171. In regard to seeing God with bodily eyes:
452 645 1786 1787

172. A creature can be elevated to the sight of God, as in fact is done for the angels and the blessed.
236 822 988 989 1106 1114 1398 1752 1786 2150 2303
173. God is incomprehensible and inexpressible.
164 205 234a 270 450 603 668 747 756 786 860 861 900 923 931 984 1015
1023 1041 1042 1075 1124 1125 1127 1128 1161 1239a 1266 1393 1505 2160 2338
174. We cannot, properly speaking, know the essence of God.
130 270 416 623 821 923 988 1048 1049 1121 1122 1123 1130 1161 2073 2074
2340
175. We do arrive at some knowledge of God through various concepts which describe Him.
192a 199b 331 423 424 455 603 786 821 894 900 908 930 985 1015 1047 1048
1049 1122 2094
176. The concepts we employ in arriving at a descriptive knowledge of God are at best extremely faulty.
760a 1047 2073
177. The concepts we employ in arriving at a descriptive knowledge of God are faulty because they cannot be understood of God in the same way in which they are understood of creatures.
270 623 754 760a 908 1028 1320 1596 2313
178. We attempt to arrive at some knowledge of the perfections of God from a consideration of His creatures, by the *way of negation*.
110 423 1047 1048 1658 2074 2340
179. We attempt to arrive at some knowledge of the perfections of God from a consideration of His creatures, by the *way of causality*.
110 455 923 931 1050 1596
180. We attempt to arrive at some knowledge of the perfections of God from a consideration of His creatures, by the *way of eminence*.
110 450 674 908 1028 1048 1266 1671 2340
181. The names of God are not synonyms.
930 933 1047 1049

GOD'S OWN KNOWLEDGE

188. God has perfect knowledge of Himself.
205 270 821 931 1161 2073 2239
189. God knows all things, not only of the present but even of the future, as with a single intuitive act.
166 177 202 397 429 471 815 822a 1059 1377 1803 2069 2313
190. God's foreknowledge is not the cause of future events.
471 663 1175 1405 1408 1547 2162 2258 2382
191. God knows all future events, even those which shall come about through man's exercise of free will.
116 1272 1405 1707 1740 1742 1928 2069 2162 2258 2359
192. God's foreknowledge of events in no way destroys or detracts from man's exercise of free will.
663 1175 1405 1707 1742 2162
193. In regard to God's foreknowledge of evil [*see also* 469 *and* 638]:
471 663 1175 1405 1547 1707 1742 2258 2359 2381
194. God knows even the outcome of future conditional events.
471 1059 1996
195. The providence of God is extended to all His creatures.
202 1014 1134 1377

PREDESTINATION AND REPROBATION

200. God desires the salvation of all men.
93b 389 1053 1202 1279 1343 1366 2030 2358
201. St. Augustine's varying interpretations of 1 Tim. 2:4:
1457 1735 1906 1927 1962 1964 1983 2030
202. In regard to the predestination of the saints:
28 28a 37a 80a 435 1947 1994 2000 2003 2246
203. According to St. Augustine, God, the merciful dispenser of grace, predestines some to eternal life.
1882 1951 1985 1988 2002
204. According to St. Augustine, predestination to faith and justification is utterly gratuitous.
1427 1428 1443 1447 1837 1946 1985 1986 1989 1990 1997 1998 2001
205. For St. Augustine predestination is a mysterious work of God.
1496 1882 1925 1949 1989 1995 2007
206. St. Augustine's idea of predestination as a call according to purpose and without revocation:
1570 1948 1949 1959 1987 1988 1990 1991 1999

207. St. Augustine's idea of a specifically determined number of the elect:
    1951   1959   1960
208. St. Augustine's idea that predestination simply does not separate those who are not saved from the *massa perditionis*
    or "lump of perdition":
    1447   1946   1949   2000
209. St. Augustine knows, however, that none are damned unless they deserve to be damned.
    1496   1735   1901   1998
210. In regard to reprobation or predestination to damnation:
    466   1722   1882
211. For St. Fulgence of Ruspe predestination is a mysterious determination of God.
    2246   2254   2255   2266
212. Predestination, though a mysterious determination of God, does not take away free will.
    1366   2254
213. The idea that predestination is in view of God's foreknowledge of merits, in St. Ambrose and Theodoret:
    1272   2162
214. God reprobates none except those whom He foreknows will sin of their own free will.
    1202   2026   2033   2162   2257   2258
215. Since God reprobates none except those whom He foreknows will sin of their own free will, it may be said that
    anyone who is damned perishes of his own negligence.
    1053   1279   2030   2113   2254   2256

THE TRIUNE GOD

THE TRINITY

230. That God is triune is clear in the Tradition of the Church even in the pre-Nicene era [*see also* 826].
    20   23   28   40   47a   80   108   112   113   117   126   128   164   165   180   191   235   256   307
    371   376   377   394a   394b   408   445   452   470   479   546   557   596   608   608a   611   681
    701   792a   1650
231. In their struggle against Arianism the later Fathers appeal to the pre-Nicene trinitarian tradition.
    757   782   792a   1107
232. The Fathers believed that they could find in the Old Testament certain hints of the Trinity, the beginnings of a
    progressive revelation even in this regard.
    180   194   377   405   789   1090   1129   1317a
233. The Fathers did especially find evidence of the progressive revelation of the Trinity in Genesis 1:26.
    31   235   361   1399   1673   1860
234. The Trinity is expressed in the formula of Baptism [*see also* 826].
    784   789   858   910r   917   1246   1682
235. The Johannine comma [1 John 5:7b-8a] cited:
    378   557   1330   2216   2251
236. In regard to the theophanies:
    127   182   290   824   864   937   1400   1653
237. Although Father, Son, and Holy Spirit are one, they are yet distinct.
    (91)   164   179   371   376   596   611   768   778   779   904   907   910o   911   915   1068   1269
    1368   1672   1682   2084   2126   2280
238. Father, Son, and Holy Spirit are distinct in such a way that in the unity of one nature there are three Persons.
    371   376   378   782   898   907   910p   911   915   926   953   997   999   1008   1017   1029   1071
    1269   1650   1668   1752   2082   2090   2132   2251   2261   2337   2362   2383   2384
239. The Most Holy Trinity is a mystery.
    204   668   779   816   834   859   878   915   996   1029   1069   1269   1672   2084   2280   2337

PERSONS OF THE TRINITY

250. Only the Father does not proceed.
    479   608   634   679   814   880   915   917   932   934   936   983   1009   1040   1081   1239a
    1657   1681   2342
251. The Son was not made.
    164   442   470   675   756   761   764   765   866   971   1081   1086   1089a   1239a   2075   2076
252. The Son was truly born of the Father.
    153   373   374   391   540   608   651f   668   674   760   765   816   823   826   866   896   902   910a
    1039   1043   1089a   1271   1325d   2085   2343
253. The generation of the Son from the Father is not free.
    153   775   1102   2106

254. Although the generation of the Son from the Father is not free neither is it forced.
    775   879   1102
255. Neither free nor yet forced, the generation of the Son from the Father is voluntary and natural.
    470   608   862   879   971   1102   2066   2068   2126
256. The Son is co-eternal with the Father.
    130   137?   153   182   189   200   205   391   393   401   442   470   608   611   651f   668   676
    679   760   761   813   816   823   877   934   935   936   1009   1014   1040   1089a   1102   1262
    1316   1317a   1325d   1460   1518   1656   1816   1859   2076   2126   2342
257. The Son is consubstantial *(homoousios)* with the Father.
    153   277   (376)   392   398   409   540   608   651f   755   756   761   765   767   767a   768   769
    783   787   792a   826   866   868   880   896   899   907   910a   910r   912   951a   952   970
    994   1043   1072   1089a   1157a   1159b   1168   1254   1262   1264   1271   1317a   1656   1677
    2015c   2106   2126   2199   2204
258. Between Father and Son there is an identity of nature and distinction of Persons.
    374   375   376   409   536   636   862   881   902   952   970   971   1053   1157a   1656   2067
259. In some way the Father is greater than the Son.
    256   374   376   608   636   679   896   915   940   1656
260. *Word (Verbum* or *Logos)* is the proper name of the Son.
    45   205   290   608   632   632a   770   787   899   910s   969   994   1264   1678   2065   2070
261. The Son is called *Wisdom of the Father*.
    137   165   182   373   460   540   674   764b   787   816   826   899   992   1264   1325d   1460
    1577   1987   2075
262. The Son is called *Word (Sermo) of the Father*.
    371   373   375   379   632   632a
263. The Son is called *Splendor of the Father*.
    18   756   768   770   1072   2343
264. The Son is called *Image of the Father*.
    536   611   674   746   764b   768   769   787   868   952   969   1006   1072   1317a   2056   2065
    2078
265. The Son proceeds from the Father by an intellectual generation.
    137   179   182   200   277   373   398   470   610   632   754   825   969   994   1677   1816   2065
    2083   2259
266. The Holy Spirit is God.
    377   680   779   784a   910a   910k   910m   910q   926   996   999   1089a   1393   1670   2078
    2089   2107
267. That the Holy Spirit is God is proved by His operation.
    780   1070   1071   1089a   1283   1285   1561   2080   2107   2114
268. The Holy Spirit is consubstantial *(homoousios)* with the Father and the Son.
    611   783   784   784a   907   910a   910f   910k   910r   940   951a   996   1040   1069   1081
    1082   1089a   1246   1286   1650   1750   2015c   2079   2114   2126   2212   2216
269. The Holy Spirit proceeds from the Father.
    164   910a   910s   915   917   983   1009   1038   1039   1082   1089a   1657   2126   2337
270. The Holy Spirit is Spirit also of the Son.
    378   388   683   783   784a   834   872   910s   915   951   1082   1099   1459   1650   2132j   2212
271. The Holy Spirit is called *Image of the Son*.
    228a   611   2078
272. The Holy Spirit proceeds from the Father through the Son *(a Patre per Filium)*.
    372   479   611   878   904   907   953   1040
273. The Holy Spirit proceeds from the Father and the Son *(a Patre Filioque)*.
    375?   861a   1067   1068   1086   1099   1284   1662   1678   1681   1681a   1839   2079   2269a
    2269b
274. Though the Holy Spirit proceeds from the Father and the Son, He proceeds in a more preëminent way from the Father.
    951   1038   1678   1681
275. The Holy Spirit is not a Son [*see also* 237].
    778   983   996   1009   1681   1681a
276. Neither is the procession of the Holy Spirit a generation.
    (907)?   917   983   996   1009   1068   1081   1681   1681a   2343
277. The Holy Spirit is Holiness itself.
    611   914   926   941   950   983   1069   1750
278. The Holy Spirit is the Gift of God.
    858   1561   1670   1678
279. The Holy Spirit is the Union in Love between the Father and the Son.
    945   1099   1582   1665

RELATIONS AND APPROPRIATIONS

280. St. Augustine, with St. Cyril of Alexandria echoing him, is able to say that each individual Person of the Trinity is not something less than the Trinity Itself.
1667 1670 2090

281. The Divine Persons are distinguished among themselves only by their relations one to another.
867 896 907 915 926 983 990 996 1009 1039 1067 1082 1264 1459 1582 1660
1670 1672 1748 2067 2085 2212 2343 2344 2346 2362

282. Because the Divine Persons are distinguished among themselves only by their relations one to another, they are co-equal as to perfection.
779 899 903 910p 1582 1677 2212 2212a 2216 2261

283. Their external operations are common to the three Divine Persons [see also 467].
235 769 779 782 834 910n 949 1037 1039 1071 1169 1186 1661 1662 2132
2207 2212a 2250

284. Creation is a work appropriated to the Word.
98 130 153 156 164 179 194 234 235 277 290 371 391 394 398 401 479 608
651f 748 761 764 764a 767a 814 910a 943 949 1086 1089a 1475a 1816 2066 2207
2352

285. Sanctification is a work appropriated to the Holy Spirit.
371 389 449 611 810b 850 853i 907 915 948 949 950 960 1282 2063 2080
2089 2099 2107 2109 2110 2114 2352 2353

286. The meaning of the word *through (per or diá):*
943 949

THE MISSION OF THE DIVINE PERSONS

290. The Son is sent by the Father.
182 376 394 398 1239a 1656 1682

291. The Holy Spirit is sent by the Son.
290 871 1682 2040 2126

292. Arian doctrine in regard to the Son:
321 608a 648 648a 648b 650 650a 651 651a 777 910h 910i 935 1659 2251

293. Sabellian doctrine:
371 376 608a 651 768 782 910g 996 2251

THE INCARNATE WORD

TRUE DIVINITY

300. Jesus Christ and His divine mission were predicted in the Old Testament [see also 51 and 81]
31 35 45 57 122 122a 127 133a 141 277 290 390 394 398 445 468a 638 664
1470 1600

301. That Jesus Christ is true God is witnessed to by pre-Nicene Tradition.
18 31 35 37a 42 45 52 69 81 98 101 112 113 117 131 136 137 160 189
191 218 222 248 277 350 377 399 401 405 406 445 468a 596 617 632 634 651a
692

302. The only Son of God is incarnate, and He is Jesus Christ [see also 80].
43 45 62 69 (91) 98 112a 117 127 136 141 191 214 218 290 328a 371 377
393 398 401 632 651f 788 823 875 907 910a 1089a 1518 2048 2059 2060
2182 2383

TRUE HUMANITY

310. The Son of God took a true human nature, not merely the appearance thereof.
39 51 62 63 63a 189 217a 343 353 357 394 405 426 445 604 680 767a 794
817 873 876 928 1076 1083 1086 1089 1110 1160 1254 1288 1400 2184 2188 2215
2289

311. Christ has a true body, formed of the substance of Mary.
51 62 112 136 277 290 353 371 389 398 611ii 711 759 817 874a 875 886a
905 995 1083 1086 1110 1245d 1479a 1518 1578 1578a 1644 2048 2059 2060 2128
2133 2138 2170 2171 2182 2183 2184 2207 2240 2281 2364

312.   Christ has a rational soul.
        394   460   461   874a   875   995   1052   1076   1083   1086   1113g   1245d   1395   1430   1517
        1818   1953   2060   2138   2149   2170   2182   2184   2207   2215   2238   2247   2289   2365
313.   Since He is of the race of Adam, Christ is consubstantial *(homoousios)* with ourselves.
        217a   239   353   394   398   604   762   788   794   828   886a   890   995   1006   1052   1159b
        1167   1517   1808   2060   2123   2124   2132e   2182a   2188   2195   2199   2240   2364   2365
314.   What were not assumed were not healed: whatever part of human nature the Son had not taken upon Himself would
        not have been affected by His work of salvation.
        221   794   817   827   906   928   1014   1018   1052   1055   1254   1289   1578   1818   2128   2149
        2240   2242   2249   2364

THE UNION OF NATURES, HUMAN AND DIVINE

320.   The Incarnation is a mystery.
        1014   1031   1103   1160   1430   1431   1953   2048   2054   2134   2138   2171   2182   2198
        2281   2362   2371
321.   The Word was not changed into nor inextricably mixed with a human nature.
        379   394   (634)   905   (1054)   1079   1086   1113k   1160   2048   2061   2124   2128   2138   2170
        2241   2312   2362   2380
322.   The Word assumed a human nature, so that now He has two natures, each distinct.
        39   189   353   379   453   482   605   1006   1055   1080   1086   1113c   1113k   1160   1267
        1288   1289   2057b   2064   2071   2088   2132f   2182a   2203   2208   2215   2248   2287c   2312
        2365   2379
323.   Though distinct, the two natures of the Word are in some way united.
        221   277   460   759   773   827   874   1001   1113k   1285   2060   2062   2131   2132g   2132h
        2132k   2199   2366
324.   The union of the two natures in the Incarnate Word is a personal or hypostatic union.
        379   393   873   1017   1110   1113   1113j   1113k   1288   1354   1431   1518   1680   1842   1859
        1916   1953   2061   2124   2128   2132b   2132c   2132d   2132f   2132g   2132h.   2132j   2132k   2132m
        2134   2170   2171   2182a   2183   2198   2238   2241   2287a   2287h   2287c   2312   2362   2368
        2379   2380   2383
326.   Theodore of Mopsuestia, in regard to the hypostatic union:
        1113   1113a   1113b   1113c   1113d   1113j   1113k
327.   Errors of Nestorius in regard to the hypostatic union.
        2056   2057a   2057c   2057d   2057e   2132a   2132b   2132c   2132d   2132e   2132f   2132g   2132h
        2132j   2132k   2132m   2132n   2171   2296a   2368
329.   This union was made in conception and is inseparable.
        218   1017   1055   1079   1113k   1680   1842   2048   2057   2060   2133   2134   2170   2171   2208
        2210   2248   2300b   2312   2368
330.   In Christ here are two wills.
        790   1074   (1113c)   1133   1309   2365   2366   2383
331.   The two wills in Christ are never contrarily opposed to each other.
        790   2203   2386
332.   In Christ there are two operations: one divine, the other human.
        277   379   759   771   773   794   817   1044   1080   1267   1288   1289   1354   2103   2289   2361   2362
        2365   2366   2383
333.   In regard to theandric operation:
        771   1651   2279   2366
334.   In Christ there is a true communication of idioms.
        460   (482)   759   771   795   830   831   874   889   1044   1055   1089   1267   1651   1859   2056   2060
        2072   2096a   2130   2132d   2132m   2132n   2170   2171   2182a   2183   2289   2296a   2312   2361   2366

CONSEQUENCES OF THE UNION OF NATURES

340.   The man Jesus Christ is not the adoptive but the natural Son of God.
        788   863   1433   1777   1811   1836   1916   2049   2077   2106   2132e   2132k
341.   Christ is utterly filled with grace and is holy in every respect.
        682   995   1208   1680   1836   1842   2071   2088   2368
342.   The Man Christ is to be adored.
        81   762   795   827   1285   2071   2087   2132h   2363   2367
343.   Christ was free of concupiscence.
        929   1953   2123   2182a   2184   2330   2386

344. Christ was free of original sin.
611ii 1089a 1808 1872 1899 1916 1929 2010 2182a 2207 2213 2247 2311 2330
345. Christ was free of personal sin.
350 357 394 482 684 929 995 1006 1087 1089a 1198 1224 1342 1406 1654
1916 2031 2132k 2182a 2213 2242 2247 2305 2365 2367 2386
346. Christ was unable to sin.
461 1089a 1721 1916 2141 2182
347. Christ had a body capable of suffering.
31 45 63 66 124 221 371 389 426 445 520 651f 772 773 828 874a 876 889
890 910a 1014 1089a 1859 2182a
348. Christ had a body subject to human infirmities.
379 771 772 817 1462
349. Christ had a body subject to human passions.
131 136 379 (426) 929 1076 1167 1267 2103 2184 2247 2249
350. Christ freely suffered and died.
830 831 889 1224 1275 1595 1654 2039 2103 2249 2305
351. Whether there was any ignorance in Christ:
204 774 992 1178 1348 1389 1410 1555 2049 2072 2238 2290 2296a 2368
352. On the beatific vision of Christ:
2238 2239

NECESSITY OF THE INCARNATION

360. If Adam had not sinned the Incarnation would not have taken place.
254 492 765 1218 1517 1929 2213 2305
361. God could certainly have effected the redemption of the human race in some other way than through the Incarnation.
767 1577 2149 2195 2204
362. The Incarnation, therefore, is a free gift of God.
99 127 1103 1517 2289
363. Although the Incarnation is a free gift of God, there is yet a certain sense in which it may be said that the Incarnation was necessary.
31 612 751 767 822b 961 1006 1675 1915 1929 2127 2182 2204 2213 2241 2311

PURPOSE OF THE INCARNATION

370. The purpose of the Incarnation and Passion of Christ is the effecting of man's salvation.
12 26 40 45 66 74 75 99 108 112 127 131 389 405a 508 651f 771 822b 901
910a 991 1089 1089a 1245a 1254 1903a 1917 2007 2307
371. The Incarnation and Passion were not intended, however, to effect the salvation of the fallen angels.
356 1369? 1843 1917 2265 2307
372. It was intended, however, that the Incarnation and Passion should serve as a manifestation of God's love of men.
98 248 822b 1103 1589 1595
373. Christ desired to serve as an example for men, to show us how to live.
201 398 401 409a 508 632 634 669 828 910s 995 1589 1715 1929 2369
374. Christ desired to redeem us from sin and from the servitude in which we were held by the devil.
31 69 89 130 133b 221 249 370 399 405 436a 492 498 669 680 684 691 848e
889 928 1007 1014 1052 1077 1085 1103 1198 1201 1218 1252 1257 1401 1527
1655 1675 1715 2031 2063 2149 2182 2195 2369
375. Christ desired to return to men the gifts of grace and immortality.
33 127 345 634 711 751 752 767 828 829 831 1016 1159b 1818 1829a 1929 2069
376. Christ desired to lead men back to the pristine state lost through the sin of Adam.
223 255 394 399 405 563 612 703 767 829 890 928 946 998 1007 1160 1185 1777 1
1857 2038 2115 2141 2188 2192 2207 2211 2242 2369 2370

THE CARRYING THROUGH OF THAT PURPOSE

380. Christ effected redemption by means of a true sacrifice.
18 33 76 80 492 498 664 669 673 751 794 910s 1201 1221 1289 1655 1915 2129
2188 2209 2270 2311
381. Christ offered that true sacrifice on the cross to God.
406 889 901 1103 2188

382. In that true sacrifice, Christ was both Priest and Victim.
    581 910s 1007 1016 1063 1221 1268 1595 1608 1745 2040 2188 2263
383. Christ effected Redemption by means of a true vicarious satisfaction.
    62 140 436a 482 552 565 664 673 691 751 767 831 906 1252 1342 1401 1675
    1903a 1916 2031 2049 2305 2311
384. The true vicarious satisfaction by which Christ effected Redemption was paid out not to the devil but to God.
    (508) (928) 1016 (1257) (1675) 2311?
385. The satisfaction which Christ made is superabundant.
    492 831 1185 2211
386. The satisfaction which Christ made is universal.
    12 224 498 (508) 664 669 751 767 906 927 998 1184 1201 1221 1252 1275 1313
    1527 2031 2149 2188
387. Christ became Mediator between God and man.
    199a 405 691 701 766 769 873 1016 1462 1500 1595 1608 1654 1766 1792 1836
    1857 1884 1891 1929 1930 2038 2182a 2184b 2188 2240 2305
388. Graces are dispensed through Christ and because of the satisfaction He made.
    7 18 61 405 1208 1274 1279 1527.
389. The graces won by Christ were dispensed even to those who found their justification in the period of the Old Law.
    45 57 61 1426 1595 1727 1857 1884 1891 2196
390. The soul of Christ descended into the lower regions.
    238 259 818 1103 1104 1369 2210 2262
391. Christ ascended into heaven in His human nature.
    191 259 371 651f 680 810a 1014 1089a 1784 2040 2211 2262 2289
392. Christ will come again to judge the living and the dead.
    31 33 101 125 191 290 328a 371 552 599a 647 651f 853c 910a 1014 1089a 2167f 2262

THE CHURCH

FOUNDATION

400. In a certain sense the Church may be said to have existed from the beginning of the world.
    82 105 435 1428 1479 1985 2295
401. Jesus Christ founded a society, with Himself its Head, which is to last forever and which is called His Church.
    20 29a 38b 105 217a 289 555-556 571 865 1479 1535
402. This Church which Jesus Christ founded serves to continue His own life on earth.
    62 256 1245d
403. In the Acts of the Apostles, St. Luke recites an authentic history of the primitive Church.
    217 268 538 1358
404. From the earliest times the Church spread thoroughout the whole world [see also 85].
    6 7 11 38 77 79 81a 93 97a 112 144 144a 187 191 192 215 257 268 405 652a
405. From the earliest times and even in its initial spread the Church showed that she was a single unified body.
    43 47a 62 77 84 93 188 192 281
406. From earliest times the Church was hierarchically constituted and showed herself as such.
    9 19 20 21 25 38a 43a 44 47a 49 50 56 58a 65 413 427 438 571 599a 1205
    1357 1371

PROPERTIES AND NOTES

410. The Church is a monarchical society.
    546 546a 573 (576b) (599a) 1242 1379 2179a 2191
411. The Church is an independent society.
    759a 1311
412. The Church is a visible society.
    97a 281 1614 2018a
413. As a society the Church consists of twofold elements, visible and invisible, called body and soul.
    97a 982 1523 1523a 1714
414. On earth the Church is mixed in her membership, having both good and wicked within her fold.
    (435) 1714
415. Heretics and schismatics, in the teachings of the Fathers, are not members of the Church.
    213 237 241 257 295a 298 308 587 589 591 593 597 601c 602 602a 1371a 1478
    1492 1523 1562 1974c 1974e 2167c 2251a 2252 2275
416. There is but one true Church of Christ.
    408 435 573 589 680 1428 1479

417. Outside the one true Church of Christ there is no salvation.
    56 226 537 597a 637 1346 1428 1492 1858 2251a 2269 2273 2274 2275

418. The true Church of Christ can be recognized by certain notes.
    587 910a 1089a 1535 1580

419. Sanctity of its leadership and members belongs only to the true Church of Christ.
    226 838 1714

420. Unity of faith and government belongs only to the true Church of Christ.
    1b 6 7 56 93 188 192 213 241 257 292 293 295 296 328a 329 435 555-556 576b
    587 588a 589a 865 910u 997a 1239a 1242 1379 1714

421. Catholicity belongs only to the true Church of Christ.
    65 79 80a 81a 435 555-556 575 587 680 838 839 1243 1422 1548 1562 1580

422. Apostolicity belongs only to the true Church of Christ.
    80a 210 213 237 292 293 296 297 298 329 341 589 680 1242 1580

423. In any individual church these notes are discoverable through her union with the successor of Peter.
    574a 587 654a 1261

THE PRIMACY

430. Among the Apostles, Peter received from Christ the primacy of jurisdiction over the Church.
    381 387 436 479a 489 555-556 571 587 592a 693a 706 810 835a 910u 1261 1379
    1526 2178a 2179a 2191

431. Peter came to Rome and died there.
    11 106a 106b 297 341 368a 439-440 611gg 647a 651aa 651cc 651dd 652b 822c 910u 10

432. Peter established his See at Rome, and made the Bishop of Rome his successor in the primacy.
    54 188 208 210 211 296 575 602a 651aa 702a 897 910u 1092 1242 1418 2178 2178a

433. The Roman Pontiffs have always laid claim to the primacy of jurisdiction.
    10a 21 25 27 28a 29 190a 592a 601a 601b 602a 860a 910u 2014 2015f 2018 2178a
    2179a 2184a 2186

434. From earliest times the Roman Church has been regarded as the center of unity.
    52 53 106c 107 187 210 211 575 580 1242 2015f

435. From earliest times it was acknowledged that supreme power over the whole Church belonged to the Bishop of Rome as successor of Peter.
    82a 107 (190a) 211 265 573 (592a) (599a) (601a) (601b) (602) (602a) 702a 702b
    806a 822c 910d 1252a 1346 1346a 1507 1892 2015f 2178 2178a 2179a 2184a

436. The title Pope is of quite early origin, but was not until later restricted in usage to the Bishop of Rome.
    568a 570b 651 1343a 2178

THE EPISCOPATE

440. Bishops are not lsss than the legitimate successors of the Apostles.
    20 21 48 49 56 65 188 209 212 237 242 257 296 341 438 602 1234 1244 2332

441. Although the bishops are the successors of the Apostles, the transmission of jurisdiction was made in various ways in the primitive churches.
    9 575 588 745g 1357 1371 2164 2165

442. In regard to the College of Bishops:
    576b 588a 599b

INFALLIBILITY

450. The Church is infallible in transmitting the teachings of Christ.
    213 295 1581

451. The Roman Pontiff enjoys infallibility when he teaches *ex cathedra*.
    294 580 1507 1892 2178

452. Bishops gathered in an ecumenical council have always been acknowledged as infallible judges of the faith.
    785 792 910b 1250 1419 2141b 2141c 2184a 2185 2186 2291

CREATION
IN GENERAL

460. God created all things.
    13a 14 85 98 110 112 117 152 154 171 178 191 194 199a 205 328a 397 402

        409   445   459   608   651r   681   748   814   896a   910u   1014   1089a   1147   1316   1490
        1564   1596   2098   2126

461. It was out of nothing (*ex nihilo*) that God created all things.
        85   111   114   129   150   171   179   194   199   275   290   323   324   325   326   327   328   363   398
        445   628   687   748   750   754   761   1014   1147   1315   1316   1317   1540   1550   1564   1711
        2075   2135   2145   2264   2310   2349

462. God alone can create.
        178   764   764a   1702   1711   1865   2136   2356

463. God creates freely.
        168   196   205   235   391   397   748   1490   1751

464. God creates in accord with divine ideas.
        1553   1803

465. God creates because He is good.
        168   231   462   884   1005   1751   2282   2349

466. God creates so that His perfections may be manifested and acknowledged.
        7   171   179   275   643   2307

467. It is the Trinity who creates [*see also* 283].
        235   1317a   1564   1662   1702   2264

468. The material world is not eternal.
        154   178   179   206   207   322   391   447   454?   761   1317   1564   1747   1757   2076   2135
        2264   2288

469. God is not the author of evil [*see also* 193 *and* 638].
        324   398   1366   1974f

470. Some ideas of Augustine on creation and the Genesis account, and his admonitions on hermeneutics:
        1541   1683   1684   1685   1686   1687   1689   1690   1692   1695   1865

ANGELS

480. There exist angels created by God.
        17   63b   83   113   156   164   165   228a   320   448   643   667   1101   1239a   1315   1316   1479
        1782   1805   1865   2350

481. In regard to the time of the creation of the angels:
        83   156   448   1101   1316

482. The angels possess by nature a certain excellence.
        18   989   1005   1148   1782   1843   2352

483. In regard to the spiritual nature of the angels:
        278   354   646   667   895   950   989   1005   1026   1152   1197   1484   1522   1774   2050   2156
        2303   2307   2320   2350   2351

484. Angels are not everywhere.
        278   781   1070   2156   2303   2353

485. Although angels excel in knowledge they do not know the secrets of men's hearts, nor do they know future events.
        2051   2303

486. The angels were created free.
        63b   142   156   244   950   1755   1782   1950   2265   2325   2351

487. Angels are able to converse among themselves.
        1197   2352

488. The angels are divided into various ranks or choirs.
        83   427   612   822   849   949   989   1125   1127   1148   1239a   1290a   1315   1316   1394   1805
        2264   2335   2355

489. The angels are elevated to the supernatural order.
        278   941   950   960   1755   2353

490. Many angels, having attained eternal blessedness, are already confirmed in goodness.
        853d   989   1755   1950   1955   1971   2266   2325

491. Many angels, having fallen into grave sin, have hastened to eternal damnation.
        191   356   446a   567   1708   1753   1843   1950   1955   2013   2265   2266   2307

492. The good angels are ministers of God and assist men in the business of working out their salvation.
        83   89   228a   446   448   895   940   1022   1217   1239a   1387   2156   2167e   2303   2354

493. There are guardian angels assigned to individuals, nations, societies, etc.
        89   430   475   895   940   1022   1387   2156   2160   2161   2354

494. The devil and the other wicked angels are able to harm men.
        69   87   112a   258   278   286   446   475   751a   853h   1022   1488   2161   2167e

MAN

500. Man is composed of body and soul.
     147   159   170   1563   2061   2062   2134   2349
501. The human soul is incorporeal.
     252   346   346a   349   355   1438   1448   1700   (2050)   2357
502. The human soul is immortal.
     (132)?   (133)?   157   168   169   206   249   252   349   355   1100   1700   2357
503. In man there is but one soul only.
     170   467?   1021   1056   2357
504. In regard to the tricotomy:
     133   148   1021   1241   1563
505. Man is free [see also 613].
     123   142   156   184   244   335   446   622   667   1151   1380   2113   2265   2357
506. The human soul is created by God.
     683   1232   1385   1395   1441   1559   1700   1879   1965   2146
507. The soul is not pre-existent to the body.
     (466)   611hh   1004   1058   1395   1456   2105
508. The soul does not spring up through the procreative process.
     (446)?   875   1385   1395   1448
509. Whether God created man immediately:
     250   360   361   611hh   687   1149   1232   1315   1696   2349
510. Woman was made from man.
     1278   1543   1702   2147
511. All men have their origin in Adam and Eve.
     1278   1813   2147
512. Man is created in the image of God.
     156   159   361   746   1673   1732   1806

FIRST MAN

520. Before the fall our first parents were endowed with certain gifts of nature not owed to them: original justice, . . .
     [see also 610].
     225   253   567   612   1318   1698   2192
521. . . . immunity from concupiscence, . . .
     224   1150   1706   1952   2122   2388
522. . . . and immunity from the necessity of dying.
     184   566   749   750   883   1150   1699   1760   1928   1956   2122
523. Adam enjoyed an excellence in knowledge.
     2011   2104   2360
524. On the origin of language:
     1051   1537
525. Our first parents, prior to their sinning, enjoyed a life of the greatest happiness.
     1762   1952   2013   2122

DIVINE WATCHFULNESS

530. God preserves all things.
     171   206   207   458   563   987   1134   1688   1688a   1694   2310   2356
531. God concurs in all the actions of His creatures [see also 690].
     1403

VIRTUES

IN GENERAL

540. The concept of virtue:
     641   1904
541. There are certain infused virtues: faith, hope, and charity.
     72   1424   1425   1469   2324
542. The virtues of faith, hope, and charity are infused with first justification.
     1425   2009

543. The infused virtues of faith, hope, and charity, infused at first justification, are capable of being increased.
      955   2328
544. Furthermore, the infused virtues can be lost.
      1469
545. Faith can subsist without love.
      1469   1679
546. In heaven faith and hope will cease, but love will remain [see also 1041].
      1057   1799
547. In regard to the infusion of moral virtues:
      1476   1849
548. In regard to the gifts of the Holy Spirit:
      910s   1332   1337

FAITH

550. The primary object of faith is God Himself.
      923   1739
551. The object of faith embraces the mysteries which exceed human reason.
      1121   1303   1613
552. Faith is intellectual assent.
      62   417   820   1429   1980   2144
553. The intellectual assent of faith is free.
      245   417   1734   1821   2144
554. The free intellectual assent of faith is firm.
      13a   62   418   972   2055   2144
555. Faith is a supernatural act.
      418   419   1204   1486
556. In regard to the faith of miracles, which is a charism:
      820   1312
557. The motive of faith is not the rational evidence of the object proposed for belief.
      417   1181   1277   1826   2055   2197
558. The intrinsic motive of faith is the authority of God revealing.
      162   173   175   359a   417   562   1179   1181   1248   1303   1321   1466   2055   2143   2197
559. A sure knowledge of its having been divinely revealed is a prerequisite to faith in any proposed object.
      417   627   629   643a   1486   2144
560. Faith is more certain than any natural knowledge.
      173   417   418   846   1223   1248   1303   1593   1970   2144
561. Faith is not opposed to reason.
      173   1429   1613
562. Faith sometimes precedes reason.
      1321   1429   1486   1499   1554   1826   2111   2144
563. Faith sometimes precedes reason and elevates it to a more perfect mode of knowledge.
      418   433   1429   1486   1746   2111   2144
564. Reason is able to demonstrate the basis of faith.
      344   627   923   924   1551   1613   1980   2143
565. When reason has been illuminated by the light of faith it can perfect our knowledge of divine things.
      433   1486   1672   2111
566. Faith must be universal, extending to every revealed truth.
      298   972   1304   1598
567. There is always some obscurity about faith, precisely because it is those things which are not seen that are believed through faith.
      417   869   1057   1223   1498   1833   2318   2331
568. For those who are of sufficient intellectual maturity faith is of absolute necessity for justification and salvation.
      289   417   886a   1445   1450   1945   2260
569. In regard to the necessity of faith in Christ the Mediator:
      1857   1884

HOPE

580. The object of hope is our future blessedness.
      1057   1187
581. Most especially the object of our hope is our future possession of God Himself.
      1474   1482

582. Hope is founded in faith and for that reason is most certain.
301a 419 864 1057 1187 1223 1913
583. The principal motive of hope is the goodness of God, from whom a reward is expected.
836 1312
584. A secondary motive for hope is our own merits.
836 1312
585. To do good for the sake of the hope of reward is an honorable way of conducting oneself, since the reward hoped for is God Himself.
1025 1312 1474 1491 1933
586. For those who are of sufficient intellectual maturity hope is necessary for justification and salvation.
1292 1512

CHARITY which is LOVE

590. Charity establishes a true friendship between God and man.
26 433 1251
591. Charity is the most excellent of all the virtues.
242 419 1025 1251 1679 1799 1933 2176
592. Charity is the root and perfection of all other virtues.
433 1363 1445 1538 1798 1933 2117
593. Perfect charity is the loving of God above all else for the sake of Himself alone.
1474 1491 1528 1538 1586 1671 1763
594. Secondary to the pure love of God is the love of neighbor because of God.
1528 1583 1586 2117
595. Charity supposes faith and is founded on it.
433 1472 1503
596. The principal motive of charity is the goodness of God.
1589
597. The proof of charity is in the actions it inspires.
1848a 2333 2334
598. Charity is necessary for salvation.
1503 1583 1860a 1943

SIN

ORIGINAL SIN

610. Our first parents, having fallen into grave sin, lost their original justice [see also 520].
225 286 567 1318 1698 1706 2013
611. Death is the effect of Adam's sin.
183 345 395 566 567 612 749 750 829 1150 1184 1245c 1325 1698 1699 1715 1760 2013 2019 2266
612. Through his sin Adam lost other free gifts.
183 225 703 1150 1727 1883 1967 2036 2122 2388
613. But in spite of his fall Adam kept free will [see also 505].
244 349 398 1022 1406 1883 2036 2038
614. The sin of Adam was passed on to all men.
224 224a 255 286 345 486 496 501 586 612 683 684 698 703 763 829 967 1077 1145a 1145b 1184 1185 1245c 1245d 1290 1306a 1341 1715 1725 1728 1791 1871 1872 1876 1877 1899 1951 1984 2007 2013 2019 2122 2123 2207
615. Original sin is transmitted by a father in the natural process of procreation.
586 1077 1290 1456 1715 1728 1870 1871 1918 1960 2007 2195
616. Original sin, as the sin of our first parents, was for them an actual and personal sin, involving free will.
1876 1877 1969 1972 2010
617. The essence of original sin, and its relationship to concupiscence:
1871 1872 1873 1887 1911 1972
618. The lot of infants who die without Baptism:
1012 1441 1456 1525 1878 1882 1901 1908 1924 1946 1997 2019
619. Errors of the Pelagians about original sin and the lot of infants who die without Baptism:
1525 1878 1967 1976 2016 2019 2025

PERSONAL or ACTUAL SIN

630. Sin is a turning away from God and a turning toward creatures.
1546 1565 1586 1605 1753 1761 1763 1904 2256
631. Sin is a negative thing rather than something positive.
1546 1549 1754
632. There are sins which are entirely internal.
119 166 239 273 352 853f 1565 1734 1885
633. Sins are distinguished as mortal and venial.
497 611s (978) 1245a 1300 1382 1536 1733 1846 1918 2233
634. There is a difference in gravity even among mortal sins.
957 1381 1442 1861 1975 2314
635. Whether numerous venial sins can coalesce into mortal sin:
1846
636. Without free consent there can be no sin.
123 244 335 1151 1406 (1454) 1549 1558 1560 1565 1718 1973 2118
637. Ignorance of gravity can be a mitigating factor in regard to the guilt of sin.
611n 611w 611x 611cc
638. God is not the author of sin, but only permits it [see also 193 and 469].
471 1263 1734 1889 2032 2118 2255 2257 2258 2326 2358
639. Sin results in the death of the soul.
184 1030 1828
640. When a sin has been committed something of the sin continues in existence even afterwards.
1873 1912

ACTUAL GRACE

NECESSITY OF GRACE

650. Grace is absolutely necessary for the performance of any good work ordered to salvation.
220 348 558 1003 1153 1219 1302 1455 1456 1569 1572 1719 1733 1791 1821
1832 1835 1855 1883 1890 1902 1903 1914 1936 1937 1938 1954 1966 2004
2200 2243 2272 2276 2359
651. Without grace man can still perform actions that are naturally commendable.
1162 1538 1733 1809 1905 2202 2244 2272
652. God never demands the impossible.
1220 1718 1720 1795
653. In what sense the acts of sinners are sins:
1450 1472 1528 1943 2037
654. In what sense the acts of infidels are sins:
1162 1463 1528 1729 1902 1903 1904 1905 2041 2042 2244 2245
655. Without grace a man cannot very long keep God's law.
1162 1719 1731 1933 1941
656. Grace is necessary even for the beginning of faith and conversion.
114 808 (892) (892a) (1155) 1165 1177 1204 (1207) (1219) 1450 1569 1571 1734
1736 1936 1940 1968 1978 1979 1980 1981 1982 1984 2004 2005 2006 2034 2045
(2052) (2053) 2163 2200 2243 2246 2278
657. Without grace a man cannot for very long resist concupiscence and grave temptation.
436 548 1191 1263 1404 1406 1592 1718 2201
658. Without a special privilege of grace no one can for very long be immune to concupiscence and entirely free even of
venial sins.
981 1509 1536 1720 1722 1733 1737 1794 1801 1846 1888 1894 1918 1921 1976
2091 2201
659. Grace is still a necessity even for a man most perfectly justified.
1404a 1792 2159 2201

PERSEVERANCE

670. All the just are able to persevere if they will it.
1177 1945 1955 1956
671. Though the just can persevere if they will it, they cannot persevere for very long without the help of grace.
485 892 1153 1956

672. Final perseverance is a great gift of God.
     79a 557a 1958 1960 1992 1993 1995 1999 2002 2005 2028
673. In what final perseverance does consist:
     1947 1992 1993 1999 2002 2028

NATURE OF GRACE

680. Even if in a less proper sense, creation, free will, and the preaching of the gospel may be termed *graces*.
     114 287 1443 1556 1736 1764 2035 2043
681. Protection from sinning, along with the other external favors of providence directed toward salvation, also pertains to grace.
     59 186 1483 1504 1592
682. Grace is an internal movement.
     833 1443 1556 1736 1764 1853 2043
683. Actual grace consists both in the enlightening of the intellect . . .
     430 548 1483 1485 1720 1722 1724 1852 1853 2034 2091 2276
684. . . . and in the inspiring of the will.
     53 420 548 1159 1458 1485 1568 1572 1576 1720 1722 1724 1736 1821 1822
     1852 1853 1955 2035 2091

NOMENCLATURE

690. Grace so coöperates *(gratia coöperans)* with the human will that a man can do nothing that is good without God's doing it along with him.
     436 465 485 1003 1219 1220 1510 1515 1571 1793 1848 1854 1893 1936 1941
     1999 2235 2278 2316 2326 2385
691. This grace that assists man's salutary actions is called *helping, coöperating*, and *subsequent grace (gratia adiuvans, coöperans, seu subsequens)*.
     1793 1914 1942 2235 2278 2326
692. The grace, however, which precedes and prompts man's salutary actions is called *summoning, arousing*, and *prevenient grace (gratia vocans, exitans, seu praeveniens)*.
     1458 1556 1572 1793 1914 1938 1942 2235 2278 2316 2326
693. The assistance which grace provides is twofold: that by which something is done, and that without which it could not be done.
     1556 1850 1954 1955 1957
694. Grace was necessary to Adam, but not in the same way before his fall as afterwards.
     1949 1952 1954 1955
695. There is a kind of grace called *sufficient grace*, which truly suffices for the producing of its effect, but which does not actually produce it.
     244 247 622 1158 1159 1188 1191 1220 1753 1925 1955 1956
696. There is another kind of grace called *efficacious grace*, which effectively moves the will.
     348 558 1568 1572 1573 1707 1890 1926 1940 1958 1979 1991 1996

GRACE AND FREEDOM

700. Grace does not destroy free will.
     244 436 446 704 1034 1151 1158 1159 1165 1188 1204 1219 1436 1510 1571
     1572 1573 1710 1722 1723 1735 1736 1821 1823 1848 1854 1856 1890 1954 1955
     1961 2359
701. Because grace does not destroy free will, with equal graces one person may succeed while yet another fails.
     247 1159 1753
702. In regard to the *victrix delectatio* or triumphant delight:
     1568 1594 1722 1724 1737 1822 1823
703. God foreknows the use that free will will make of grace.
     1740 1830 1948 1985 2033
704. To some God issues His call of grace in a way that is best suited to them if they are to coöperate with His grace.
     1427 1573 1574

GRACE AS A GIFT

710. Grace can conquer all the demands of nature.
     1939 1982

711. Grace is freely given: *i.e.*, it is gratuitous.
(808)? (1155) 1355a 1443 1451 1452 1456 1458 1473 1496 1791 1807 1837 1851 1857 1889 1974 1974a 1994a 1999 2005 2034 2044 2045 2253
712. It is proper that we pray for grace.
507a 1355a 1724 1795 1796 1801 1821 1941 2201
713. It is possible to win the graces of conversion and final perseverance with prayers of supplication.
699 1456 1827 1940 1993 1994 2001

DISTRIBUTION OF GRACE

720. In a mysterious but just determination God distributes His graces to men unequally.
1456 1496 1821 1984 1995 2028 2277
721. God never abandons a man unless that man first abandons God.
1792 1889 1954 1960 2026 2232 2255
722. Hardheartedness is never visited by God upon anyone, except as a punishment for previous sin.
1830 1907
723. To all sinners, however hardened, sufficient grace is given for them to be converted if they would but will it.
1220 1405 1830 2097 2232
724. To no one, not even to infidels, does God deny sufficient grace for faith and for salvation.
12 622 1158 1313 1461 1539 1791 1968 1986 2020 2046 2047 (2277)
725. Pelagian errors on free will:
1411 1412 1413 1414 1415 1416 1495 1856
726. Pelagian errors on the nature of grace:
1412 1413 1443 1851 1939 2008 2020
727. Pelagian errors on the necessity of grace:
1355 1356 1411 1413 1718 1855 1888 1891 1894 1902 1976 2019
728. Pelagian errors on the gratuity of grace:
1450 1851 1978 1989
729. Semi-Pelagian errors:
1978 1981 2003 2021 2022 2024 2052 2053 2278

HABITUAL GRACE

THE SUPERNATURAL ORDER

740. Among the gifts which God bestows upon creatures some are natural and some are supernatural.
253 699 813 941 950 960 1027 1185 1318 1433 1755 2106 2115 2265 2359

JUSTIFICATION

750. In justification the permanent supernatural gift of habitual grace is infused.
251 253 449 1145a 1282 1319 1698 1701 1715 1730 1732 2063 2080 2099
751. In justification sins are truly blotted out.
146 407 1256 1886 1910 2009 2298
752. In justification man is renewed internally.
32 36 219 548 607 835 1011 1144 1203 2080 2089 2106 2109 2193
753. In justification man receives within himself the indwelling Holy Spirit.
36 158 159 219 251 449 607 683 770 780 813 853a 872 944 1071 1186 2107 2114
754. In justification man becomes a sharer of the divine nature.
40 412 613 770 780 787 788 944 1171 1283 1468 2063 2079 2106 2107 2193
755. In justification man becomes the adoptive son of God.
407 766 770 788 813 946 948 1145a 1171 1187 1273 1433 1468 1777 2106
756. In justification man becomes an heir of the heavenly kingdom.
607 1145a 1187
757. In justification man becomes a friend of God.
433 1187 1203
758. It is by faith that a man is justified.
16 48 57 173 245 310a 428 481 910r 1024 1163 1185 1445 1450 2163 2260 2327
759. Man is not justified by works.
16 (176) 699 2163
760. Although it is by faith and not by works that a man is justified, works too are necessary for his justification.
15 16 428 481 564 1024 1163 1310 1362 1515 1590 1827 2167a 2233c 2327

761. Habitual or sanctifying grace is lost through mortal sin.
158   683   770   1701   1944
762. Man can never in this life be certain of his justification.
1374   1800   2296

MERIT

770. The just man can have true merit.
68   123   246   311   836   889a   966   1247   1383   (1414)   1449   1452   1477   2316   2326
771. The just can merit eternal life.
173   176   396   564   1319a   1453   1498   1502   1575   1807   1937
772. The just can merit an increase of grace.
1446   2027   2328
773. But not even the just can merit justification itself.
1446   1449   2027   2044
774. Among the conditions for meriting is the promise of God.
962   1477   1511
775. Besides the promise of God and the state of grace another condition of meriting is free will.
123   156   1380
776. Besides the promise of God and free will, another condition of meriting is the state of grace.
1449   1575

MARY

779. Mary is truly the Mother of God, . . .
42   223   256a   701a   711   (1113d)   1400   2059   2060   2064   2125   2241   2242   2312
780. . . . the *deipara* or *theotokos*.
680   788   824   1017   1020a   1086   1113b   2054   2058   2060   2125   2132a   2171   2364   2371
2371b   2378   2379   2383   2387   2390
781. Mary conceived as a virgin (*virgo ante partum*).
42   112   122a   127   134a   141   191   222   223   224   277   328a   330   358   359   371   380   389
394   398   408   495   633   634   711   788   817   864   874a   875   886a   910a   910s   995   1017
1077   1086   1289   1325d   1361   1430   1518   1578a   1610   1614   1680   1808   1899   2054
2057   2058   2060   2064   2171   2177   2182   2194   2195   2240   2241   2281   2289   2300b
2311   2372
782. Mary was a virgin during the birth (*in partu*).
(359)   710a   1014   1289   1327   1430   1518   1808   1975   2177   2182   2194   2241   2242   2289
2312   2331   2372
783. Mary remained a virgin after the birth of Christ (*virgo post partum*).
(380)   767a   1020a   1073   1089a   1111   1361   1518   1643   1974d   2048   2133   2177   2194
2288b   2289   2372   2383   2390
784. Mary is the New Eve, the coöperatrix in the mystery of the Redemption.
141   224   358   1578   1644
785. The holiness of Mary is entirely unique.
(927)   1325a   1643   1794
786. Mary was conceived immaculate, *i.e.*, without original sin.
719   1314   1794   (2242)   2336a   2336b   2336c   2389
787. The body of Mary was assumed into heaven.
2288a   2288b   2390

SACRAMENTS

IN GENERAL

790. Sacraments are outward signs which confer the grace they signify.
181   303   590   601b   1179   1423   1424   1432   1475   1524   1601   1647   1744   1847
791. Sacraments are physically constituted of things and words, called respectively the matter and the form.
1062   1329   1817   1834
792. Among the sacramental rites the imposition of hands signifies in a special way the conferring of grace [*see also* 906, 958 *and* 959].
304   362   568b   569   595   601b   611v   919   1236   1295   1359   1627   2300a
793. Even before the covenants and under the law of nature there was some remedy, instituted by God, against original sin.
1909   2306

794. Even under the Old Law there were sacraments, but they did not confer grace of themselves.
    1419   1475

795. Circumcision was a sacrament of the Old Law, prefiguring Baptism.
    134   1646   1875   2306

796. The Sacraments confer grace more abundantly upon a better disposed recipient.
    809   848b

797. If an obstacle is present when the Sacraments are received grace is not conferred; but when the obstacle is removed the Sacraments revivify and grace is then received.
    1621   1625   1637   1638   2269   2300a

798. The Sacraments of Baptism, Confirmation and Holy Orders imprint an indelible spiritual character.
    712   808   847   968   1011   1233   1240   1282   1332   1337   1620   1642   1713   1867

799. Because Baptism, Confirmation and Holy Orders confer an indelible spiritual character they are never to be repeated.
    308   314   592a   593   651n   1617   1621   1623   1627   2269   2300a

800. The Sacraments confer grace from the power, present in the rite, of the Holy Spirit.
    303   607   683   835   947   1242a   1282   1329   1423   1834   2110

801. Christ is the author of the Sacraments, each of which He instituted directly.
    1301   1338   1419   1638   1814

802. Morally the Sacraments are actions of Christ, who makes use of the ministry of men in performing those actions.
    1169   1242a   1280   1339   1638   1810

803. The validity of the Sacraments does not depend upon the faith of their minister [*see also* 830 *and* 962].
    (308)   (592)   (594)   (596)   (599b)   (601a)   (601c)   (602)   (919)   1242a   (1281)   (1293)   1360   1621
    1628   1858

804. The validity of the Sacraments does not depend on the probity of their minister; . . .
    1169   1189   1616   1624   1635   1645   1713   1810   2300a

805. . . . but one who administers a Sacrament when he is not himself in the state of grace does so illicitly and is guilty of sacrilege.
    1616   1624

806. In adult recipients of the Sacraments the intention of receiving is required for validity.
    1632   1639

807. Moreover, for a licit and fruitful reception of the Sacraments on the part of an adult, certain dispositions are necessary
    504   1645   1647   1737a   1862

808. The Fathers knew all of our seven Sacraments.
    299   362   848a   1419   1635   1844   2100

809. In regard to the washing of feet (*lotio pedum*):
    611y   690   1331   1336   1834

810. The Fathers are witness to the fact that there was, especially in regard to the Sacraments, a rule of secrecy (*disciplina arcana* or *arcani disciplina*), the arcane discipline.
    274   394i   807   811   834a   954   1084   1166   1199   1239   1520   1815   1838   2151   2157

811. Besides the Sacraments there are certain sacred things or rites called Sacramentals, which also are of value for sanctification.
    394i   1241   1536   1888   1921

BAPTISM

820. Baptism is a true Sacrament, instituted by Christ.
    4   34   126   299   302   329   362   491   681   690   1242a   1244   1297   1301   1617   1647   2100
    2251a

821. The Baptism of John was not a Sacrament.
    305   690   1634   1810

822. The remote matter of Baptism is natural water.
    4   92   126   302   303   367   394i   810a   954   1330   1395a   1817

823. The proximate matter of Baptism is the washing in water.
    4   126   307   394i   810a   1395a

824. There is witness to the washing having been done by immersion, by infusion, and by aspersion.
    4   34   92   304   394i   547   590   812   840a   841

825. The triple washing is not of necessity: but it is a usage of greatest antiquity.
    4   367   394i   840a   947   954   1368   2292

826. In the form of Baptism it is essential that there be a distinct expression of God as Three and One [*see also* 234].
    4   126   219   307   394i   500   597   601d   647c   651y   745d   840a   858   945   1000   1281   1330   1368
    1368   1410   1638   2015c   2271   2300a

827. Baptism conferred in the name of Jesus, lacking the Trinitarian formula, is held to be invalid.
    500   597   945

828. In regard to the minister of solemn Baptism:
   65   310   394i   594   601   601c   1108   1120   1236   1244   1359
829. Any man, using the requisite matter and form and having the intention of baptizing, can validly confer Baptism; but he does so licitly only when he does so in a case of necessity.
   310   366   611u   1359   1618   1628   1639
830. Even heretics can baptize validly [*see also* 803].
   (308)   (591)   (592a)   (593)   (599b)   (600)   (601a)   601d   (602a)   647c   1360   1492   1621   1623
   1625   1626   1636   1637   1639   2014a   2015c   2251a   2269   2273
831. Baptism is necessary for all in respect to salvation, whether they be infant or adult.
   92   135a   302   306   310   (310a)   496   501   586   601?   752a   810a   811   1206   1323   1324
   1330   1439   1525   1536   1716   1717   1862   1878   1881   1882   2016   2019   2251a   2269   2271
832. In the case of adults the desire for Baptism can take the place of actual Baptism in water.
   (1012)   1328   1629   1630
833. In the case of infants or adults, martyrdom can take the place of actual Baptism in water.
   309   493   597a   598   811   1010   1139   1513   1630   1759   2269
834. A fit subject for Baptism is any person not yet baptized.
   126   201   585   1324   1862
835. The Church has always acknowledged that even infants are capable of receiving Baptism.
   201   394i   496   585   1011a   1012a   1145a   1324   1439   1440   1632   1705   1715   1725   1862
836. The effect of Baptism is spiritual regeneration, which consists in the remission of every sin with the punishment due it, and the infusion of first grace.
   34   87   92   93b   126   181   187a   220   302   304   312   362   394i   407   491   493   501   548
   594   597a   613   683   812   818e   910a   968   1011a   1012a   1089a   1145a   1240   1295   1301
   1331   1335a   1336   1395a   1404a   1536   1622   1715   1725   1726   1768   1864   1874   1918
   2121   2184b

CONFIRMATION

840. Confirmation is a true Sacrament.
   174   304   362   390   547   592   595   698   725   842   1233   1240   1244   1332   1337   1358   1647
   2015d   2100
841. The remote matter of Confirmation is blessed oil (chrism or myron).
   174   304   394i   698   841   954   1062   1240   2015d
842. The proximate matter of Confirmation is the anointing made with chrism on the forehead, in the form of a cross.
   174   299   304   394i   592   745q   842   847   954   1844   1847   2015d
843. In regard to the ordinary minister of Confirmation:
   394i   595   601c   611ee   1244   1359   2015d
844. In regard to the priest as extraordinary minister of Confirmation:
   547   592   611ee   2294
845. There is an obligation, however less strict, of receiving Confirmation.
   547   592   611ee
846. The effect of Confirmation is the more abundant pouring out of the graces and gifts of the Holy Spirit [*see also* 548].
   362   745q   841   842   842a   1240   2100

EUCHARIST

Real Presence

849. The Sacrament of the Eucharist was instituted by Christ in memory of His passion and death.
   135   708   725   1063   1192   1195   1270   1390   1519   1587   1604   1652
850. In the words recounted by John (6:48*ff*), Christ promised that He would give Himself, His own flesh and blood, in a real sense, as food and drink.
   408   491   559   870   916   1270   1365   1480   1587   1824   2116   2131   2214
851. Christ is really present in the Eucharist under the appearances of bread and wine.
   54a   56   64   128   187   187a   234   249   362   367   394i   410   490   707   708   845   846   848
   853j   870   1063   1113f   1179   1192   1194   1195   1207   1333   1334   1479a   1519   1524
   1652   1815   2151   2166   2214   2371
852. The truth of the Real Presence is evident from the words of institution.
   128   232   240   300a   689   707   843   974   1084   1113e   1113f   1179   1239a?   1340   1464   2101
   2371
853. Some Fathers occasionally referred to the Eucharist as a sign or figure of the body of Christ, . . .
   337   343   394i   504   1239a   1424   1566   2371
854. . . . and even of His Mystical Body, the Church.
   589a   1780a

855. The presence of Christ in the Eucharist does not depend upon the faith and dispositions of the recipient.
(504)? (707)? 1633 1820
856. The bread and wine, through the words of consecration, are changed into the Body and Blood of Christ.
128 249 802 840 843 844 850 1035 1062 1113e 1113n 1137 1157 1270 1333 1339
1340 1520 2101 2151 2371
857. In the Eucharist Christ is really present, but in a spiritual manner.
410 1084 1179 1334 1365 1480
858. Christ is present in the Eucharist, entirely in each of the two species.
318
859. Christ is present in the Eucharist, entirely in every particle of each of the two species.
367 490 707 853k 1035 1113h 1222
860. The matter of the Eucharist is bread and wine.
6 128 129 187 249 394i 581 582 671 707 802 840 1062 1113f 1113n 1340 1519
1524 2100
861. A small amount of water is to be added to the wine before the consecration.
128 129 240 249 410 583 1113n 1340 2371
862. The Fathers regarded the form of the Eucharist as consisting either of the words of Christ, . . .
128 1157 1207 1260 1339 1340
863. . . . or of the epiclesis; . . .
234 840 842 850 954 1113f 2151 2371
864. . . . or, less precisely, they refer to it as the *prayer* or *blessing*.
128 504 802 1035 1270 1333 1520 1652 2139
865. The Eucharist is a permanent Sacrament.
301 318 916 2139
866. The minister of the confecting of the Eucharist is a priest.
65 (366) 647e 671 1207 1260 1339 1345 1357
867. In offering the Sacrifice of the Mass the priest functions as another Christ.
584 1260

Communion

868. In regard to the minister of the distribution of the Eucharist:
128 129 394i 552a 916 1236
870. In a broad sense eating of the Eucharist is a necessity for the soul.
845a 1716 1717 1866 2016 2234
871. In the ancient Church it was generally the custom that Communion was taken under both species.
6 7 128 187 436a 552a 845 846 853*l* 1035 2237
872. Examples of Communion under only one species, however, are not totally lacking.
318
873. It was the practice of the early Church that the faithful received the Eucharist daily.
301 436a 559 916 1519
874. Only the baptized may receive the Eucharist.
6 128 1716
875. For a licit and fruitful reception of the Eucharist it is necessary to be in the state of grace.
7 8 368 504 551 552a 569 853m 974 1180 1532 1536 1633 1780a
876. It was the custom already in the ancient Church to fast before receiving Communion.
1420
877. The Eucharist was so instituted that it might be received in the manner of food, for the refreshment of the soul.
7 187 362 394i 408 410 436a 707 916 1113n 1166 1593 1652 2101 2131
878. Through Communion the just become, in a certain sense, concorporeal and consanguineal with Christ.
249 843 845 853e 853k 870 1035 1137 1166 1180 1194 1524 1593 1824 2116 2206
879. The Eucharist is a pledge of resurrection and of life eternal.
43 234 249 436a 559 1035 2371
880. The Eucharist both signifies and assures the unity of the Church.
6 56 848c 1166 1194 1239a 1519 1824
881. The Fathers did not countenance intercommunion.
6 2371a

The Mass

890. The Mass is a true Sacrifice.
21 232 233 320 382 552a 584 851 1019 1063 1118 1183 1192 1193 1222 1239a
1260 1424 1844 1977 2270

891. The Mass is a re-enactment of the Sacrifice of the cross.
    582 1222 1239a 1604 1745 2270 2323
892. The Sacrifice of the Mass was prefigured in the sacrifices of the Old Law.
    135 233 1193 1222 1600 1604 1744 1866 2270
893. The Sacrifice of the Mass was prefigured in a special way in the sacrifice of Melchisedech.
    581 671 1390 1977
894. The Mass was announced beforehand in the prophecy of Malachias.
    8 135 232 1977
895. Christ is the Victim offered in the sacrifice of the Mass.
    853 1118 1183 1192 1193 1222 1260 1424 2323
896. Christ Himself offers the Mass through the ministry of the priest.
    1157 1207 1260
897. The Mass is a Sacrifice offered for adoration, thanksgiving, propitiation, and supplication.
    232 367 851 853 1173 1206 1239a 1339 1516 1744 1866 1930 1977 2270 2323

Liturgy and Law

898. There were liturgical regulations even in the early Church; . . .
    19 19a 367 394e 651x 651z 671 745k 745l 745r 853k 853l 954 954a 1233
899. . . . and other regulations, seemingly arbitrary, but really prompted by prudence, in view of the necessities of good order.
    611o 611p 611z 647b 647f 647i 651g 651h 651i 651j 651k 651l 651m 651o 651u 651v 651w 702a 745m 745n 745o 745p 910c 910d 910j 1419a 2015a 2233b

PENANCE

900. The Church has received from Christ the power of remitting or of refusing to remit sins.
    387 584a 602 611e 611f 611i 637 855a 1113p 1119 1234 1244 1287 1293 1297 1345 1386 1480a 1526 1579 2121 2184b 2251b 2332
901. This power extends to all and every sin committed after Baptism.
    59 385 (386) 561 577 578 1245 1294 1298 1501 1532 1533 1874 1919 2252
902. Adultery, murder, and apostasy or heresy were regarded as more grave than other sins.
    81c 93a 383 385 568 576a 576b 611k 611q 611bb 611cc 611dd 919e 919i 1245a 1501 1532 1536 2015 2184b
903. In regard to blasphemy against the Holy Spirit:
    1174 1444 1501 2321
904. In the ancient Church public penance was imposed for the more grievous public crimes.
    315 385 568 568b 569 578 611a 611l 611m 651q 651r 651s 651t 745b 922a 1434 1435 1532 1536 2233 2233a
905. Less grave sins were remitted without public penance.
    485a 497
906. Reconciliation was made through the imposition of hands, ordinarily administered by the bishop.
    386 568b 569 570 611s 647c 651n 745c 752a 1435 1864
907. There are indications that forgiveness through public penitential acts was granted only once to any one penitent; . . .
    81b 86 87 314 315 386a 497 611r 1300 1435
908. . . . but there are indications also, and even clear statements, that the private reception of sacramental forgiveness was repeatable.
    314 317 485e 497 561 637 685 1230 2165b
909. In regard to private absolution, granted in the imminent danger of death:
    570 576 651s 752a
910. Repentance is a true virtue, by which a man detests and grieves for his sin, and intends to repair what was, in a certain sense, an injury done to God.
    27 86a 315 1494 2233b 2336
911. Repentance is necessary in order to obtain forgiveness of sins.
    90 103 315 386 611n 1132 1310 1480a 1919 2332
912. Contrition, which is sorrow for sin motivated by perfect charity, always and immediately by its very nature justifies.
    26 434 493 1846 2176
913. Contrition is able even to take away entirely the punishment due sin.
    1305
914. Attrition, which is sorrow for sin motivated by the fear of punishment, is a good act and suffices, in respect to sorrow, for the obtaining of absolution.
    434 1025 1143 1487 1514
915. For attrition to suffice for the receiving of absolution, it is necessary that a purpose of amendment accompany it.
    1797 1885

916. Some kind of confession, not made to God only, but external, is required for the remission of sins.
 3 8 26a 37 192b 193 315 316 477 485a 493 551 569 570 685 1164 1245a 1298 1299 1375 1480a 1846 2121 2184b 2189a

917. Some passages in Chrysostom, however, are interpreted by some as indicating that Chrysostom did not require confession to a priest; and there are passages in Socrates and Sozomen that indicate that for a time the practice of confession to a priest was abandoned in some places.
 1131 1132 1136 1145 1164 1196 2165a 2165b

918. For absolution there is required a distinct accusation of sins.
 485a 494 553 1245b 1259 1386 2189a 2332

919. A declaration of sins joined to penance:
 485a 493 1136 1259 1494 2189a

920. Confession was made privately to a priest.
 485a 493 553 685 975 977 1113p 1132 1136 1259 1375 1386 2189a 2233a

921. With confession made privately, the priest was obligated not to make public knowledge the sins confessed.
 685 1113p 1132 2023 2189a

922. Even when guilt is taken away the whole temporal punishment due to sin is not always taken away.
 1845 2309

923. There remains after absolution the necessity of making the satisfaction demanded by God's justice.
 313 315 584a 1305 1434 1494

924. The form of absolution in the ancient Church seems to have been deprecative.
 1287 1627 2184b

925. The minister of the Sacrament of Penance is a priest only; . . .
 73? 315 394a 551 553 578 975 977 1119 1120 1244 1293 1294 1295 1297 1386 2184b

926. . . . but a deacon might, in case of necessity, be the minister of reconciliation, . . .
 611s

927. . . . and Cyprian of Carthage seems to have allowed in such cases that confession even might be made to a deacon, but whether or not with absolution given by the deacon is not clear.
 570

928. Penance is necessary for all who have fallen into grave sin after Baptism [see also 911].
 314 561 1095 1536 1864

929. Venial sins can be remitted by charity, by prayer, and by good works.
 493 563 564 707 1113m 1536 1781 1888 1921 2233

930. Venial sins can be forgiven also in the fruitful reception of the Eucharist.
 1113m

931. Sins forgiven never revive.
 1256 (1622)

Indulgences

935. Something of the canonical penance could be remitted through the intercession of the martyrs.
 387a 570

936. There exists in the Church a treasury of merits from which indulgences can be applied to sinners in respect to the punishments due their sins.
 552 1296

SACRAMENT OF THE ILL

940. Extreme Unction, the Sacrament of the Ill, is a true Sacrament, the effect of which is to blot out the remains of sin and to strengthen both soul and body.
 493 698 1120 1241 1295 2015e 2092 2234

HOLY ORDERS

950. Orders is a true Sacrament.
 919 1062 1617 1642 2190

951. In the Church the clergy constitute a rank distinct from the laity.
 11 48 49 50 300 366 438 477a 611aa 651g 745h 753 919 919b 1062 1236 1345 1350a

952. Episcopate, priesthood, and diaconate constitute the major orders.
 43a 44 47a 49 50 58a 70a 394c 413 427 546a 611j 611k 745m 1205 1236 1350

953. Bishops are constituted in an order superior to that of priests.
 19 43b 394c 546c 1108 1205 1236 1238 1357? 1359 (1371) 1394 2164 2165

954. Deacons are the helpers of bishops and priests in the sacred functions.
9 19 20 43a 48 84 128 294c 546a 1231 1236 1357

955. Subdeacons were the helpers of deacons; and they were constituted in a rank established by the Church.
70a 394h 546a 745j 745m 1236

956. Besides subdiaconate there were other orders also, called minor orders.
70a 300 394g 546a 570a 745i 745m 1236

957. In the ancient Church women were able to be consecrated to God in a special way as deaconesses or widows; but they received no order in the proper sense, and were not ordained.
70a 300 394f 413 477a 546a 651y 745f 1112 1231 1236 1265b

958. The matter of Orders is the imposition of hands.
394a 394d 588 1108 1205 2179

959. The form of Orders is the prayer which is conjoined to the imposition of hands.
394a 394b 394c

960. The minister of Orders is the bishop only.
394a 394b 394c 601c 753 910e 1108 1234 1236 1237 1357

961. The minister of episcopal consecration is a bishop, and from earliest times three bishops were regularly required.
394a 651j 1205 1235 1237

962. Even heretics can validly ordain; . . .
(592) 651n (919) 1360

963. . . . but valid Baptism is a necessary prerequisite to a valid reception of Orders.
651y

964. In the Church it was already the custom in antiquity to impose celibacy on clerics in major orders or at least to prohibit their marrying a second time.
299 366 381 611t 647g 919d 919h 1096 1350 2188a 2293 2319

965. The effects of the reception of Orders are the augmenting of grace, the imprinting of a character, and the conferring of spiritual power.
237 394a 1062 1119 1120 1236

966. The Church can establish impediments to the reception of the Sacrament of Orders.
651g 651h 651o 651p

MATRIMONY

968. The ends of Matrimony are the begetting of offspring, the mutual help of the spouses, and the providing of a remedy against concupiscence.
433a 507 818c 818d 1094 1253 1640 1642 1867 1869 2233

969. From earliest times the Church has regarded abortion as a most grievous crime, . . .
1a 396a 919a 919f

970. . . . and contraception, too, as a grievous sin against the ends of marriage.
396a

972. Christian marriage is a true Sacrament.
67 320 384 420a 420b 505 1094 1176 1245d 1249 1253 1342a 1640 1812 1867 1876 2108 2155 2374

973. Marriage is perfected by the mutual consent of the spouses. There was, therefore, a true marriage between Mary and Joseph.
1326 1361 1610 1868

974. Matrimony effects a bond which is completely indissoluble.
86 119 320 420 506 507 611b 611d 642 854 919g 921b 921c 922 1002 1308 1322 1341a 1351 1352 1388 1861 1863 1864 1867 2015 2017 2155 2297

975. The indissoluble bond of Matrimony cannot be broken, not even on account of adultery on the part of one of the spouses.
86 (342) 507 611c 642 854 921a 921c 922 (1341a) 1351 1436a 1737a 1861 1863 1869

976. The Pauline Privilege case:
506? 611d 1190 1307 1341b 1436a

977. The Sacrament of Matrimony effects an exclusive bond.
167 186 271 281a 1097 1176 1322 2017

978. Polygamy was tolerated, however, in the earlier Old Testament history.
1641 1867 2155

979. In regard to second marriages:
88 119 167 366 382 477a 506 611u 651n 745a 818d 919c 1097 1325b 1349 1354a 1354b 1378a 1579 1790

980. The Church is competent to establish matrimonial impediments.
320 384 611g 611h 611i 647d 647h 745e 918 919d 1307

981. The Church establishes matrimonial impediments apart from any consideration of civil law.
1308 1352 1867

982. A vow of chastity is an impediment to subsequent marriage.
    568 1115 1378 1789 2015
983. Matrimony is good and lawful, a holy estate; . . .
    818c 1077 1115 1116 1253 1349 1361 1378 1789 1812 1876 1974b 1974c 2155 2374
984. . . . but it is surpassed in dignity by celibacy and virginity.
    67 433a 516a 818c 1020a 1077 1116 1253 1325c 1327a 1349 1361a 1379 1789 1975
    2167b 2374

ESCHATOLOGY

DEATH

990. Death is the separation of the soul from the body.
    252 345 349a 683 1030 1031 1772
991. After death there is no longer any possibility of meriting or demeriting.
    103 560 561 576 578 693 886 887 966 980 1138 1172 1200 1325 1364 1934a
    2268 2321

PARTICULAR JUDGMENT

995. The soul undergoes the particular judgment as soon as it leaves the body.
    (646) 886 956 1200 1880
996. Even before the general judgment souls are already in blessedness or in torment.
    132 (259)? (351)? 352 446 (646) 721 886 887 1109 1829 1930 1971 (2140) 2234a
    2320

PURGATORY

1000. A place of purgation exists where those souls of whom further expiation is required undergo temporary punishment.
    352 646? 956 1013? 1061 1467 1544 1737a 1776 1780 1920 1930 2233 2321
1001. The souls of the dead detained in purgatory can be aided by the suffrages of the living.
    187 187a 367 382 852 853 1109 1206 1239a 1513 1516 1780 1930 1934
1002. Purgatory will not continue beyond the day of general judgment.
    1776 1778

END OF THE WORLD

1010. Various signs will precede the end of the world.
    10 832 832a 1771
1011. The dead will rise, . . .
    10 13 13a 51 54 74 112 147 155 157 169 173 190a 249 250 252 272 276
    301a 328a 345 363 364 446 680 681 687 721 836 872 910a 1064 1065 1089a
    1100 1232 1276 1522 1768 1785 2153 2167f 2375 2376
1012. . . . not the just dead only, but all the dead.
    (63)? (64)? 124 191 290 365 395 646 647 694 837 1232 1829 1922 1922a 2019
    2112 2267 2390
1013. The dead will rise in their same bodies.
    104 120 155 345 365 395 446 468 686 836 837 885 1088 1522 1785 1880
    1923 2375
1014. Origenism, in regard to the final apokatastasis:
    456 457 463 464 467a 468 1013 1033 1353 1373 1384 1402
1015. Origenism, in regard to spiritual fire:
    463 464 1013 1306 1370
1016. Millenarianism or chiliasm was admitted by some Fathers, . . .
    138a 260 261 338 447? 647 658 1407 1521 1769
1017. . . . but was rejected by others.
    138a 263? 658 1769 2154

GENERAL JUDGMENT

1020. After the end of the world there will take place the general judgment.
    74 155 364 396 579 694 1172 1456 1768 1880 2140 2376

HELL AND PUNISHMENT

1030. Those who die in mortal sin are thrust into hell.
41   317   579   980   1206   2233   2321a
1031. In hell, besides the pain of sense through true corporeal fire, there is also the pain of loss, in the deprivation of God.
1772   1932   2266
1032. In hell, besides the pain of loss in the deprivation of God, there is also the pain of sense, through true corporeal fire.
41   78   98a   100   106   115   121   124   166   176   273   276   284   317   346   396   437   560
646   837   958   1013   1036   1065   1138   1258   1370   1774   2167e   2320
1033. The fire of hell torments both the souls of the damned and the demons.
124   356   579   646   1013   1370   1402   1525   1774   2266   2320
1034. The punishment of the damned is eternal.
41   78   100   102   106   115   121   124   176   191   239   273   276   284   290   317   396
437   446   560   579   646   837   976   1013   1060   1384   (1402)   1525   1772   1775   1779
1802   1931   1932   2267   2317   2322   2376
1035. Although it is eternal, the punishment of the damned is not of equal severity for all.
697   976   1778   1860a   1924   1931   2167e   2322
1036. In regard to the mitigation of punishment:
273   396   560   1036   1932
1037. The notion of limbo reprobated as being of Pelagian origin:
1878   1976

HEAVEN AND BLESSEDNESS

1040. The object of blessedness is God only.
53a   1591   1743   1749   1788
1041. Perfect blessedness in heaven consists in seeing and loving God.
236   301a   579   891   1552   1753   1786   1788   1971   2376
1042. The blessed are not able any more to sin.
693   1802   1931   1956   2012
1043. Blessedness is eternal and cannot be lost.
102   176   191   239   276   284   290   396   468   579   693   910a   976   1089a   1552   1674
1749   1756   1779   1788   1802   1931   1950   2154
1044. The bodies of the blessed will be glorious and immortal.
166   338   395   468   837   883   885   1520a   1522   1698   1760a   1785   1788   2267
1045. In regard to accidental blessedness:
78   176   579
1046. There will be various degrees of blessedness, in respect to merits.
696   1383   1502   1831   1931   2308

Numbers **1**, **2**, or **3** in boldface refer to the volume of *The Faith of the Early Fathers*; numbers in ordinary face are page references. Numbers followed by an *n* refer to footnotes on the page indicated by the number. Numbers preceded by *DI* are references to propositions so numbered in the Doctrinal Index, which immediately precedes this General Index. Roman numerals following a name (as in Innocent XIII) and the words *a*, *an*, and *the* are ignored in the alphabetic arrangement of this index.